THEY CAME TO BOURNEMOUTH

Some famous residents and visitors

by

RITA M. POPHAM, A.L.A.

Bournemouth Local Studies Publications
The Teachers' Centre 40 Lowther Road
Bournemouth

1983

The material for this booklet was originally researched for a talk, with slides, given to the volunteer tourist guides of Bournemouth, in my capacity as Local Studies Librarian of Dorset County Library, East Area.

For it I drew extensively on the contents of the Bournemouth Local History Collection at the Lansdowne Reference Library. The sources there, - books, Pamphlets, newspapers, etc. - are too numerous to list as a bibliography.

Rita M. Popham, A.L.A.
February 1981

ISBN 0 906287 36 7

C O N T E N T S

The ilustrations are by courtesy of the Dorset County Libraries.

PORTMAN LODGE. Built by Mr. Tregonwell in 1810 to house his butler.

INTRODUCTION

Although evidence of people living in the Bournemouth area for many years has been quite well documented, this booklet is based almost entirely on the nineteenth and early twentieth centuries. It has not been possible to include all the personalities and local names associated with the town, and some selection has had to be made.

Of course, being a seaside town, Bournemouth has attracted a vast number of people, some very well-known, but the choice has been confined to those who have contributed to the amazing growth of the town or have made a lasting impression on it.

In the early 1800s very little of present-day Bournemouth existed and most of the local inhabitants lived in the small villages along the Stour Valley. There was little sign of occupation along the coast between the historic towns of Christchurch and Poole, just one or two scattered buildings, but otherwise it was open heathland.

All this began to change after the Christchurch Inclosure Act of 1802, which allowed for the enclosure of the common and wastelands in the neighbourhood of that town. Three Commissioners were appointed to carry out the provisions of the Act and prepare an Award, setting out details of allotment of land. This followed in 1805, and the main purchasers of land for sale were three of the local landowners, Sir George Ivison Tapps of Hinton Admiral, William Dean of Holdenhurst, and James Harris, 1st Earl of Malmesbury. More of these presently.

* * * * * * *

A VIEW OF BOURNEMOUTH FROM THE HÔTEL MONT DORE.

THE PLEASURE GROUNDS NEAR THE PIER.

BROOKSIDE.—Brookside, standing in its own grounds near the entrance to the pleasure grounds from the Pier, as long as two of its stones shall remain together, will ever be regarded by many devout Christians with respect almost akin to the feeling which we pay to sacred places, because in this house the Rev. John Keble, the author of the *Christian Year*, passed the last days of his life on earth, and he here peacefully "fell asleep in Jesus on the morning of the Ascension, 1866."

THE FOUNDER OF BOURNEMOUTH

The gentleman often referred to as 'The Founder of Bournemouth', Lewis Dymoke Grosvenor Tregonwell, was born in 1758, Son of Thomas Tregonwell of Winterborne Anderson, in Dorset. As Captain of the Dorset Yeomanry (a volunteer cavalry force) Lewis was appointed in 1801 to command the defence of the area, including Bournemouth, Poole and Wimborne.

He came from an old Dorset family established at Milton Abbey in the 16th century by Sir John Tregonwell, who had been born in Cornwall. The family originated at Manaccan in that county, and Tregonwell Farm and Tregonwell Mill are still to be found there.

Lewis Tregonwell's home was Cranborne Lodge, Cranborne, Dorset. His first wife, Katherine, daughter of St. Barbe Sydenham, of Priory, Devon, and Combe, Somerset, died in 1794. He married, secondly, in 1800, Henrietta, daughter of Henry Portman, of Orchard Portman, Somerset, and Bryanston, Dorset. In 1810 he visited Bourne Chine, with Mrs. Tregonwell, whilst on holiday at Mudeford, near Christchurch. His wife was very taken with the area and after further visits that same year Lewis Tregonwell negotiated the purchase of 8½ acres of land from Sir George Tapps, for which he paid just over £179. On part of this (now the east side of Exeter Road) he erected his mansion, occupied for the first time in 1812. This house was used as a holiday home and was also let to friends and relatives. It became known as Exeter House (it was let to the Marchioness of Exeter in about 1820) - later it was extended and altered, but it is not difficult to recornise it today as the Royal Exeter Hotel. A plaque on the wall of the hotel records his connection with it. Also on his land he built Portman Lodge and Terrace Cottage, the former now the site of the old Hants & Dorset Bus Station; the latter part of the Hotel Merville. In 1809 Sir George Tapps had built a small inn at Bourne and called it 'The Tapps Arms'. Tregonwell acquired it, rebuilt it and changed its name to 'The Tregonwell Arms'. It was demolished in 1885 and its site is now Post Office Road, Bournemouth.

Lewis Tregonwell died at Cranborne Lodge in 1832, aged 73, and was buried in Winterborne Anderson. In 1846 his remains were reinterred in the family tomb in St. Peter's Churchyard, Bournemouth.

* * * * * * *

IMPORTANT LAND-OWNING FAMILIES

The Inclosure Award of 1805 has already been mentioned and the fact that property was acquired by William Dean of Littledown House, Holdenhurst. William Dean acquired 400 acres of the West Cliff, more land around Queens Park, and a large tract between Old Christchurch Road and Stewart Road (Dean Park, etc.). One of the Award Commissioners was William Clapcott, his son-in-law, a member of the banking firm Dean, Clapcott and Castleman of Wimborne. The Dean Estate passed to William Clapcott, and his son assumed the family name of Dean. The property was inherited by his nephew, James Edward Cooper, who adopted the surname 'Cooper-Dean' in 1888. He died in 1921 and some of the Littledown Estate was developed for building; many street names in the district are place-names of the Meon Valley in Hampshire where his nephew, James Edward Cooper, had his home. Descendants of the family still own considerable areas in the town, and plans are under discussion for the future development of the Littledown Estate.

The family seat of the Earls of Malmesbury was at Heron Court, sometimes known as Hurn Court, situated across the River Stour from Throop. The estate was inherited by James Harris in 1795. He had been created Baron Malmesbury in 1788 and later Viscount Fitzharris and Earl of Malmesbury in 1800. He spent his life in the diplomatic service and was Ambassador in several European capital cities; he was also Lieutenant-Governor of the Isle of Wight and Lord Lieutenant of Hampshire. The 1st Earl was never a permanent resident at Hurn Court, but his son, James Edward Harris, the 2nd Earl, devoted his life to the

Hurn Court Estate and was probably responsible for changing the name of the house to Heron Court. He was a member of Parliament and, amongst other posts, Governor of the Isle of Wight.

The 5th Earl, also James Edward Harris, succeeded to the title in 1899. Shortly before his death in 1950 he had decided to dispose of Heron Court because of high taxation and the cost of upkeep, and had moved to Winchester. After his death the house was sold and concerted into a boys' school.

The gate piers to the house are topped by herons. There was a heronry on the estate and there may be a connection between the place name HURN and the word HERN - the old name for heron. Heron Court Road is situated on land acquired by the 1st Earl under the 1805 Award.

The other important landowners already mentioned were the <u>Tapps</u> of Hinton Admiral, near Christchurch. The family acquired the Manor of Christchurch (including the site of Bournemouth) in 1708, and when this land was enclosed Sir George Ivison Tapps became the principal beneficiary under the Award of 1805, and he also purchased land at Bournemouth at the same time. He bought just over 200 acres for a little over £1,050. This was land between the sea and the main road stretching approximately from Derby Road, on the East Cliff, to the Highcliff Hotel, on the West Cliff. He died in 1835 and was succeeded, as 2nd Baronet, by his son, George William, who in that year assumed the name and arms of Gervis and became known as Sir George William Tapps-Gervis. (The present Baronet bears the names of Tapps-Gervis-Meyrick).

The new Sir George, M.P. for Christchurch from 1832-1837, was responsible for the development of his Westover Estate at Bourne Mouth in 1835-1840. Westover - meaning the western bank - derived from the Old English 'west + pfer', a bank or boundary.

ARCHITECTS, BUILDERS & BUSINESS MEN

Sir George Tapps-Gervis brought in as architect for his development plans Benjamin Ferrey, youngest son of Benjamin Ferrey, senior, (Mayor of Christchurch in 1840). Born in 1810 the younger Ferrey was educated at Wimborne Grammar School and, even as a boy, was interested in drawing in the Minster. He was articled to Augustus Pugin the elder, famous for his architectural drawing and engraving. He set up in practice in London, and in 1834 brought out 'The Antiquities of the Priory of Christchurch, Hants', for which he did some fine drawings. Ferrey produced plans and drawings for the proposed marine village of Bourne, some of which was accomplished and some not. Several buildings designed by Ferrey were erected, namely the Westover Villas, 1836-1838, along the line of Westover Road, and the Bath Hotel, opened by Sir George Tapps-Gervis on Queen Victoria's Coronation Day in 1838. The Bath Hotel was extended in 1880 after purchase by Mr. Merton Russell Cotes, who added the prefix 'Royal'. Ferrey went on to build up an enormous architectural practice, his work including Dorchester Town Hall, Dorset County Hospital, and All Saints and Holy Trinity Churches (also at Dorchester); the new facade for West Stafford House; churches at Plush, Osmington, Melplash and Tarrant Hinton; alterations and a new chancel for St. John Evangelist, Holdenhurst; and much restoration work at Wells Cathedral. He died in 1880.

Another well-known architect connected with Bournemouth was George Edmund Street, born in 1824. Changing his mind from his first intention to take holy orders, he became an architect, and his first church was Par, in Cornwall. He was engaged by the first vicar of St. Peter's, Bournemouth in 1845, to extend the small building opened in 1843. The original St. Peter's was never demolished and the various stages were added until the spire was finally completed in 1879. Street had a large practice and designed many churches and other buildings, including the Royal Courts of Justice in the Strand, London Other local connections include East Parley Church; schools in Bournemouth; restorations to St.James' Church, Pokesdown and Canford Church; and Kingston Church, Purbeck.

A successful speculative builder, Henry Joy, came to Bournemouth in the middle of the 1800s as a journeyman-carpenter. He was especially well known for the development of the area of the town containing the Rustic Bridge. This bridge was erected by Thomas Shettle in 1853 as a way across a glen, 20 ft. deep, from Gervis Place to Old Christchurch Road. Henry Joy's project was to erect an Arcade in its place, and this was begun in 1866. It was known locally as 'Joy's Folly' as it was considered that it would not be a viable proposition. An Arcade was completed in 1873 and when the roof was glazed over it became a popular shopping precinct. Joy was also the builder of Westbourne Arcade, the Quadrant property (later J. J. Allen's) and Southbourne Terrace (the site of W. H. Smith). He died in 1906 and is buried in Wimborne Road Cemetery.

After a breakdown in health Thomas James Hankinson came to Bournemouth in 1858. He was a London man, born in 1831, who worked there for the firm of solicitors who were agents for the Durrant Estate in Bournemouth. He established himself as a bookseller and stationer at Victoria House in Exeter Road. He also ran the Victoria Library (a circulating, subscription library) which adjoined the house. In 1865 he established an estate agency at this address until, in 1875, the business was transferred to Richmond Chambers at the bottom of Richmond Hill (premises just vacated by the Wilts & Dorset Bank), Here Hankinson was concerned mainly with auctioneering and estate agency. The Victoria Library continued until the early 1890's, and Hankinson published a series of local guide books from 1876 to 1892. He was on the Board of Commissioners (who ran the town) from 1873-1890, latterly as its Chairman. When Bournemouth became a Borough in 1890 T.J. Hankinson became the town's first Mayor. He died in December 1905. His eldest son, Charles, became an author, writing under the pseudonym 'Clive Holland'.

Joseph Cutler has been described as one of the liveliest and most provocative characters in the public life of the town. Born in 1830 at the Horse and Groom Inn, Christchurch, son of a fisherman and rabbit dealer, he began in the family trade. He emigrated to Australia during the gold rush but later returned to England. On medical advice Cutler came to Bournemouth in 1865 and soon set up as a builder. Joseph Cutler's house, 'Muriel', built in 1871, at the junction of Exeter Road and Upper Terrace Road, was strongly criticised as a disfigurement to the neighbourhood. This he stoutly defended in the local paper! He built other houses such as Durley Dene, West Cliff Road, and Boscobel Towers, Terrace Mount. He worked 'hard and indefatigably' for the Bournemouth, Swanage and Poole Steamboat Company formed in 1881; he supported many local schemes, proposing a local fire brigade in 1866 and volunteering to lead it; he just as vigorously opposed other schemes such as that for an undercliff drive.

He was elected to the Board of Commissioners, and on that occasion presented sixty chestnut trees to the town - planted in Invalids' Walk and around tennis courts. He later served as a Councillor and Alderman. He died in 1910 and was buried in the Wimborne Road Cemetery, close to the magnificent monkey-puzzle and golden holly avenue planted along the main drive at his suggestion some years earlier.

Among the well-known names in the history of the town is that of John Elmes Beale, born at Weymouth in 1849, the son of a captain of a small ship. His father was subsequently lost at sea. John was apprenticed to a Weymouth draper and then worked in Sherborne. in 1878 he married Sarah Brickell at Shaftesbury, and after returning to Weymouth for a while, they came to Bournemouth in 1881. Later they moved to a house called 'Bridge End' in Parsonage Road. In November 1881 he opened his Fancy Fair at 3, St. Peter's Terrace, with a small stock of fancy goods. This small shop was soon extended into the yard behind and there were further extensions into neighbouring premises. A five-storey building was erected on part of it.

J. E. Beale was elected Mayor for 1902-3 and 1903-4. In 1885 he had introduced Father Christmas to his customers and in 1912 the first procession took place. The following year Father Christmas arrived by aeroplane!

J.E. Beale died in 1928, but further shop extensions and rebuilding took place and a fine nine-storey block was opened in 1931. This building survived until World War II when it was destroyed in an air-raid in May 1943 and had to be entirely rebuilt.

In 1876 the Bath Hotel, Bournemouth was purchased by Merton Russell Cotes (born in 1835), the proprietor of the Royal Hanover Hotel, Glasgow. He settled in the town, and in 1894 (as he describes in his autobiography 'Home and Abroad') acquired land "to build a house after my own heart ... my ideas were realised at last, and I built on the corner plot of the East Cliff ... and called it 'East Cliff Hall'. When completed and furnished, I gave it to my wife as a birthday present". The house, designed by J.F.Fogerty, was built by Messrs. William Hoare & Son. Russell Cotes became a member of the Board of Commissioners, and was Mayor for 1894-5. He took a leading part in the town's development and was a keen supporter of the Undercliff Drive and Pavilion schemes. He and his wife were great travellers and enthusiastic collectors of pictures and art objects which they brought back from abroad. On the day of the opening of the first section of the newly-completed Drive (6th November 1907) he presented his collection to the town. At the same time his wife presented their residence, East Cliff Hall, in which the treasures were preserved, to form an Art Gallery and Museum under the control of the Corporation, for the benefit of the general public. As a result they were both made Honorary Freemen of the Borough in 1908. The following year Mr. Russell Cotes was given a knighthood for his services to the town and to the word of art - his loan collection of paintings and drawings having been exhibited in most of the country's main cities and towns.

Lady Russell Cotes died in 1920 but the family continued to live at East Cliff Hall until Sir Merton's death in 1921. The family's handsome mausoleum can be found close to the Wimborne Road Cemetery Chapel.

* * * * * * * *

VISIONARIES, A SMUGGLER AND A PRIEST

Mary Anne (sometimes spelt Marianne) Talbot and her sister, Georgina Charlotte, were living in Grosvenor Square, London, with their father, Sir George Talbot, 3rd Baronet (1763-1850). In the 1840s they decided to move from the grey climate of the capital, and so came to Hinton Wood House on the East Cliff at Bournemouth. Miss Georgina already owned Forest House and Little Forest House not far away.

The two sisters noticed the distressed state of the local people on the outskirts of the town, but found that handing out money did more harm than good. As a result of this Georgina acquired a piece of land from the Meyrick Estate and from William Driver just over the county border in Dorset, to provide for the 'working and labouring poorer classes'. The estate was later officially named Talbot Village and administered by Trustees. Between 1850 and 1862 nineteen cottages were built, each having an acre of land. The whole inclosure of the village was 465 acres, including five farms and uncultivated land for cattle grazing. In 1862 seven almshouses were built and endowed, and a school erected. In 1868 three acres were set aside for a church and churchyard. The Church of St. Mark was begun, but Georgina died in February 1870 without seeing it completed, and she was the first to be buried in the churchyard. Her sister, Mary Anne, saw to the completion and furnishing of the new church. She died in 1885.

The founder of the first circulating library and stationer's shop in Bournemouth was John Sydenham, a bookseller, of Poole, whose business at the Pier

Approach was established in 1840, adjoining the Belle Vue Boarding House (later Hotel) opened two years earlier.

He was also the publisher, also in 1840, of Bournemouth's first guide book 'The Visitor's Guide to Bournemouth and its Neighbourhood'. It was the circulation of this little guide which brought the new marine village to public attention. A series of guide books, written and illustrated by Philip Brannon, was published by Sydenham between 1855 and 1890.

From 1877 the name of the firm changed to Sydenham's Royal Marine Library. Other members of the family were concerned in the business and John Sydenham's eldest surviving son, also John, was the author of 'The History of the Town and County of Poole', published in 1839. In January 1846 he founded and edited the Poole and Dorsetshire Herald.

Another son, David, was a pioneer in the promotion of steamer excursions from 1868 and was local manager of Messrs. Cosens & Co. of Weymouth. His great-nephew, Reginald, was the proprietor of Sydenhams Printing Works in Oxford Road, and also of the Royal Marine Library when it was disposed of in 1925.

Some way from Bournemouth town centre big things were happening in the east. The district had been noticed by Dr. Thomas A. Compton, (born 1838), who had begun practising in Bournemouth in 1866. He saw it as a promising site for a new resort. In 1870 he purchased about 230 acres, with more than a mile of coastline, chiefly from a General Cleveland, and used the name 'Southbourne' for the first time. He subsequently formed several companies to develop the area which at that time consisted mainly of fairly good farm land and two small woods. The only buildings to be found were three small cottates and a Coastguard Station.

Roads and houses were built; in 1874 a Winter Gardens opened in Belle Vue Road (today the site of Bolton Road); the first part of St. Katherine's Church was completed in 1882; in 1883 the first Tuckton Bridge was completed (a wooden structure, rebuilt in 1905). In the same year the Southbourne Land Company began the construction of an Esplanade and sea-wall; in 1888 six large houses were built on the Esplanade, and a pier was opened, erected by the Southbourne Pier Company.

Unfortunately in December 1900 heavy gales buffeted the sea-wall and the pier was severely damaged. The Esplanade became dangerous and the houses were pulled down. The following year the sea-wall collapsed. The pier, having been made derelict by subsequent storms, was also declared dangerous and was demolished in 1907.

In his early days in Bournemouth Dr. Compton lived near the Lansdowne and from 1888-1892 in one of the ill-fated houses on his Esplanade at Southbourne. He moved to Parkstone where he died in 1925.

One of the most notorious local smugglers and the subject of many tales and legends was Isaac Gulliver. He was the principal character in a novel 'Branksome Dene' by Hugh Walmsley, and in a play 'The Gentle Smuggler', written by Joan Pitts, a local author.

Gulliver was born in 1745 at Semington, near Trowbridge, in Wiltshire, son of Isaac and Elizabeth Gulliver. It is probable that his main activities as a smuggler in the Bournemouth area took place between 1758 and 1778. It is also probable that he was referred to in the Gentleman's Magazine of 1763 as "one particular smuggler who alone cheats the Customs of more than £20,000 a year'. At one time, it was said, he owned three large ships, and his convoy of pack-horses stretched for two miles across the heathland as he smuggled silk, tea, brandy and tobacco. Various properties are supposed to have connections with Gulliver, for instance 'Howe Lodge', in Kinson, where he lived for a time. This house was reputed to have an underground chamber and a secret tunnel. It was demolished in 1958 to make way for road and housing estate. Gulliver's Farm, West Moors, also has connections with the smuggler.

In 1782 a royal proclamation extended a pardon to smugglers, and Gulliver turned his attention to the legitimate wine trade. Having retired from this he lived in Wimborne in a house in West Borough, now 'Gulliver's House', where he died in 1822. His grave slab can be found in the centre aisle of the Minster.

The first Vicar of St. Peter's Church, Bournemouth (from 1845-1880) was Alexander Morden Bennett. Born on 11th October 1808 at Morden College, Blackheath, (where his father, Rev. Alexander Bennett was college treasurer), he later studied at Worcester College, Oxford, obtaining his B.A. and M.A. before becoming a priest in 1832. His first assistant curacy was at Withington, near Cheltenham. He held several posts before coming to St. Peter's in 1845. In that same year he married as his second wife (the first having died in 1842) Marianne, daughter of Captain Henry Hopkins of Hubborn Lodge, near Christchurch. The small church at Bournemouth, built in 1843, was duly consecrated on 7th August 1845, and the new curate lived at Mudeford until the new Parsonage was completed. One of Bennett's first works was to start a school, and the foundation stone was laid in 1850.

Mrs. Bennett died in 1852 and their daughter in 1853, leaving Morden Bennett with two young sons.

Morden Bennett engaged the architect G.E. Street to prepare plans for the extensions to St. Peter's and they worked together for more than twenty-five years. The last great work which Bennett saw accomplished was the completion of the spire at the end of 1879. The joy of the parishioners was soon marred by the sudden illness and death of their Vicar on 19th January 1880. One local clergyman estimated that there must have been nearly 3,000 people at the burial service when Alexander Morden Bennett was laid to rest close to the church he had built and served.

St. Peter's Church in 1865

Mr. T. J. Hankinson

Mr. Joseph Cutler.

BY THE SEA

O. IV.—BOURNEMOUTH.

NEWLYN'S ROYAL EXETER HOTEL, BOURNEMOUTH.

MUSICIANS, ARTISTS AND WRITERS

Municipal music in Bournemouth really began in 1893 when the Council applied to Lieutenant Dan Godfrey, the famous Bandmaster of the Grenadier Guards, about the supply of a suitable band to perform in the town's Winter Gardens. The request was passed to his son, Daniel Eyers Godfrey, a well-reputed conductor, just returned from a tour of South Africa. The younger Dan, born in London in 1868, came from a family in which several members held prominent positions in the world of military music. After school and a visit to Germany, Dan Godfrey entered the Royal College of Music in 1885 and became a scholar in the clarinet. He too moved into military music, becoming conductor of the London Military Band, and Bandmaster of the Corps of Commissionaires. His time in South Africa was a complete change, as musical director of an opera company.

At the beginning of 1893 Dan Godfrey signed a contract to provide a string section to play at the Bournemouth Winter Gardens, and a military band to perform on the Pier. They made their debut at the Winter Gardens on 22nd May, and the following year Dan Godfrey gave up his other engagements to become resident Musical Director to the Bournemouth Corporation. In 1895 the now well-known series of Symphony Concerts was established with an increased number of musicians. Under Godfrey's direction the first permanent Municipal Orchestra in the country became famous, and now it has a world-wide reputation for fine music.

In 1922 Dan Godfrey was awarded a Knighthood for

his valuable services to British music. He retired as Director to the Bournemouth Municipal Orchestra in 1934 and died in 1939, and is buried in St. Peter's Churchyard.

Charles Barnard Groves also played an important part in the musical history of the town. Born in 1915 he became a chorister at St. Paul's Cathedral at the age of 9, and on leaving school he studied at the Royal College of Music. The organ was his greatest interest but at the College he became interested in accompanying and obtained an accompanist post with the B.B.C. In 1943 he was appointed conductor of the B.B.C. Review Orchestra and the following year took charge of the B.B.C. Northern Orchestra. After an exchange visit to Australia in 1950 he came to Bournemouth in 1951 as Musical Director to the Corporation and Conductor of the Bournemouth Municipal Orchestra. He saw the Orchestra through a difficult period when there were union disputes and the Corporation voted to disband it owing to rising costs. Groves' personality was largely responsible for the loyalty of the Orchestra which he managed to keep together and it was eventually reformed as the Bournemouth Symphony Orchestra under the control of the Western Orchestral Society Ltd. He saw the progress of the Orchestra's regional scheme and its success with audiences of schoolchildren and young people.

Thinking it was time to move on, Groves resigned in 1960 and became resident musical director of the Welsh National Opera Company in 1961, but remained principal conductor of the Bournemouth Municipal Choir until 1968. Groves was knighted in 1973 and is now Musical Director of the English Opera Company.

This next section is concerned with literary connections. Many of those mentioned were resident only for a short while, but some of them produced significant works while here or went on to become famous.

Born in Brighton in 1872 Aubrey Beardsley, on leaving school, worked in a surveyor's office and then for an insurance company. He evolved his own style of black and white drawings and illustrated several books. His associations with Oscar Wilde and his circle led to some unpopularity. In 1896 some of his finest art work was done, but Beardsley developed tuberculosis which brought him to Boscombe seeking a cure. He arrived in July and stayed at 'Pier View' near Boscombe Pier. It was whilst staying there that he wrote to a friend recording the body of a large whale being washed up on the beach at Boscombe. Beardsley moved from Boscombe to Bournemouth, in late January 1897, to the house called 'Muriel' in Exeter Road (built by Joseph Cutler some years earlier.) It was at this address that he was received into the Roman Catholic Church by the Priest of the Church of the Sacred Heart. His last letter from Bournemouth was dated 6th April 1897, and a few days later he and his mother left for France. They settled in Menton where Aubrey produced some remarkable drawings. It was at Menton that he died on 16th March 1898, and was buried in the cemetery there.

A plaque on 'Grantchester Dene', number 12, Littledown Road, records Bournemouth's link with Rupert Brooke, the poet. Born in 1887, he made several visits to Bournemouth as a boy and young man. His grandfather, the Rev. Richard England Brooke, retired from Bath to Bournemouth in 1895. Here he took the house, 'Grantchester Dene', in Littledown Road, and with him lived his two unmarried daughters. It was during a visit here in 1896 that, through reading a copy of Browning, Rupert Brooke discovered poetry. His grandfather died in 1900 but the two maiden aunts remained in the house. Several letters from Bournemouth appear in Brooke's published letters, including one of 1906 in which he describes the town as "this strange place, which is full of moaning pines, and impressionist but quite ungentlemanly sunsets. With other decrepit and grey-haired invalids I drift wanly along the cliffs". He was only 18!

Visiting his aunts in the summer of 1907 he discovered the name 'Lulworth' on a local map and decided to spend a short holiday there, staying in rooms above the Post Office. One letter recalls "Tomorrow I'm going to the most beautiful place in England to work. It is called West Lulworth. I have made seven poems on it ... "

War broke out in 1914 and Brooke joined the Royal Naval Division. Just before Christmas he paid his last call to 'Grantchester Dene' whilst stationed near Blandford. In March 1915 his battalion was sent abroad but in April Brooke went down with acute blood poisoning whilst in the Mediterranean. He died on board ship on 23rd April and was buried the same evening on the island of Skyros in the Aegean Sea. The plaque was unveiled at 'Grantchester Dene' in October 1965.

There has been an increase of interest recently in the Russian Colony at Tuckton, and several articles written. Count Vladimir Chertkov, a disciple of the great writer and social and religious thinker Leo Tolstoy, was banished from Russia as a result of this, and came to England in February 1897. He settled first at Purleigh with other followers of Tolstoy, who were publishing a magazine on the principles of Tolstoy's teaching. After disagreements Chertkov left Purleigh and came, with his family, to Bournemouth where his mother already owned a house called 'Slavanka', used for holidays. Chertkov was able to buy 'Tuckton

House' (in Saxonbury Road) with land adjoining, and the property known as 'the old Waterworks' nearby. It was at the latter premises that a printing press was set up to print essays and articles of Tolstoy's, whose publication was prohibited in Russia. These were distributed throughout the world, and a 16-page newspaper, in Russian, was also produced by this press. Joined by a number of other Russian exiles the colony in 1905 numbered about thirty. In 1908 Chertkov was given permission to return to Russia where he died in 1937 at the age of 82. The colony broke up soon after Chertkov's departure and the house sold in 1913 and the site redeveloped. Chertkov's mother spent the end of her life at 'Slavanka' which she had sold to a Christian community. She died in 1922 and was buried in Christchurch Cemetery.

A local poet who has gone virtually unknown and unrecognised is Cumberland Clark. Born in 1862 he spent his early years travelling widely, especially in New Zealand and Australia, in formerly unexplored terretory, and working on the land. During the First World War he was appointed as an Army lecturer, and by 1938 had published no fewer than sixty-seven books, some on Shakespeare, the Empire, sonnets and poems. He came to Bournemouth following the death of his wife, and his 'Bournemouth Song Book' was first published in 1929. At the publication of his 'Book of a Thousand Songs' in 1935 the Weekly Post said

> 'Mr. Clark's industry and versatility are extraordinary. He is a man of ideas, some poetically beautiful, some idealistic, and others humorous and witty ... the author ranks as one of the principal poets of the world'.

In 1935 Clark erected his own memorial, in pure white marble, in Boscombe Cemetery - thereby saving relatives and friends any trouble and expense after his death. On it he described himself as 'poet, historian and dramatist'.

During the Second World War he wrote verses about the achievements of the armed forces and other patriotic themes.

He lost his life on Good Friday, April 1941, when, during an enemy air-raid, a bomb fell on his flat in St. Stephen's Road.

More well-known is the novelist and playwright, John Galsworthy. He attended a small preparatory school, 'Saugeen', in Bournemouth from the age of nine until he was fourteen, when he entered Harrow school.

His stay in Bournemouth led to several visits by his whole family which are recorded in 'The Life and Letters of John Galsworthy', by H.V. Marrot.

The school he attended from 1876 was in Derby Road, close to St. Swithun's Church. The building no longer stands, having made way for redevelopment.

The novelist and poet, D.H. Lawrence, spent a month in Bournemouth in the early part of 1912. He came to recuperate after an illness and stayed at 'Compton House', a boarding-house in St. Peter's Road, from 6th January to 3rd February. During his stay he revised and re-wrote a story called 'The Saga of Siegrried', preparing it for publication under the title 'The Trespasser'. He wrote several letters, to his friends and fiancée, from Bournemouth, full of the day-to-day happenings at the boarding-house, his fellow boarders and the owners. The weather during his stay was not good but after three beautiful days he wrote 'I am very sensitive to the exquisite atmospheres of down here...' The site of Compton House is now a modern office block of the same name.

The Shelley Park estate at Boscombe was purchased in 1849 by Sir Percy Florence Shelley, only surviving son of the poet, Percy Bysshe Shelley and his wife, Mary Wollstonecraft Shelley. The residence at the time of Sir Percy's buying the estate was known as 'Boscombe Lodge'. The new owner set about rebuilding it 'under the direction of Mr. Creeke. The apartments are lofty and ample in their proportions, and the internal fittings up and arrangements are admirable (Brannon's Guide, 1855). Shelley changed the name to 'Boscombe Place' and later to 'Boscombe Manor'. The house included a private theatre where performances were given to audiences composed of Sir Percy's personal friends. Sir Henry Irving and Sir Herbert Beerbohm Tree, both famous actors, appeared on this stage. Sir Percy died in 1889. Many relics and manuscripts of Shelley, the poet, were preserved at 'Boscombe Manor', and it is said that the poet's heart had been saved from the funeral-Pyre (after he was drowned in the Gulf of Spezzia) and was preserved at Boscombe Manor, until Lady Shelley died in 1899 when it was placed in the family tomb at St. Peter's, Bournemouth. This tomb has become one of the most interesting literary shrines in the country as it also contains the remains of Mary Shelley (Sir Percy's mother), the author of 'Frankenstein', and of her parents, both famous authors.

A monument to Shelley, the poet, sculptured by Henry Weekes, was refused a place in St. Peter's Church and was erected in Christchurch Priory. It went through several changes - as a school, as a wartime A.R.P. headquarters, part of the Bournemouth Technical College, and now in 1981 as a branch of the Bournemouth & Poole College of Art.

There is a direct link between the Shelley

family and Robert Louis Stevenson as there is in existence a photograph of him taken by Sir Percy Shelley in 1886.

Stevenson arrived in Bournemouth in August 1884 staying at a number of addresses for a few weeks at a time, before finally moving into a house in Alum Chine Road (now number 61) in April 1885 which his father had purchased in the January. The house, called 'Sea View', Stevenson renamed 'Skerryvore' after the lighthouse built by the family firm in Scotland. A portrait by John Singer Sargent was painted inside the house during the summer. Several important works were written during Stevenson's Bournemouth period, including 'Kidnapped' and 'Dr. Jekell and Mr. Hyde'. During 1885 Stevenson visited Thomas Hardy at Dorchester and received a visit from Henry James. Stevenson's health had not been good for some time and doctors were divided in their opinions as to whether he should stay in this country or go abroad. In the end he decided to remain so as to be near his father who was in ailing health, but in May 1887 Stevenson's father died in Edinburgh. After this Stevenson had no reason to stay in England and felt free to go to whatever climate his doctors recommended, and so on their advice he left Bournemouth in August 1887 for London on route to America. The house, 'Skerryvore', no longer stands as it was bombed during the Second World War in an air-raid on 15th November 1940 and was later demolished. In 1954 the Bournemouth Corporation acquired the site and laid it out as a memorial garden, marking out the footings of the house and erecting a model of the Skerryvore Lighthouse.

Born in 1844 Paul Verlaine became an aspiring poet in his native France, but the way of life he led brought him to Court in Brussels and in 1873 he was sentenced to two years imprisonment. On his release in January 1875, his past unknown in England, he arrived at Stickney School in Lincolnshire in April to take up a teaching post. His mother arrived to join him in 1876 and then, through a London teaching agency, Verlaine was engaged as a French and Latin master at a private school in Bournemouth. This school was St. Aloysius College founded by Frederick Remington at 2 Westburn Terrace, Poole Road. The school later moved to Surrey Road to a house which is now number 24, on the corner of Queens Road. Whilst in Bournemouth Verlaine wrote two poems - one called 'Bournemouth'; the other 'La Mer de Bournemouth' - both dated 1877. A cartoon by Max Beerbohm appeared in the magazine 'Poet's Corner' in 1904, entitled 'Paul Verlaine (Usher in Private School at Bournemouth, 1877-78). We know these dates to be inaccurate because by September 1877 Verlaine was teachine in France, but in 1879 he was back in Hampshire, at a school in Lymington until his return to France in 1880. In a magazine of 1894 he published his 'Notes on England. Myself as a French Master', in which he describes his 'visits' in Hampshire with a description of Mr. Remington's school and the neighbourhood.

****

ROYAL CONNECTIONS

Bournemouth has had its Royal visitors too ... in fact in 1888 the town hosted two Queens at the same time! The first to arrive was the Queen of Sweden and Norway, Sophia Wilhelmina. She was no stranger to Bournemouth having spent the early part of 1881 at 'Crag Head' on the East Cliff. She had come then in the January but was recalled to Stockholm when the King was taken ill. The King, Oscar II, returned with her in May and his stay resulted in an improvement in his health so he was able to visit several places of interest in the neighbourhood. On the 25th May the Kind laid the foundation stone of the ,Mont Dore' Institution. The purpose of this establishment was to provide a course of treatment called the 'Mont Dore Cure', named after the area in central France where it was first commenced. The Bournekouth Visitors' Directory described 'the idea of erecting in a healthy locality on the south coast an institution for the reception of invalids and others of the upper class, requiring a change of air; or for visitors on pleasure, or residents who might desire to embrace the residential club system, and free themselves from the cares of household management, with a system of baths of approved use'.

Although until then there had been no special acknowledgment of the royal visit, this event was announced as a 'public reception' and the townspeople were asked to decorate their houses. The route from 'Crag Head' was duly decorated with bunting and a triple triumphal archway stretched across the roadway at the juntion of Gervis Place and Old Christchurch Road. The foundation-stone-laying was followed by a luncheon at the Town Hall, then on the site of the present Criterion Arcade in Old Christchurch Road. The 'Mont Dore' became the new Town Hall in 1921. The site of 'Crag Head' is now a block of flats of the same name built in 1973.

The royal couple left Bournemouth in May 1881 but the Queen returned to the town on 20th February 1888, again for the benefit of her health. While she was here (until 11th June) arrangements were made for the wedding of her second son, Prince Oscar, to a Swedish commoner, Ebba Munck. The Bishop of Winchester had agreed to the service of the Church of Sweden being performed in St. Stephen's Church because it was the only Church of England church in Bournemouth at that time not consecrated or licensed for the solemnisation of marriage according to the rites of the Church of England. The service was preceded by a civil ceremony at Christchurch and after the marriage the bridegroom, who had given up his claims to the thrones of Sweden and Norway, became known as Prince Oscar Bernadotte.

It was under this name that he and his wife signed the Visitors' Book of Newlyn's Royal Exeter Hotel when they called on Elisabeth, Empress of Austria and Queen of Hungary who was staying there. The Empress, her daughter (the Archduchess Marie Valérie) and their suites arrived in Bournemouth on 10th April 1888 on a special train from London. Although there was no special reception a great number of people assembled to greet the arrivals. Six carriages and pairs were needed to convey the visitors and according to the local newspaper (The Bournemouth Observer) 'There was an enormous quantity of luggage. For the conveyance of this three of the huge vans which Mr. Allen uses for the removal of furniture were required'. Thirty-six rooms of the Royal Exeter Hotel were taken over. The Empress signed the Visitors' Book, as did a number of local people and visitors who called on her. Elisabeth did not venture far during her stay and spent most of the time walking on the sands.

On her departure from the town on 16th April the Empress was presented with a portfolio of views of the town and it was reported that she 'was delighted with Bournemouth and that she hoped to pay it a visit again before long; she thought it was one of the most charming places she had ever been in'.

Unfortunately a return visit was not to be undertaken and the Empress, the wife of Franz Josef I, was assassinated by an anarchist in Geneva in September 1898.

Another royal visitor who came to Bournemouth, but this time incognito, was Edward, Prince of Wales, later King Edward VII. His relationship with the actress, Lillie Langtry, has in recent years become the subject of several books and a television series. Emilie Charlotte Le Breton, only daughter of the Very Reverend William Corbet Le Breton, was born in Jersey in 1853. She married Edward Langtry, a ship-owner, in 1874. They moved to London in 1877 where Lillie was soon noticed by the Prince of Wales and became his mistress. He provided for her a residence in Bournemouth to which he made secret visits. This residence was 'The Red House' in Derby Road, later to become the 'Manor Heath Hotel'. A small foundation-stone is marked 'E.L.L.1877', and another stone, on the tower, has 'E.L.1881' on it. Other evidence points to this house being the right one, and after the television series on Edward VII the hotel was renamed the 'Langtry Manor Hotel'. It promotes 'Edwardian dinners', and Lillie's ghost has even been reported!

There can be few towns, one would imagine, that could claim to have rescued Kaiser Bill, but this happened in Bournemouth, or rather in a small village just outside, in 1907. Kaiser Wilhelm II of Germany arrived at Hinton Admiral Station on 18th November for a three-week visit to Highcliffe Castle, near Christchurch. The castle was built in the early 1800s by Lord Stuart de Rothesay, and the Kaiser was staying with his descendant, Edward Stuart Wortley. Each day the party of visitors would be taken out to neighbouring places such as the New Forest, Beaulieu and Lymington. On 20th November His Imperial Highness motored to Bournemouth and through the Lower Pleasure Gardens to the Pier Approach. The motorcade, cheered by a large crowd, then drove along the newly-completed section of the Undercliff Drive which had been formally opened two weeks before, and returned via Bath Hill to Highcliffe.

On 28th and 29th November the orchestra of the Kaiser's yacht, which was moored in the Bay, performed at the Winter Gardens.

It was during one of the drives into the countryside that the Kaiser's car passed through Kinson, towards Longham, along Millhams Lane. Only a footbridge crossed the small tributary of the River Stour, near the Church - all other traffic had to negotiate the muddy ford, and it was here that the royal car became stuck. Local villagers came readily to the rescue and pushed the Emperor to safety. This incident gave rise to a poem being published in the Bournemouth Graphic of 12th December - one verse running:

When in flood 'tis no place for a bloater,
Much less for a nobleman's motor,
Jess Short and Bill Hicks
Did the work of quite six,
And, with others, they managed to float 'er.

* * * * * * *

OTHER FAMOUS NAMES ...

Come and visit the giant! An advertisement in the Bournemouth Observer of 3rd June, 1893 announced that Chang, the celebrated Chine Giant, would be 'At Home' morning and evening, daily at his address in Southcote Road. Chang stood at the height of 8 ft 2 ins. After a life of appearing in variety entertainments Chang Woo Gow retired to Bournemouth in 1890, firstly to a temporary home in Derby Road, and then to 'Moyuen', a house he had bought (now number 6) in Southcote Road. One of the reasons he settled in the area was that he suffered from consumption of the right lung. The local climate suited him and he sometimes went away on professional visits. He had travelled widely and was very popular. His wife, an Australian, died on 27th June 1893, which very much depressed him, and his own death occurred on 5th November of the same year, at the age of 52. The funeral took place at the Wimborne Road Cemetery and it was reported that the coffin measured 8 ft 4 in x 2 ft 6 in. He left two sons, aged 14 and 16, then at school in the town, who were the only relations at the funeral as neither Chang nor his wife had any other family in the country. There were, however, a large number of friends present.

Another giant among men was only a young man when he stayed in the locality. Winston Churchill (later statesman and Prime Minister) at the age of 18, came to stay in the summer of 1892 at 'Branksome Dene', in Alumhurst Road, which belonged to his aunt, Lady Wimborne. She had lent the family her house and estate at Bournemouth which included forty or fifty acres of pine-covered heathland. It also contained a deep chine spanned by a rustic bridge. Churchill

CRAIGHEAD.

EAST CLIFF FROM THE PIER.

records in his book 'My Early Life' that he, his brother and cousin were playing in the area when the other two began to chase him. He ran onto the rustic bridge but was trapped by his companions and unable to escape. He climbed over the balustrade hoping to reach one of the trees. He unfortunately misjudged his position and fell 29ft on to hard ground. Winston was badly injured and was unconscious for three days. It was three months before he left his bed. This accident could have been a tragedy and the country's future might have been quite different!

Bournemouth like Patagonia? The famous naturalist Charles Darwin came to Bournemouth in September 1862. His son had had scarlet fever, and his wife contracted the disease on their way from Kent. They stayed at 'Cliff Cottage' on the South Cliff, a picturesque thatched building belonging to the Drax family of Charborough Park. In letters written to friends he expressed a longing to get back to his work, and it was in one of these that he wrote

> 'This is a nice but barren country, and I can find nothing to look at. Even the brooks and ponds produce nothing. The country is like Patagonia'.

He was able to return home by 26th September. The cottage was pulled down in 1876 but its name is commemmorated in Cliff Cottage Road, formerly the main drive to the house.

Another visitor who stayed in the town for a short while was Benjamin Disraeli who was in his second term of office as Prime Minister. He suffered from the gout, so the Queen and his doctor recommended him to spend the winter of 1874-75 in Bournemouth. He stayed at the Bath Hotel and although it was a particularly cold winter and he complained that he was unable to get his rooms up to 60 degrees, he was decidedly better when he left in January.

The great statesman, William Ewart Gladstone, also came to the town for the sake of his health. He stayed at 'Forest House' in Grove Road, from 22nd February 1898. In March, however, it was found that his illness was incurable and that he had not long to live. He made his last Communion in church at St. Peter's on 3rd March, and shortly afterwards returned home to Hawarden in Wales, where he died on 19th May 1898.

It is perhaps unfortunate that many people seemed to have come to Bournemouth for their health, and promptly lost it!

Another such was the Reverend John Keble. He became Vicar of Hursley, near Winchester, in 1836, and for the next thirty years Hursley was to be his home. Keble was the author of a number of well-known hymns and the very popular devotional work 'The Christian Year', first published in 1827. By the early 1860s Mrs. Keble's health was giving cause for alarm and visits to a number of resorts took place in the hope of relieving her chest complaint. In the summer of 1865 it became apparent that the Kebles would have to move from Hursley and they came 'on trial' to Bournemouth where her health began to improve. As a result on the 11th October 1865, the day after their thirtieth wedding anniversary, they removed to Bournemouth. They stayed firstly in a house on the South Cliff and then in another near the Pier Approach called 'Brookside'. The house still stands but is now an annexe to the White Hermitage Hotel. Keble worshipped daily at St. Peter's Church, generally occupying a seat in the South

Transept. In 1866 Keble himself became ill and after only a week he died on 29th March, and was buried at Hursley. Mrs. Keble survived him by just six weeks and she was buried beside her husband. Early in 1867 a large window was fixed in the South Transept of St. Peter's, in commemmoration of Keble, and in 1906 the transept itself became a memorial to him when it was converted into a chapel and named the 'Keble Chapel'.

Bournemouth played a part in the birth of wireless. Guglielmo Marconi began his experiments in 1896 near Bologna, in Italy, and after applying for a provisional patent continued them in London. The Wireless Telegraph and Signal Company was formed in July 1897, and an experimental station was put up at Alum Bay on the Isle of Wight. Early in 1898 another station was erected at Bournemouth in the garden of a house called 'Madeira' on the South Cliff. Experiments were made to the Isle of Wight, Swanage, and ships at sea, and the first paid wireless message, sent on behalf of Lord Kelvin, was sent from Marconi's station at Alum Bay to his station at Bournemouth. Marconi later moved his apparatus to 'Sandhills', the house next door to 'Madeira'. Later in 1898 a station was established at the Haven Hotel, Sandbanks, Poole. This station was maintained until 1926 and many of Marconi's experiments were carried out there.

Another pioneer came to Bournemouth - this time in the field of aviation. As part of the Centenary Fetes of Bournemouth in 1910 the International Aviation Meeting was held on land between Southbourne and Hengistbury Head.

One of the aviators attending was the Hon. Charles Stuart Rolls, who, in partnership with the engineer,

Frederick Royce (who had made his first motor-car in 1904) formed the famous firm of Rolls-Royce. A number of flying events had been arranged in July 1910, and on the second day of the Meeting, 12th July, Rolls took part in an Alighting Competition. Competitors had to try to land on a marked spot on the field. Rolls took off in his Wright aeroplane but in attempting to make his landing misjudged the height and the plane hit the ground. The tail broke off, the machine collapsed, and the pilot was killed. He was 33.

This event, of course, made national news-headlines and public mourning as Rolls was the victim of the first flying accident in this country. He was buried at his family home at Llangattock in Monmouthshire and a statue was erected in Monmouth, showing Rolls holding a model aeroplane. In July 1978 a memorial stone was placed in the grounds of St. Peter's School, Southbourne, close to the spot where Rolls was killed.

Many people have come to Bournemouth since the town began a relatively short time ago - for business, for health, for pleasure. Just some of these have appeared here to show why they came and, perhaps, what part they played in the development of the history of a 'small marine village', called BOURNE MOUTH.

* * * * * * *

ALPHABETICAL LIST OF FAMOUS RESIDENTS AND VISITORS

Continued/

EVEREST

1863

KÜRŞAT BAŞAR

1963 yılında İstanbul'da doğdu. İ.Ü. Felsefe Bölümü'nü bitirdi. Birçok dergi ve gazetede yöneticilik yaptı. *Cumhuriyet*, *Yeni Yüzyıl*, *Star*, *Akşam* gibi birçok gazetede köşe yazıları yazdı. 90'lı yıllarda başladığı televizyon programlarına halen devam ediyor.

1989 yılında yayınlanan ilk kitabı *Kış İkindisinin Evinde*'yle *Haldun Taner Öykü Ödülü*'nü aldı. 2011 yılında kurduğu "Kürşat Başar Orkestrası"yla *Keşke Burada Olsaydın* ve *Kaldığımız Yerden* adlı iki albüm yayınladı.

KİTAPLARI:

1989 *Kış İkindisinin Evinde* (öykü) (Haldun Taner Öykü Ödülü)
1990 *Konuştuğumuz Gibi Uzaklara* (roman)
1992 *Sen Olsaydın Yapmazdın, Biliyorum* (roman)
1996 *Aşkı Bulmanın ve Korumanın Yolları* (roman)
2000 *İğreti Yaşamlar* (yazılar/denemeler)
2003 *Başucumda Müzik* (roman)
2006 *Çok Güldük Ağlamayalım* (yazılar/denemeler)
2006 *Sanki Bir Roman Kahramanı/Doğan Hızlan* (biyografi)
2014 *Yaz* (roman)
2018 *Bazen Unutmak İstersin* (deneme)
2019 *Aklımda Hep Sen* (roman)

KÜRŞAT BAŞAR

Aklımda Hep Sen

§

Yayın No: **1863**
Türkçe Edebiyat: **753**

Aklımda Hep Sen
Kürşat Başar

Kapak tasarımı: Füsun Turcan Elmasoğlu
Sayfa tasarımı: M. Aslıhan Özçelik

1. Basım: Haziran 2019 (100.000 adet)

ISBN: 978 - 605 - 185 - 405 - 2
Sertifika No: 43949

Baskı ve cilt: Melisa Matbaacılık
Matbaa sertifika no: 12088
Çiftehavuzlar Yolu Acar Sanayi Sitesi, No: 8
Bayrampaşa/İstanbul
Tel: (0212) 674 97 23 Faks: (0212) 674 97 29

EVEREST YAYINLARI
Alemdar Mahallesi Ticarethane Sokak No: 15 34110
Cağaloğlu-İstanbul
Tel: (212) 513 34 20-21 Faks: (212) 512 33 76
e-posta: info@everestyayinlari.com
www. everestyayinlari.com
www. twitter. com/everestkitap
facebook.com/everestyayinlari

Everest, Alfa Yayınları'nın tescilli markasıdır.

Aklımda Hep Sen

Tren uçsuz bucaksız ormanların arasından geçiyor. Beni, bu bilmediğim ülkenin sonbaharından, kırmızı, sarı yaprakların, düzenli bir hayatı simgeleyen küçük evlerin, kasabaların arasından gitmem gereken yere, son istasyona taşıyor.

Belki benim için de son istasyona...

Görüntüler hızla geçiyor yanımdan. Burada, olduğum yerde duruyorum aslında ama tam da hayat gibi, nelerle karşılaşacağımı bilmediğim bir geleceğe doğru gidiyorum.

Bir yandan da geçmişi izliyorum ve anlar hızla gelecekten geçmişe doğru yanımdan akıp gidiyor.

İşte şimdi burada, sanki elimdeki dürbünle uzaklara bakıyormuş gibi biraz puslu, biraz titrek görüntüleri izliyorum ve kendimi oralarda, geçmişte bir yerlerde görüyorum.

Uzak geçmişi bugüne getiren bir dürbünle...

Olup biten ne varsa anlatmak istiyorum, anneannem derdi hep, hayat fırtınadaki bulutlar gibi geçip gidiyor ve siz değişen görüntülere, ışığa bakarken birdenbire kendinizi bambaşka bir yerde buluyorsunuz.

Nerede mi?

Nerede olacak?

Hayatın sonunda tabii...

Üstelik hayatın sonunda olsanız da olmasanız da, bir gün gelip geçmişe bakmak, en azından zaman zaman bir yerlerden çıkıp gelen ve birbirine bağlanmayan anıları, oraya buraya, karmakarışık çekmecelere, dolaplara tıkıştırılmış dosyaları, belgeleri toplar gibi yeniden yaşamanızı sağlar.

Belki benim için biraz erken ama bu garip yolculuğun sonunda ne olacağını ben dahil hiç kimse bilmediği için en azından unutmak istemediğim şeyleri yeniden biraraya getirmek istiyorum.

Kimbilir belki de tutunabileceğim tek şey bu olduğu için...

Ne olursa olsun, iyi ya da kötü, içlerinden bazıları kaybolup gitse de anılar aşinadır bize...

O yüzden onların yanında rahatım, çünkü dediğim gibi bir sonraki durakta ne olacağını bile bilmiyorum.

Karşı koltukta oturan yaşlıca şişman yabancı uyukluyor. Parmaklarını birbirine kenetleyip göbeğinin üstüne koymuş, arasıra başparmağını çeviriyor, dışarı bakıyor, yeniden gözlerini kapıyor. Ara ara dalıyor, iç geçiriyor. Giyimine, haline, tavrına bakılırsa (eski moda ama kaliteli yün takım, klasik çizgili kravat, yakasında, benim bilmediğim ama herhalde bir aidiyete işaret eden rozet) hayatını iyi geçirmiş birine benziyor. Uzun bir evlilik, çocuklar hatta torunlar, pazar günleri ailecek toplandıkları güzel, bahçeli bir ev...

Öyle mi?

Kimbilir. Hiç kimse aslında göründüğü gibi değil. Belki de aklıma bile gelmeyecek garip bir hayatı oldu ve gözlerini kapadığında herkesten gizlediği hayatının ayrıntılarını düşünüyor. Belki yaşamın bir yerinde geri alınamayacak yanlış bir karar verdiğini...

Yeniden dışarı bakıyorum, trenin ritmine göre sallanıyoruz yerimizde, kimi zaman tekdüzeleşen, kimi zaman değişen o sesle birlikte görüntüleri eşleştirmeye çalışıyorum. Kendimce bir oyun işte...

Evimden çok uzaktayım.

Zaten benim evim var mıydı, gerçekte hiç oldu mu ondan da emin değilim. Tek bildiğim, herhalde tam da bu yüzden, kendi içimde bir ev kurduğum.

Evet evim var, içimde, benimle her yere gelen bir ev.

Zaten asıl önemli olan da budur belki.

Annem evine çok düşkündü. Bütün hayatını o evin içine eşyalar, anmalıklar, biblolar, süsler doldurmakla geçirdi. Gittiği her yerden ne bulduysa alıp o eve koydu. Neredeyse artık bize yer kalmayacak kadar çok eşyanın içinde, orada sonsuza dek yaşayabileceği bir ev yaptığını sanmış olmalı.

Eski kralların yalnızca bir odada yaşasalar da kendilerine devasa saraylar hatta öldükten sonra da korunacakları muhteşem mezarlar yapmaları gibi...

Ama onlar nasıl bir hayat yaşayacaklarına ve nasıl öleceklerine karar verdikleri halklarını ve düşmanlarını korkutmak için yapmışlardı bunları.

Anneminki yalnızca başa çıkamadığı ya da asla sevemediği dünyadan kaçma ve kendisine ait mükemmel bir hayat kurma çabasıydı herhalde.

Şöyle dönüp bakınca insanın hayatında belirli günler, anlar, resimler ötekilerin önüne geçiyor. Yaşarken aklınıza gelmeyecek rastlantılarla, yalnızca birkaç saniyelik bir gecikmeyle değişen geleceğin dönüm noktaları aslında sayılı resimle anlatılabiliyor.

Evet evet tam da eski filmlerdeki dış sesin tonlamasıyla, 'kader denilen örümceğin ağlarını ördüğü' anlardan bahsediyorum.

Benim çocukluğumda habire 'iç gösteren gözlük' diye birşey çıkartırlardı. Gazetelerde bile böyle haberler çıkar, buna inanan da çok olurdu.

Keşke kaderin ağlarını gören bir gözlük bulsalardı.

İyi olmaz mıydı?

Evet çok uzaklarda, bilmediğim bir yerde, bilinmeyen bir yolculuktayım ama keyfim yerinde ya da en azından ben hala öyle sanmak istiyorum.

Tren sallandıkça gözlerim kapanıyor, yarı uyur yarı uyanık bir haldeyim.

Her zaman olduğu gibi gerçekle düşün arasında…

Ben…Ebru…

Dediğim gibi benim evim içimde.

Onu ne zaman yaptığımı çok iyi hatırlıyorum. İşte o, zaman içinde kafamda değiştirip farklılaştırsam da unutulmaz resimlerden biri, belki de en önemlisi, okuldan eve geldiğim o sıradan günlerden biri.

Okul evimize çok yakındı. Her gün Seda'yla birlikte yürüyerek gider çıkışta da yine yürüyerek eve gelirdik.

Seda bir sokak ötemizde otururdu.

Uzun, sıkıcı bir yaz daha bitmişti. En azından artık ortaokula gideceğimiz için mutluyduk. Büyümüştük işte sonunda.

Seda, eteklerinin altına çıt çıt dikip okuldan çıkınca eteklerini katlayan ablaları anlatıyordu. Biz de yapar mıydık? Yapardık tabii annem farketmezse...

"Annem mi etmeyecek," dedim, "delirdin herhalde, ne çıt çıtı, düğme yerinden iplik çıksa farkeder o..."

"Ben yaparım," dedi Seda. Ne garip o konuşmayı hala hatırlamam...

Çünkü ilk kez, annesi olmadığı için mutluymuş gibi söylemişti bunu...

Eve geldim. Annem her zamanki gibi okulda neler olduğunu sordu, ben de her zamanki gibi geçiştirdim. Neden çocuklara okulda olanları sorarlar bilmem. Çocuklar, iş yerinde bugün ne oldu diye sorar mı büyüklere?

Kurabiyeyle meyve suyu getirdi annem. Elimi yüzümü yıkadım, üstümü değiştirdim, çünkü beş dakika bile formayla otursam laf edeceğini bilirdim.

Annem saçını topuz yapmıştı, anlaşılan yine kuaföre gitmişti benden sonra. Mutfakta yemekle uğraşırken ödev var mı, Seda nasılmış gibi sorular sormaya devam ediyordu.

"Matematikse baban gelmeden birazını yap istersen sonra televizyona dalacaksın yine..."

Henüz oniki yaşındaydım ve kaç yıldır artık bu konuşmalara alışmıştım. Annelerin işi bu gibi görünüyordu, söylenmek... Ama annem başkalarından biraz daha fazla söyleniyordu galiba, bana, babama, herkese...

Her nedense hiç birimiz bir türlü onun istediği mükemmellikte olamıyorduk.

Yine de artık öğrenmiştim, özellikle eve girdiğim zaman onunla biraz konuşmazsam, kendi dünyama çekilirsem işi iyice abartır, bütün gece bunu mesele ederdi.

O yüzden laf olsun diye, bildiğim halde, "Fatma nerede anne?" diye sordum.

Elinde bez mutfaktan çıktı, anlaşılan tam yerinden yakalamıştım.

"Nerede olacak yine bugün erken izne çıkacağım diye tutturdu, sürekli bir hastalık, bir gün annesi, bir gün dedesi, bir gün bilmemnesi... Derdi bitmiyor bunun..."

Aklım tabii ki başka yerdeydi ama dinliyor gibi göründüm çünkü anlaşılan bugün de Fatma'ya takmıştı.

"Yok göndereceğim ben bunu da, kadın bulmak kolay değil, gelen gideni aratıyor..." Yanıma gelip saçlarımı okşadı sonra da kokladı eğilip.

"E, sen terlemişssin, ne yapıyorsunuz okulda anlamıyorum ki, teneffüste yine koşturdunuz değil mi?"

"Yok anne sıcaktı işte ben ne yapayım?"

"Neyse neyse baban gelmeden bir duşa gir bari... Dur şu böreği fırına koyayım da... Seversin sen bak ıspanaklı börek var..."

"Yaşasın..."

İşte böyle bir gündü. Ötekilerden pek farkı olmayan...

Ben okuldan gelirim, bu konuşma benzer şekilde her gün tekrarlanır, akşama doğru babam gelir, o fazla konuşmaz, benim kafamı okşar öper, üstünü değişir, ajansı açar, annem yine ona da olan biteni anlatır, belki nadiren birileri gelecekse hazırlık yapılır yoksa akşam ben odama gider ders çalışırım, onlar içerde oturur, televizyon izler, sonra da yatma saati...

Özellikle maç varsa babam onu kaçırmaz, annem her ne kadar söylense de maç sonrası tartışmalarını bile kendi kendine sanki duyacaklarmış gibi onlara cevap yetiştirerek izlerdi.

Nasıl anneme göre kimse tam istediği gibi değilse babama göre de hemen herkes aptaldı, salaktı, budalaydı hatta çok kızdığı zaman söylediği şekliyle 'habenneka'ydı.

Politikacılar, gazeteciler, sporcular, artık akla kim geliyorsa hepsine sinirlenirdi.

Ama onun siniri bile fazla üst perdeden değildi.

Bazen annem, "Canım sen niye sinirleniyorsun ilgisiz adamlara, sana ne?" dediği zaman, "Doğru doğru bunlara sinirlenmeye bile değmez, sen bana çay koy," diye iki dakika önceki sözlerinden vazgeçerdi.

Ayda birkaç kez de babamın iş seyahatleri vardı. O zamanlar ya annemin bir arkadaşı gelir ya ikimiz yalnız kalırdık. O zaman hiç adeti olmasa da ya benimle yatar ya da geç yatmama izin verirdi.

Eğer yatmak istemezsem ve ısrar ediyorsa tam yatacakken ona olmadık bir soru sorardım. Ölümden sonra hayat var mı gibilerinden... O zaman kuşkuya kapılır, bana cevap vermesi gerektiğini düşünürdü ve en az bir yarım saati daha uyumadan geçirebilirdim.

Babamın seyahatleri her günkü hayatımı biraz değiştirdiği için ve tabii bana mutlaka kimsede olmayan hediyeler getireceği için iyiydi.

Şikayetçi miydim bu hayattan? Bilmem... Pek farkında değildim. Bizimkisi de böyle bir hayattı işte. Ama sanki şu salondaki kahverengi koltuklar bile yıllardır süren bu düzenden yorgun hatta üzgün gibi gelirdi bana.

Banyoda biraz oyalandım. Hayatta en sevdiğim şey bugün bile sıcak sudur. Su üstüme aksın öyle saatlerce oturabilirim.

Banyodan çıktım, annem saçlarımı kuruttu, fırçaladı, topladı, masa kuruldu, kapı çaldı.

Babam geldi.

Uzun boylu, yapılı bir adamdı babam. Şişman değildi ama iri yarıydı. Saçları erkenden beyazlaşmış ama dökülmemişti. Onları kısa kestirir, kendi gençliğindeki Cary Grant gibi oyuncuların tarzını beğenirdi. Pek fazla konuşup gülmezdi. Aslında yüzünden ne düşündüğünü tam anlayamadığınız insanlardandı. Kızdı mı, sevindi mi, nadiren belli ederdi. Genel olarak suratı asıktı.

Tok, kısık bir sesle konuşurdu. Sesi öyle anneminki gibi inip çıkmazdı. Yine annem gibi eliyle koluyla da konuşmazdı. Sakin bir adamdı kısacası.

Sanki her zaman çok derin konular düşünürmüş de günün birinde bütün bunları birdenbire anlatacakmış gibi bir hali vardı.

Gerçi hiç anlatmadı, ayrı...

Zaten annem öyle bir düzen kurmuştu ki, babamın belki başka türlü davranma şansı da kalmamıştı. Başkalarıyla konuşurken bile ondan üçüncü şahıs olarak, Kemal Bey diye sözederdi.

Manavdan birşey alırken bile "Kemal bey onu sevmez, sen şunlardan ver," diye konuşurdu.

Sanki babamın kendi istekleri yoktu, onun yerine hepsini annem bilirdi.

Ben de babamla siz diye konuşurdum. Bu annem için asalet göstergesi miydi, bir tür disiplin miydi bilmiyorum. Başka çocuklarla babalarını görüp aklım erdiğinde sormuştum. O zaman da bunun saygıyla ilgili olduğuna dair uzun bir nutuk dinlemiştim.

Babam küçükken benimle oynardı. Haftasonları gezmeye giderdik. Beni at gibi sırtına alıp dolaştırır, ellerimden tutup çevirerek uçak oynatır, tatillerde denizde omuzuna bindirip gezdirirdi.

Galiba o zamanlar daha çok gülerdi.

Gece yanlarında uyumak istesem annemin tüm karşı çıkmalarına rağmen babam izin verirdi.

Sonra buna kesin bir yasak koydu annem.

Ben büyümeye başladım ve babamla oyunlar da giderek azaldı. Sonra artık bazen keyfi yerindeyse yanına çağırır, kendince hoşuma gideceğini veya birşeyler öğreneceğimi düşünerek aldığı kutu oyunlarını oynamak isterdi. Ben bazılarından çok sıkılsam da onunla oynamak için sesimi çıkartmazdım. Bana soru sorduğunda aslında ona neler anlatmak isterdim ama yapamazdım.

Babam geldi beni öptü, annemi öptü, içeri geçti. Biraz sonra annem de yanına gitti.

Yemeğe oturmadıkları için merak edip içeri gittim, odalarının kapısı aralıktı, benim odamın hemen yanındaydı.

"Seyahate mi gidiyorsun, birden mi çıktı bu, söylemedin," dedi annem.

"Evet," dedi babam.

"Nereye peki?"

Ses gelmedi.

"Ne oldu Kemal bey bir terslik mi var?" dedi annem.

Bir terslik vardı, evet. Çocuklar konuşmaları bazen anlamaz ama belki seslerden olup biteni sezerler.

Annemin sesinde bir gariplik vardı.

Babamsa konuşmuyordu.

"Birşey olmadı," dedi sonunda, "gidiyorum, kendinize iyi bakın, sonra konuşuruz."

Ben odama geçtim, babam elinde bavulla dışarı çıktı, kapıdan beni gördü, gelip öptü ama aceleyle, başımı okşadı her zamanki gibi… Sanki bana söyleyecekleri varmış da bir an düşünüp vazgeçmiş gibi geldi bana.

Kapıdan çıktı gitti.

Her zamanki gibi seyahate mi gidiyordu? Öyleyse annem niye onu uğurlamamıştı?

Annemin yanına gittim.

Yatağın yanındaki koltuğa oturmuştu.

Loş odada öylece oturuyordu.

"Anne," dedim, "nereye gidiyor babam? Seyahate mi?"

O zaman bana baktı. Titreyen bir sesle,

"Evet kızım," dedi, "seyahate..."

İnsanın babası ölür.

İnsanın babası, annesi boşanır.

İnsanın anne, babası kavga eder, sonra biri öfkeyle çıkar gider.

İnsanın babası seyahate gidiyorum diye bir gün ansızın çıkıp gider mi?

Benimki gitti.

Hiçbir şey söylemeden.

O an'ı, onun kapıdan çıkıp gitme anını şimdi hayal meyal hatırlıyorum, nedense bazen bir an dönüp bana bakmış gibi geliyor, bazense bunu sonradan uydurduğumu düşünüyorum.

Ama insan öyle bir bakışı kendi kendine uyduramaz...

Annem yemekte konuşmadı. Gözü bir yere takılmış gibi televizyona baktı ve sessizce yemeğini yedi. Ben bir terslik olduğunu biliyordum ama anlamamış gibi yaptım.

Belki de böyle düşünmek o an işime geldi. Yani babamın her zamanki gibi iş gezisine gittiğini ve tabii ki bir iki gün sonra geri geleceğini düşünmek...

Belki de sorsam annemin duymak istemeyeceğim şeyler söyleyeceğinden korktum.

Hep korkarım kötü şey duymaktan.

O yüzden sormam.

Hala bugün de öyle...

Annem ki her zaman, en kötü olayda bile istifini bozmayıp kendi gibi davranmayı bilirdi, şimdi konuşamıyordu. Benim bildiğim annem ne olursa olsun benimle her zamanki gibi konuşup sorun yokmuş, herşey yolundaymış gibi yapardı. Ama yapamıyordu.

Kimseyi aramadı.

Kimseyle konuşmadı.

Sonunda, "Yemeğim bitti, ödevimi yapayım," diyince, "Tamam," dedi sadece.

Allahın cezası matematik ödevinin kafama girmesi pek mümkün değildi o akşam ama uyduruktan çalıştım işte. Sonra biraz kitap okudum...

Bilmediğim bir ülkede, bilmediğim bir zamanda, mahallenin çocukları karşı çeteler kurmuş birbiriyle savaşıyordu. Anlamsız yere acıklı bir kitaptı.

Annemin kuralları: Her akşam en az on sayfa...

İçeri gitsem? Onunla konuşsam? Neler olup bittiğini sorsam?

Keşke anneannem olsaydı, o herşeyi çözerdi.

Bilemedim ne yapacağımı...

Biraz daha oyalandım. Annem içerde sevdiği diziyi izliyordu.

Sonra gelip, "Ödevler bitti," dedim. Kontrol etmek istemedi bu kez.

Giyinirken yanıma geldi, çantamı topladım, ödevleri, kitapları koydum. Yatarken yanımdaki küçük lambayı açtı, lambanın içinden şelale akardı, onu izleyerek uyurdum ben. Beni öptü, okşadı, biraz yanımda kaldı, ben de ona sarıldım çünkü üzgündü. O söylemese de ben biliyordum. Sonra dönüp kıvrıldım ve uykuya dalmış gibi yaptım ki, gitsin.

Çünkü ağlamak istiyordum. Nedenini bilmiyordum ama ağlamak istiyordum ve onun görmesini istemiyordum.

Biraz sonra üstümü örtüp alnımdan öptü ve gitti. Şelaleyi kapadım, yorganı kafama çektim ve ağlamaya başladım.

Kimsenin bana açıklama yapmasına gerek yoktu.

Ben karanlıkta ağlayıp uyurken annem bütün gece salonda oturmuş.

On yedi yılda yarattığı bu mükemmel düzene bakarak... İstanbul'un en güzel manzaralarından birine bakan, ünlü tasarımcıların imzasını taşıyan mobilyalar, en pahalı ağaçlardan lambriler, dünyanın dört bir yanından tek tek toplanmış biblolar, objeler, resimler, heykellerle doldurulmuş bir ev...

Yıllarla kurulmuş bir hayat.

Mumlara, sürekli yenilenen renkli çiçeklerle dolu kristal vazolara, gümüş ve kristal şekerliklere, tablalara, geçmiş hep bizimle kalsın diye zamandan kesilmiş fotoğrafların konulduğu çerçevelere, en küçük ayrıntılara kadar tıka basa doldurulmuş bu evde öylece oturmuştu karanlıkta.

Belki bütün bu yılları düşünerek... Belki bundan sonrasını düşünerek... Belki de düşünemeden...

Bazen annem o bayat konulu, dokunaklı eski filmleri izlerken ağlardı. Ben de o komik filmlere ağlamasına gülerdim. O zaman bana, "Günün birinde sen de bunları anlayacaksın," derdi.

Gerçekten de insan bazı şeyleri ancak "günün birinde" anlayabiliyormuş.

Kendi başına gelince, hayatı biraz daha öğrenince, en beklenmedik şeylerin olabileceğini görünce, yaşananların hiç de öyle gülüp geçilecek gibi olmayabileceğini farkedince herhalde...

Ve bir gün gelip, onlar ne kadar basit, ne kadar sıradan, ne kadar uydurma anlatılırsa anlatılsın, hatta bir reklam filmine sığdırılmış ya da uydurma bir şarkının sözleri haline getirilmiş olursa olsun artık gülemiyormuşsunuz...

Ben de anladım ama çok sonra...

Babam o akşam öylesine çıkıp gitti ve bir daha da hiç gelmedi.

Birkaç gün geçti. Sonra birkaç gün daha geçti. Yavaş yavaş neler olduğu ortaya çıkmaya başlayıncaya kadar bekledik.

Annem onun belki birşeye kızdığını, belki işle ilgili sorun olduğunu, hatta belki bize söyleyemediği bir hastalığa yakalandığını düşündü.

Ama çok geçmeden gerçekleri öğrenecektik.

Çoğumuz zaman zaman yaşadığımız hayatı tümüyle değiştirebilmeyi, yeniden başlasak nasıl olacağını hayal etmişizdir.

Büyük ikramiye kazananların ortadan kaybolduğuna dair hikayeler bana hep bunu hatırlatır.

Ama babama ikramiye çıkmamıştı. Amcamla ortak şirketlerinin hesabını zaman içinde gizlice yurtdışına aktarmış, orada kimsenin bilmediği bir hayat kurmuş, ev almış, evlenmiş, belki yeni bir kimlik bile edinmişti.

Amcam onun peşine düşmedi. Her nedense kendisinden çalınan parayla da ilgilenmedi. Galiba kardeşinin bu yaptığından o denli utandı ki bu konuda hiç konuşmadı.

Zaten bizimle de görüşmedi.

Yengem öldükten sonra yaşlı bakıcısıyla oturduğu evinde birkaç yıl sonra hayatını kaybetti. Cenazesine sadece üç beş kişinin geldiğini duyduk.

Anneme bir tanıdığımızın, onun son yıllarını sürekli içerek ve uyuyarak geçirdiğini söylediğini hayal meyal hatırlıyorum.

İnsan hayatını değiştirmek isteyebilir değil mi?

Benim anlayamadığım, bunu neden anneme söylemediğiydi. Ne olursa olsun boşanmak isteyen birini yanınızda zorla tutamazsınız. Birkaç kez bunu anneme sormak istedim ama soramadım. Bu konuyu açmanın onu her zaman fazlasıyla inciteceğini düşündüm.

Yıllarca güvendiğiniz, hep yanınızda olan birinin, çocuğunuzun babasının hem yalancı hem de sahtekar çıkması o kadar utanılacak birşeydi ki amcamın da annemin de bu konuda hiç konuşmaması belki en doğrusuydu.

Sanırım her ikisi de bu durumu açıkça söyleyip konuşmanın asıl kendilerine hakaret, hayat boyu inandıklarını boşa çıkaran inanılmaz bir felaket olduğunu düşünüyorlardı.

Ben uzun zaman bunları bir biçimde bize açıklayacağını düşündüm. Parayla mı ilgiliydi? İşlediği suçun ortaya çıkacağını düşündüğü için mi kaçmıştı yalnızca? Yoksa orada aşık olduğu bir kadının ona artık son bir şans vermesi, onu zorlaması yüzünden mi böyle yapmıştı?

İnsan en azından mektup yazıp bunları anlatamaz mıydı?

Ama bilmiyordum ki, özellikle duyguların, insan davranışının çılgınca savrulmalarının aslında böyle basit açıklaması yoktur. Deli gibi sevdiğiniz birine onun sizi neden öyle sevmediğini sorduğunuzda vereceği cevap neyi açıklayabilir ki?

Ve açıklasa bile sahiden sizi rahatlatır mı?

Annem yine de uzun süre bunlara inanmadı.

Herkese hatta Seda'ya bile babamın uzun bir iş seyahatine gittiğini söyleyerek oyalandık.

Ama sonunda anneannem geldi ve duruma el koydu.

Doğrusu o günlerde tam olarak ne düşündüğümü, ne hissettiğimi hatırlamıyorum. Şaşkındım galiba. Çok üzülmüş müydüm? Bilmiyorum. O ilk geceden sonra ağladığımı da sanmıyorum.

Sürekli gelen gidenlerle bu konu konuşuluyor, herkes ben gelince fısıldamaya başlıyor, kimileri babamın bir maceraya kalkıştığını, zamanla hatasını anlayıp döneceğini, kimileri namussuz bir kadına kapıldığı için yakında zaten kapıya konulacağını, paraları bitince kadının onu bırakacağını, kimileri de beni özleyip nasıl olsa yakında arayacağını söylüyordu.

Büyüdükçe, yıllar geçtikçe bunları unuttum. Ya da galiba unuttuğumu sandım. Öylesine derin, sonsuz bir uçuruma gömdüm ki tüm bunların üstesinden rahatlıkla geldiğimi sandım. Öyle ki artık babamın yüzünü bile doğru dürüst hatırlamıyordum. Bir keresinde Seda, "Peki ben ne yapayım, benim annem de babam da yok ve onları hiç görmedim," demişti. Öyle ya, babam da kazada ölmüş olabilirdi. Bunu böylece kabullenmek çok mu zor?

Evet zormuş.
Bunu ancak yıllar yıllar sonra anlayabildim.

Yine de bu sorular, nasıl bunca yıl herkesten gizli bir hayat daha sürdürdüğü, nasıl en sevdiklerinin hayatını ve parasını çalıp yine de herşey yolundaymış gibi davranabildiği, nasıl böylesine bir parçalanmışlıkla yaşayabildiği soruları aklımdan hiç çıkmadı.

Ta ki, Ferhat'ın sergisine gidip o resmi görene kadar.

Dev tuvalde sayısız insan figürü... İşçiler, köylüler, kadınlar, erkekler, sanatçılar, ünlüler, çıplak kadınlar, çarşaflı kadınlar, sporcular, zenginler, yoksullar, sarışınlar, esmerler, güzeller, çirkinler... Her türden insan vardı bu resimde...

Ama hepsinin yüzleri farklıydı. Bir taraftan bakınca başka, biraz eğilince başka bir yüzünü görebiliyordunuz insanların.

Aslında korkunç bir resimdi. Çünkü bir yüzüyle gülerken bir yüzüyle ağlayan, hem sevimli hem ürkütücü yüzlerdi bunlar.

Bana önce çok komik birşey hatırlattı. Tuvalete girdiğimde çocukluğumdan beri yer döşemesine bakarım ve çizgilerde, kendiliğinden oluşmuş damarlarda yüzler, desenler bulmaya çalışırım.

Ama bu dev resmin başka bir özelliği vardı. Yüzleri değişmeyen yalnızca aralarda görünen küçük çocuklar ve hayvanlardı.

O zaman Ferhat'ın burada ne anlatmak istediğini düşünmeye başladım. Bu resim bizim dışarıya verdiğimiz fotoğrafla gerçek kimliğimizi, belki farklı kimliklerimizi, gizlenmiş yüzlerimizi anlatıyordu.

Çocuklar ve hayvanlar başka kimliklere gizlenemez.

Onlar bizi bir başkası olarak kandırmazlar.

Yanıma geldi ve şaşkın şaşkın bakakaldığım resmin önünde benimle birlikte eserine baktı. O sırada sergiyi gezenler, bir kadınla bir erkeğin konuşmasını dinliyorlardı. Banttan verilen bu konuşma oldukça garipti. Çünkü söylenen sözler farklı anlamlara çekilebilirdi. Aynı konuşmayı herkes farklı biçimde yorumlayabilirdi.

"Ne o," dedi, "bütün figürleri tek tek inceliyorsun galiba?"

Ona baktım ve ağlamamak için kendimi zor tuttum.

Resmin altında bir yazı vardı. Bu resmi artık yaşamayan bir arkadaşına ithaf etmişti.

Ve ben o arkadaşının kim olduğunu biliyordum.

Onu ihbar eden ve ülkesinden kaçmasına neden olan kişiydi o.

"Bu herkesin bir başkası olduğu bir dünyanın resmi mi?" diye sordum.

"Bir başkası mı?" dedi, gülerek, "Hayır, birçok başkası olduğu bir resim.."

Ama bu çok sonraydı...

Şimdi düşünüyorum da gerçekten çok garip geliyor bütün bunlar.

Hani insanın filmlerde gördüğü, gazetelerde okuduğu ama benim başıma gelmez dediği türden...

Ama gelmişti işte.

Hayatı boyunca işiyle evi arasında yaşayan, iş gezileri dışında pek bir yere gitmeyen, fazla arkadaşı olmayan hatta hiç arkadaşı olmayan silik bir adamın yıllar sonra birdenbire çıkıp gitmesi, yeni bir hayata başlaması bugün bile beni şaşırtıyor.

İtiraf edebilirim artık. Belki de babam olmasa, başka biri olsa bu hikaye bana ilginç gelirdi.

Ama sanırım o zaman gelmedi.

Çünkü birkaç ay sonra görünürde herhangi bir belirti yokken birdenbire yere düştüm ve mosmor kesildim. Konuşamadım, hareket edemedim. Beni hastaneye götürdüler ve birkaç saat sonra kendime geldim.

Belki de hastalığımın babamın gidişiyle ilgisi yoktu ama ben öyle inandım.

Ve birşeye inandığım zaman dünyanın en büyük saçmalığı da olsa ne yazık ki ne derseniz deyin benim için farketmez.

Ve elbette ne olursa olsun bir çocuk hastalandığında, korktuğunda, kendisini yalnız hissettiğinde babasının yanına geleceğine inanır ve bekler.

Yalnızlık dedim.

Artık bunca yıl sonra bunu söyleyebilirim, yalnızlığın ne olduğunu, gerçekte ne anlama geldiğini bilen pek az kişiden biriyim.

O zamanlar bütün bunların tam anlamıyla farkında değildim tabii... Hayat yine de devam ediyordu. Ama annesinin masal kahramanı, okulun en sevilen, kıskanılan başarılı kızı, gözlerine, saçlarına herkesin sokakta yürürken bile methiyeler düzdüğü Ebru'ya tıpkı o gereksiz yere hüzünlü masallardaki gibi birşey olmuştu, nazar değdi, büyü yapıldı dedikleri gibi birşey...

İyi ama o büyüyü bozacak, belki bir öpücükle herşeyi eski haline getirecek biri var mıydı?

Yoksa o, yalnızca biz küçük kızların, hayatı ne olursa olsun bir gün daha sürdürebilmesi için uydurulmuş bir masal mıydı?

Bence çok da önemli değil. Önemli olan böyle bir masala inanmak isteyip istemediğiniz çünkü. Ben böyle bir masala inanmak istiyordum.

Ama daha önce anlatmam gerekenler var.

Birdenbire bütün hayatımız değişti.
Bizde masalın tersi oldu.
Herkesin gıpta ettiği prenses bir anda Külkedisi'ne dönüşüverdi.

Anneannem (ki ona herkes gibi benim de Sare Hanım dememi ister, anneanne, nene, abla gibi laflardan hoşlanmazdı) Emirgan'da tepeden denize bakan, ağaçların içinde, oldukça eski, iki katlı bir evde oturuyordu.

Bizim evle karşılaştırınca onun zengin mi yoksul mu olduğunu pek anlayamazdım. Çünkü evin kendisi gibi eşyalar da oldukça eskiydi. Hatta o zamanlar artık her eve giren televizyon bile yoktu.

Ama buna karşılık belki de gördüğüm en güzel tablolar, heykeller, porselenler, kristal avizeler, mobilyalar da oradaydı. Evet gardırop, komodinler kurt yenikleriyle doluydu, bazen oradan buradan sular damlardı ama evin tavanları bile inanılmaz güzellikte ahşap işlemelerle bezeliydi.

Sonradan o evin aslında çok ünlü bir mimarın evi olduğunu, öldüğü zaman dedemin satın aldığını öğrenmiştim.

Bazı haftasonları orada kalırdım. Bazen de yaz aylarında daha uzun süreliğine... O bakımsız bahçe benim için masal ülkesine açılan kapı gibiydi. Orada kendi kendime oyunlar oynar, kendime dair hikayeler uydurmaya bayılırdım.

Sürekli bahçede kaybolup bulunmak bu oyunların en hoşuma gideniydi. Ve ancak yıllar sonra evdeki telaşın aslında tümüyle beni kandırmak için kurgulandığını, kimsenin benim kaybolmamdan korkmadığını öğrenecektim.

Ama aslında bu evin özelliği kapının neredeyse sürekli açık olmasıydı. Gelen giden eksik olmazdı. Salondaki büyük masa hemen her akşam dolar, dönemin ünlü yazarları, sanatçıları gelir, yenilir içilir, sabahlara kadar sohbet edilirdi.

Ben onu anneannem olduğu için sevmezdim. Ona herkes gibi ben de hayran olduğum için severdim. O zaten tanıdığım kimseye benzemezdi. Bana da torunu ya da küçük bir kız gibi davranmazdı.

Annemden o kadar farklıydı ki nasıl olup da annemin onun kızı olduğunu bugün bile anlayamam.

Hani şu eski filmlerdeki gibi annemin başkasının kızı olup da evlatlık verildiğini duysam hiç şaşırmam.

Yan evdeki Yıldız Teyze anneannemden hiç çıkmazdı. Evin hizmetine bakan Saniye gelen gidenden bunalıp arada bir gitmeye kalkışır ama sonra yine kendiliğinden çıkıp gelirdi. Onun bu gidip gelmeleri eğlence gibiydi.

Sare Hanım arada mutfağa girip özel bir yemek yapmak istemezse elini birşeye sürmezdi. Evin içinde sürekli "Saniye, Saniye" diye seslenişi duyulurdu.

Artık kendisini bir anlamda evin sahibi gibi gören Saniye de bu duruma çok alıştığından, önce ortada görünmeyip onu bağırtır, anneannem ne istediğini unutursa ne ala, unutmaz da sesini yükseltirse, dalga geçerek, "Tamam tamam bir saniye," diye çıkagelirdi.

Gelip giden insanların hepsinin ayrı özellikleri, tuhaflıkları, hem de bana göre çok acayip huyları olmakla birlikte Saniye belki de bu evdeki en komik tiplerden biriydi.

Gelenlerin çoğunu sanki o da sanat ortamında yetişmiş gibi tanır, kim ne yer ne içer, kim hangi meyveyi sevmez, kim hangi gün gelir, kim kiminle karşılaşmak istemez, kimler biraraya gelirse kavga çıkar hepsini bilirdi.

Konuklar hakkında da kendi fikirleri vardı. Kimini hiç sevmez, kimine hayran, kimiyle uzun uzun sohbetler eder, kiminin dedikodularını anlatmaya bayılırdı. Hangisi sinsi, hangisi çıkarcı, hangisi iyi insan bunları kendince garip işaretlerden çıkartıp edebiyat eleştirmenlerinin karakter analizi yapması gibi ortaya atıverir, anneannemi çok güldürürdü.

Sare Hanım, babamla annemin evlenmesini istememiş, evlendikten sonra da pek görüşmemiş, ben doğduktan sonra araları biraz düzelmişti.

Babamın da ondan hoşlandığını sanmam. Çünkü ne zaman beni çağırtsa sinirlenir, göndermek istemez, "Kaç yaşında kadın, her akşam ayyaşları, komünistleri masaya topluyor, yakışıyor mu, küçücük çocuğun bunların arasında ne işi var," diye söylenir ama sonunda mecbur kalıp yollardı.

Kırk yılın başı karşılaştıklarında bu arkasından atıp tuttuklarını yüzüne söyleyemez, çıtı çıkmadan oturup onu dinlerdi.

Zaten Sare Hanım'ın böyle bir özelliği vardı. O açık yeşil, parlak gözleriyle baktı mı yerinize çakılıverirdiniz. Gözlerimi ondan aldığımı söylerdi hep.

Ayrıca onun kimseden çekinmesi yoktu, tepesi attı mı aklına geleni pat diye söyleyiverir ama sonra biraz zaman geçince bu sefer "Tüh ben ne yaptım, durup dururken ne diye kalbini kırdım, böyle de söylenmez ki," diye üzülür, hediyeler hazırlar, gönül almaya çalışırdı.

Belki de annemle aralarındaki en önemli farklardan biri de buydu.

Annem adeta tüm dünyayı bir düzene uydurmaya çalışır, daha doğrusu düzen bozulmasın diye uğraşır, herşey yolundaymış, iyiymiş gibi yapardı.

Özellikle haftasonları oraya gittiğimde akşamüzeri büyük kristal avizeler yanar, sofra yavaştan kurulmaya başlanır, Sare Hanım da içeri gidip giyinirdi.

Bu tören hiç değişmezdi.

Bazen yanına gidip onun giyinip makyaj yapmasını izlerdim. O zamanlar benimle sohbet etmeyi sever, bana kumaşların özelliklerini, hangi rengin hangi renkle uyacağını anlatırdı. Arada bir terzi Perihan Teyze gelir, elbiseler dolaptan çıkar, tadilat yapılır, yeniden özenle yerlerine yerleştirilir, birtakım dergilerden patronlar çıkartılıp senenin modasından kumaşlar sipariş edilirdi.

Bir keresinde bir kumaşı yüzüme sürerken yanıma gelip ne yaptığımı sordu. "Dokunuyorum," dedim. O zamanlar farkında değildim ama sonradan anladım ki garip bir biçimde dokunma ve koku alma duyum çok gelişmiş. Bunu ilk anneannem farketmişti.

Kumaşları bugün bile bir uzman gibi ayırdetmemin, çoğu insanın duyamadığı kokuları duymamın ve herşeyi hatta insanları bile dokunuşla, kokularıyla tanımamın nedeni herhalde bu olsa gerek.

Anneannemin çoğu oldukça eski ama belli ki döneminin oldukça pahalı, gösterişli giysilerinin doldurduğu büyük gardırobu benim en büyük zevklerimden birini oluşturdu.

Onları giymesem de çıkartıp dokunmaya, sonra onlara bakarak biraz değiştirdiğim modellerini çizmeye başladığımda herhalde ortaokul sıralarındaydım.

Annem, küçük bir bebekken bile kumaşları ayrıdedebildiğimi, biraz sert ya da kaba giysiler giydirmeye çalıştıklarında ittiğimi, ağladığımı, yumuşak özel giysiler gördüğümde gülümseyip elimi yüzümü sürdüğümü söylemişti. Tabii eve gelip giden teyzeleri kokularına göre ayırdığımı da...

Sare Hanım gezmeyi pek sevmezdi. Genellikle herkesin ona gelmesini isterdi. Bu nedenle de en üzüldüğü şeylerden biri çok sevdiği şapkalarını kullanamamasıydı.

Ayda yılda bir, kıramayacağı birinin sergisine ya da oyununa gitmek için çıkar, ondan da pek memnun kalmazdı.

Bir keresinde ünlü bir şair öldüğünde cenazeye gitmesi gerekmiş, "Aman neyse fırsat çıktı, şu şapkamı takabilirim artık," diye sevinmişti.

Zaten onun yaşamla ve ölümle ilişkisi çok garipti. Biri öldüğünde onu sevse bile çok fazla üzülmez, "Eh zaten bin yaşına gelmişti, bu kadar içmeseydi, kazık kakacak değil ya," diyebilirdi. Bana öyle gelir ki hayatın içinde ne varsa onu öylece kabullenmiş ve hiç şaşırmazmış gibi bir hali vardı.

Kimbilir belki de bu onun hayata katlanma biçimiydi.

Çoktan ölmüş olanlar ve yabancılar da dahil ünlü sanatçıların, yazarların hayatı hakkındaki konuşmalar sanıyorum onu en çok heyecanlandıran konulardı.

Örneğin bir yönetmen geldiğinde eski, sevdiği bir filmini nasıl çektiğini anlattırır, en küçük ayrıntılara kadar sorar ve sanki o filmin içine girmiş, hatta orada oynarmış gibi herkesi unutur giderdi.

Kimi zaman hararetli tartışmalar olur, siyasi kavgalar çıkar, kimi zaman şarkılar söylenir ve gece geç saatlere kadar uzardı.

Bu gecelerde bana hiçbir zaman, "Hadi bakalım artık yatağa" ya da "Bunlar çocuklara göre şeyler değil kızım," filan demezdi. Ben canım ne zaman sıkılırsa o zaman gider yatardım. Annemin bütün tembihlerine rağmen...

İçkiyi ve sarhoşluğu sevmem. Sare Hanım küçük, renkli kristal kadehlerde şarap ve bazen de büyükçe bir kadehte konyak içerdi ama çok fazla değil. Bir anlamda içermiş gibi yapardı. Kadehi ağzına götürür ama sanki değdirip tadına bakıp geri koyar böylece bütün gece içermiş gibi görünürdü.

Galiba içmekten çok uzun zayıf parmaklarıyla o zarif kadehleri tutmak hoşuna giderdi.

Bazıları gecenin sonunda merdivenleri zor inerken o gayet sakin saat kaç olursa olsun Saniye'den kahvesini ister, Yıldız Hanım'la sohbet edip biraz dedikodu yaptıktan sonra yatardı.

Ne de olsa her akşam gelen gidenle ilgili konular olur ve bunlar sanki önemli bir toplantıdan sonra değerlendirilmesi gereken şeylermiş gibi tek tek ele alınırdı. Ayrıca gelenler bir anlamda sınavdan geçer, kimilerinin, Yıldız Teyze'nin deyimiyle, "ayağı kesilir"ken, bazıları yeniden davet edilir, bir süre uzak kalan biri varsa acaba kırıldı mı diye meraklanılırdı.

Haddini aşan, sesi biraz fazla çıkan, değer verilen bir konuk hakkında ileri geri konuşanlar da Sare Hanım'ın "biraz soğutalım arayı" sözüyle ortadan kayboluverirlerdi.

Çok kızdığı biri için, "münasebetsiz", "sersem" belki en fazla "hödük" sözcüklerini kullanırdı.

Şiirlerini okumaya uğraşan şairlerden ve kendini övüp duranlardan pek hoşlanmazdı.

"Kendini ne anlatıp duruyorsun yahu, yaşadığın tuhaf olayları anlat da eğlenelim münasebetsiz adam," diye kızardı sonradan.

Tabii güne başlama saati de bizim evdekinden çok farklıydı. Ancak öğle saatlerinde uyanır, kahvesini ister, Saniye önceden sarılmış sigaralarından birini uzun ağızlığa yerleştirip getirir ve ne yemek yapacağını sorardı ki işte her seferinde onu çileden çıkartan da bu soru olurdu.

"Görüyorsun bu kadın beni delirtmek için mahsus yapıyor, sabahın köründe akşama ne yeneceğini mi düşüneceğim, akılları fikirleri yemekte," diye söylenir ama kahvesi bittikten sonra neşesi yerine gelip akşama neler yapılacağına dair emirlere başlardı.

Zaten geçe kalmaz Yıldız Teyze de gelirdi. Akşama özellikle çağırılmış biri varsa ya da ilk kez gelen bir misafir, onun için mutlaka farklı yemekler düşünülürdü.

Bu arada anneannem genellikle ya yarım kalmış romanını okumaya devam eder ya da yeni gelen imzalı kitaplara ve sanat dergilerine göz gezdirirdi.

Dedem çok erken ölmüş ve ona fena sayılmayacak bir miras kalmıştı. Zaten okul yıllarından beri sanata, edebiyata çok meraklıymış. Annemi büyütüp evlendirdikten sonra evini yazarlara, sanatçılara açmış.

Hatta pek fazla dile getirilmese de şu garip şiirleri yazan ve sonra biraz komik bir biçimde ölen ünlü şairle de büyük bir aşk yaşamış.

Eğer doğruysa adamcağız bir gece sarhoşken kendi kendine aklına gelen bir şiiri mırıldanırken karanlıkta belediyenin açtığı çukura düşmüş ve kimse bulamadığı için de orada ölüp kalmıştı.

Aslında şimdi uzaktan bakınca daha iyi anlıyorum ki Sare Hanım bütün o ağırlığına, herkesin hem dostu hem hamisi gibi davranmasına karşın sık sık aşık olurdu.

Çünkü onun için aşk, hayatın bir gün daha sürmesi için gereken tek duyguydu.

Önemli olan o aşkı yaşaması değil, yalnızca hissetmesiydi.

Bunu, gelen kimi insanlara daha farklı bir ilgi göstermesinden, ertesi gün Yıldız Teyze'yle fısır fısır onun hakkında konuşmasından, o geleceğinde giyinirken biraz daha fazla özenmesinden ve tabii ki gözlerinden anlardım. Daha doğrusu o zaman bunu anlamazdım ama bir farklılık olduğunu bilirdim.

Çünkü o yemyeşil gözleri, bilmem makyajın da etkisiyle mi sanki birden başka biçimde parlardı.

Gece sona erdiğinde renkli giysilerini çıkartıp makyajını silerken onu görmemi pek istemezdi.

Uyandığı zaman bile hep bakımlıydı ve sanıyorum onu dedem bile gerçek haliyle tam olarak görmemiştir.

Ben görmüştüm ve bana aynadaki o birbirinden çok farklı iki yüz büyük bir hüzün vermişti.

Rimeller, pudralar, ruj silindikçe sanki hayatın güzel yüzü çekilip gidiyor ve geriye soluk, yorgun, bitmiş bir hayat kalıyor gibi gelmişti.

Gerçek hayatımız gibi...

Şimdi hala gecenin bitmesini sevmem.

Acaba neden?

Acaba neden kaybolmak isterdim? Neden hep gizli geçitlerin peşindeydim? Öğledensonra uykusundan uyandıklarında evin içinde bile neden bir yerlere saklanıp herkesin beni aramasını, meraklanmasını isterdim?

Anneannemin eviyle annemin evi benim için iki ayrı dünyaydı.

Ama asıl neden şu ki, burası benim gizli hayatım gibiydi. Burada başka bir Ebru'ydum. Evdekinden, okuldakinden farklı...

Ve ne garip, çok küçükken bile bunun farkındaydım.

Sare Hanım benim bu küçük oyunlarımdan hiç sıkılmaz, her seferinde "Ay şimdi düşüp bayılacağım, yine nereye gitti, kayboldu, Saniye bahçeye baktınız mı, bana biraz kolonya verin yine tansiyonum çıktı," diye numaralar yapar, ben artık bir süre sonra korkup ortaya çıkınca ya da bulununca da, "Ah yaramaz çocuk çok korkuttun beni, ya seni bulamasaydık, hiç mi acımıyorsun bu yaşlı kadına," diye beni kucaklardı.

Tabii ben de inanır, yaptığımdan utanıp onu öperdim. Kucağında yatarken yumuşacık giysilerine başımı koyar, o güzel kokuyu duyardım ve kendimi hiç hissetmediğim kadar iyi hissederdim.

Ben en çok akşamüstüleri severdim.

Çünkü o saatlerde ev canlanır, ışıklar yakılır, akşam için hazırlıklar başlardı. Kendisi gibi beni de mutlaka giydirir, saçımı örer, kurdela takar, annemi delirten ne kadar renkli, parlak kıyafet varsa giymeme izin verirdi.

Derdi ki, "Gündüzleri bizim beynimizde bir bekçi vardır, akşam olunca onun mesaisi biter, bizi de rahat bırakır, bu yüzden akşamlar güzeldir..."

Terzi geldiği zaman sevdiğim renklerden bana da etekler, bluzlar, elbiseler dikilirdi.

Ben de sanki gelen konuklardan biriymişim gibi havaya girerdim.

Zaten evin maskotu gibi her gelen de benimle ilgilenir, sohbet eder, hediyeler getirirdi.

Babamın gidişinin üstünden birkaç ay geçip ben bir gün ansızın düşüp bayılınca birşeyler değişti. Sanki birdenbire büyüdüm. Sare Hanım en ünlü doktorları buldu, ama onlar bende birşey bulamadılar.

Bir sürü tetkikler yapıldı. Onlar pek bir sonuç vermeyince benimle uzun uzun konuşup babamı, annemi, nelerden korktuğumu, duygularımı sorup duran, bana garip garip şekiller, resimler gösteren doktorlarla buluştum.

Bazen dalıp gidiyordum ve başım çok ağrıyordu, bazen uyurken vücuduma dikenler batıyormuş gibi uyanıyordum, bazen sanki yere düşecekmişim gibi başım dönüyor ve oturduğum yerde kalakalıyordum. Bazen konuşmalar, çevredeki sesler inanılmaz derecede yükseliyor, kulaklarımı kapamak istiyordum.

Ve o zaman konuşamıyor, adeta kilitleniyor, olduğum yerde mümkünse karanlıkta öylece kalmak istiyordum.

Bazen uyandıktan sonra neler olduğunu hatırlamıyordum. Aslına bakarsanız gördüğüm rüyalarla gerçekleri birbirine karıştırdığım oluyordu.

O sıralar tam olarak hissettiğim şey korkuydu.

Çok korkuyordum.

Bütün o doktorlar, psikologlar bana iyi gelmiyordu. Aksine onları görünce daha kötü hissediyordum. Annem sürekli ya ağlıyor ya "Mutlaka nazar var, kurşun mu döktürsek," gibi anneannemi delirtecek sözler söylüyordu.

Bir tek onu isterdim yanımda o anlarda. Çünkü anneannem elimi tutar, konuşmazsam konuşmaz, bazen bana ilgisiz hikayeler anlatır, saçlarımı okşar ve kötü birşey yokmuş, ben hasta değilmişim gibi davranır, ben sorunca da "Herkesin birtakım hastalıkları vardır, kimisi doğuştan, kimisi sonradan olur, bunlarla başa çıkacaksın, bunların seni yenmesine izin vermeyeceksin," derdi.

Ne garip belki de benim halime en çok üzülen oydu ama ben onun bunu hiç umursamadığını sanırdım. Sonra birden kalkar, "Hadi bakalım toparlan, bu akşam sana bir sürprizim var," derdi.

Genç bir oyuncu çağırır, sevdiği bir piyes alır, benimle karşılıklı oynamasını isterdi örneğin. Ve sanki bir yönetmen edasıyla, "Hayır hayır, onu öyle tonlamayacaksın şekerim, sözleri öyle üstüste sıralama, hisset, sessizlikler çok değerlidir, bir an bekle sonra söyle o cümleyi," gibi uyarılarda bulunurdu.

Sanırsınız ki birkaç gün sonra perde açılacak ve biz sahneye çıkacağız.

Sonra o an geçer, ben de hastalığı mastalığı unuturdum. Yeni atak gelene kadar...

Sanırım onun üzüntüye, acıya tahammülü yoktu. Bunları sıradanmış gibi konuşsa da görmek istemezdi. Sanki elinde sihirli değnek varmış ve herşeyi halledebilecekmiş gibiydi. Belki de bu yüzden anlı şanlı koca yazarlar, sanatçılar özel hayatlarındaki sorunları bile gelip ona anlatırlardı.

Pek anlatmazdı ama öğrenebildiğim kadarıyla bu tutumunun nedeni dedemdi. Dedem zamanında çapkınlıklarıyla ünlüymüş. Sare Hanım'ı çok üzmüş. Ve çok genç yaşta geçirdiği bir felç yüzünden yatağa bağlanmış. Anneannem yıllar boyunca ona bakmak zorunda kalmış. Tabii dedem bu durumu kaldıramadığı için de gün günden huysuzlaşmış. Ölümü de oldukça acılı ve üzücüymüş.

Biz annemle üst kata yerleştikten sonra da Sare Hanım alışkanlıklarını değiştirmedi.

Tabii ki annem bu evdeki yeni durumdan hoşnut değildi. Hem gelen gidenlerden hoşlanmaz, hem anneannemin otoritesine karşı gelemez hem de benim onların yanında oturmamı istemezdi.

Ama anneannem bir bahaneyle beni çağırır, ben de annemin "yine mi?" suratına ve "hayır bu kılıkta inemezsin aşağıya," laflarına aldırmadan aşağı koştururdum.

Galiba hem anneannemin bu kez feci şekilde haklı çıkmasından, hem elimizde kalan parayla artık geçinemeyeceğimizden, hem de bana olan düşkünlüğü nedeniyle aslında bütün bunlara katlanmak zorunda kaldı ve iyice kendi içine döndü.

Bir süre sonra da bu hayata alıştı.

Böylece bu evde iki ayrı hayat başladı.

Üst katta annemin yine eskisi gibi kurduğu özenilmiş, bezenilmiş, dış dünyanın kötülüklerinden uzak, temiz, sessiz dünyasıyla, alt katta daha aldırışsız, çok daha rahat, kalabalık, gürültülü ve renkli bir hayat...

Kimbilir belki zaten insanın hayatı da böyle olmalı...

İstediğinizde üst kata, istediğinizde alt kata gidebileceğiniz bir hayat.

O yılların içinden gelen iki kişi daha var.
Seda ve Tolga.

Babamın gidişinden sonra kendimi iyice derslere vermiştim. Hatta annem bile bu duruma şaşırıyor, eskiden her dakika ödevleri sorarken şimdi "Kızım yeter artık gözlerin kanlandı, biraz dinlen, yarın çalışırsın," gibi ona pek uymayacak sözler söylüyordu.

Her nedense o sıralarda okul birincisi olmak ve bursla yurtdışına gitmek gibi bir düşünce oluşmuştu bende.

Galiba anneanneme gelen bir yabancı dil profesörüyle konuşmalarımızın da etkisi vardı bunda. Vahit Hoca kendi alanında dünya çapında çalışmalar yapan birisiydi ve benim mutlaka çok iyi bir okula kabul edileceğimi, bu imkanı kullanmam gerektiğini söyleyip duruyordu.

Ama ne gariptir ki dil okumayı düşünürken beklenmedik bir rastlantıyla o sıralar kimsenin aklına gelmeyen bambaşka bir okula gidecektim.

O yıllardaki tek yakın erkek arkadaşım Tolga da benim gibi edebiyata, sanata meraklıydı. Şiirler, kısa öyküler yazıyor, günlük tutuyordu. Lisenin ikinci yılında onunla birlikte okul dergisi çıkartmaya başladık. Dergi dediysem tabii fotokopiyle çoğaltılan on, oniki sayfalık birşey.

İçinde kendi yazılarımız, başka yazarlardan alıntılar, resimler, desenler vardı. Birkaç kişi de yazılarını, kitap tanıtımlarını verirdi.

Hatta son sınıfta dergi epeyce havalı olmuş, dergiyi okuyanlar adeta bir tür klan gibi ayrıcalıklı bir havaya bürünmüştü. Öyle ki yazı ya da desen vermek isteyenleri ince bir elemeden geçiriyor, sıraya koyuyorduk. Dergi fazla sayıda basılmadığı için de en başta bizi izleyenler ötekilere binbir nazla okutuyordu. Hatta komik ama derginin korsanı bile çıkmış, bir arkadaşımız edindiği kopyayı çoğaltmıştı.

Tolga'yla bizi herkes sevgili sanıyordu. Ama değildik. Doğrusu o kadar yakın arkadaş olmuştuk ki artık birbirimize karşı ne hissettiğimizi tam anlayamıyorduk belki de.

Seda'ya kalsa Tolga bana kesin aşıktı ama bunu söylemeye çekiniyordu. Aramızda bir tür aşk vardı belki de çünkü her sabah onu görmek beni mutlu eder, geleceğini söyleyip gelmediği zamanlarda (ki bunu sık sık yapardı) içim sıkılır, evin içinde dolaşıp beklerdim.

Arada böyle sudan nedenlerle bozuşur, birkaç gün surat asardık. Sonra mutlaka bana bir mektup yazardı. Ben mektubun geleceğinden emin bir şekilde durumu uzatırdım. Ama neden böyle yaptığımı şimdi pek bilmiyorum, galiba bunu oyun gibi görüyordum çünkü aslında ona karşı o anlamda bir çekim hissetmiyordum ve bunu gayet iyi biliyordum.

Zaten nasıl hissedecektim ki. Tolga eşcinseldi.

Ve bunu hiçbir zaman açıkça söylemese de bana anlattığı kimi şeylerden hatta yazdıklarından gayet iyi biliyordum. Belki annesi ya da başkaları da hissediyordu ama onlara durumu hiç açık etmezdi.

Bir biçimde anladığımı biliyordu ve bu ikimiz arasında kabullenilmiş bir sırdı.

Yine de bu aşk oyunu beni mutlu ederdi, sanırım onu da...

Hatta kıskançlıkları vardı. Beni beğenen ya da görüşmek isteyen biri çıktığında mutlaka ona çeşitli kulplar bulur, çaktırmadan iğneler, oğlanın öyle açıklarını bulup çıkartırdı ki çocuk daha benimle ikinci buluşmasına kadar gözümden düşmüş olurdu.

Açıkçası kendimi onun yanında o kadar rahat ve iyi hissederdim ki başkalarıyla konuşurken zaten sıkılır ve bir an önce onun yanına gidip anlatmak isterdim. Hatta bir keresinde bizden büyük ve okulda pek beğenilen o çocukla birkaç hafta flört etmemin en önemli nedeni belki de buydu. Yani buluştuktan sonra gidip Tolga'yla onun dedikodusunu yapmak...

Üstelik çocuk hakkında sanki gerçek aşığımmış da beni delice kıskanıyormuş gibi öyle şeyler söylerdi ki gülmekten gözlerimden yaş gelirdi.

Gariptir, Seda en yakın arkadaşımdı ama onunla bu kadar rahat değildim.. Örneğin Tolga'yla aklımıza ne gelirse en açık şekilde konuşurduk ama Seda'yla bazı konular hep tabuydu.

Benzetmek gerekirse Seda biraz anneme, Tolga'ysa anneanneme benzerdi.

Zaten anneannem Tolga'ya bayılırdı. Tolga ona gelirken çiçekler alır, nereden buluyorsa antika kalemler, defterler, kitaplar getirirdi.

Tabii Sare Hanım'ın gözdesi olup ara sıra akşam yemeğine çağırılmak ve adeta taptığı yazarlarla, şairlerle tanışmak onun için çok büyük olaydı. Yani anneanneme olan düşkünlüğünün belki de asıl nedeni buydu.

"Ne ince ruhlu çocuk bu Tolga," derdi anneannem.

Sanırım o durumu çoktan anlamıştı. O yüzden de bir tek o hiçbir zaman bana aramızda aşk olup olmadığını sormadı.

Ne yapayım ki huyum böyle, birşeyi anlatırken birden aklıma başka konular geliyor ve böyle daldan dala atlayarak zamanı, mekanı, insanları birbirine karıştırarak, aslında çok iyi bildiğim ama karşımdakinin bir türlü anlayamadığı bir kurgu oluşturuyorum.

Daha doğrusu bir kurgu bile oluşturamıyorum.

Neyse ki yazar olmaya kalkışmadım. Herhalde kimse yazdıklarımdan anlam çıkartamazdı.

Gerçi şu da var ki ben hayata benzemeyen romanları sevmem. Çünkü hayatın o romanlardaki gibi düzenli, bizim istediğimiz gibi bir kurgusu yok.

Var mı?

Tolga yıllar sonra yazdığı romanında belki de benim dediğimi yapmaya çalıştı. Çocukluğumuzu, gizli oyunlarımızı, büyüyünce yüzümüzü kızartacak ayrıntıları, kendi ikili hayatını, belli belirsiz bir biçimde anlattı. Ama öylesine karmakarışıktı ya da öylesine gizlenmeye çalışmıştı ki okuyanlar anlamadı.

Galiba hayat romanlara benzemiyor.

Sokağa çıkıyorsunuz ve aniden hiç beklenmedik birşey oluveriyor.

Birine deli gibi aşık oluyorsunuz ve o birdenbire ortadan kayboluyor.

Birinin hep yanınızda kalacağını sanıyorsunuz ama işte akşamüstü bavulunu toplayıp yolculuğa çıkıyor.

Hayatınızın yolunda olduğunu, çok mutlu olduğunuzu, hep böyle devam edeceğini sanıyorsunuz ama bir gün düşüp bayılıyorsunuz ve hayatınız tümüyle değişiyor.

Yoksa bu herkes için böyle değil mi?

Belki değil.

Annemin söylediği gibi hep garip olaylar benim başıma mı geliyor?

Böyle sanki hayatının romanını yazar gibi kendi özel dürbünüyle zamanın ötesinden geçmişe bakınca insan tüm ayrıntıları anlatmak zorunda hissediyor...

Çünkü aslında bizi yakından tanıyanlar bile gerçek hayatımızı, sayısız ayrıntıyı, gizlenmiş duyguları, unutulmuş anları, kırıklıkları, gizli mutlulukları, kaçamak bir bakışı, bir yerde rastlayıp sonra hiç görmediğiniz ama her nedense yıllar içinde ara sıra hatırladığınız o gülümsemeyi bilmiyor...

Yavaşlıyor tren, görevli gelip biletlerimizi soruyor. Karşımdaki yolcu uykusundan uyanıyor. Ben dalgınlığımdan sıyrılıyorum. Ağaçların içinde sevimli bir köy mü, kasaba mı? Biraz duruyoruz.

Ferhat'ı ilk gördüğümde lisenin son sınıfındaydım. Bahar gelmişti ve artık dersler bitmek üzereydi. Bahçedeki büyük manolya öyle güzel kokuyordu ki... Karşı tepedeki korunun içinde mor salkımlar, erguvanlar yeşillerin arasında eşsiz bir manzara resmi gibiydi.

Korunun içinde yüksek kuleleriyle benim perili köşk dediğim eski evin camları açılmıştı. Temizlik başladığına göre yaz geliyordu.

Bir cuma akşamüstüydü.

Tolga'yla okuldan çıkınca eskicilerin olduğu sokağa gitmiştik. O yine hediyeler almış ben de anneanneme güzel bir sigara tabakası bulmuştum.

Geldiğimde Sare Hanım'ın bahçedeki hasır koltuklarda uzun saçlı biriyle oturduğunu gördüm. Adamın arkası bana dönüktü.

"İşte benim neşem de geldi," diye el salladı anneannem beni görünce. Yanlarına doğru yürürken bana döndü ve o zaman onu gördüm.

Eve gelip gidenlerden değildi. Onu ilk kez görüyordum. Beni görünce ayağa kalktı, elini uzattı, anneannem bizi tanıştırdı.

"Bu benim torunum Ebru, bu yakışıklı beyefendi de yakında resim tarihini değiştirmeye hazırlanıyor," dedi.

"Belki de resmi tarihi..." diye güldü o...

Garip ama nedense elimi sıkarken yüzüne bakamadım. Tuhaf, bugün bile anlatamayacağım bir bakışı vardı, derin, sert hatta vahşi denilebilecek bir bakış. Uzun boyluydu. Geniş omuzlu, elmacık kemikleri çıkık, geniş alınlı, uzun saçlı, büyük burunlu, avurtlar hafif çökük ve belki biraz yorgun...

Yaşı belli olmayan insanlardandı.

Geri dönüp eve çıkmak istedim ama anneannem durdurdu, "Gel gel otur nereye gidiyorsun, bizimle çay iç, sonra çıkarsın."

Ne yapacağımı bilemedim ama üstümdeki formayla burada oturmak istemediğim kesindi.

"Ben çıkıp anneme haber vereyim bir de üstümü değişip geliyorum, hem sana sürprizim var," deyip fırladım.

Gerçekte insan birinden ilk görüşte neden etkilendiğini tam olarak bilir mi? Ben bilemem. Üzerindeki ceketin kumaşından, o bakıştan, durgun ve sakin bir halde, yumuşak ama güçlü sesiyle "Memnun oldum," deyişinden mi? Kimbilir.

Yukarı çıktım, anneme aşağı ineceğimi söyledim ve odama gidip üstümdekileri herhalde birkaç saniyede çıkartıp fırlattım. O yine sorular soruyordu, hepsine yine klasik cevapları yetiştirdim ki konuşma uzamasın.

Terlemiş miydim biraz? Ama vakit yoktu. Pamuğa parfüm sıkıp koltukaltımı sildim, rengarenk desenli uzun gömleğimle bol bir pantolon geçirdim üstüme. Bu pantolonu alırken altına giyecek ayakkabı bulamadığım için kendime kızdım. Sonra mantar topuklardan birini ayağıma geçirdim, saçlarımı biraz dağıttım, aynaya baktım, eh işte idare ederdi, zaten yapacak fazla birşeyim de yoktu.

Tabakayı aldım, annemin "Misafir kimmiş, fazla kalma, yemek yiyeceğiz," laflarını geçiştirip doğruca aşağı indim.

Anneannem tabakayı pek beğendi, beni öven sözler söyledi. Ferhat, gelen çoğu misafir gibi bana okulla ilgili, derslerle ilgili, nelerle uğraştığımla ilgili sıradan soruları sormadı. Ben geldiğimde aslında bir filmle ilgili konuşuyorlardı. Filmin sonundaki sahnede iki kişi tenis oynuyordu ama ortada tenis topu yoktu, filmi bilmediğim için ne anlattıklarını tam olarak anlamıyordum, anneannem "Evet bazen ben de bunları beğeniyorum ama doğrusunu söylemek gerekirse Alain Delon'un filmlerini izlemeyi tercih ederim, belki de ben sinemayı hayatın yansıması değil de daha güzel kurgulanmış hali olarak görmek istiyorum," dedi.

O zaman Ferhat güldü, "Haklısınız, aslında sanat için de aynısı söylenebilir, belki roman da doğada gezdirilen bir ayna değildir," deyip birden bana döndü, "Siz, nasıl filmleri seviyorsunuz?" diye sordu.

Onları dinlerken aslında dalmış onu izliyordum. Yakalanmış gibi kızardım.

Gözlerimi kaçırdım, fincanı masaya bıraktım, "Galiba rüya gibi olanları," dedim.

"Rüya gibi mi?"

"Evet, aslında olmayacak şeyleri biraraya getiren filmleri, beni başka bir yere götüren filmleri severim..."

"Ne güzel bir tanımlama değil mi Sare Hanım," diye anneanneme döndü. Döndü ama aslında bir yandan bana baktığını hissediyordum.

Şu salak gözlükleri gözümden çıkarmak istiyordum ama bu sefer de onu göremeyecektim.

"Yaa işte bizim Ebru böyledir, hem biliyor musun okulda çok güzel bir dergi çıkartıyor, sanat dergisi..."

"Yok yok bizimki fotokopi, zavallı birşey," dedim..

"Niye öyle söylüyorsun gayet de güzel, kendi arkadaşları da yazıyor, aa bak Ferhat'la bir röportaj yapsanıza dergiye, güzel olmaz mı?"

Bir an sustum.

"Kimler kimlerle yaptılar, pek havalı dergi canım,"

"Anneannemin sayesinde," dedim,

Bardağını yerine bırakıp arkasına yaslanırken döndü ve uzun parmaklarını içinden geçirdiği saçını arkaya attı. Sanki müziğin durduğu bir anda obuacının nefes alması gibiydi.

"Tabii memnun olurum, ne zaman isterseniz," dedi, gülümsedi.

Kısık bir sesle ciddi ciddi cevap verdim:

"Zaten son sayımız olacak, ben de sevinirim..."

İşte aynen böyle oldu. Onlar yeniden kendi konularına döndüklerinde acaba kaç yaşında, acaba evli mi, acaba sevgilisi var mı, bunları düşünüyordum. Belli etmediğimi sanarak gözucuyla ona bakıyordum ve bunları neden düşündüğüme kesinlikle anlam veremiyordum.

Çocukluğumdan beri bir köşede durup insanlara bakarım. Yüzlerini, konuşmalarını, bakışlarını incelerim. Kendimce onlarla ilgili hikayeler uydururum.

Onun yüzünde birşey vardı, bakışlarında mı, gülüşünde mi, konuşmasında mı bilmiyorum.

Bazı şeyleri hissederiz, düşünürüz, biliriz ama kimseye söylemeyiz.

Bunu ona asla söylemedim, başkasına da, hatta belki kendime bile ama o akşamüstü orada otururken sanki elimde olmayan bir güç beni ona çekiyordu ve bu duyguyu daha önce bilmiyordum.

Aklımda ne vardı, bir an önce onu Tolga'ya anlatmak ve en kısa zamanda onunla röportaja gitmek.

Anneannem birlikte gittiğimiz sergiyi anlatıyordu. Makara bantların sarıldığı kundura boyama sandıkları, bir araya getirilip altına şiirler yazılmış objeler, ahşap levhalara nakşedilmiş büyük harfler...

"İyi ama bunun neresi resim, insan en azından desen çizebilmeli şekerim, herhalde ben artık iyice yaşlandım, bunlardan anlamıyorum," diye söyleniyordu.

Ferhat, her zamanki yumuşak konuşma tarzıyla, "Böyle söyleseniz de aslında hep farklı şeyler yapan insanları destekliyorsunuz, ben de bunu merak ediyorum, neden?" diye sordu.

Biz çay içiyorduk, o kristal bardakta içki içiyordu. Konuşurken bardağın içindeki buzu yuvarlıyordu.

"Evet bakma sen benim böyle söylendiğime," dedi anneannem, "herkes deli deli şeyler yapmazsa hayat boyu aynı filmi izleriz değil mi? Bak benim evimde hep natürmortlar var ama meyve sebze de bir yere kadar..." Ve o ünlü kahkahalarından birini atıp ağızlığına yeni bir sigara taktı.

İçkisi bitmişti, anneannemin Saniye diye bağırmasına az kalmıştı, kalktım, bardağını aldım, "Yenisini getireyim ben size," dedim.

"Aslında kalksam iyi olur," dedi, "akşam oluyor, daha fazla rahatsız etmeyeyim."

"Aa, ne güzel sohbet ediyoruz, getir sen getir kimse gitmiyor," dedi anneannem.

Güldüm. Yakında öğrenirdi o da...

Sare Hanım istemezse kimse bir yere gitmiyor.

Gidip mutfaktan içkisini doldurdum, buzlarını koydum, geldim, ama verirken elim titredi, birden alttan elimi tuttu, gözgöze geldik, karnımdan başıma kadar içimden ateş geçti sanki, kısacık bir an, hayatın içinde anlamı olmayan bir an, ama anlamı vardı, o elimden bardağı alıp teşekkür ederken...

Evet o anda birşey oldu ama ne olduğunu ben anlamadım.

Onsekiz yaşımın yazı…
Belki de hayatımın en mutlu zamanı…
Artık kocaman bir kızdım ve üniversiteye gidecektim.. Hem de nereye…

Bir gün anneannemin bir arkadaşı gelmiş ve çizimlerimi görmüştü, sonra kumaşlara olan ilgimi dinleyince Londra'da moda okulunda ders veren ünlü bir modacıyı tanıdığını ve bazılarını ona yollamak istediğini söylemişti.

Seniha Teyze ülkenin en ünlü markalarından birinin sahibinin eşiydi ve aslında o markayı birlikte kurmuşlardı.

Anneannem buna pek sevindi. "Seniha öyle kolayına beğenmez, mutlaka bunun arkasından birşey çıkacak, bak görürsün ben sana hep söylemez miydim," dediyse de fazla üstünde durmadım. Hatta ertesi gün unuttum gitti. Zaten biraz aklım havalardaydı o sıralarda. Ne de olsa okul bitiyordu, o sıkıcı kış sabahları erkenden kalkıp eski, soğuk, karanlık okula gitmeyecektim artık.

Tolga'nın dediği gibi, "o pasaklı tuvaletlerde ellerimi yıkarken titremekten kurtuluyorum ya başka ne isterim…"

Annem benim yurtdışına gitmemi istemiyordu. Madem dil okuyacaktım burada da güzel okullar vardı. Aslında orada yalnız kalacağım düşüncesi onu huzursuz ediyordu.

Ama son zamanlarda kendimi daha iyi hissediyordum ve bayılmalar, kasılmalar, kendinden geçip sonra unutmalar azalmıştı.

Taner Amca'nın verdiği ilaçlardan mı, birden büyüdüğüm için mi, artık eskisi kadar karanlıkta babamla karşılaştığım anı kurup, ona neler söyleyeceğimi düşünüp ağladığım geceler azaldığı için mi bilmiyorum ama Tolga da bir yıl içinde çok değiştiğimi söyleyip duruyordu.

Tolga'nın annesi eğer yurtdışına gideceksek ikimizin aynı yere gitmesinin iyi olacağını söylüyor, buna göre tercih yapmamızı istiyordu. Orada ikimizin oturacağı küçük bir ev tutabileceklerini söylüyordu ki bu düşünce annemin aksine bizi sevinçten deliye çevirmişti.

Hatta oturup sanki yeni evlenecek çiftler gibi neler yaparız, evi nasıl döşeriz, onlara kadar düşünmeye başlamıştık.

Tolga'nın babası çok zengindi. Ben hiç yurtdışına gitmemiştim. O çocukluğundan beri kışları kayağa, yazları birtakım ünlü tatil kasabalarına giderdi. Ama aklındaki şehir Londra'ydı.

Zaten bana, "Sen ne okuyacağına karar ver okulu bul gerisi kolay," diyordu. Çünkü onun umurunda bile değildi üniversite okumak. Yalnız başına kalabilmek, kendi hayatını kurmak, yazar olmak istiyordu. Sırf babası istiyor diye okula yazılacaktı işte.

Ben de anneannemi işliyordum ki annemi ikna edebileyim.

Ama Sare Hanım'ın bazı konularda kimselere belli etmeden alttan alta bir plan yaptığını, kafasına koyduğunu ne olursa olsun gerçekleştirdiğini unutmuştum.

Bu konudaki tek hüsranı annemdi ve sanırım bu nedenle de ona hep kızgın kaldı.

"Annen de senin yaşındayken sözümü dinleyip dışarda okusaydı böyle manasız bir ev kadını olmayacak kadar akıllıydı, üstelik başına bütün bunlar gelmeyecekti..." diye bazen söylenmeye başlar, sonra birden, "Aman neyse bunlar geçmişte kaldı, ben geleceğe bakarım, geçmişle uğraşa uğraşa hayat geçiren budalalardan değilim..." diye kestirip atardı.

Sonra bir gün beni karşısına alıp, "Sana bugün büyük bir sürprizim var," dedi.

Ben meraklandım. Ama o kahvesini, sigarasını içmeye devam etti ve biraz sonra kapı çaldı.

Meğer o günden sonra Seniha Teyze'yle sürekli konuşmuşlar ve sözünü ettiği Londra'daki ünlü modacıyla bağlantıya geçmişler. O çizimlerimi gördükten sonra ve tabii şimdi anlıyorum ki Seniha Teyze'nin torpiliyle beni okula almayı kabul etmiş.

İçeri elinde koca bir dosyayla Seniha Teyze girdi. Her zamanki gibi enerjik, bakımlı, (bayılırdım onun saçlarını yapışına, sanki hiç yokmuş gibi duran makyajına, giysilerine...) yüksek perdeden sesiyle bizi selamladı.

Anneannem gerçekten heyecanlandı.

"Eee, herşey tamam mı Seniha?" dedi.

"Tamam tamam Sare Hanım, hepsi tamam, yalnız şu belgeler doldurulacak ve bir de özel mektup yazılacak, sonra kısa bir hazırlık dönemi o kadar..."

"Peki konuştuğumuz gibi de oldu mu?"

"Aynen öyle oldu benden kurtulur mu, tam burslu gidecek..."

Ben şaşkın şaşkın onlara bakıyordum.

Evet benden sözediyorlardı ama öyle kaptırmışlardı ki sanki orada olmayan biriyle ilgili konuşur gibiydiler.

Sonra Seniha Teyze bana döndü:

"Evet Sare Hanım işte geleceğin ünlü modacısı karşımızda oturuyor şu an..."

Anneannem bana sarıldı ama ben hala şoktaydım.

İşte böyle öğrendim hangi okula gideceğimi...

Şimdi o akşamüstünü, her zamanki gibi birilerinin gelmesinin beklendiği aslında sıradan bir akşamüstünü, tabii ki o an farkına varmadıysam da hayatımı tümüyle değiştiren bu iki olağanüstü kadının karşısında oturduğum o günü bütün ayrıntılarıyla hatırlıyorum.

"Saniye Saniye, gel gel, bize zarif bir alkol getir bakalım da kutlayalım yahu sabahtan beri fenalık geçirdim burada zaten beklemekten, bak yine tansiyonum fırlayacak..." diye içeri seslendi anneannem...

Ben tabii annemden bahisle, bu işin o kadar kolay olmayacağını söyledim ve Sare Hanım'ı iyice kızdırdım.

"İşte şekerim bu bizim milletçe huyumuzdur, güzel bir hadise olduğunda hemen arkasından ne fenalık çıkar diye düşünürüz, kızım bu huyu hemen bırak, önce güzel haberin tadını çıkart gerisini sonra düşünürüz..."

Annem aşağı gelip haberi aldığında yüzü asıldı, hem sevindi hem üzüldü, Seniha Teyze'nin heyecanla okulu anlatması karşısında pek itiraz da edemedi. Tabii benim de onlarla birlikte kadeh kaldırmama şöyle bir ters baktı ama ses etmedi.

Belki de aklından, kızının gerçekten ne kadar büyüdüğü, yaşadıklarımızdan sonra bunun aslında önemli bir başarı olduğu geçiyordu ama kaygıları her zamanki gibi ağır basacaktı.

Bana mı öyle geldi bilmiyorum ama kadeh tokuştururken gözleri dolmuş gibiydi.

Tolga haberi aldığında Ajda'nın son çıkan şarkısını dinliyordu.

Onun küçükken başlayan 45'lik merakı o haldeydi ki sanırım en büyük koleksiyonlardan birine sahiptir. O plakların başında ne çok zaman geçirirdi. Bir şarkı başladığı an hemen devamını söylerdi.

O sıralar okuldakilerin çoğu yabancı şarkılar dinlerken o daha çok Türkçelere meraklıydı. Ve tabii ki en sevdiği de Ajda'yla Sezen'di.

Yeni bir plak aldığında onu defalarca dinlemekten bıkmazdı.

Onun için ağırdan aldım, bir haberim olduğu belliydi ama ne?

En sonunda dayanamayıp söyledim. Neredeyse, kalkıp hani filmlerde piyango çıkınca göbek atarlar ya sevinçten öyle oynayacak sandım.

Sanki okulu tam burslu kazanan ben değildim de oydu.

Hemen koşup annesine haber verdi ve annemi ikna etme işi onun üstüne kaldı.

Okuldaki notlarım çok iyiydi ama yine de okul daha bitmemişti, Tolga da bana kızdı, niye sürekli kaygılanıyorum diye...

Ayaklarım yerden kesilmişti ama yine de inanamıyordum bütün bunlara.

Bizimki o andan sonra Londra'yla ilgili ne bulduysa getirip neredeyse gitmeden kentin her yerini bana öğretmeye başladı.

Komikti halimiz. Bir yandan sürekli aynı Ajda şarkısını dinliyor bir yandan kitaplara bakıp nerelere gideriz, hangi müzikali izleriz, hangi müzede ne var onları konuşuyorduk.

Ama işte diyorum ya hiçbir şeye tam sevinemem ben. Çünkü mutlaka çok mutlu olduğumda bir terslik olur. Hem de hiç beklenmedik bir terslik... Anneannem bu huyuma ne kadar kızsa da bu böyle...

Biz annemin çıkaracağı arızalarla uğraşırken asıl darbe Tolga'nın babasından geldi. Bu yaşta bir kızla erkeğin aynı evde kalmasının doğru olmadığı şeklinde bir ifadeyle...

Öyle ya biz bunu hiç düşünmemiştik. Çünkü tabii ki annesi de dahil hepimiz (söylemesek de) onun durumunu biliyorduk. Ama babası bilmiyor ya da kabul etmiyordu.

Zaten ölene kadar da etmeyecekti.

Ev tutmak yerine pansiyonda kalmamız düşünüldü önce.

Sonra şeytan Tolga'nın aklına daha parlak bir fikir geldi. Ev ona tutulacaktı. Ben de pansiyonda kalıyor olacaktım. Ama aslında birlikte oturacaktık. Babası gelirse de o zaman düşünürdü bir çare...

Hatta bir keresinde, "Canım en kötüsü, yakalanırsak, evleneceğiz deriz, buna da laf edecek hali yok, hatta hoşuna gider," demişti de şaşkın şaşkın yüzüne bakakalmıştım.

"Aman korkma uyduruktan..." diye güldü sonra...

O hayatı boyunca bir başkası gibi yaşadığı için sır saklamayı, yalan söylemeyi neredeyse oyuna dönüştürmüştü. "Yalan da sanattır, herkes söyleyemez, çünkü bir yalan mutlaka başka yalanları getirir ve birini unutursan domino taşları gibi bütün hepsi üstüste yıkılır," der hatta bununla övünürdü.

Ben yalan söylemeyi pek bilmem. Utanırım söylemek zorunda kalınca. Gözlerimi kaçırırım, kızarırım, anlaşılır yani ne çevirdiğim. Aslında sonradan çok düşündüm bunu. Korktuğumdan değil, neden yalan söylemem gereksin diye düşünürdüm. Karşımdaki kim oluyor da ona yalan söylemek zorunda kalıyorum diye kızardım kendime.

Yalan söylemem ama çok şeyi gizlediğim doğrudur. Hayatımı da doğru söyleyeceğim diye herkese açıklamak zorunda değilim.

Belki anneme duyduğum tepkidendi bu. Çünkü annem sürekli yalan söylerdi ama anlamsız yalanlar. Biri geleceğinde istemiyorsa, istemem demez, "Akşam bir akrabamız geliyor," gibi mazeretler uydururdu. İnsanları kırmamak için böyle davranmak gerektiğini söyler, bunu bir nezaket kuralı gibi görürdü.

Anneannemse tam tersi... "Kimseyi memnun edecek halim yok, isteyen gelir benimle oturur, istemeyen oturmaz, kocama yalan söylememişim, elin adamına ne diye söyleyeyim?" derdi.

Tolga eğer günün birinde babasına gerçeği söyleseydi belki de hayatı bambaşka olabilirdi. Ama söyleyemedi.

İşte biz o günlerde böyle bir ruh hali içindeydik. Gelecek planları yapıyor, yakın gelecekteki gizli saklı hayatımızı nasıl kuracağımızı düşünüyor, geceyarılarına kadar kendi kendimize kurduğumuz bu oyunla belki de gerçekte olacağımızdan daha mutlu oluyorduk.

İşte Ferhat'ın bizim eve geldiği akşamüstünün hemen ertesinde oldu bütün bunlar.

Belki komik ama ben onun bana uğur getirdiğine inanıverdim.

Birkaç gün sonra Tolga'yla birlikte onun evine gittik. Tolga beni almaya geldiğinde şöyle baştan aşağı süzdü. Kızardım. Aslında epey denemeden sonra kendimce son derece sıradan giyinmiştim. Bir iki yerinden yırtık son moda bol paça pantolon, üstüne bol ipek gömlek ve püsküllü güderi ceket, ayağımda da salaş, bağlanmamış botlar vardı. Ve gömleğin açık düğmelerinden görünen büyük, renkli taşlardan kolye...

"Pek havalıyız bugün," dedi sadece ama şeytanın kuşkulandığına emindim.

Bahçedeki konuşmayı anlatırken o kadar da dikkatli davranmıştım oysa ki...

Büyük taş merdivenlerden çıkıp daracık çıkmaz sokağa girdik. Birkaç küçük kız lastik oynuyordu. Sessiz, eski, yoksul bir mahalleydi. Yalnızca kızların oynarken bağırışları duyuluyordu.

"Evet işte burası," dedi Tolga, demir bahçe kapısının önünde durup.

Kapıyı itti, içeri girdik. Bakımsız bahçede heykeller, garip ahşap parçaları, eski ve herhalde kullanılmayan bisiklet, hafifçe esen rüzgarın getirdiği çiçek kokuları, büyükçe bir malta eriği...

Bahçenin içinde tek katlı, gecekondu gibi bir evdi.

Kapıyı çaldık.

Ses çıkmadı.

"Burası olduğuna emin misin?" dedim.

"Evet, tam da uçuk ressama göre değil mi, 8 numara yazıyordu adreste..."

Yeniden çaldık.

Üzerinde uzun beyaz gömlek ve ıslak saçlarla açtı kapıyı... Boynunda bir havlu vardı.

"Gelin gelin, hoşgeldiniz, kusuruma bakmayın..."

Girdik ve bizden izin isteyip saçlarını kurulamaya gitti.

Şöyle bir etrafa baktım. Hayatımda bu kadar çok eşyanın olduğu bir yer sanırım hiç görmemiştim.

Ama ne gariptir ki bütün bu kalabalık insanın gözünü rahatsız etmiyordu. Özellikle uğraşılmamış olsa da belki seçilmiş eşyanın niteliğinden ötürü bütün bu birbirine benzemez parçalar yerli yerinde gibi görünüyordu.

Benim doğup büyüdüğüm ev, annemin mükemmellikle donattığı, herşeyin birbiriyle uyumlu olduğu klasik senfoni gibiydi.

Anneannemin evi, biraz daha karmaşık ve eski de olsa yine de kulağınızı rahatsız etmeyen modern bir eser gibiydi.

Ama burası hayatımda hiç görmediğim, birbirine hiç uymayan parçaların biraraya getirildiği, ahşapla camın, mermerle kağıdın, dev insan figürleriyle ne olduğu anlaşılmaz küçük bibloların, eski bir film afişiyle astronot giysilerinin, kırık bir bisikletle teneke bir arabanın, bilinmeyen yerlerin eski haritalarının, hani o şairin "Kardeşim su versin ona, susamış," dediği tahta atın, korkunç yüzlü kuklalarla canlı gibi duran bebeklerin, azraille meleğin, kavanozların içindeki ceninlerle kadim uygarlıkların ölüm törenlerinin, rönesans duvar resimleriyle çizgi filmlerin içiçe geçtiği dünyadışı bir yer gibiydi.

Asıl olanla taklidin, yaşamla ölümün, iyilikle kötülüğün, masumiyetle sapkınlığın, gerçekle rüyanın içiçe geçtiği, ancak sizin bakışınızla, o anki algınızla anlam kazanan bir sanat eseri gibiydi.

Adeta bir rüya gibi...

Çünkü rüyaları biz biçimlendiremeyiz. Birbiriyle ilgisiz, zamandan, mekandan kopuk, görülmüş ya da hiç bilinmeyen şeyler biraraya gelir ve kendimizi çekilmesi imkansız bir filmin içinde buluruz.

Sarhoşluk gibi...

Sınırların kalktığı, bilinen bütün biçimlerin bozulduğu, sözcüklerin artık ne anlama geldiğinin bile anlaşılamadığı, başka dünyaya geçmiş gibi hissettiğiniz başka bir ruh hali...

Tam da benim gibi...

Rüyadan uyanırken hep huzursuz olurum. Çocukluğumdan beri... Sanki bir yere gitmişim ve yeniden bu dünyaya geri geliyormuşum gibi... Çoğu zaman çarpıntıyla uyanırım ve orada bıraktığım puslu görüntüleri, insanları unutup yeniden uyandığım, tanıdığım, bildiğim gerçeğe dönmek için biraz zaman geçirmem gerekir.

Ben aşık olmak nasıl birşey bilmiyordum.
Üstelik bunu bilmediğimi de bilmiyordum.
O uçuşan kelebekleri, birini görünce heyecanlanmayı, kalp çarpıntısını, yüz kızarmasını filan aşk sanıyordum ben.
Bir de tabii elele tutuşup gezmeleri, akşam olup gitmesin diye ikide bir saate bakmaları, olur olmaz konuşmalarla hiç sıkılmadan oturmaları...
Birine yalnızca bakmanın, onun kokusunu hatırlamanın, gün içinde yanımdayken birşeyi söyleyiş biçiminin, elinin basit hareketinin, gömleğinin kırışıklığının, saçlarını karıştırmasının, olur olmaz anlarda yeniden aklına geleceğini bilmiyordum mesela.
Ya dünyanın öteki ucundan hatta yılların içinden bile onun kokusunu duymayı?

Ve bütün bunların beni garip bir biçimde heyecanlandırmış olmasını, sabahları sanki birşey olacakmış gibi uyanmamı, yüzümde durduk yerde beliren saçma gülümseyişi, birileriyle konuşurken dalıp gitmelerimi ve söylenenlerin umurumda bile olmayışını anlayamıyordum.

Sonra o geri geldi...

Saçları hala biraz ıslaktı. Yine uzun beyaz bir gömlek giymişti. Ayakları çıplaktı. Bize kahve yaptı. Oturup sigara yaktı.

"Evet," dedi, "şimdi, soru mu sormak istersiniz, sohbet etmek mi?"

Ne diyeceğimizi bilemeden birbirimize baktık Tolga'yla...

Sanki bana fazla sormayın, ben soruları sevmem, der gibiydi.

Tabii yine de bir sürü soru sorduk. Çünkü gelmeden önce onun hakkında birbirinden çok farklı hikayeler anlatıldığını duymuştum. Daha ilk resimleriyle birdenbire büyük olay yaratan, bir anda ünlü ressamların önüne geçen ama kendi sergisinin açılışına bile gelmeyen, ortada görünmeyen bu adam hakkında herkes konuşuyordu.

Kimine göre bütün bunlar planlanmıştı. Böyle gizemli bir hava yaratarak resimlerine çok daha yüksek fiyatlar koyacaktı. Kimi onun çılgınca resimler çizen ve ne çizdiğinin farkında bile olmayan delinin biri olduğuna inanıyor, kimi, düzene karşı bir anarşist olduğunda ısrar ediyordu.

Annesi çok küçükken ölmüş ve ona teyzesi bakmıştı. Babasının tek başına hem ona hem hasta kardeşine bakacak durumu yoktu.

Erkek kardeşi zihinsel engelliydi. Babası Erzurum'a tayin olunca o Van'da teyzesinin yanında ilkokulu okumuş ve onca yıl babasını ve kardeşini belki bir ya da iki kez görebilmişti.

Annesini çok hatırlamıyordu. Ama teyzesini annesi kadar çok sevmişti.

Yoksullardı.

"Aslına bakarsanız uzun zaman bunun farkında değildim," dedi. "Herkes yoksuldu çünkü, sonuçta yemeğimiz vardı, okula gidiyorduk, sokakta oynuyorduk, yazın nehirde yüzüyorduk, kırlarda dolaşıyorduk, bir eski radyo vardı, oradan dinlediklerimiz de bize masallar dünyasından öyküler gibi gelirdi... O kadar uzaktı bizim gerçeğimizden..."

Durup bir an sanki o günler gelmiş, şu an yanıbaşımızdaymış gibi baktı ve gülümsedi, "Ne zaman ki insan başka şeyler görüyor o zaman çaresizliğin, yoksulluğun ne demek olduğunu anlayabiliyor, ne zaman ki başkalarının evlerini görüyor, kendi eşyalarının ne kadar zavallı olduğunu farkediyor."

Tolga'yla birbirimize baktık. İki şımarık çocuk. Hep bir eli yağda bir eli balda büyümüş. Şimdi böyle bir adamın karşısında oturmuş ona sorular mı soruyorduk?

"Ben ortaokulu bitirdiğimde babam yeniden evlendi. Ölen eşinden yüklüce mirasa konmuş bir kadınla. Beni de yeniden yanına almaya karar verdi tabii. Bu kez teyzem deliye döndü, aslına bakarsanız biraz deliydi de gerçekte ama pek belli olmazdı, sakin, içine dönük, durduk yerde ağlayan kadınlar vardır ya öyle bir kadındı zaten. Benden ayrılacağını duyunca artık ağlaması hiç kesilmedi. Sonunda ben de bir karar verdim ve onun yanında kalacağımı, yazları ya da tatillerde de babamın yanına gideceğimi söyledim. Sanırım yeni anne de buna pek üzülmedi."

Bir an aklıma babam geldi.

"Babanızın evlenmesini nasıl karşıladınız?" diye sordum.

Kahvesinden bir yudum aldı. Kafasını kaşıdı. Bana değil uzak bir noktaya bakarak cevap verdi:

"Bilmem, galiba o zaman bunu çok önemsemedim, sanki içimden ben ona zaten küsmüştüm ve duygusal anlamda o konu benim için kapanmıştı, daha doğrusu ben öyle sanıyordum. Bir oğlanın babasıyla böyle bir konusu tabii asla kapanmıyor yalnızca saklıyorsun ve orada seni bekliyor, yıllar sonra yeniden beklenmedik biçimde karşına çıkmak üzere..."

Belki bir kızın da babasıyla... diye geçirdim içimden... Devam etti, "Onlar İstanbul'daydı ben Van'da. Ama artık parası vardı babamın yani daha doğrusu karısının... Onun için de ilk tatilde onların yanına gitmem için otobüs bileti geldi. İlk kez bu kadar uzun bir yolculuğa çıkmıştım ve tek başıma pencereden yollara, sanki bırakılmış, terkedilmiş gibi görünen uçsuz bucaksız topraklara, ekili tarlalara, telefon direklerine, yoksul evlere, güzel evlere, kimi zaman insanın içini burkan bozkıra, kimi zaman yemyeşil küçük köylere bakarak ve elimdeki deftere gördüklerimi çizerek geldim. O yolculuğu hiç unutmam. Belki ilk uzun yolculuğum olduğu için, belki kısa da olsa tüm hayatımı ilk kez kendi başıma yeniden gözümde canlandırdığım için, belki birçok hayatın içinden geçerken aslında kendi yaşadıklarımın öyle çok da acıklı, çok da bana özgü olmadığını ilk kez anladığım için, bilmem..."

Sanki sesi titredi gibi geldi bana... Tolga hayranlıkla ona bakıyordu.

Birden kalktı, "Burası fazla sessiz," dedi, gözlerini mi sildi acaba, eski bir pikaba bir plak koydu, sert, sigaradan kalınlaşmış sesli adam Fransızca şarkı söylemeye başladı. Sürgün edilmekten, bir bavulla yaşamaktan ya da ülkesinin artık o bavul olduğu gibi şeylerden sözeden bir şarkıydı.

Sanki tüm bunları anlatmak için yıllardır bizi beklermiş gibi, sanki az önce soruları sevmem diyen o değilmiş gibi, sanki biz yokmuşuz ve kendi kendine konuşuyormuş gibi kaldığı yerden anlatmaya başladı.

Öylesine canlı anlatıyordu ki sanki o ana, o zamana birlikte gitmişiz, biz de onunla oradaymışız gibi hissediyorduk.

Çok sonra bana o gün bütün bunları gerçekten de yıllar sonra ilk kez bize anlattığını söyleyecekti.

"İstanbul'da beni otogardan babam aldı. Henüz benim için yeni olan, farklı olan tek şey inanılmaz kalabalıktı. Sanki herkes üstüme geliyormuş gibi korkmuştum. Bu kadar çok insanın aynı anda yollarda yürümesi, bu kadar çok arabanın dolaşması hiç filmlerdeki gibi değildi...

Hem ürkütücü hem de heyecan vericiydi.

Aslına bakarsanız çok fazla film de izlemiş değildim. Kasabadaki sinemaya bir ya da iki kez gitmiştik. İstanbul'u da ilk izlediğim o siyah beyaz filmde görmüş ve aşık olmuştum. Sanki benim için dünyadaki en eşsiz yer gibiydi."

Kahve getirdi. Müziğin sesini biraz kıstı.

Sonra devam etti.

"Babamın yeni evi bizimkine benzemiyordu. Bilmemne palas diye havalı, yeni bir apartmanın bahçe katındaydı. Oldukça büyüktü ve benim için de ayrı oda hazırlanmıştı. Kardeşim beni yadırgadı, huysuzlandı, belki gerçekten hatırlamadı belki de içinden bana küsüp unutmuştu... Köşede oturup bu yabancıya yadırgayan gözlerle bakıp elindeki ipliklerle oynamaya devam etti.

Cici annemiz babamın yaşlarında, giyimine meraklı, süslü, püslü bir kadındı. Gür bir sesi vardı. Kendinden emin, kesin cümlelerle konuşuyordu.

Babamın onunla sırf parası için evlendiğini herkes gibi herhalde o da biliyordu. Ama ben bugün bile onun niye babamla evlendiğini anlayabilmiş değilim."

Ne garip diye düşündüm, bambaşka insanlar benzer şeyler düşünüp, beklenmedik biçimde benzer şeyler yaşayabiliyor, hissedebiliyor demek ki...

"Çünkü babam neredeyse hiç konuşmayan, saatlerce gazetenin verdiği bulmacaları çözüp sıkılmayan, sonra uyuyakalan biriydi. Evlendiği için ona kızmadım, en azından kardeşimle ilgilenen biri var diye düşündüm..."

O insana huzur veren, yumuşak ama etkileyici sesiyle bunları anlatırken ben sanki radyo tiyatrosu dinler gibi garip bir ruh haline girmiştim.

Bir an, hiç beklenmedik biçimde, normalde herkes sorularıma son derece basit, sıradan cevaplar verirken onun yıllardır beni tanırmış gibi böyle hayatını anlatması beni irkiltti. Sanki gizlice onun çekmecelerini karıştırmış, günlüğünü okumuş gibi suçluluk duydum.

"İşte orada ilk akşam yemeğimizi yerken galiba ilk kez yoksulluğun farkına vardım. Masanın üstünde sallanan kristal avize bile gözümü alıyordu. Elimi, ayağımı nereye koyacağımı şaşırdım. Bir sürü çatal bıçak, bardak, üstüste konmuş tabaklar, porselen takımlar, sanki kadıncağız eski bir ihtişamı sürdürmeye çalışır gibiydi."

Aklıma annem geldi tabii...

"Aslında o gece hemen oradan çıkmak ve geri dönmek istiyordum. Kendimi hiç bir zaman bu kadar rahatsız, bu kadar yabancı, bu kadar ait olmadığım bir yerde bulmamıştım. Karşımda oturan bu adam benim babamdı ama aslında onu hiç tanımıyordum, bu benim kardeşimdi ama o da beni tanımıyordu, bu kadınsa tümüyle yabancıydı. Bana sorulan sorulara (ki babamdan çok kadın soruyordu) kısa kısa cevaplar veriyordum. Şimdi size verdiğim cevapların tam aksine..."

Gülmesiyle birden sanki bir rüyadan uyandım.

"Siz tabii benim doğup büyüdüğüm yerleri bilmezsiniz," dedi.
"Hayır," dedi Tolga benim yerime, "gitmedik hiç..."
"Bir yere gitmekle, orada yaşamak, bazı şeyleri görmekle onu anlamak çok farklı, her gün sokaklarda dilenen çocukları görürsünüz ve belki üzülürsünüz ama onların aslında ne yaşadığını asla bilemezsiniz, tıpkı benim de bunca zenginliğin içindeki insanların bir resme dünyanın parasını verip, yanlarında çalışan bir işçinin zar zor geçindiği maaşını düşürmek için uğraşmasını anlayamamam gibi..."

Çocukken bir odun parçasını yontarak heykeller yaptığını anlattı. Bazen bir koyun, bazen ağaç, bazen neye benzediğini kimsenin anlamadığı figürler yontuyordu.
Okuldaki öğretmenlerden biri yaptıklarıyla ilgilenmiş, onu resim çizmesi için yüreklendirmişti.

"İyi bir öğrenciydim, çünkü yapacak pek işim yoktu, yılbaşında okul kitapları alındığı zaman hepsini okurdum, anlamasam da okurdum, ilgimi çeken cümlelerin altını çizerdim, şiirleri, hikaye parçalarını ezberlerdim, anlamadığım bir formül olduğunda sayısız kez yeniden çözmeye çalışır ve sonunda kendime göre çözerdim. Sonra karpuzlardan, kabaklardan bile heykeller yapmaya başladım. Öğretmenim onları alıp okulda sergiliyordu. Bir gün bana büyükçe bir defterle siyah, kalın kalemler getirdi. Ben de çizdim. Öyle çok çiziyordum ki defter hemen bitti. O zaman gidip okuldaki teksir kağıtlarını alıp onların arkasına çizerdim.

Benden manzarayı, keçileri, çobanları, uçsuz bucaksız otlakları çizmemi isterlerdi. Onları da yapardım ama neye benzediği bilinmez garip şeyler çizmek daha çok hoşuma giderdi ya da ne bileyim içimden öyle gelirdi."

"Neye benzediği bilinmez mi?" diye sordu Tolga...

"Evet, onlar benim rüyalarımdı..."

Sonra büyük masaların üzerinde üstüste yığılmış bir sürü çizim gösterdi bize. İnsanı öyle hemen içine alan, renklerini beğendiğiniz ya da size alıp evinize asma isteği veren resimlerden değildi bunlar... Şaşırtıcı, karışık, içiçe geçmiş figürlerle, renklerle, yazılarla dolu, o güne kadar pek de görmediğim türden şeylerdi. İlk bakışta tam olarak ne olduğunu anlamıyordu insan. Hani bir buluta bakıp ondan biçimler oluşturmaya çalışmak gibiydi.

Bir köşede tahtadan yontulmuş bir araba üzerine paslı bir tel takılmış. Yanında, çiviler çakılmış, üzerine futbol sahası çizilmiş bir tahta parçası...

"Bunlar sizin gerçek oyuncaklarınız mı?" diye sordu Tolga.

Güldü.

"Evet," dedi, "top alamadığımız için bozuk parayla bu tahta sahada maç yapardık. Bu arabayı da ben yaptım. Kılıçlar, tüfekler daha bir sürü oyuncak yaptım ama birçok şey gibi onları da bir yerlerde bıraktım ya da belki birilerine verdim... Bende kalan bunlar..."

Anneannem Ferhat'ı ilk gördüğüm akşam sonradan bana onun tutuklandığını, kısa bir süre önce hapisten çıktığını söylemişti.

Sormak istedim.

"Önemli değil," dedi, "bizim gibi ülkelerde farklı görüşleri savunan herkes neci olursa olsun bir gün devlet zulmüne uğrar, hatta devleti yönetenler bile..."

Ve daha fazlasını soramadan sözü değiştirdi, o bize sorular sormaya başladı.

Tolga'nın makinasıyla birlikte ilk fotoğrafımız çekildi. Hala duruyor o fotoğraf. Ben yanında biraz küçük kalmışım, o da elini omuzuma koymuş ve biraz eğilmiş, o gülüyor bense şaşkın şaşkın bakıyorum.

Çıktık. Akşam biraz serinlemişti. Yürürken Tolga bana döndü, "Nasıl adam bu, resmen çarpıldım," dedi.

"Bilmem," dedim, "resimleri gibi galiba..."

Yoksa... Rüyaları gibi mi?

Ama o gün kısa kısa resim parçaları gibi anlattığı çocukluğunda çok daha fazlasının olduğunu ancak uzun zaman sonra öğrenebilecektim.

Evet bir anda hayatım değişmişti. Büyümüş müydüm? Bence öyleydi. Bu, sabah akşam, uyandığımda, yattığımda içimde hiç kesilmeyen çarpıntı büyümenin heyecanı mıydı?

Annem her ne kadar anneannemin bu yaptığından hiç memnun olmasa da yavaş yavaş ikna olmuştu. Belki de ona böylece yeni bir uğraş doğmuştu.

Tabii ki onun da Londra'ya gelip en azından bir süre bizimle kalacağından hiç kuşkum yoktu. Ama buna da razıydık.

Çünkü bu sayede Tolga'nın babası da itirazlarından vazgeçmiş, ona yalanlar uydurmamıza gerek kalmamıştı.

Zaten evde Meral Teyze'nin sözü geçerdi.

Ev nerede tutulacak, nasıl olacak, nasıl döşenecek bunları ikisi uzun uzun konuşuyor hatta bazen iki kaynana gibi bozuşuyorlardı.

Meral Teyze, o eski püskü Londra evleri olmaz, mutlaka yeni ev olmalı, ısınmalı, her tür konforu olmalı diyordu.

Annem üç oda olmasında ısrarcıydı. Tabii ki bir odaya onlar geldiklerinde yerleşeceklerdi.

Ayrıca okula yürüyüş mesafesinde olmalıydı. Öyle geceleri filan güvenilir bir semt olması şarttı.

Sare Hanım bu işlere hiç karışmadı. "Meral bilir ne yapacağını, uzatmaya gerek yok, bulur o, becerir," diye kestirip attı. Onun için hedefe ulaşılmış, mesele kapanmıştı.

Onun asıl ilgilendiği başkaydı. Eski dergiler çıkartıyor, bana modeller gösteriyor, kumaşlar hakkında bilgi veriyor ve daha çok çizmemi istiyordu.

Hatta ona kalsa terzi Perihan Hanım geldiğinde biraz dikiş öğrensem iyi olacaktı.

Bense dediğim gibi bütün bunlar sanki benim hayatımın dönüm noktası değilmiş gibi aldırışsız bir havadaydım.

Zaten Tolga söylemişti, biz kendi isteklerimizde ısrar etsek de işe yaramayacaktı.

"Bırak annem istediğini yapsın sonra biz yerleşince kafamıza göre değiştiririz," diyordu.

Benim aklımsa o resimlerin içindeki adamdaydı.

Bunu kimseye söylemeye cesaretim yoktu hatta belki kendime bile ama böyleydi.

Şimdi artık bunca yıl sonra rahatlıkla söyleyebilirim.

İlk gördüğümden beri onu düşünmeden geçen tek günüm bile olmadı.

Aslında bu eve gelip giden yazarların, sanatçıların hepsi değişik, çekici, ilginç insanlardı. İçlerinde çok etkileyici olanlar hatta hayran olduğum insanlar da vardı. Ama o güne kadar ara sıra öylesine aklıma gelse de hiç birine karşı böyle hissetmemiştim.

Örneğin çok hayran olduğum bir oyuncu vardı. Oyunlarına da gitmiştim, yemeğe geldiğinde o davudi sesiyle konuşurken hayran hayran ona bakarken yakalardım kendimi.

Anneannem de benimle eğlenir, bazen öylesine sorar gibi, "Akşama kimler geliyor?" dediğimde, "Ayol sen asıl soracağını sorsana hadi iyisin seninki geliyor akşam," diye gülerdi.

Ben de utanır kızarıp bozarırdım ve "Canım ne var bunda pek hoş adam doğrusu ben de olsam beğenirim ama daha senin sıran değil bu işlere..." diye cümleyi bağlardı.

Sonunda o da bir gün yanında pek havalı oyuncu bir kızla gelmiş ve ben de kendimce ona küsüp bu hayale bir son vermiştim.

Sonra o kadınla evlendi. Kadın çok ünlü bir oyuncu ve şarkıcı oldu. O yakışıklı adamsa oldukça genç yaşta kansere yakalandı ve kısa sürede öldü.

Ne garip, o akşamı, ona kendince aşık olmuş ve sonra da kendince küsmüş küçük kızı belki de hiç hatırlamadan...

Böyle ne çok hayat var aklımda.

Eve gelenlerin çoğu tanınan insanlar olduğu ve gelecekte daha da ünlü olduklarından onların hayatını, neler yaptıklarını sonraki yıllarda izleme şansım oldu.

Bazılarının bir köşede ezik büzük oturup söze bile giremezken yıllar sonra üst perdeden atıp tutan, kimseleri beğenmeyen insanlar olduğunu, bazılarının hararetle savunduğu tüm düşüncelerin tam tersi bir yere savrulduğunu, bazılarının geçmişlerini anlatırken aslında bambaşka yalanlar uydurduğunu, kendilerinden çok şey beklenen bazılarının da yokolup gittiğini gördüm.

Şimdi düşünüyorum da bir çocuk, bir genç kız için çok farklı bir ortamdı bu. Hepsi, yaratan, çılgınca düşünceleri olan, çoğu zaaflarına kapılmış ve sanki bununla mutluymuş gibi davranan, dünyanın her yerinden, tarihin her döneminden bilgiler getiren ulaklar gibi insanlarla oturmak, onların kendi aralarındaki tartışmaları, konuşmaları, dedikoduları dinlemek gerçekten de çok garipti. Ama o sıralar bu benim sıradan hayatımdı, bütün bunların farkında bile değildim.

Bir yılbaşı akşamı annemle yemek yedikten sonra aşağı indim. Tabii ki annem gelmeyecekti ama anneannem için yılbaşı önemli bir gündü.

Bu kez oldukça kalabalıktı. Hatta kapı açıktı ve birileri geliyor, birileri gidiyor, sürekli içkiler yemekler geliyor, herkes birileriyle sohbet ediyordu.

Daha onyedi yaşındaydım ama üzerimdeki gece elbisesiyle, topuz yapılmış saçlarımla pek havalı hissediyordum kendimi. Hatta oldukça parlak, kırmızı ruj da sürmüştüm.

O gece genç bir şairle ve arkadaşlarıyla uzun uzun sohbet ettim. Hatta biraz da sarhoş oldum. Benim çok sevdiğim yazarlardan, şiirlerden sözediyordu.

Kimi çok ünlü yazarların hayatlarına nasıl son verdiğinden açıldı sonra konu. Birinin damarlarını keserken son şiirini yazdığından, birinin tüm istediklerine sahipken artık bu dünyaya bunca acıya daha fazla dayanamıyorum diyerek suyun içinde yürüyüp gittiğinden, bir başkasının günlüklerinin sonunda intihar ettiği için kitabın yarım bir cümleyle bittiğinden sözediliyordu.

Hatta bir ara anneannem yanımıza gelip biraz dinledikten sonra, "Ah tabii gençler toplanmış ölümden sözediyorlar, yaşlılar ölümden hiç sözetmez, hatta duymak dahi istemez, içim sıkıldı," diyerek gitti.

Ben o akşam o şaire de aşık olmuştum.

Ama iki gün sonra ondan bir haber geldi.

Akşamüstü evinde arkadaşlarıyla otururken kalkıp içeri gitmiş ve pencereyi açıp aşağı atlayarak intihar etmişti.

Bu beni beklenmeyecek biçimde etkiledi. Nasıl olur da böyle hoş, bilgili, yetenekli, herkesin çevresinde pervane olduğu genç adam böyle bir delilik yapardı?

Yoksa o gece bunu yapacağını bilerek mi bu konuları açmıştı?

Acaba o gece cesaretimi toplayıp onunla görüşmek istediğimi söylesem intihar etmekten vazgeçer miydi?

Şöyle yazmıştı öldükten sonra masasının üstünde bulunan son şiirlerinden birinde:

Zamandan bir parça daha koptu
Akşam bana, yarın da böyle olacağını söylüyor
Nedensiz bir hüzün
Belki de bu yüzden
Nedensiz bir ben
Belki de bu yüzden

İnsan arkadaşlarıyla oturup sohbet ederken, gülüp eğlenirken birdenbire içeriye gidip pencereden atlar mı?

Bunu düşünmek bana derin bir hüzün vermişti. Hala da veriyor.

Üstelik acıklı olan, uzun süre içeride kahkahalar atıp eğlenen arkadaşları ne olduğunu farketmemiş ve ancak kapıya polis gelince anlamışlardı.

Hayat bütün bu sorulara cevap vermeyi zorlaştırıyor. Ama ben o zaman ona kızdım. Ne olursa olsun bir daha istediklerimi ertelememeye de belki o an karar verdim.

Belki de Ferhat'ın atölyesine yeniden gidecek cesareti toplamamın aslında bununla ilgisi vardı.

Söyleşinin çıktığı dergiyi alıp Ferhat'a gidecektim ama Tolga da gelmek istiyordu tabii. Hatta olur olmaz zamanlarda ondan sözedip canımı sıkıyordu. "Acaba gerçekte nasıl biri, sevgilisi var mı, çok mu çapkın, gerçi evde bir kadın yaşıyormuş gibi gelmedi bana ne dersin, bence çok sevgilisi vardır, kesin birşey," diye iyice sinirlerimi oynatıyordu.

Sare Hanım da birkaç kez, "Ferhat nerelerde acaba epeydir görünmedi, arayıp çağırmak lazım," demişti ama ben onun adı geçince hemen lafı değiştiriyordum. Kızardığım anlaşılacak diye ödüm kopuyordu.

Tolga'yla annesinin eve bakmak için Londra'ya gittikleri zamana kadar oyalandım.

Niye beni beklemedin derse, aman ne bileyim aklıma esti gittim işte, diyecektim.

O cuma gecesi neredeyse hiç uyumadım. Hatta gitmekten vazgeçecektim. Kalbim şimdiden böyle atıyorsa onu görünce ellerimin titreyeceğinden emindim.

Saçlarımı nasıl yapsaydım, toplasam mı açsam mı, yeni aldığım yazlık elbisemi mi giysem yoksa daha derli toplu pantolon gömlek gibi mi? Makyaj yapmasam daha iyiydi bence, böyle şeylerden pek hoşlanacak birine benzemiyordu.

Aman belki de dergiyi elimden alıp bana güle güle diyecekti. Belki de evde birileri olacaktı.

O zamandan beri kalkıp Sare Hanım'ı ziyarete gelmediğine göre tabii ki benim düşündüklerimden habersizdi.

Ama ne komik, kendi kendime film kişisi gibi rol yazıyordum, belki de onu şaşırtacak şeyler yapmalıydım, insanlar önce beğenmese de şaşırdıkları şeylerle daha çok ilgilenir. Biraz serseri, biraz umursamaz, rahat bir kız gibi mi olmalıydım acaba? Yoksa aksine daha ağır, hanım hanımcık mı?

Eh aslında ikisi de bendim. O yüzden fazla rol yapmaya gerek kalmayacaktı. En önemlisi açık mı olmalıydım –ki buna çok şaşıracağı kesindi– yoksa gizemli biçimde onun beni merak etmesini mi sağlamalıydım?

Evet bu ikincisi daha iyiydi.

Bir yandan bunları kuruyor bir yandan da "Ne aptalsın adam kimbilir kaç kadın tanımıştır, senden kaç yaş büyük, anında anlayacak niyetini ve gülüp geçecek," diyordum.

Sonra bu düşünceyi hemen kovalıyordum çünkü kendi kendime yazdığım romanı bozuyordu.

Hem aşk zaten hayallerden oluşmaz mı?

Aşk ne zaman biter diye kitaplar yazıyorlar bir de... Ne zaman bitecek, hayal kurmayı bıraktığınız zaman... Hayal gerçeğe döndüğü zaman...Kırıldığı zaman...

Aman çok biliyorum sanki...

Kendi kendime dedim ki (galiba artık sabah oluyordu ve bayılmak üzereydim) madem ki sen günlerdir anlamsız biçimde mutlusun, onu düşünmek sana iyi geliyor, kendini böyle rollere sokup ilk kez nasıl bir kadın olduğunu düşünüyorsun ve bu seni bugüne dek olmadığı kadar heyecanlandırıyor, bunu yaşayacaksın.

Hem en kötü ne olabilir ki? Bana kötü kız gözüyle mi bakar? Utanmaz küçük liseli mi der? Hiç sanmam. Yalnızca korkabilir.

En önemlisi korkmamasını sağlamak...

Hem ne yapıyordum ki, dergiyi götüreceğimize ona söz vermemiş miydim o gün?

Kapıdan bırakacaktım işte... Davet etmezse zaten biriyle buluşmaya giderken uğradığımı söyleyecektim.

İşte sabaha kadar böyle gelgitlerle uğraşırken yine gerçekle düş birbirine karıştı.

Ne güzel bir cumartesi günüydü.

Denizin kokusu, martıların neşesi, ışığın dünyaya sanki yeni bir ruh veren canlılığı, çiçek kokuları...

Tabii yola çıkmam epey zamanımı aldı. Öğlene doğru uyanabildim ve gözlerimin şişi gitsin diye Sare Hanım usulü çay banyosu yaptım.

Sonra aşağı indim. Sare Hanım her zamanki gibi uzun, renkli çiçekli sabahlığıyla oturmuş kahvesini içiyor.

"Gel bakalım gel, bu ne güzellik böyle hayrola nereye?" diye sordu.

"Arkadaşlarla buluşacağız," diye belki de ilk kez yalan söyledim ona.

Şöyle bir süzdü beni sonra "Git içerden benim ilk çekmecemden kırmızı küçük kutulardan birinde yeşil küpeler var biliyorsun, onları getir," dedi.

Getirdim. Kulağıma taktı.

"Hah şimdi oldu," dedi, "çok yakıştı..."

Kızardım.

İncecik ipekliden kısa bir elbise vardı üstümde, renkli geometrik desenler, yeşiller, maviler, bejler, çok severek almıştım.

"Aaa ama bu ayakkabılar olmamış ki bunun altına," dedi.

"Uff biliyorum ama bulamadım başka birşey," dedim.

"E, hani sana lacivert beyazlı üstünde kurdela olan ayakkabılar almıştık onları giysene..."

"Gündüz gündüz mü?" dedim. Hem çok özenmiştim hem de özenmiş görünmek istemiyordum çünkü. Düz basit bir ayakkabı giymiştim.

"Canım ne gündüzü akşamüstü artık giyebilirsin, yalnız çantasını da al, geç kalmazsın değil mi akşam misafir var."

Onu yanağından öptüm. "Kalmam kalmam," dedim.

Arkadaşlarımla sinemaya bu kılıkta gitmeyeceğimi biliyordu bence. Belki de okuldaki çocuklardan biriyle buluşacağımı düşünmüştü.

Mor salkımlı eski duvarların önünden geçip evine geldim.

Elimde dergi ve çantamda da küçük bir hediye vardı.

Nedense ona yakışacağını düşünmüştüm. Çok sevdiğim rengarenk ipek fular. Beyaz gömleğinin üstüne takar mıydı?

Sonradan öğrenecektim ki yaşlı mahalle terzisi dikiyordu gömleklerini. Ve hepsi beyaz, uzun, çok güzel ince pamukludan.

Evin önünden geçtim, biraz yürüdüm tekrar geri döndüm.

Sokak duvarlarından birine o sakallı, kızıl yıldızlı beresiyle Che Guevara'yı çizmişlerdi. Kocaman bir duvar resmi... Altında sloganlar... Kahrolsun...

Kapıyı çaldım. İçerden yüksek sesle klasik müzik geliyordu. Kapıyı açtı, pek de şaşırmış gibi değildi.

"Ben," dedim, "dergiyi getirecektim ya..."

"Hoşgeldin," dedi ve girmem için yana çekildi.

"Arkadaşın yok mu?"

"Tolga mı? A, hayır o Londra'ya gitti..."

Gelince bakalım bu yaptığımı ona nasıl anlatacağım...

Yine kahve kokusu...

İlk oturduğum eski koltuğa oturdum.

Birşey yapmam gerektiğini düşünerek hemen dergiyi uzattım.

"Güzel kahvem var, ister misin?" diye sordu.

İsterim.

"Sade?"

Sade.

Saçımla oynuyordum yine. Saçınla oynama Ebru diyordum ama oynuyordum.

Kahveleri getirdi, beyaz düz porselen fincanlar...

"Ne güzel kokuyor," dedim.

"Ben de seviyorum, belki tadından çok kokusunu..."

Dergiyi karıştırdı.

Fincanı alırken elim titredi, yerine bıraktım.

Gördü.

"Sıcakmış biraz," dedim.

Bir an hemen çıkıp gitmek istedim.

Sessizlik olmasın diye, "Sokakta, duvardaki resmi siz mi çizdiniz?" dedim.

Kalkıp müziğin sesini kıstı.

"Guevara'yı mı? Hayır, ben kahramanlarla pek ilgilenmem... Ve zaten sonunda kahrolan sistemler olmaz. Hep insanlar kahrolur..."

Koltuğun ucuna doğru oturdu. Yakın.

"Sare Hanım nasıl, uzundur göremedim onu," dedi.

"İyi, o da sizi soruyordu..."

Bakalım buraya geldiğimi duyunca ne olacak? Umarım görüşmezler...

"Çok şanslısın biliyorsun değil mi," dedi, anlamadım, "böyle bir anneannen olduğu için..."

"Ah evet, biliyorum," dedim, "belki de tek şansım..."

"Onunla oturup konuşmak bile insanı rahatlatıyor," dedi sonra durdu, "tek şansım mı dedin?"

"Evet..."

"Belki başka şansların da vardır da henüz farkında değilsindir," dedi.

Utandım. Ne demek isteğini anladım.

Ne garip, böyle karşılaşmalarda, "Ee nasıl gidiyor," filan gibi sorular sorulur. O sormuyordu.

Ne diyeceğimi bilemedim. Çantamdan fuları çıkarttım.

"Size bunu getirdim ama bilmem takar mısınız?"

"Bana mı?" Aldı, okşadı, sonra hemen boynuna taktı...

"Takarım tabii çok güzelmiş, teşekkür ederim, galiba beni fazla renksiz buldun..?"

Güldük.

"Sadece beyaz gömleğin üstünde güzel durur diye düşündüm..."

"Durdu mu?" diye sordu...

"Evet, çok güzel, nedense size vermek istedim," dedim.

"Bir ressama verilecek en güzel hediye... Renkler ve desenler..."

"Her gün çiziyor musunuz yoksa aklınıza esince mi?"

Soruya bak! Neden resim diye sorsan daha iyiydi... Oynama su saçınla...

"Her gün çizerim bazen deftere bazen tuvale genellikle karalamalar yaparım..."

"Yolda gelirken aklıma bir soru geldi?" dedim.

"Öyle mi?"

"Sen neşeli bir ilkyaz cumartesisinin resmini yapabilir misin Ferhat?"

İlk kez kahkaha attı.

Ve ben de ona ilk kez "sen" demiş oldum.

"Bak bu resmin adı bile yeter, hemen yapmalıyım..."

Kahveden bir yudum aldım, elim titremedi. Biraz rahatladım. En sevdiğim fularım boynunda, karşımda oturmuş gülüyordu.

Sonra nasıl oldu bilmiyorum ama kendimi ona Londra planlarını, yeni okulu, tasarım merakımı, kokuya ve dokunmaya olan zaafımı anlatırken buldum.

İkinci kahvenin yanında birer küçük kadeh konyak geldi.

Çok mu konuşuyordum?

"Galiba şöyle bir resim geldi aklıma, erguvanlar, mor salkımlar, ayva ağaçları, çocuklar, yerde yuvarlanan bir kedi, ona ağacın üstünden bakan bir karga, denizle içiçe girmiş bahçeler ve bu fuların renklerinde boyanmış bir bisiklete binen sen... Ne dersin?"

Ne mi derim? Bu adam benim aklımı mı okuyor?

"Belki de resmin içinde resmi çizen ve çizerken gülen ressam..."

Neydi bu?

"Madem ki resmi sen ısmarladın istediğini söyleyebilirsin," güldü, "Da Vinci de siparişle resim çiziyordu.."

Neydi?

Herhangi bir cumartesi günü, koskoca bir adamla sıradan bir konuşma mı?

Hiç tanımadığım biriyle ilk kez yalnız konuşurken aniden hayallerin içine girmek mi?

Sanki o kapı kendiliğinden açılmıştı. Düşünmeden, dün geceki gibi planlar yapmadan, öylesine, kendiliğinden... O kadar kendiliğinden ki, düşünsem aklıma gelmeyecek şeyler söylüyordum ve o da sanki beni yıllardır tanırmış gibi onlara benim beklediğim cevapları veriyordu.

Ya da hiç beklemediğim...

Evet orada onun yanında otururken, hatta daha gelmeden önce bile sanki bütün bunların böylece, kendiliğinden olacağını hissetmiştim.

Ben buraya gelirken ne istediğimi biliyordum.

O bilmiyordu.

Konuşurken, geçmişten, birbirinden çok farklı hayatlarımızdan, komik anılardan sözederken, o gözlerime bakarken, ben onun gülüşüne, eski şarkılar çalarken, yavaş yavaş akşam olurken tek bildiğim zamanı durdurabilmeyi, burada bu anın hiç geçmemesini istediğimdi.

Ve ne gariptir ki bundan böyle de hep bunu isteyecektim.

Sanki yıllardır böyle oturup konuşuyormuş gibi...

Bütün bu karmaşanın içindeki huzuru sanki önceden bilirmişim gibi...

Öyle bir an geldi ki kucağına uzanmak ve hiç konuşmadan öylece kalmak istedim.

Beni öpmesini istedim.

Bunları ve itiraf etmeliyim, daha fazlasını da...

Akşam oluyor, gitmem gerekiyor.

Bir an önce buradan kalksam iyi olacak diyordum kendi kendime.

O güne kadar böyle şeyler hissetmemiştim.

Hem şaşkındım hem de bu duygunun kaybolmasını istemiyordum.

Tıpkı bahçedeki gizli dehlizde ilk kaybolduğum günkü gibi... Hem korkuyordum hem de devam etmek, başka neler olduğunu görmek istiyordum.

Oraya ne zaman girsem gizemli, bana ait, kimsenin bilmediği bir dünyaya girmiş olurdum. Sonra oradan gerçek dünyaya dönerdim.

Belki de bu iki dünya arasındaki gidiş gelişler benim sonraki hayatımı belirledi.

Nasıl bir duyguysa, bütün düşünceler, kaygılar, korkular silinip gitmişti aklımdan, buradaydım, sanki her zaman olduğu gibi birlikteydik, bir an onun da benimle aynı şeyleri düşündüğünü, istediğini sanıyor sonra kendimi toparlayıp konuşmaya devam ediyordum.

Hiç tanımadığı biri insanda nasıl böyle bir etki yaratabilir ki?

Ama durumu idare ettiğimden, içimden geçenleri ona belli etmediğimden emindim.

İşte karşısında oturmuş kendinden emin genç bir kadın olarak onunla her konuda konuşuyor, sohbet ediyordum.

Söz bir türlü dönüp dolaşıp ikimize gelmese de...

Önce gözleri gülen insanlar vardır. O da onlardandı. Bazen çok ciddi birşey söylüyor, zaten konuşurken doğruca gözlerime bakıyor ve ben o gözlerin içinde kaybolup gidiyordum, susuyor ve gözlerinden aslında şaka yaptığını anlıyordum. Arkasından gülmeye başlıyor, kendi söyledikleriyle alay ediyordu.

Kendi kendime bir yandan konuşmayı sürdürürken bir yandan hayaller kuruyordum. Onunla uzakta, bizi kimsenin tanımadığı yerlerde olduğumu düşünüyordum. İçimden de gülüyordum tabii... Hem kendi halime hem onun bütün bunlardan haberi olmayışına...

Aslında birdenbire aklımdan geçenleri olduğu gibi söylesem bence çok gülerdi.

"Ben çok şey anlattım ama sen bana anlatmadın," dedim birden. Aslında anlattıklarının çok daha derininde olanları duymak istiyordum.

"Benim hayatım pek de neşeli değil," dedi, "anlatırsam sıkılırsın..."

"Hayır, sıkılmam, benimki de öyle sayılmaz aslında..."

Sonra anlatmaya başladı.

Aslında beş kardeşlerdi ama üç kardeşi ondan önce ölmüştü.. Onun hatırladığı ağabeyi de altı yaşındayken hayatını kaybetmişti. Anne babası akraba evlliği yaptığı için...

"Bir tek ben ve kardeşim hayatta kaldık. Ama kardeşim de zeka özürlüydü. Bizim oralarda dedikleri gibi moron..."

Birdenbire aklımdaki herşey uçup gitti. Bütün o konuşmalar, sanatla, ünlü isimlerle ilgili söylediklerimiz bitti. Dalgın dalgın anlatmaya devam etti...

"Evet insanlar acımasızdır. Ne tuhaf, çocuklar da öyle.

Bazen insan kendisine bile doğruları itiraf edemez. Tek başına kaldığı anlarda bile bazı şeyleri başka türlü görmeye ya da gördüğünü düşünmeye çalışır.

Ama aslında yıllar boyu Mehmet'ten utandım. Yanımda bir yere gönderdikleri zaman ondan nefret ettim. Yürürken önde giderdim ki kalabalıkta birlikte olduğumuzu anlamasınlar. Ama o tek başına kalakalırdı ve dönüp onu almak ve elini tutmak zorunda kalırdım.

İnsan kardeşinden utanır mı? Utanılacak birşey yaparsa utanır değil mi?

O ne yapmıştı ki?

Yalnızca anlatmaya çalışırken, sevinince, üzülünce, başka çocuklar gibi heyecanlanınca, onlar gibi sözcükleri kullanamadığı için garip sesler çıkartır, elleriyle garip hareketler yapar, bazen kendine zarar verir, bazen bir yerlere saldırırdı ve insanlar ondan korkardı.

Çocuklardan birinin yanına giderdi örneğin, bir kızın, bir bebeğin ve aslında istediği onu sevmek ya da onunla ilişki kurmaktı ama korkuturdu onları.

Kim korkmazdı ondan biliyor musun?

Hayvanlar."

Ansızın buradan bambaşka bir yere, onun hayatına, onun gizli tüneline girmiştik sanki ve ben yalnızca dinliyordum.

"Hayvanlar mı?" dedim.

"Evet," dedi, "çünkü hayvanlar bizim gibi acımasız sözdizimini bilmez. Birinin renkli, birinin çirkin, birinin şişman olduğunu bilmez. Belki zayıf olan orada zaten yaşayamadığı için..."

Gözlerinin dolduğunu hissettim. Elini yüzünde gezdirdi, bana bakmadan anlatmaya devam etti:

"Köpeğimiz vardı küçükken. Mehmet en çok onunla anlaşırdı. Sanki o köpek, Panço, onun her halini bizden iyi anlardı. Üzgünse yanına gider, kucağına kafasını koyar, kendisini sevdirir, neşeliyse onunla koşar zıplar, gülüyor ve deli deli hareketler yapıyorsa o da havlayıp bağırarak ona eşlik ederdi.

Çok küçüktü daha. Belki beş yaşında ya var ya yoktu. Bir gün okuldan dönüyorduk. Her yer kar içindeydi. Öyle çok kar yağmıştı ki ertesi gün, sonraki gün hep okullar tatil edilmişti. Yolda yürürken biz kartopuna daldık ve ben Mehmet'i unuttum. Neden sonra baktım ki ortada yok. Deliye döndüm. Her yere baktık bulamadık. Mehmet yok. O an bunun ne olduğunu anlamamıştım. Sorumluluk muydu? Babama ne söyleyeceğim miydi? Hayır. Kalbim deli gibi atıyordu ve hayatımda belki de hiç böyle korkmamıştım. Ölecek olduğum zaman bile böyle korkmadım hayatımda. O zaman tabii bilmiyordum ama onu gerçekten sevdiğimi anladığım an, o andı bence.

Sonra onu bir ağacın altında bulduk. Neredeyse donmuş halde oturmuş elindeki karı yemeye çalışıyordu hala."

Onu dinlerken düşünüyordum. Nasıl olmuştu ya da ne zaman, birilerini güzel, birilerini çirkin, birilerini bize uygun, başkalarını farklı görmeye başlamıştık? Nasıl olmuştu da onları hep yoksaymaya hatta yoketmeye çalışmıştık? Bu hep böyle miydi?

"Nerede şimdi, ne yapıyor?" diye sordum.

"Babamın yanında, zaman zaman gidip görürüm onu... Ne yazık ki onu görmek hala beni üzüyor... Ve o da benden uzak duruyor."

Sonra yine zamanın içinden geçti, buraya geldi. Bana baktı, gülümseyerek, "Ne yaptın sen bana böyle, çenem düştü, seni evden merak ederler..." dedi...

Evet ederler... Kalktım.

Kapıdan çıkmadan önce karşılıklı durduk. Birden sarılıp onu dudaklarından öptüm. Şaşkın kalakaldı sonra beni kucakladı ve öpmeye devam etti. Ve ben merak edenleri, nereye gideceğimi, nereden geldiğimi, bundan sonra olacakları hepsini unuttum...

Hayır, tabii ki böyle olmadı. Bu sadece aklımdan geçti.

Karşılıklı durduk, elimi sıkıp beni yanaklarımdan öptü, kokusunu duydum ve bir daha hiç unutmadım, gülümsedi, birşey söylemeyecek miydi, ben söylese miydim, söylemedi, ben de söyleyemedim.

Öylece arkamı dönüp yürüdüm.

Tren sallanarak ilerliyor, karşımdaki adam uyukluyor, hatta ara sıra derin bir iç geçiriyor rüyasında, ben yine pencerelerden dışarı bakıyorum ama dışarıdakileri görmüyorum da sanki trenin camlarında kendi kısa hayatımın filmini izliyorum.

Kısa dedim evet ama bu kadar kısa zamanda neler olmuş.

Üstüste yaşananlara böyle uzaktan bakıp düşünmeye sanki fırsat olmamış...

Bu anlattıklarımın üzerinden yıllar yıllar geçmiş...

Buraya gelirken kararlıydım.

Bütün bunlar olmasa kimseyi dinlemeyip bu ameliyata girmeye kesin karar vermiştim.

Ama şimdi içimde başka bir duygu var. İlk istasyonda inmek, geri dönmek, onun yanına gitmek istiyorum. Belki de bu garip rastlantıların bana söylemek istediği birşey var.

Yazık ki onun ne olduğunu hala anlamıyorum.

Doktor bana bir keresinde, "Tam olarak ne hissettiğini anlatabilir misin?" demişti.

"Yorgunum," demiştim, "sanki çok yaşlıyım ama genç bir kadının bedenindeyim."

Ve böyle daha fazla sürdüremeyeceğimi biliyorum. Bunu biliyorum.

Onun için buraya geldim. Onun için bunu yapmalıyım.

Kucağımda çocukluk arkadaşım Puska var. Adının neden Puska olduğunu benim bile hatırlamadığım, küçük tüylü oyuncağım...

Bazıları geçmişini unutmak ister, anıları siler, onların yerine başka anıları, belki başkalarının anılarını koyar, kendisine tıpkı bir roman kahramanı gibi farklı, yeni bir geçmiş yaratır.

Bazılarıysa benim gibi çocukluğuyla yaşar.

Gülüyorum bazen kendi halime.

Tıpkı küçük bir kızken Puska'yı nasıl her yere götürdüysem, nasıl onu unuttuğum anda geri dönüp almak için kıyametleri kopardıysam, şimdi de çocukluğum sanki onun gibi yanımda her yere benimle geliyor, benimle oturup kalkıyor, benimle uyuyor, uyanıyor.

Kızardı babam, Puska'yı sanki aileden biriymiş gibi yemeğe otururken bile baş köşeye yerleştirmeme, onu her yere götürmeme...

"Koca kız oldu hala elinde bu ne idüğü belirsiz oyuncakla dolaşıyor..." derdi.

Ne idüğü belirsiz mi? Puska'ya bakardım ama biz onunla anlaşmıştık, büyüklerin söylediklerine aldırmayacaktık, onun için üzülmediğini bilirdim.

İşin tuhaf yanı, onu bana kimin aldığını, onu nereden bulduğumu kimse hatırlamıyor...

O kadar oyuncağım varken bu boz renkli, fil mi köpek mi, kedi mi tavşan mı olduğu belli olmayan tüyleri tiftik tiftik olmuş hayvana neden böyle düşkün olduğumu da kimse bilemiyordu zaten.

Çok da derdim değil. Kaç yaşına gelmiş kadının hala yanında oyuncakla yatmasını garip bulan varsa da bulsun. Yaptığım pek çok şeyi de garip buldular, onlara da aldırmamayı çoktan öğrendim.

Ben kimseyi yargılamam, kimseye neden böyle yaptın, neden öyle yaptın diye sormam, birilerine zarar vermiyorsa, kötülük etmiyorsa kimsenin saçmalıklarını çekiştirmekle zaman geçirmem. Baktım ki çok sıkıldım, ondan uzaklaşırım olur biter.

Bunları kimden öğrendim? Tabii ki anneannemden.
Belki biraz da tam ne olduğunu anlamadığımız ama hepsini izlediğimiz ilk gençlik yıllarımın Fransız filmlerinden...

Yaşlılık nasıl birşey diye sormuştum Sare Hanım'a bir keresinde...

"Ben nereden bileyim, yaşlı değilim ki," diyecek sandım her zamanki gibi şakaya vurup ama öyle yapmadı. Bir an durdu, yüzü asıldı,

"Şöyle birşey, önce etrafındaki konuşmalardan sıkılıyorsun, sonra eşyalar, eskiden çok değer verilen ıvır zıvır saçma gelmeye başlıyor, sonra ertelenmemesi gerekenler, yapılması gerekenler, uyulması gerekenler saçma geliyor, sonra giyinip kuşanıp bir yerlere gitmek saçma geliyor, sonra bu aşk meşk meseleleri saçma geliyor ve sonra hepsi saçma gelmeye başlıyor. Hiç birşey yapacak takatin kalmıyor."

Ona baktım. Birden canlandı, eski haline döndü,

"O yüzden ben her gün böyle giyinirim, her akşam insanları çağırırım, bütün ışıkları yakarım, başka şeyler düşünmeye zamanım kalmayacak kadar meşgulüm... Ha bir de yavaş yavaş unutursun ama ben bundan şikayetçi değilim, unutmak hiç de fena sayılmaz..."

Zaten bana her zaman derdi ki, "Sakın oturup da kafana takılanları fazla düşünme, hep uğraşacak birşeylerin olsun, insanlar bazen seni yalnız bırakır, o zaman kendi kendine oyalanmayı bilmelisin, böylece hiç sıkılmazsın..."

Ben de öyle yaptım. Düştüğüm zaman, sabah kalkıp yürüyemediğim zaman, olup bitenleri hatırlayamadığım zaman, ışığa bakamayıp günlerce karanlıkta oturmak zorunda kaldığım zaman, çok canım yanıp ağlasam da güçlü olmaya çalışarak geçen zamanlarda hep bunlar geçecek, bir kere daha olmuştu, yine oluyor, korkmayacaksın, dedim...

Aslında hayatı fazla ciddiye almadığımı, aldığım zamanları gençlik döneminde geride bıraktığımı, sonra da her zaman herşeyin üstesinden gelebilecek bir gücüm olduğunu düşündüm. Çünkü eğer içinde o güç varsa, olup bitenlere ne olursa olsun direnerek çıkıp gidebiliyorsan, vazgeçmeyi öğrenmişsen sonunda istediğin gibi yaşamayı başarıyorsun ve artık seni kimse çok fazla değiştiremiyor.

Sonra doktor bana, "Bazen hepimiz böyle hissederiz aslında," dedi, "derken birşey olur ve yeniden gençleşiriz, bu kararı verdikten sonra çok güçlü olmalısın, sen inanmazsan bizden fazlasını bekleme..."

Evet güçlü olmalıyım. Buraya kadar gelirken nasıl olduysam öyle... Ve üstelik oldu, beklenmedik birşey oldu ve gidip o çiçeği, yılanbalığına kaptırmadan almam gerekiyor, ölümsüzlüğün o gizli çiçeğini... Kimseye söylemek yok.

Hadi gel Puska, yine hatırlamaya çalışalım unuttuklarımızı, kimbilir belki görmediğimiz daha çok işaretler vardır orada...

Tolga Londra'dan heyecanla döndü. Yeni evi, oturacağımız semti, hemen yakında her sabah kahvaltı edeceğimiz küçük kafeyi, hatta oradaki sempatik garsonu anlatıp duruyordu. Epeyce alışveriş yapmıştı, odanın her tarafına aldıklarını yaymış bana gösteri yapıyordu. Tabii bana da yeni moda rengarenk gömlekler, pantolonlar, kocaman taşlı kolyeler, kitaplar almıştı. Çok komikti gerçekten de... "Okuldakilere söylemeyelim gözleri kalır," diye beni ciddi ciddi tembihliyor, tahtalara vuruyordu.

Üşenmedi bana aldıklarını tek tek denetti. Bazılarını çok beğendi bazılarına burun büktü. "Senin de biraz göğüslerin mi büyüdü ne, bunu kaldır, değiştiririz gidince," diyordu.

"Keşke benim kardeşim olsaydın," dedim.

"E zaten öyle sayılırım," diye bana sarıldı.

Ev aslında eşyalıydı ama yine de annesine bir sürü şey aldırmıştı tabii.

"Biraz eski püskü ev ama yeri şahane," diyordu, "yürüyerek her yere gidebiliriz, bisiklet alsam mı dedim ama o da havamı bozar, ne diyorsun?"

Gülüyordum, ne diyeceğim...

"Evet bence de bu kıyafetlerinle bisiklete binip paçana halka takman hoş olmaz..." dedim...

"Eee sen neler yaptın?" dedi sonunda o uzay stili yuvarlak koltuğuna gömülüp.

"Hiiç," dedim, "aynı şeyler işte, ha Ferhat'a dergiyi götürdüm bu arada..."

Gözleri açıldı birden...

Gömüldüğü koltuktan zor fırladı.

"Ferhat'a? Dergiyi mi götürdün? Şimdi hemen hemen anlatıyorsun herşeyi..."

"Ne var canım, dergiyi götürdüm işte... İstemişti ya..."

"İstemişti ya... Tabii tabii... Seni şimdi parçalarım. Hemen anlat diyorum!"

Kızacağını düşünmüştüm ama gülmeye başladı.

"Çabuk diyorum..."

Resimleri, anlattıklarından bazılarını... Tam anlatıyordum ki, eliyle ağzımı kapadı...

"Sen benim gözlerime bir baksana," dedi, "başlatma şimdi resimlerden mesimlerden..."

"E ama bunları konuştuk..."

"Koca adam oturup sana saatlerce bunları niye anlatsın, zaten ben ilk gün anlamıştım,"

"Neyi anladın canım, oturduk sohbet ettik işte ne olacak..."

"Oturduk sohbet ettik, ne olacak," diye taklidimi yaptı.

"Off çok heyecanlı... Biraz ayrıntı rica etsem..."

"Tolga" dedim, "bırak ayrıntıyı filan, beni dinle, kimseye söylemek yok, gülüp dalga geçmek de yok... Birşey oldu..."

Birden o da ciddileşti.

"Ne oldu? Çabuk söyle?" dedi.

"Galiba, ben aşık oldum.."

"Sen insanı delirtirsin sahiden, onu anladık, bilmediğimi söyle, adamdan haber ver..?"

"Ne haberi vereyim bir şey bilmiyor ki..."

"Aman ne komik! Küçük hanım giyinip süslenmiş çok lazımmış gibi koştura koştura dergiyi götürmüş, beş saat oturup sohbet etmiş adam da anlamamış... Delirdin herhalde!"

"Ya sahiden de böyle oldu, çıkarken yeniden görüşür müyüz diye bile sormadı..."

"E sormamıştır tabii, ortada Sare Hanım var, çekinmiştir..."

"Öyle midir?"

"Yok değildir, senin vazgeçilmez sohbetinle çok eğlendiği için oturmuştur o kadar saat..."

"Dalga geçmek yok dedim, ne bileyim belki de ayıp olmasın diye öyle yaptı... Zaten sonunda seni evden merak ederler deyip sepetledi..."

"Korkmuştur," dedi.

"Benden mi?"

Onun kaş kaldırma hareketi vardır... Aslında komik olur ama o ciddi konuşurken yapar. Bir kaşını kaldırdı:

"Bilmem," dedi, "belki de kendisinden..."

Neden bütün bunları hemen Tolga'ya anlatırdım da Seda'nın haberi olmazdı?

Çünkü o herşeyi yargılardı.

Küçük, düzenli bir dünyanın içinde kalmak isterdi, belki de kendisini orada güvende hissettiği için...

O kadar çok konuşurdu ki sonunda herkesi yanından kaçırmayı başarırdı.

Küçükken bile çok bilirmiş gibi ahkam keserdi. Üstelik bunları öyle keskin söylerdi ki cevap da veremezdiniz.

Herkes hakkında kesin yargıları vardı. O kız içten pazarlıklı, o oğlan sinsi, öteki kompleksli, bu ruh hastası...

İnsanların kağıttan kesilmiş formlar olmadığını, herkesin içinde, kendisi de dahil, çok farklı insanlar olduğunu, kimsenin aslında ne kötü ne de iyi olduğunu anlamak istemezdi.

Böyle davrandığı için kimse de onu sevmezdi. Neredeyse tek arkadaşı bendim. Ben onu olduğu gibi kabul etmiştim. O benim tuhaf kızkardeşimdi. Ne yapalım ki böyleydi. Dediklerini pek umursamaz ama değiştirmek için de çabalamazdım. Garip bir biçimde beni sahiplenmişti. Herkesin bana zarar vereceğinden, beni inciteceğinden korkardı.

Anne babasını bir kazada kaybetmiş, o arabadan bir tek o sağ çıkmış, sonra da bütün hayatını dul teyzesiyle geçirmişti.

Neyse ki o kazayı hatırlamayacak kadar küçüktü.

Daha ilkokulda bile tombuldu. Sonraki yıllarda iyice şişmanladı ve neredeyse bütün hayatını o kilolarla uğraşarak geçirdi.

Belki kimse bilmezdi ama hayatı çok zordu. Aksi, huysuz, otoriter bir teyzeyle, kıt imkanlarla tek başına ayakta durmaya çalıştı her zaman. Kendisini orada sığıntı gibi gördü. Belki gerçek bu değildi ama önemli olan onun öyle hissetmesiydi.

Ve üstelik ne olursa olsun güçlü görünmeye, erkek gibi davranmaya çalışırdı. Kıvırcık kısa saçları ve iri yapısıyla zaten hep erkek fatma'ydı o.

Bir keresinde ona çok kızıp, "Yeter artık, herkes kötü değil, sen de mükemmel değilsin, kimse mükemmel değil, başkalarını değil, kendini değiştir yapabiliyorsan," diye bağırmıştım.

Birkaç hafta benimle konuşmadı. Sonra bu söylediklerimin bir anlamı olmadığını düşünüp ona küçük porselen bir biblo aldım. Çünkü kendisiyle başbaşa kalıp mutlu olduğu anlar porselen koleksiyonuyla geçirdiği zamanlardı. Bir *tinker bell* biblosuydu ve kurduğunuz zaman müzikle birlikte dansediyordu.

Onu koleksiyonunda özel bir yere koydu ve çalan müziği de hiç unutmadı.

Bazen insanlara dışardan bakıp onlarla ilgili yargılara varırız. Ben Seda sayesinde kimseyi böyle yargılamamayı, o görüntünün altında hiç bilmediğimiz bir hikaye olabileceğini öğrendim.

Onun altın gibi bir kalbi vardı aslında. Yalnızca kendini korumak için onu ortaya çıkartamıyordu. İncinmekten korkuyordu. O yüzden ne lastik ya da ip oyunlarına ne yakartopa katıldı. Bence çok istese bile köşeye oturup kitabını okumayı tercih etti.

Niye ona anlatmadım yaşadıklarımı? Çünkü hemen neyin yanlış neyin doğru olduğunu söylemeye başlayacak, kaygılanacak, başımın etini yiyecekti.

Ne işim vardı koca adamla... Üstelik sanatçı... Mutlaka beni "kötü niyetlerine" alet edecekti. Başka ne olabilirdi ki? Beni kullanıp, hahaaha, buruşturulmuş mendil gibi kenara atacaktı...

Onu asla görmemeliydim, arasa bile telefonuna çıkmamalıydım.

Elbette bunları söyleyecekti. Tıpkı annem gibi. Sanki ben bilmiyorum da...

Onun için ona söylemedim.

Bu Tolga'yla aramızda sır olarak kalacaktı.

Biz onunla çocukluğumuzdan beri en gizli şeyleri bile paylaşmıştık ve kimseye söylememiştik. Ben bir erkeği o da bir kızı ilk kez çıplak görmüştük. Birbirimize dokunmuştuk. Hatta öpüşmüş ve bunun çok anlamsız olduğunu düşünüp çok gülmüştük.

Sahiden de kötüydü.

O benim doktorculuk arkadaşımdı.

Bir keresinde poposuna sahiden de iğne batırmıştım.

İlk sigarayı da ilk içkiyi de onunla içmiştik.

İlk çıplak fotoğraflara onunla bakmıştık.

Okulda otururken birden içimden birşeyler aktığını hissedince öğretmenin kulağına söyleyip tuvalete gittiğim gün de önce onun haberi olmuştu.

Artık büyümüştük ve bunları hiç konuşmasak da birbirimizi çok iyi tanıyorduk. Ve artık o da bana sempatik garsonu rahatlıkla anlatıyordu.

Evet sahiden de büyümüştük...

Şimdi mezuniyet zamanıydı, sonra...
Sonra hayat yeni başlıyordu...
Yeni bir hayat...

Şimdi dönüp bakınca diyorum ki bütün bunlar yalnızca basit rastlantılar olabilir mi?

Herhalde bir hafta sonraydı. Tünel'e çizim için kağıt, kalem almaya gitmiştim.

O eski otelin önünden geçiyordum ve birden pencereden onu gördüm.

Otelin lobisinde, pencerenin önünde bir masada oturmuş birşeyler çiziktiriyor ya da yazıyor ve kahve içiyordu.

Yok bu herhalde bir yanılsamaydı.

Geçtim biraz yürüdüm. Geri döndüm.

Gerçekten o muydu? Öyleyse o da beni görmüş müydü? Gördüyse şimdi yeniden oradan geçmem doğru olmayacaktı...

Elimde kocaman resim defterleri, boyalar, otele döndüm.

Kapıdaki adam bana gülümsedi, ben de gayet rahat içeri girdim. Sola döndüm ve onun oturduğu yere geçtim. Evet oydu.

En köşede, pencerenin önünde tek başına oturuyordu. Zaten içeride bir başka masada üç kişi oturuyordu. Başka kimse yoktu.

Sanki çok gizli birşey yapıyormuşum ve o da bunu biliyormuş gibi titriyordum ama onu görmemiş gibi başka bir masaya yöneldim, elimdekileri masaya koyup oturdum.

Dalmıştı. Her ne çiziyorsa onunla meşguldü.

Gizlice onu izliyordum. Sonra bir an önündeki kadehten bir yudum aldı ve alırken beni gördü.

Gözgöze geldik.

Ne yapmalıydım?

Evet biliyorum aşk, insanların kalbine ok atan tombul, küçük melekle tasvir edilir.

Bebek aşk tanrısının haşarı bir biçimde gülümseyerek attığı ok günün birinde kalbinize saplanır.

Ama kimse kalbine saplanmış görünmez ok yüzünden çektiği acıyı anlatmak için doktora gitmez. Sanki tıpkı o simgedeki gibi acının da mutlulukla birlikte geldiğini herkes bilir.

Ani bir kalp çarpıntısı, yürek sancısı, göğüs sıkışması... Sıradan bir günde paniğe kapılmanız gerekir değil mi? Ama şimdi hiç de öyle gelmiyordu.

Aksine ben şimdi kendimi başkalarından çok farklı, özel bir duyguyla ödüllendirilmiş gibi hissediyordum.

Yoksa kalkıp bana doğru yürüyor mu?

Başım dönüyor. Bulutların üstündeyim ama kalbim sıkışıyor, ayağa kalkıyorum ve "Hemen kendine gel Ebru," diyorum, ne güzel rastlantı, ne rastlantısı, bu saatte kimselerin gelmediği otelin lobisinde, artık işarete gerek var mı, bir kanıta? Kendimi yokuştan aşağı son hızla gider gibi hissediyorum işte. Başka kanıt gerekir mi?

Ve bunun adı yok. Korku mu? Mutluluk mu? Yalnızca heyecan mı?

Gülümseyerek karşımda duruyor. Ayağa mı kalksam, ne yapsam diye düşünüyorum ama kıpırdayamıyorum.

Önümdeki boyalara, kağıtlara baktı ve "Ne o sen de mi resim çiziyorsun yoksa?" diye sordu.

Merhaba, nasılsın, burada ne arıyorsun filan yok.

Biraz sonra kendimi orada küçük bir masada bu hiç beklenmedik anda onunla yine sanki yıllardır tanışıyormuşuz hatta sözleşip buluşmuşuz gibi konuşurken buldum.

Onu tanıyorlardı çünkü pek kimselerin olmadığı saatlerde buraya gelip oturuyor, birşeyler karalıyordu.

Birden dedi ki, "gel yukarı çıkalım, otelin terasında inanılmaz bir manzara vardır bu saatte..."

Yukarı çıktık.

Gün batıyordu.

Eski İstanbul'un üzerinde.

Karşı kıyıdaki camlara güneş vuruyordu.

Anneannemin en sevdiği şiiri hatırladım.

"Başkadır bu akşam bütün akşamlardan / güneşin vehmi saraylar yaratır camlardan".

"Bütün bunlar bir ressam için bulunmaz şeyler değil mi," dedim.

"Bilmem," dedi, "akıl hastanesinin küçük penceresinden inanılmaz bir gökyüzü çizen ressamlar da vardır. Galiba önemli olan ne gördüğün değil, ona nasıl baktığın..."

Söylediği resmi hatırladım. Ama söylemedim. Dünyanın en ünlü ressamlarından birinin benim çocukluğumda çizdiğim resimlere benzer bir resmiydi. Lacivert gökyüzü, sarı ay, hepsi yerli yerinde ama ressamın gördüğü gibi...

"Acaba bende ne görüyorsun?" diye sordum.

Kızardım.

O manzaraya baktı. Sonra bana döndü, elini uzattı, gözlüğümü çıkardı.

Şaşırdım.

Gözlerime baktı.

"Bazen birine bakarsın ve yalnızca onu görürsün, güzeldir, çirkindir, şişmandır, zayıftır... Bazen gözlerine bakarsın ve onu değil kendini görürsün... Aslında insan neye bakarsa baksın kendini görür. Onun için aynı yerle ilgili herkesin farklı izlenimi vardır."

"Ama," dedim, "soruma cevap vermedin..."

"Belki de vermesem daha iyi," dedi.

Sessizlik oldu. Garson gelip birer kahve daha getirdi.

Niye, diye sormalıydım, sormadım.

Saçlarımı yüzümden çekti, yüzümü okşadı, ben de onu öptüm.

Evet bu kez gerçekti.

İnsanın kalbine bir ok saplanması ve aynı anda acıyla mutluluğu birlikte hissetmesi...

Hayır, bu kez doktora gitmeme gerek yoktu.

Bir sabah... Bütün pencereler açık... Tüller uçuşuyor... Serin, güzel bir ilkbahar günü. Bahçede kuşların neşesi... Uzaktan bir gemi gür sesiyle selam vererek geçiyor.

Sare Hanım üstünde ipekli, çiçek desenli sabahlığıyla koltuğunda oturuyor.

Annemle mezuniyet için ne yapılacağını, bana nasıl bir elbise dikileceğini konuşuyorlar.

Galiba konuyla en az ilgilenen benim.

Zaten bana soran da yok.

"Bütün kızlar pembe giyecekmiş, çok güzel kumaşlar getirdi Perihan, muhakkak ince olmalı şöyle dökümlü yerlere kadar..." diyor anneannem.

Kahvesini içiyor annem, "Bilmem ki acaba kabarık mı olsa etekleri pek severim ben..."

"O ne öyle gelinlik gibi, evlenmiyor ya kız, mezun oluyor, kabarık etek olmaz..."

Annem susuyor.

Yıldız Teyze, "Kapatsana sen de fincanını, senin de falına bakayım..." diyor.

Kapatıyorum.

"Yarın sen ortadan fazla kaybolma," diyor anneannem, "Perihan gelecek, hem kumaşlara bakalım hem de ölçünü alsın hemen başlasın.."

"Zaten ne kaldı şunun şurasında..." diyor annem, "acaba hazır mı alsak, çok güzel elbiseler var Nişantaşı'nda... Artık kimse elbise diktirmiyor..."

"Ben diktiriyorum efendim," dedi anneannem, "herkese göre yapılmış elbiseden ne hayır gelecek, olmaz öyle, tam üstüne göre ölçülüp biçilir dikilir, modeline de insan kendi karar verir.."

Sare Hanım varken tabii annemin sözü geçmeyecek, Perihan Teyze gelecek, yine her zamanki gibi annem söylenecek ama boşuna...

O çoktan elbisenin modelini bile kafasında seçmiştir.

"Ama siz gidin bir ara da ayakkabı bakın, en mühimi o... Vakıa önce renge karar verelim..."

"Var ayakkabım anneanne," diyorum, "yeni aldık daha..."

"Kadında ayakkabı en mühim şeydir. Bir ayakkabı bir kadını alır başka bir kadına çeviriverir. O topuğun iki santimi insanı değiştirir. Ayakkabı seçemeyen kadından hayır gelmez, ben bunu bilir bunu söylerim, değil mi Yıldız?"

"Evet evet hep söylersiniz Sare Hanım," diye onayladı Yıldız Teyze.

Ben güldüm.

Annem bozuldu çünkü çoğu zaman düz ayakkabılar giyer ve anneannem ona "Sanki selvi boylusun bir de bunları giyiyorsun, cüce gibi geziyorsun ortalıkta, bilmem kime çektin..." diye söylenirdi.

Birden dedim ki, "Ben mezuniyet elbisemi kendim çizmek istiyorum..."

Sare Hanım öksürdü, suyundan bir yudum aldı, elindeki sigarayı söndürürken şöyle bir bana baktı.

"Aman kızım olur mu öyle, Perihan getirince modellerin içinden sen seçersin..." dedi annem.

"Dur dur bakayım," dedi Sare Hanım, "nasıl gelmedi bu benim aklıma, çok iyi fikir, tabii ya, kızı moda mektebine yolluyoruz, sonra burada terzilere elbise çizdiriyoruz..."

"Zaten çizdiğim bazı modeller var onların üstünde biraz daha çalışırım tabii Perihan Teyze bana yardım ederse..."

"Aman bayıldım bu fikre, hem de ilk modelini kendin giymiş olacaksın..."

Sonra bana baktı, ne düşündüyse, "Gelsene bakayım sen benim yanıma," dedi, gittim, eliyle uzandı gözlüğümü çıkarttı.

Bir an şaşaladım. Sanki daha dün yaşadığım an gibi... Sanki o anı o da görmüş gibi kızardım...

"Artık bu gözlükleri de atalım gitsin, kızın dünya güzeli gözleri görünmüyor, lens diye birşey çıktı biz hala gözlükle dolaştırıyoruz, bir ara Metin Bey'e gidin de halledin şu işi..."

"Gözlük yakışıyor ona, değil mi Ebru?" dedi annem.

"Bilmem ki..."

"Sen benim dediğimi yap canım, gözlük kimseye yakışmaz, yaşlanınca takılır o kadar, artık o genç kız oldu dörtgöz diye dalga geçilecek zamanı geçti, hatta yarından tezi yok ben de geleyim beraber gidelim benim de yakına baktırmam lazım, bahane olsun..."

Güldüm. Sahiden de ilkokulda ne çok dalga geçerlerdi benimle dörtgöz diye...

Ama asıl garip olan bir gün önce Ferhat'ın da aynı şekilde gözlüğümü çıkartıp gözlerime bakmasıydı.

"Gel bakalım falın neler söylüyor," diye fincanı eline alıp bakmaya başladı Yıldız Teyze.

"Saniye, bana biraz daha su getir kızım, ilacımı da ver," diye içeri seslendi anneannem. Kesik kesik öksürüyordu.

"Burada sanki kış geçmiş gibi bulutlar dağılmış, bak nasıl güzel bir parlaklık doğmuş... Aaa maaşallah pırıl pırıl olmuş her yer..."

"Sen manzarayı geç de başka ne var ondan haber ver," dedi anneannem bana göz kırpıp. İçimden, ne biliyor, yoksa Ferhat ona söyledi mi diye bir ürperti geçti. Ama ne zaman söyleyecekti ki? Telefon etmişse? Yok yok söylemez.

"Bak şurada, görüyor musun?"

Eğilip baktım fincana birşey göremedim, "Şurada hemen uzun boylu zayıf biri var..."

Sare Hanım'a baktım. Annem pek ilgilenmemiş, elindeki gazeteyi okuyordu, "Havalar daha da ısınacakmış, bahar günü çöl sıcakları geliyor yazmışlar..."

Anneannem ona şöyle bir baktı, "sen de gazeteye mi inanıyorsun, Noel Baba'ya inanmak gibi yahu gazeteye inanmak... Gelmez, birşey olmaz, sen devam et Yıldız..."

"Biraz uzaktan gelmiş ya da uzağa gidecekmiş gibi... Ama elini de sana uzatmış. Bak sen de buradasın işte gördün mü?"

Baktım sahiden de bu sefer gördüm. Buyurun bakalım. Her gün bakılan falla dalga geçer misin?

"Ee nasıl uzaktaymış peki anlamadım..."

"Orasını bilemem, uzakta işte, hem uzak hem yakın, geliyor mu, gidiyor mu anlayamadım..."

"Tolga'dır o canım," dedi annem lafa karışmış olmak için...

"Tolga mı? Ayol ne Tolga'sı, duymuyor musun uzun ince adam diyor..." dedi anneannem...

Saniye ilaçla suyu getirdi. O da meraklandı, "Kısmettir kısmeti çıkmış besbelli..." dedi.

"Ne kısmeti canım, nereden çıkartıyorsun," diye sinirlendi annem, zaten onun söze girmesinden hiç hoşlanmaz, anneannemin onu çok şımarttığını söyler dururdu.

"Başka ne olacak?" dedi Saniye ona hiç aldırmadan giderken, "Koca kız oldu kısmettir o kısmet..."

İşi dalgaya vurdum, "Kısmetse de var mı yok mu belli değil anlaşılan daha karar verememiş..."

Gülüştük.

Fal faslı da böylece kapanmış oldu.

Kapanmış oldu ama ben şaşırmıştım. Hala anneannemin birşeyler öğrendiğinden kuşkulanıyordum.

Önce gözlük sonra uzun, ince adam...

Tam da ona rastladığımın ertesi günü...

Belki de insanın aklı neye takılıysa birileri onu anlayabiliyordur.

Kalkarken fincanları alıp içeri götürdüm. Saniye küçük masaya oturmuş yaprak sarıyordu.

"Ooo akşama yaşadık desene," dedim, bayılırdım sarmaya...

"Güzel kızım sana yapıyorum zaten şimdi anneannene sorsam yine kızacak bu saatte bana akşamı soruyorsunuz diye, en iyisi dedim ben bildiğimi okuyayım, beğenmezse de artık köfte patates ne varsa yersiniz..."

İçerden Sare Hanım'ın sesi geldi, "Bak duyuyorum buradan seni Saniye, daha sağır olmadım şükür..."

Saniye fısıltıyla, "Maşaallah bilmez miyim ondaki kulak filde yoktur..." diye beni güldürdü.

Tam fincanları musluğun yanına koyuyordum ki yeniden bakmak geldi içimden.

Fincanı aldım baktım. Sonra bir daha baktım. Bu nasıl şey?

Ben duruyordum ama o yoktu.

Faldaki adam bir anda silinip gitmişti.

O akşam ünlü bir şairle eşi de geldi yemeğe. Fransa'da uzun yıllar yaşamış olan bu adam ilgimi çekmişti çünkü alışılmadık şeyleri son derece normalmiş gibi söyleyiveriyordu.

Konu elbette onun unutulmaz aşk şiirlerine ve aşka geldi sonunda...

Saçlarını hep kocaman topuz yapıp, kalın dudaklarını da koyu kırmızı boyayan romancı Nazlı Hanım,

"Şiirlerinizde hep aşk var ama sanki daha çok aldatma var, ikisi hep birlikte midir?" diye sordu.

"Öyle değil midir?" dedi Cemal Bey, "Daha en baştan bile birbirini aldatmaz mı aşıklar? Hatta kendilerini de... Aşk birini olmadığı gibi görmektir..."

"Ama ben daha çok ihanetten sözediyorum," dedi Nazlı Hanım.

"Kadınlarla erkeklerin aldatması farklıdır," dedi Cemal Bey, "erkekler için aldatmak yoktur aslında, onlar oyun peşindedir, öyle ki bunun sonuçlarının ne olacağını bile fazla düşünmezler..."

"Ama aldatılmak vardır değil mi?" dedi bir başkası...

"Erkekler için mi? Evet, boynuzlanmak dediğiniz şey... Orada anlarlar ne olduğunu ancak..."

"Peki, kadınlar için nedir?" dedi şairin eşi...

Sessizlik oldu, herkes cevabı bekledi. Şair sakin sakin suyunu içti, sigara yaktı...

"Kadınlar için sevgi isteğidir, kaçıştır, yeni bir başlangıçtır, aşktır... Bir kadın asla yatağa girerken kaçamak yapmak, çapkınlık yapmak için girmez...."

"Yok ben buna inanmıyorum, pek çok kadın var yalnızca seks için yatağa giren ve ertesi gün ortadan kaybolan..." dedi Nazlı Hanım.

"Çok sarhoştur hatırlamıyordur," dedi biri, gülüştüler.

"Belki başka ülkelerde örneği çoktur. Ben daha çok bizdeki durumu söylüyorum," dedi şair, "bizim kadın erkek rollerimiz farklı... Misal, ben küçükken asla bir kızla yatabileceğime inanmıyordum. Anahtar hep kadınların elinde çünkü. Onlar da biz de bunu biliyoruz. Onun için de erkek fırsatını bulduğu an, en istenen, beğenilen erkek bile olsa o geçmişteki eksiği kapatmaya çalışıyor..."

Şairin eşi biraz bozuldu galiba... "Sen de öyle mi yapıyorsun Cemal Bey," dedi.

"Fırsatını bulsam ben de yaparım emin ol," dedi adam gayet rahat.

"Hem herkes bilmez mi bunu," dedi, "ilk kez bir kadınla yattığınızda eğer herşey iyi gitmiş bile olsa, ertesi sabah erkek oradan kaçmaya çalışırken kadın şimdi ne olacak diye düşünmeye başlar..."

Bunu masadakilerin bazıları doğruladı, bazıları karşı çıktı.

Nazlı Hanım, "Peki ya aşk Cemal Bey, siz ki en güzel aşk şiirlerinin şairisiniz..."

"Evet ama aynı zamanda, çok aşık bir kadın, erkeğin felaketidir, diye yazan da benim.."

"Yani aşk kadınlara ait birşey mi?"

"Böyle de denebilir, çünkü bir içgüdüyü, yalnızca doğanın bizden beklediği bu eylemi ancak kadınsı bir incelik böylesine özel, böylesine eşsiz hale getirebilir. Ancak bir kadın yanındaki çirkin, sevimsiz, huysuz adamı böylesine yüceltebilir..."

Karısı içkisinden bir yudum aldı... Yüzü asıldı. "İşte Cemal Bey'in dahiyane fikirleri böyle..."

Bozulmuştu belli ki.

"Niye hayatım, sana iltifat ediyorum, benim gibi çirkin, sevimsiz, huysuz bir adama bile aşık olabildin diyorum..."

Siyah kalın çerçeveli gözlükleri ve hep siyah takım elbisesiyle gezen genç yönetmen,

"Aman üstad," dedi, "şaşırtıyorsunuz bizi, siz hiç aşık olmadınız mı, erkekler aşık olmaz nasıl denebilir, ya Romeo ne olacak, ya Abelard?"

Şair gülümsedi, "Aşkı için dağları delen Ferhat'ı da örnek verebilirdiniz genç dostum," dedi, "elbette ben de aşık oldum ve diyorum ki erkekler aşık olduklarında kadınsı yanları öne çıkar, onları o hale getiren içlerindeki kadındır..."

Büyük bir ilgiyle dinliyordum.

Ferhat deyince ürperdim.

Sare Hanım, "Bakın bu hoşuma gitti," dedi, "bence haklısınız, bu erkek milleti ancak aşık olduğu kısa zaman içinde adama benzer..."

Kahkahalar patladı.

Cemal Bey, "Biliyor musunuz dünyada en çok kullanılan simge nedir?"

Markalar söylendi, tarihten örnek verenler oldu...

O ana kadar hiç konuşmamıştım. Kendimi tutamadım.

"Kalp mi?" dedim...

Bana döndü, "Bravo," dedi, "genç hanım doğru söylüyor, evet tabii ki kalp... Okul sıralarının üzerinde, ağaçlarda, parklardaki banklarda, duraklarda, duvarlarda, kartlarda, aklınıza gelecek her yerde ona rastlarız. Kimi bir okla yaralıdır ve üzerinde iki ismin baş harfleri yer alır. Kimi ne yazık tam ortadan kırılmıştır. İnsanlar birbirlerine seni seviyorum yazmak yerine kalp işareti yapılmış kartlar atarlar."

Birden aklım başka yere gitti.

Küçük bir kız çocuğuyken kalbim babama aitti. Çok sürmedi. Ortaokula gittiğim ilk yıl birkaç sıra uzağımda oturup kağıtlara kalpler çizen ve üzerine ismimi yazan, şimdi yüzünü bile hatırlamadığım o çocuk sayesinde kalbimin yerini tam olarak belirleyebildim. Göğsümün solundaydı ve anlaşılmaz biçimde bu çocuğun dönüp bana baktığı her an deli gibi atmaya başlıyordu.

Bu duygu yıllar içinde gelip gidecekti. Her keresinde onun gerçek olup olmadığını, birini gerçekten sevip sevmediğimi kanıtlayan bir işaret gibi kalbim sıkışacak, nefesim hızlanacaktı.

İnsanlar bazen birbirine "Acaba ona aşık mıyım?" diye sorar. Oysa aşkın kanıta ihtiyacı yok. Birini gördüğünde yokuştan aşağı çılgınca koşar gibi bir duygu hissediyorsan, kalbin yerinden fırlıyorsa aşıksın...

Hatta kimi zaman onu görmeye bile gerek kalmaz. Yalnızca telefonun başında ondan haber beklerken de aynı duyguyu yaşayabilir insan...

Bu duygu mutluluk, heyecan, coşku gibi özlediğimiz isimlerle ifade edilebildiği gibi beklenmedik bir anda birdenbire hüzün, keder, acı gibi sözcüklere de dönüşebilir.

Hepimiz şaşmadık mı? Kısa süre önce kalbimizin çılgınca çarpmasını sağlayan şu adam, şu kadın nasıl olup da şimdi yalnızca kalp ağrısına dönüşüverdi?..

Nazlı Hanım onun sözlerine ekleme yaptı.

"Hatırlar mısınız, okul yıllarında sevgililer birbirine kalple birlikte aynı zincire takılmış küçük bir anahtar verirlerdi. Bilmem hala veriyorlar mı? Kalbimin anahtarı sende demekti bu."

"Ah," dedi şairin eşi, "ne yazık pek az erkek o anahtarı doğru kullanma yeteneğine sahip..."

"Aksine çoğu kalbinizi açacak yerde öylesine kilitler ki artık açmak için çilingir gerekir..." diye güldü Nazlı Hanım.

"Kalbimin anahtarı sende" kolyesi mi.. Ne şeker... Hiç görmemiştim...

Sare Hanım, birden uzun süredir herkesi dinleyip konuşmayan, sürekli masadaki mezelerden tırtıklayan kel, şişman adama döndü, "Ama Fazıl Bey siz hiç konuşmuyorsunuz halbuki bu sizin alanınız..."

Fazıl Bey kalp doktoruydu.

"Aman efendim," dedi, "bizim için kalp beyefendinin şiirlerindeki gibi değil, emme basma tulumba... Bizim için önemli olan çarpması, artık çarpsın da ne sebeple çarparsa çarpsın..."

Herkes güldü.

Genç yönetmen, "Aztekler kurbanların kalplerini canlı canlı söküp çıkartıyorlardı. Bugün onlara acımasız katiller gözüyle bakabiliriz ama kalbin önemini anladıklarına şüphe yok..." dedi...

"Bugün de yüz yıllar sonra kalpleri söküyoruz," dedi Fazıl Bey, "ama bir başkasına takmak ve onu yeniden hayata döndürmek için...Yine de bazı hastalar kimin kalbini taktığını merak ediyor ve onun huylarını edindiğine inanıyor..."

"O zaman söyleyin bakalım sevgili doktor, madem kalbin bu duygularla ilgisi yok, neden sevgiliyi görünce kalbimiz yerinden fırlayacak gibi çarpıyor...?" dedi anneannem.

"Kalpten değil de beyinden gelen emir nedeniyle... Heyecan, korku, öfke gibi duygularda da olduğu gibi... Gelip de sigara içmiyorum, her gün spor yaparım, sapasağlamım ama bakın kalbimde görünmez bir ok var ve canım yanıyor diyen hasta görmedim. Ama geçmiş zamanda bu yüzden doktora giden çok kadınlar varmış.?"

"Peki gelse ne ilaç verirdiniz?" diye sordu Nazlı Hanım.

"Aşkın ilacı mı? Hanımefendi siz söyleyin, böyle bir ilaç olsa da onu içmek isteyen hasta çıkar mı? Dünyada o kalp çarpıntısından daha güzel ne vardır?"

Doktorun bu sözleri beğeni topladı.

"Ancak kadınlarla erkeklerin çarpıntısı biraz değişiktir," dedi Cemal Bey, gülerek, "alın size örnek, bir kadının kalbi bir kağıda bakarken çarpar mı?"

"Kağıt mı?"

"Evet, belki bir aşk mektubuysa, ya da ayrılık..."

"Peki ya erkeklerin?" diye sordu yönetmen...

"Erkeklerin kalbi kağıda basılmış çıplak kadın resmine bile deli gibi çarpmaya başlar, işte aradaki fark bu kadar açık..."

Herkes gülüşmeye başladı, konu dağıldı...

Ben dalmıştım. Hepimize okullarda gösterdikleri gibi, damarların içine girip çıktığı, kanla beslediği, kanı pompalayarak hayatı devam ettiren bir kas yumağı..

Hepsi bu mu gerçekten?

Peki bunca makina, içimizi gösteren filmler, herşeyi ölçen aletler bizim için özel olan birini gördüğümüzde saatlerce koşmuş gibi atmasının nedenini söyleyemiyor mu?

Ya da beklenen telefon gelmediğinde duyduğumuz o tanımsız yürek sıkışmasının nedenini?

Evet burada her akşamki gibi konuşmaları dinliyordum ama şimdi tıpkı benim gibi Ferhat'ın da içinde kendiliğinden bir çarpıntı duyduğunu ve hem huzursuz olup hem de gülümsediğini düşünüyordum.

Sonra anneannem kendisine imzalı gelen şiir kitabını açtı ve okudu: "Bakın ne güzel yazmış şair, bence aşk mevzuunu bununla kapatalım: *"Ah aşkların çocuk bahçesi neden ömrün çok kısa?"*

Gerçekten öyle mi?

Çok mu kısa?

O gece sabaha kadar oturup birşeyler çizdim. Az çok herkesin ne giyeceğini biliyordum. Birbirine benzer uzun elbiseler... Etekleri yerlerde sürünecek.

Bütün kızlar kalın tafta etekleri elleriyle tutarak masal prensesi havalarında gezinecek...

Birkaç oğlan baloya benimle gitmek istemişti ama ben Tolga'yla gidecektim. Tolga kendisine Londra'dan yakaları kırmızı, siyah bir smokin almıştı. Üstünde aynı o renklerde kelebekler olan papyon. Çok şekerdi. Tam ona göre.

"Emin ol hepimizden çok sen ilgi çekeceksin," dedim.

"Babam ceketin yakasına ne der bilmiyorum ama papyonu görünce kesin delirecek... Artık bu yılın modası buymuş filan diyeceğim. Neyse ki annem bayıldı..."

Bir sürü şey çizdim, bir sürü modele baktım ama yine de asıl istediğimi bulamadım.

Sonunda tül etekleri yerlere kadar inen, üstü omuzları ve göğüsleri kapatan bir elbise çizdim.

Mezuniyetten çok sanki kendi çizdiğim elbiseyi giyecek olmak beni heyecanlandırmıştı.

Aslında bir dönem bitiyordu hayatımda.

Buna bu kadar sevinmeli miydim, bilmiyordum.

Her gün okula git, öğretmenlerle iyi geçin, derslerine çalış, böylece günler geçip gidiyordu.

Annem hele ki anneannem varken benden rahatı yoktu.

Artık büyümüş, akşam sofralarında ünlü yazarlarla, sanatçılarla birlikte oturuyor hatta söze bile karışıyordum.

Ben konuşmasam bile çoğu zaman onlar bana sorular soruyordu zaten.

Şimdi bir anda kendimi yalnız, güvensiz, boşlukta hissediyordum.

Hiç bilmediğim bir kentte, yabancıların içinde yeniden başlayacak olmak bir yandan heyecanlandırsa da aslında korkutuyordu beni. Neyse ki Tolga vardı.

Sanki son hazırlıklarını yapıp bilinmeyen yerleri keşfe çıkan kaşifler gibi hissediyordum kendimi.

Farkettim ki ben öyle maceraların, keşiflerin insanı değilim. Ben herşeyin istediğim gibi, alıştığım gibi olmasını seviyorum.

Dünyayı gezip her yeri görmek isteyen değil, olduğu yerde kendisine yeni dünyalar kuran biriyim ben.

Böyle masanın başında uyuyakalmışım, sabah bir ara gözümü açıp kendimi elbiselerle yatağa attım.

Ertesi gün Perihan Teyze geldi. Ona birkaç model gösterdim ama kendi istediğimi söyledim.

"Çok güzel olmuş, bayıldım ama bilmem annenler ne der, bunun göbeği açık," dedi.

"Aman sen annemi karıştırma Perihan Teyze," dedim, "anneanneme sorarız..."

"Çok müşterim oldu ama Sare Hanım gibisini hiç görmedim," dedi, "o kumaşı bilir, neyin neyle giyileceğini, hangi rengin neyle gideceğini, nereye ne seçileceğini hepsini bilir, sen de ona çekmişsin..."

"Kimmiş o çok bilmiş bakayım," diye Sare Hanım salona girdi.

Çizimler yerlere saçılmış, kumaş örnekleri...

Gözlüğünü taktı, önce çizimlere baktı. İki tanesini eline aldı, oturdu.

"Ne diyorsun Perihan," dedi, " bu daha okula gitmeden olmuş, bunların ikisi de birbirinden güzel..."

"Ben birini seçtim aslında ama.."

"Seçtiysen ne soruyorsun?"

Böyleydi işte o.

"Dur bakayım ben bileyim hangisini seçtiğini..."

Biraz daha baktı ve benim seçtiğimi ayırdı.

"Bunu mu?"

"Yaaaa," dedim, "evet, beğendin mi?"

"Bu omuzlardan arkaya dönerse böyle durur mu, hareket edince bozulur mu Perihan?" dedi.

"Yok bozulmaz da..."

"Eee..?"

"Bilmem ki mezuniyet gecesi ya, bunun göbeği açık..."

"Ne olmuş göbeği açıksa?"

"Yani bilmem ki pek böyle elbise dikmiyoruz mezuniyetlere..."

"İyi ya şimdi dikersin işte... Bayıldım ben buna... Benim göbeğim güzel olsa ben bile giyerim..."

Sonra çizimi ona uzatıp içeri seslendi, "Saniye Saniye kızım, her sabah kahveyi yeniden mi söyleyelim, bugün de kahve içiyorum, birdenbire bu sabah çay içmeye karar verecek değilim..."

Sonra gözlüklerini çıkartıp arkasına yaslandı, "Belki," dedi, biraz daha o bandı genişletirsin göbek kısmı daralır anladın mı?"

"Anladım," dedi Perihan Teyze...

"Bu omuzlardan gelişini ne güzel çizmişsin, Sophia Loren'in buna benzer elbisesi vardı bir filmde, sen ver bakalım şu kumaşları şimdi onu seçelim..."

Perihan Teyze pembenin neredeyse her tonundan kumaş parçalarını ona uzattı.

"Böyle uçuşan bahar gibi olmalı, giydirirler kızları şimdi ağır ağır kumaşlarla yürüyemezler, hışır hışır taftalarla, yok yok uçuşsun şöyle gençliği, ilkbaharı anlatsın, yürüdükçe uçar gibi görünsün... Meleklere benzesin benim kızım..."

Saniye kahveyi getirdi.

"Durun şunu içeyim de kendime geleyim, daha afyonum patlamadı, annen şimdi göbek diye konuşur durur, bana bak sakın gevşeme, bu elbise olacak o kadar... Bir de bunun altına ayakkabı seçelim gidip offf çok işimiz var daha göz doktoruna da gideceğiz, neyse aynı yerde ikisi de birarada çıkar, hemen sen ölçü al Perihan, başla... Saniye Saniye ilacım evladım, ilacımı da ver.."

"Getiriyorum büyük hanım.."

Saniye'nin böyle huyları vardı, anneannemi delirtmek için özellikle yapıyormuş gibi...

"Büyük hanım mı? O ne yahu, o nereden çıktı? Ne büyük hanımı... Nereden öğreniyorsun böyle acayip lafları, hanımın büyüğü küçüğü ne, saray mı burası? Haşmetmeap de bari... Hey Allahım sen bana sabır ver..."

Onların ikisinin bu hali beni öyle güldürürdü ki, yalnızca her sabah konuşmalarını dinlesem keyfim yerine gelirdi.

Ama yakında gidecektim ve artık bu sabah keyfi olmayacaktı. Bir an içim burkuldu. Ya gidersem ve anneannemi bir daha göremezsem...

Zaten aklıma iyi birşey gelmez ki...

Ne çok zaman geçti. Ne çok şey unuttum. Ne çok şeyi artık hatırlamadığım için üzüldüm.

Ama elbette o günü, o sabahı, o akşamı, o geceyi en küçük ayrıntılarına kadar hatırlıyorum.

Elbisem bir akşam önce geldiğinde Perihan Teyze hala üzerinde düzeltmeler yapıyor, anneannem fenalık geçiriyor, annem yine "hazır alsaydık keşke"lerine devam ediyordu.

O akşam evin içinde Yıldız Teyze ve Saniye'nin de katılmasıyla tam bir kadınlar partisi vardı. Sonra Tolga'yla Seda uğradılar. Seda'nın elbisesi daha düz, kapalı bir elbiseydi. Benimkine biraz şaşırdı. Tolga'nın övgüleri karşısında biraz da bozuldu gibime geldi. Ama o sırada bunun üzerinde pek fazla durmadım.

Neyse ki geceyarısını geçerken elbise hazırdı.

Annem bana çok güzel, üzeri minik taşlarla süslenmiş küçük bir saat hediye etti.

Sare Hanım da eski, küçük incilerden kolye ve küpelerini...

Sonra içeri gitti, o çok sevdiğim yakut yüzüğü alıp geldi. Parmağıma taktı.

Evet birşey eksikti.

Hiç düşünmediğimi sandığım halde aslında sürekli bir burukluk gibi içimde birşey eksik...

Ne olduğunu hepimiz biliyoruz ama söylemiyoruz.

Yarın herkesin babası orada olacak.

Benim babam tabii ki gelmeyecek.

Yoksa gelir mi?

O sıralar belki de gelir diye düşünmüş müydüm? Evet itiraf etmeliyim ki düşünmüştüm.

En azından kızının mezuniyetine gelir belki diye...

Bunca doğumgünümde, yılbaşında aramış mıydı ki?

Ama kimbilir belki haberi bile yoktu. Belki zamanlamayı bile hatırlamıyordu.

Yine de o gece orada hem söylenip duran, hem gülüp eğlenen, başta annem, o elbisenin içinde beni gördükçe ağlayan kadınların arasında kendimi mutlu hissettim.

Ertesi gün saçlarımın toplanması, o gergin topuzun yapılması ne kadar sürdü bilmiyorum ama bir ara neredeyse imdat diye bağıracaktım.

Sonunda hafif bir makyajla herşey tamamlandı ve hep birlikte deniz kenarındaki otele doğru yola çıktık.

Hem kendimi çok güzel hissediyordum hem de niye bu kadar heyecanlı olduğumu anlamayıp kendi kendime gülüyordum.

Sanki bir mucize olacakmış gibi...

Oldu da...

Denizden ılık rüzgar esiyor, gün henüz batmamış, güneş ilerde kızıla dönmüş bir top gibi boyuyor gökyüzünü... Otelin bahçesinde pembeler içinde genç kızlar, siyahlar içinde genç erkekler...

Daha bahçeye girer girmez, heyecan hissediliyor. Anne babalar, öğretmenler kendilerine ayrılan masalarda oturuyor, birtakım duygulandırıcı konuşmalar yapılıp derece alanlar açıklandıktan ve tabii bitmek bilmez fotoğraf çekimlerinden sonra onlar gidecek ve burası bize kalacak.

Tolga heyecandan yerinde duramıyor, oradan oraya koşturuyor, kim kiminle gelmiş, kim ne giymiş, kimin saçları çok komikmiş anlatıyor, "Bu gece sarhoş olacağız ona göre, tam dağıtmak niyetindeyim," diyordu.

Üstüne biraz dar gelen pırıltılı kırmızı yakalı smokini ve rugan ayakkabılarıyla hemen ilgi odağı olmuştu.

Yıllardır okuldaki tüm kızların korkulu rüyası Nedret Hanım bir ara yanıma gelip beni şöyle bir süzdü, "Son moda mı bu elbise?" diye sordu.

Ama artık tırnaklarıma bakacak, küpelerimi çıkartacak, saçlarıma karışacak zaman geçti Nedret Hanım...

"Hayır," dedim, "ben çizdim, yakında moda olacak daha olmadı..."

Suratını asıp gitti. Seda'yla Gülgün daha gitmesini beklemeden kahkahayı patlattı.

"Aman bundan kurtulduk, bak ben bunu unutmuştum," dedi Seda...

"Tabii unutursun," dedi Gülgün, "sana hiç karışmazdı da ondan, tam istediği öğrenciydin..."

Seda bozuldu. Şu anda da herhalde Nedret Hanımın en beğeneceği kılıkta gelmişti. Boğazına kadar kapalı uzun bir elbise, kısacık topuklar, kısa saçlar... Makyaj yok.

Gülgün durumu toparlamak için, "Aman hadi gel biraz dolaşalım, bizim gibi yalnız gezen yıldızlar var, herkes çift gelmedi..." diye elinden tutup onu sürükledi.

Sare Hanım ön masaların birinde kraliçe gibi oturmuş, etrafı inceliyordu. Annem elinde mendil sürekli ağlıyor, onu sinir ediyordu.

İşin kötüsü Saniye de anneme uymuş, beni gördükçe "Ah benim güzel kızım bugünleri de mi görecektik, daha dün erik isterim diye okuldan gelen bücürün haline bakın," diye o da ağlıyordu.

Söylemem gerekir ki evden çıkmadan aynada kendime bakmak hoşuma gitmişti. Artık gözlüklerim de yoktu. Tolga'nın demesine bakılırsa bütün oğlanlar benden sözediyordu.

"Ohooo, farkında değil misin kızım, herkesin radarındasın, yanına gelmeye çekiniyorlar ama merak etme şu tören bitsin burada kuyruk olacak bak iddiaya giriyorum... İstersen eski zamanlardaki gibi kendine dans defteri yap..."

"Aman eğlence çıktı sana, sen kendine bak, şu kılıkla bizi gölgede bıraktın, asıl herkes sana bakıyor..."

"Herkesi bilmem de sen babamın suratına bak, birşey de söyleyemedi, ala ala bunu mu aldınız Londra'dan demekle kaldı ama neyse ki notlarım iyi..."

"Bana bak sen keşfetmişsindir her yeri, gizlice birer sigara içelim mi, var mı öyle bir yer?"

"Olmaz olur mu, gel benimle, garsonların çaktırmadan sigara içtiği bir balkon buldum bile çoktan..."

Annemlere, ellerimi yıkamaya gidiyorum dedim, kalabalığın arasından kimileriyle selamlaşarak, kimileriyle biraz konuşarak, kimileriyle sadece gözgöze gelerek geçip arkadaki balkona gittik. Tam oraya giderken elinde tepsi dolusu şampanyayı taşıyan garsonla karşılaştık, "Hah işte biz de seni arıyorduk," dedi Tolga, hemen iki bardağı kapıverdi.

"Delisin sen," dedim.

"Biz kendi kutlamamızı yapalım da önden, gerisine bakarız," dedi.

Denizin kenarında, gün batarken, kırmızı renkler yavaş yavaş laciverde, mora dönüşürken, hafif bir esintiyle boğazdan geçen gemilere, teknelere bakarken, elimizde geniş şampanya kadehleri...

"İşte sonunda büyüdük..." dedim.

"Evet, sonunda..." dedi Tolga ve kadeh kaldırdık...

Konuşmalar yapılırken, müdür, okul aile birliği başkanı, vakıf başkanı, birincilikle mezun olan oğlan, ağlayanlar oldu. Doğrusu ben pek duygulanmadım bu konuşmalardan. Bir dönem kapanmıştı hayatımızda ama çok da umurumda değildi. Bir keresinde gelecekte okulun ortadan kalkacağını, insanların evlerinde istediklerini öğreneceğini anlatan bir ödev yazmıştım.

Her ne kadar babamın gitmesinden sonra kendimi derslere verdiysem de okulu hiçbir zaman sevmedim.

Uyulması gereken kurallar, hiç sevmesem de ezberlenmesi gereken şiirler, hiç anlamasam da öğrenmem gereken formüller, sabahın körü kalkıp yola düşmek, seni inciten, aslında hiç biraraya gelmek istemeyeceğin öğrencilerle birlikte yıllar geçirmek zorunda kalmak, bazı öğretmenlerin senin üzerinde otorite kurmaktan duyduğu zevki görmek ve ses çıkartamamak, sürekli sınava çekilmek, sürekli kendini kanıtlamak zorunda olmak, aklına gelen ama söylememen gereken sözleri yutmak, birilerinin senden şanslı olduğunu, birilerinin senden zengin olduğunu, birilerinin senden güzel ya da başarılı olduğunu öğrenmek...

Hayatın küçük modeli miydi bu?

Öyleydi.

Ama ben zaten hayatın bu halini de sevmiyordum ki...

"Buraya, bütün bu formülleri öğrenmeye gelmiyoruz aslında," demişti Tolga bir keresinde, "buraya gelecekte kimseyi rahatsız etmememiz için istenen kalıba girmeye geliyoruz..." Haklıydı belki de...

"Mezuniyet ödevinde, okulun artık anlamını yitirmiş bir yer olduğunu uzun uzun anlatmasaydın belki birincilik konuşmasını sen yapıyor olurdun," diye burnumu sıktı Tolga...

Güldüm.

"İyi ki olmamışım çünkü herkese teşekkürle dolu bu sıkıcı konuşmayı yapamayacaktım..."

"Aman iyi oldu, yoksa rezalet çıkabilirdi..."

Sonunda tören bitti, annem yine ağlayarak beni öptü, onları uğurladık. Tolga, Seda'yla ikimizi eve bırakacağını söyledi.

"Ama bu bizim gecemiz, biraz eğleneceğiz, geç kalırsak merak etmeyin," dedi..

Ama annem tabii ki uyumayacaktı. "Çok geç kalmayın," diye tembihlemeyi unutmadı.

Ara sıra başkalarıyla biraraya gelip sohbetler ettik, belki biraz geçmişten ama daha çok gelecekten...

Bazıları bizim gibi yurtdışına gidecek, bazıları üniversite sınavının sonuçlarını bekleyecekti.

Önce epeyce tepindik. Geç saatlerde orkestra biraz daha yumuşak, eski şarkılar çalmaya başladı.

Biraz sarhoş olmuştum galiba. Ama başım dönmüyordu. Bir iki çocukla dans etmiş, iltifatlar hatta buluşma teklifleri almıştım. Galiba herkese mavi boncuk dağıtıyordum. Seda arada yanıma gelip yine polislik yapıyor, fazla içme, bu çocuk sana fazla sarıldı, herkes sana bakıyor gibi klasik cümlelerini kuruyordu.

Tolga nasıl becerdiyse okulun en komik çocuklarından Fıy fıy Uğur'u alıp yanımıza getirdi ve Seda'yla dans etmesini sağladı.

"Başka türlü seni kurtaramayacaktım," dedi ve biz de dansa başladık.

Keyfim o kadar yerindeydi ki o an beni ancak gecenin bitmesi üzebilirdi. Hani çocukken arkadaşınız gelir, önce ne oynayacağınızı bilemezsiniz, o bir oyun ister, siz bir başkasını, sıkılırsınız, sonra gün biterken tam ne yapacağınızı bulmuşken ve mutluyken anneniz gelip onun gitmesi gerektiğini söyler, işte böyle bir ruh halindeydim.

Gerçi dans ettiğim Tolga'ydı ama bu gece hiç bitmesin istiyordum.

Evet babam tabii ki gelmemişti. Sırf bir kadehi bu yüzden kafaya dikmiştim. Bunu unutmak istiyordum artık.

Başımı Tolga'nın omuzuna koymuş onun ritmine uyuyordum. Yavaş yavaş dönüyorduk. Herkes etrafımızda dönüyordu. Işıklar dönüyordu.

Yine dalmış gitmiştim.

"Bir tek dönmeyen bana sensin..."

Şarkıyı dinliyordum, "Yok artık," dedi Tolga birdenbire...

Başımı kaldırdım. "Ne oldu?" diye sordum.

"Şuraya bakar mısın sen biraz," dedi ve beni çevirdi.

Dans ettiğimiz terasın arkasında düzenli kesilmiş çalılar ve sonra da çim bir alan vardı.

Çalıların arkasında öylece durmuş elleri ceplerinde bize bakıyordu.

Önce hayal görüyorum sandım.

Onu çevirdim.

"Gerçekten o mu?" dedim.

"Asıl ben sana sorayım, gerçekten o mu?"

"Yok olamaz," dedim.

"Sakın bana haberin olmadığını söyleme…"

"Yemin ederim yok."

Nasıl olabilirdi ki? Herhalde içimden geçen ama aklıma gelecek en son şeydi bu.

Yok canım benim için gelmiş olamazdı. Herhalde yine oteldeki başka bir davete gelmişti. Belki de benim burada olduğumu da bilmiyor, öylesine bu eğlenceyi izliyordu.

"Neler saçmalıyorsun," dedi Tolga, "gelmiş adam bildiğin, seni arıyor…"

"Beni oraya doğru götür ama belli etme," dedim.

"Aman yarabbim," dedi, "tarihe tanıklık ediyorum şu an…"

Sonra beni yavaş yavaş kenara doğru götürdü.

"Sakın beni çevirme," dedim, "sakın…"

"Gördü galiba," dedi, "bu kadar aynı renkte giyinmiş kızın içinde seni görmesi de ayrı mucize ya…"

"Sakın sakın, çevirme beni," dedim.

Birden beni bıraktı. Birkaç adım attı. Öylece kaldım, ne yapmam gerektiğini bilemedim, mecburen ona doğru döndüm.

Doğruca onun yanına gitti ve elini sıktı.

Ben de şaşırmış gibi arkasından yürüdüm.

"Ne güzel rastlantı," dedi Tolga, "siz misiniz, değil misiniz diye bakıyorum ben de…"

"Evet ne güzel rastlantı, otelde bir sergi vardı ona gelmiştim, biraz hava alıp sigara içmeye çıkınca bu eğlenceli topluluğu gördüm, hangi okul diye sordum, söylediler, o yüzden bakıyordum belki sizi de görürüm diye.."

Yanına gittim, elimi sıktı.

"Ne güzel elbise, çok hoş görünüyorsun…" dedi.

"Kendisi çizdi," dedi hemen Tolga…

"Gerçekten mi? Tebrikler... Bir periye benzemişsin.."

O an gerçekten peri gibi kanatlanmış mıydım, utancımdan kızarmış mıydım, evet tabii ki, ne yapacağımı şaşırmış halde elim ayağıma mı karışmıştı bilmiyorum. Hem onunla konuşmayı sürdürmek istiyordum hem de sanki herkes bizi görüyormuş gibi bir an önce geri dönmem gerektiğini düşünüyordum.

Ama zaten karanlıktı, kiminle konuştuğum şu an kimsenin umurunda bile değildi.

Bir an sessizlik oldu. O yalnızca bana bakıyordu.

"Ben Seda'ya bakıp geliyorum," dedi Tolga ve birden ortadan kayboldu.

Biz karşılıklı kalakaldık. Aramızda bodur bir çalılık vardı.

Neydi bu? Gerçekten bir sergiye mi gelmişti? Herhalde benim mezuniyetime gelmiş olamazdı. Bundan haberi bile olamazdı.

Belki de biraz sarhoş olmasam soramazdım ama sordum.

"Burada ne arıyorsun?" dedim.

Hiç duraklamadı.

"Seni arıyorum," dedi.

"Beni mi?"

Çalılıklar aramızda yasak gibi duruyordu. Ayışığında orkestra yavaş, eski aşk şarkıları çalıyordu, artık kimse hoplayıp zıplamak istemiyordu, yalnızca sarılmak istiyorlardı çünkü dans ederken...

"Bu bizim güzel sırrımız, hiçbir zaman unutulmayacak..."

Güzel sırrımız...

"Seni buradan kaçırmaya geldim," dedi sonra. Şarkı devam ediyordu yüksek sesle...

"Kimse bilemez kalbin içindekileri çünkü..."

"Kaçırmaya mı, nereye?"

"Bilmem, ister misin? Sen onu söyle..."

İstemek mi? O an aklımda ne varsa uçup gitti. İstemez miyim? Bu, herhalde bu gece isteyip de gerçekleşeceğini düşüneceğim son şeydi. Ama nasıl yapacaktım ki...

Tolga geldi. Birden kafamı topladım.

"Ben dedim, Ferhat'la sergiye bakmaya gideceğim, birazdan gelirim..."

Kulağıma eğildi, "İki saat sonra burada ol, seni bekleyeceğim, Seda'yı ben idare ederim," dedi.

"A tamam," dedi sonra yüksek sesle, "biz daha buradayız, görüşürüz..."

Çalıların bittiği yere kadar eteklerimi tutarak yürüdüm, dönüp onun yanına gittim, birlikte yürümeye devam ettik konuşmadan. Nereye gidiyorduk? Ne yapmak istiyordu? Bunları soracak halde değildim.

Rıhtıma doğru yürüdük. İskelenin yanında küçük, külüstür bir balıkçı motoru çalışır halde bekliyordu. Şaşkın şaşkın bakıyordum. Kaptan bizi görünce halatı çekti, tekne iskeleye yanaştı, elini uzattı, Ferhat öteki elimi tuttu, kendimi teknede buldum.

Kimse bilemez kalbin içindekileri...

Ay, kenarından ısırılmış parlak bir elmaya benziyordu. Denizin üzerinde kıpırdayan ışıklar.

O şarkı hala çalıyordu biz uzaklaşırken...

Sonra yalnızca motorun gürültüsü kaldı.

Sallana sallana gidiyorduk.

Yine beyaz gömleği, üstünde eskimiş keten haki ceket. Rüzgarda saçları yüzüne düşüyor. Eliyle geriye atıyor sürekli.

"Nedenini bilmiyorum ama bu gece seni görmek istedim," dedi.

"Sen her istediğini istediğin zaman yapan biri misin?" dedim.

"Eğer elimden geliyorsa evet..."

Ben de bu gece seni görmek isterdim. Ama bunun olacağını hiç düşünmemiştim. İçimde bilmediğim bir duygu vardı. Birşey olacağını biliyordum sanki ama ne olacağını değil.

Beklediğim biri vardı ama o gelmedi.

Sen geldin.

Aklıma en son gelen şey geldi. Yoksa başıma mı demeliyim? Çünkü bu gece ayışığında, bu şarkı çalarken, ben artık dedikleri gibi "kocaman bir kız olmuşken" sanki masaldan çıkıp gelen prens elimden tutmuş gibi, beni bilmediğim yerlere götürecekmiş gibi...

Aslında bilmiyorsun ama çoktan beni bilmediğim yere götürdün bile diyorum içimden.

Ben şimdi oradaydım, bilmediğim o ülkede, belki de varolmayan, kimsenin bilmediği, gizlenmiş, dokunulmamış bir yerde...

Elimi tuttu. "Üşüyor musun?" dedi.

"Hayır," dedim, aslında üşüyordum hatta titriyordum ama aynı anda o kadar yanıyordum ki neden titrediğimi anlayamıyordum.

Ceketini çıkartıp omuzuma koydu.

Aslında söylemek istediğim ne çok şey vardı, bu gece ne çok konuşmuştum ama şimdi konuşamıyordum. Ne diyeceğimi, ne demem gerektiğini bilemiyordum.

Daha biraz önce dedikodu yapan, Tolga'yla dansederken yakışıklı oğlanları, havalı kızları çekiştirirken kahkahalar atan kıza ne olmuştu birdenbire?

"Demek nedenini bilmiyorsun?" dedim sonra.

Duymamış gibi, "Gözlüklerini çıkartmışsın," dedi.

Evet bu daha iyiydi. Başka şeylerden sözetmek.

"Evet anneannemin ısrarıyla..."

Aklıma onun da Sare Hanım'ın da gözlüklerimi çıkartması geldi. Bilemezdi tabii...

Işıklar içindeki yalıları, karanlıkta dev gölgeler gibi geçip giden gemileri, yaz gecesi eğlencelerinden gelen şarkıları arkamızda bırakıp sakin, sessiz bir koya geldik.

Kaptan motoru susturdu.

Sanki birden başka bir ülkeye gelmiş gibi olduk.

Arkaya gelip bize birer kadeh doldurdu. Benimle tanıştı. Sonra yerine geçerken radyoyu açtı.

Yalnızca ayışığının aydınlattığı sessiz koyda yalnız biz vardık şimdi.

Artık titremiyordum. Buradaydım. Onun yanında. Neresi olduğu umurumda bile değildi. Hatta şu an buradan daha uzaklara, bizi kimsenin bulamayacağı bir yere gidiyoruz dese gider miydim? Evet, bence giderdim.

Tekne durgun suda sallanıyordu. Yanımda oturmuş birlikte radyodan gelen müziği dinliyorduk.

Dün gece son anda elbisenin son düzeltmeleri yapılırken, bugün kuaförde, sonra Tolga'yla dans ederken aslında herşey olması gerektiği gibiydi. İşte biraz sonra Tolga, Seda ben eve dönecektik, belki Tolga biraz bizimle oturup gecenin dedikodularını anlatacaktı ve sabah hepsi bitmiş olacaktı.

Ama öyle olmadı.

Sonra birden o çıkıp geldi.

Demek sabahtan beri içimde hissettiğim adeta bana gizlice haber verilmiş olan buydu…

Artık ben o pembeli kızlardan biri değildim.

Yanımda öylece oturuyordu. Elimi tutuyordu hala. Elim ısındı elinde. Kulağına uzandım, "Beni yine öpsen ne olur?" diye sordum.

Bir rüya görmüştüm.

Dalgaların kıyıya çarptığı kıyıda hemen kumların üzerinde bir evde oturuyorum, Ferhat var yanımda, kalabalık, annem sürekli emirler yağdırıyor, yemekler geliyor, insanlar eğleniyor, sonra kıyıya eski büyük bir vapur geliyor ama iskele yok, yolcular doğruca suya iniyor, yürüyerek aramızdan geçip gidiyorlar, annem sinirleniyor, nasıl olur da tanımadığımız bunca insan evimizin içinden geçer diye, anneannem onu susturuyor, bak diyor ne güzel vapur, benim çocukluğumdaki vapurlardan, meraklanma kimse bize birşey yapmaz, bırak geçsinler, hatta isteyenler gelip bizimle otursun, birden deli gibi yağmur bastırıyor, herkes içeri kaçışıyor, ben diyorum ki, denize girelim, bizi yağmurdan da, fırtınadan da deniz korur, ikimiz suya giriyoruz ve suyun ne kadar sıcak olduğuna şaşırıyoruz, suyun altında çıplak olduğumu hissediyorum ve çok utanıyorum, neyse ki anlamadı diyorum, ama bir dalga geliyor, o beni tutuyor, çok su yutuyorum hep başıma gelir bu diyorum, gel diyor, şurası daha karanlık bizi kimse görmez, niye gizleniyoruz, gizlenmemiz gerekir evet hatırlıyorum, kucağındayım, çıplağım, beni bir mağaraya götürüyor, denizin içindeki mağarada, korkuyorum biraz, artık sesler yok, kimseyi duymuyoruz, karanlıkta, mağaranın içinde, dev bitkiler var, suyun içinde büyümüş, çizgi romanlardaki garip canavarlara benzetiyorum onları, suyun gelgitiyle canlı gibi hareket ediyorlar yavaşça, kaygan kayaya yaslanıyor, ben ona sarılıyorum, dudaklarından öpüyorum, büyük bir dalga geliyor ve birden kendimi başka kayalara çarparken buluyorum, suyun içine batıyorum ve korkuyla uyanıyorum.

Onun cevap vermesini beklemedim. Gözlerimi kapadım ve onu öptüm.

Bildiğim tek şey, hiç kimse için böyle hissetmediğimdi.

Herhalde dans devam ediyordu, önce Seda sonra Tolga paniklemiş olmalıydı, saatler geçmişti, artık saati bilmiyordum, sonra annem kaygılanmaya başlayacaktı, başım dönüyordu ve bütün bunları aynı anda düşünmek istemiyordum, bu o garip rüyalarımdan biriydi belki ama uyanmak istemiyordum.

Yüzümü tuttu iki eliyle, beni öptü. Saçlarımı okşadı.

Ne garip, benim gibi onun da tedirgin olduğunu anlıyordum artık.

Hatta benden daha çok.

En kötü ne olabilir ki diyordum. Kısa hayatım boyunca yaptığım en acayip şey bu muydu? Öyle olsun. Bir kez de ben böyle birşey yapsam ne olur?

Kötü kız mı olurum?

Birine aşık olmanın nesi kötü?

Hem üstelik kim beni suçlayabilirdi ki?

Aşk öyle sizin karar verdiğiniz birşey değildi.

İnsanın başına gelen birşeydi.

Kaza gibi birşey...

Belki şimdi birdenbire fırtına kopar ve bizi açık denize atabilir, geri dönemeyeceğimiz bir yerde denizle gökyüzünün birleştiği karanlık bir anda yokolup gidebilirdik.

Bunu belki kimseye anlatamazdım ama aslında anlatsam anlamazlar mıydı? Herkes bilmez miydi bunu?

Tam da buydu işte... Öpmek istemek ve öpünce neden istediğini anlamak. Çünkü onu öpseydim ve bu beni mutlu etmeseydi aşık olmadığımı anlayacaktım. Gerçek böyle birşeydi.

Ona sormak istediklerim var mıydı? Vardı. Ama şu an hepsi anlamsız geliyordu bana. Hem sözler neye yarar ki? Yanımdaydı işte. Üstelik de beklemediğim bir anda. Onunla konuşmak, merak ettiklerimi sormak, aklımdan geçenleri anlatmak... Hayır, ilgilendirmiyordu beni bunlar.

Onu gördüğüm ilk günden beri öpmek istiyordum ama bunu kendime bile itiraf edememiştim.

Sözler, gülüşler, anlatılanlar, anılar, yüz ifadeleri... Hayır, benim için gerçek olan yalnızca kokular ve dokunuşlardı.

Boynunu kokladım ve dudaklarını öptüm.

Başka hiç birşey...

Koku ve dokunuş... Beni hiç yanıltmadı...

İnsanı düşünceler yanıltır, duygular değil.

Karanlık denizde, sallanan küçük teknede, yalnızca ayışığının pırıltıları, eski şarkılar, yapılması gerekenler, uzak durulması gerekenler, bize öğretilmiş olanlar, üstümde pembe tüllerden bir elbise, bana şimdi buradan gidiyoruz ve geri gelmeyeceğiz dese hayır demeyeceğim bir adam, büyük bir hata mı, korkulması gereken birşey mi, bilmiyorum, bildiğim yalnızca kalbimin nasıl çarptığı, ona kimse kural koyabilir mi, kimse kalbimin yalan söylediğine beni ikna edebilir mi, ama asıl önemlisi onun beni öperken yalan söylemediğini anlamam...

Nasıl mı? Bunu o an benim yerimde olmayan kimse bilemez. Ben biliyorum artık.

Geri dönmeliyim. Niye? Dönmek istemiyorum. Ama dönmelisin. İçimdeki polis mi bu? Akıllı yanım mı? Yarın böyle düşünmeyecek miyim? Kendimi yarın kötü mü hissedeceğim? Ama o bana ne yapıyor ki... Yalnızca sarılmış öpüyor. Bunu ondan ben istedim.

Kendi kendime diyorum ki, bu nasıl bir öğreti? Gerçekte ilk günden beri istediğin adamla öpüşüyorsun ama kafanda hala bunlar var. Bunları silebilir miyim? Hepsinden kurtulabilir miyim?

Bir dalga geliyor ve tekne sallanıyor. Ayrılıyoruz. Ellerim hala ellerinde.

"Gemi geçti, aldırmayın," diyor kaptan.

Beni omuzlarımdan tutuyor. Yüzüme bakıyor. Sanki içimden geçenleri anlamış gibi...

"Tolga seni bekliyor," diyor, "dönsek iyi olur..."

Evet dönmemiz gerekiyor.

Rüyalar biter. En sevdiğimiz, uyanmak istemediğimiz rüyalar da korkunç kabuslar da..

Bu bir film değil. Buradan çıkıp denize açılıp, kimsenin bilmediği yerlere gidip bir hayat kurmak ancak filmlerde olur. Çocukken çok sevdiğim kitaplardaki gibi... Bilinmeyen uçsuz bucaksız buz kütlelerinin üzerinde ya da sıcacık gizli bir koyda, kendi halinde yaşayan ve dünya umurunda olmayan insanların unutulmuş kasabasında...

Eğilip yeniden öpüyor.

Olsun, belki de filmlerde olmadığı kadar uzağa gittim bu gece, belki masallarda olmadığı gibi garip şeylerle karşılaştım, belki rüyalarımda görmediğim kadar eşsiz bir duygu yaşadım.

Ne olmuş!

Kıyıya yanaştık. Gece bitmişti. Karanlıktı.

Biraz geç kalmıştık.

İyi ki de kalmıştık.

Ben, Ebru, pembe, biraz ıslanmış tüllerden elbisemle, aydedenin gülümsediği karanlık denizde, kimselerin olmadığı, kimselerin bizi görmediği bir yerde, hayatımın yeni bir dönemine girdiğim bu gecede, hayatımda ilk kez istediğimi yaptım. Kimseye sormadan, kimseyi umursamadan, ne istiyorsam onu yaptım.

Biraz üşümüş, biraz ıslanmış, elini tutarken, boynuna başımı koymuş, dalgalara karşı geri dönerken, biraz başım dönerken, kendi kendime dedim ki bunu yaptığın için pişmanlık duymayacaksın.

Duymayacağım.

Kim ne derse desin.

Söz mü?

Söz.

Nasıl becerdiyse Tolga, Seda'yı birileriyle yollamış, benimle sonra buluşacağını söylemiş ve herkes gittikten sonra tek başına otelin barında oturup beni beklemişti.

Ve tabii ki zil zurna sarhoş olmuştu.

Yine de geldiğimiz zaman bizi karşıladı.

Garip smokini, çözülüp sallanan komik papyonu ve jöleli saçlarıyla hem de sallanarak o kadar komik görünüyordu ki, gecenin bu saatinde gülmeye başladım.

Ferhat bizi eve bıraktı.

Tolga'ya, "Bana bak sen de geliyorsun, beraber oradan bir yere gittik, biraz fazla kaçırdık, tamam mı?" dedim.

Annem tabii ki uyumamıştı.

Ama her nasılsa söylenmedi.

Tolga dili dolaşarak, "biraz geciktik kusura bakmayın, ne de olsa mezuniyet," diye içeri girdi.

"Ben kahve yapayım," dedi annem.

"Sen yat anne," dedim, "ben yaparım."

Önemli olan "sağ salim" gelmemizdi. Annem gidip yattı.

Kahveleri getirdim.

Tolga ceketini, kelebekli papyonunu çıkartmış, salondaki koltukta yayılmıştı.

"Kahve filan istemiyorum," dedi, "iki saat tek başıma barda içki içtim, şimdi bana değişik bir hikaye anlatsan iyi olur..."

"Ne anlatayım," dedim, "beni balıkçı teknesiyle gezdirdi, çok güzeldi.."

"Gezdirdi mi? Sen bana baksana, sarhoşum diye benimle dalga geçme istersen, ne oldu diyorum..."

Gülüyordum.

"Ne olduğunu bilmek mi istiyorsun?"

Bir sigara çıkardı, yaktı, neredeyse yere düşecek gibiydi...

"Söyleyeceğim ama zaten yarın hatırlamayacaksın..."

"Bana bak, bütün gece seninle uğraştım, o şapşal Seda başımın etini yedi, ayrıca annemlere de hep beraber Ebru'ya gidiyoruz, orada kalacağım diye yalanlar uydurdum, bana güzel birşey söylemezsen rezalet çıkartırım, herkesi uyandırıp ne haltlar karıştırdığını söylerim anladın mı?"

Bunları ağzı dolaşarak söylüyordu, o kadar tatlıydı ki gülmemek için zor duruyordum.

Ama o anda birine bunu söylemek istediğimi farkettim.

"Ben," dedim, "onu öptüm..."

"Onu mu soruyorum," dedi, "çizgi filmlerde de herkes birbirini öpüyor."

"E, ne soruyorsun?"

Çok sarhoştu. Birden değişti yüzü, "O yaşlı çapkın seni kullanacak, keşke gitmene izin vermeseydim, keşke suratına yumruk atsaydım..."

"Aaa, ne o, kıskandın mı yoksa?"

Sigarasını söndürdü.

"Oraya gittiğimiz gün biliyordum. Anlamıştım ben bakışlarından. Şimdi söyle bana sahiden ne düşünüyorsun?"

"Ben ona aşık oldum," dedim, "hatta ben olmadım, ne olduysa kendiliğinden oldu, o beni öpmedi, ben onu öptüm, asıl sen şimdi söyle bana ne olacak?"

"Ne demek ne olacak? Adam kalkmış senin mezuniyetine gelmiş, tekne tutmuş, dünyanın en adi adamı değilse..."

Bir an durdu...

"Ki değil..."

"Eee...?"

"Sana bir tek şey söyleyeceğim... Keşke bu gece bütün bunlar benim de başıma gelseydi..."

Ben anlatmaya devam ediyordum ama baktım sızmış bile...

İçerden battaniye getirdim. Üstünü örttüm.

Gidip saçımı açtım. Takılarımı çıkardım. Makyajımı sildim. Soyundum. Aynada dantel çamaşırlarımla kendime baktım.

Gülümsedim.

Ben artık büyük bir kızım.

Şimdi ne yapıyor diye düşündüm. Acaba onun aklından neler geçiyor. Onun yanında olmak istedim.

Ve o an farkında değildim belki ama birinin hep yanında olmak istemek hiç de sandığımız kadar iyi değildi.

O gece uyuyamam sandım ama yorgunluktan mı, deniz havasından mı, biraz içkiden mi bilmem daha kafamı yastığa koyar koymaz uykuya dalmışım.

Hem ne uyku.

Rüyamda Seda beni arayıp televizyondaki filmi izlememi istiyordu ısrarla... Açıp filmi izliyorum. Filmin sonunda adımın geçtiğini duyuyorum. Yabancı bir filmin içinde benim adımın geçmesi çok garip. Sonra Seda gelip beni alıyor ve tanımadığım bir yere gidiyoruz. Beni neden oraya getirdiğini soruyorum ama cevap vermiyor.

Küçük bir eve giriyoruz. Hiç tanımadığım insanlar var salonda. Eski eşyaları olan, orta halli bir ev. Yerdeki halılar yer yer yolunmuş, yırtılmış. Yaşlıca bir adamla kadın oturuyor. Bunları tanıyor musun diye soruyor Seda. Tanımıyorum. Bak diyor, onlar senin gerçek annenle baban. Ürperiyorum rüyamın içinde. Şaşkın şaşkın bakıyorum. Kadın ağlıyor, adam hüzünlü. Nasıl olur diyorum? Bunca yıl benden gizlendi mi bütün bunlar? Arkada orta yaşlarda, topluca, yeşil gözlü bir kadın oturuyor. "Peki beni tanıyor musun?" diye soruyor. Tanımıyorum. Hiç görmedim bu kadını. "Hayır," diyorum.

"Ben gerçek Ebru'yum," diyor.

Çarpıntıyla uyandım. Ne biçim rüya bu böyle dedim kendi kendime... Gerçek Ebru mu? Gerçek anne babam mı? Kadının yüzü uzun süre gözümün önünden gitmedi.

Saate baktım. Öğlen olmuş.

Uyandım ama hala sersem gibiydim. Sıcak suyun altına girdim ve yere taşın üstüne oturdum. Suyun altında durmaktan çok ne sakinleştirebilir beni? Kafamı toplamaya çalıştım. Rüyanın etkisinden çıkıp dün geceyi düşündüm. Tolga? Uyanmış mıydı? Ya uyku sersemi anneme ağzından birşey kaçırırsa? Yok yok yapmaz öyle şey...

Bütün bunlar nasıl olmuştu?

Sanki bir film sahnesi gibi...

Böyle şeyler gerçekte olur muydu?

Ama rastlantı değildi bu kez. Hepsini önceden ayarlamıştı.

Bunu yapmasını hiç beklemiyordum. Hem nasıl cesaret etmişti ki? Ya gitmeseydim? Anneanneme söyleseydim?

Üstelik ayrılırken bana kimse bilmesin, gizli kalsın filan bile dememişti. Belki de umursamıyordu.

Bir pantolon gömlek geçirdim üstüme...

Tolga çoktan gitmişti. Annemin pek kuşkulanmış bir hali yoktu. Benim gecenin en güzel, en zarif kızı olduğumdan sözediyordu. Belli ki babamın gelmeyişinin, hiç konuşmasak da beni üzdüğünü düşünüyordu. Bu halini bilirim. Eğer öyle olmasa mutlaka göbeğimin açıklığından topuklularla zar zor yürüyüşüme, yemeklerin kötülüğünden müziğin yanlış seçilmesine kadar laf ederdi şimdi.

Tam sorulara başlayacakken aşağı anneanneme kaçtım.

Kahvesini almış, gazetelere göz gezdiriyor. Beni görünce yakın gözlüklerini çıkardı.

Gittim onu öptüm.

"Aman aman prensesimiz nihayet uyanmış, sen de bana benzemeye başladın galiba artık, kahvaltı ettin mi, getirsin Saniye..."

"Ben alırım," dedim, mutfağa gidip kendime kahveyle çörek aldım.

"Olur mu bunla, ye biraz bak geç olmuş, güzel kahvaltı et..."

"Yok yok, yeter bu bana şimdilik," dedim.

Gazeteleri katlayıp kaldırdı. "Tek iç açıcı haber yok. Ne diye okuyorum hala bunları bilmem..."

Kahvemden bir yudum aldım. Galiba olup bitenler bizi ya da beni hiç ilgilendirmiyordu. Gazete de okumuyordum zaten.

"Eee, neler yaptınız bakalım bizden sonra, aldığım haberlere göre kafalar bulunmuş..."

"E işte dans filan derken... Hele Tolga düz yürüyemiyordu, görmeniz lazımdı, çok komikti hali..."

"Bakıyorum gözlerin parlıyor hala, dün akşam bütün iltifatları topladın değil mi?"

"Bilmem..." dedim.

Gözlerimin parladığı anlaşılıyor muydu sahiden?

"Yalnızca dans edip eğlendiniz mi, başka değişik hadise yok mu?" dedi birden, az daha kahveyi döküyordum.

"Yok, ne olsun ki başka?"

"Bilmem, sordum yani ne bileyim, mesela bugün buluşacağın biri var mı?"

Gözlerine baktım. Yoksa biliyor mu?

"Yoo, belki Tolga'yla Seda'yla buluşuruz..."

"Aman Seda dedin de, yazık aklımıza gelmedi, onun elbisesini de biz diktirseydik keşke neydi o acayip elbise Victoria döneminden gelmiş gibi..."

Rahatladım.

"Evet benim de aklıma geldi görünce ama ne bileyim kendisi bulmuş, hiç de sormadı..."

"Nasıl sorsun zavallı, imkanları da yoktur ki, sana daldık onu unuttuk..."

Bu yaşta bunları bile atlamıyordu. Gerçekten de onun için üzüldüğünü hissettim.

"Bazen yakın arkadaşlar arasında da kıskançlıklar olur, biliyorsun değil mi?"

"Seda mı? Yok canım o beni kıskanmaz. Hem bütün gece dans etti durdu. Keyfi yerindeydi yani... Siz eğlendiniz mi?"

"O manasız konuşmalarla mı eğleneceğiz. İçim kıyıldı. Bizim milletin mikrofon bulunca birden dünyayı kurtarma çabası nedir bilmem... Ama zaten sizin gecenizdi, ben senin yaşında olacaktım ki bak bakalım dans nasıl ediliyor..."

Aklım tabii ki başka yerdeydi ama her zamanki gibi onunla konuşmak beni rahatlattı. İçimdeki suçluluk duygusu uçup gitti. Benim yerimde olsa aynını yapacağından emindim. Hatta delirip olan biteni ona anlatmayı bile düşündüm.

Tabii yapmadım.

Ne olacaktı şimdi?

Beni evden arayamazdı. Ben de sersem gibi telefonunu almamıştım. Çat kapı evine gidecek halim de yok. Off ne salağım. O tüllerin içinde ayışığının altında Külkedisi gibi dolaşırken bütün bunları unutmuştum.

Al bakalım sana, atlı araba kabağa dönüşüverdi.

Ben dalmışım.

"Bu Yıldız da kayboldu ortalıktan, akşama misafir var, aa bil bakalım kim geliyor akşam?" dedi.

"Kim?" dedim.

"Hani Ferhat vardı ya sizin röportaja gittiğiniz ressam..."

Herhalde o an domates rengini almış olmalıyım. Kalbim çarpmaya başladı ve göğsümden başıma kadar bir sıcaklık yükseldi.

"Aa öyle mi?" diye kekeledim.

"Evet. Ne zamandır yoktu ortalarda. Senin pek sevdiğin şairimiz de geliyor... Akşam kaybolma yani...Sen de geliyorsun..."

Hayır bilmiyor. Off neyse...

Yüzüme şapşal bir gülümseme geldi oturdu. Bu adam hep böyle şaşırtacak mıydı beni? Deli. Tam da onu nasıl göreceğimi düşünürken...

Hiç gelmez olur muyum?

İşte bu yolculukta yanımdan geçip giden görüntüler gibi, o günleri hatırlarken de böyle hızla, üstüste nasıl geçtiğini düşünüyorum.

Öyle hızlı ki ayrıntıları tutamıyorum. Günler birbirine karışıyor. Küçük bir an bazen büyük resmin önüne geçiyor nedense...

Ne garip, güzel şeyler hep çabucak geçip gidiyor da acılar hayat boyu bizimle kalıyor.

Belki insan hayatın içindeki güzel anları toplayıp bir bavula koyabilseydi o zaman gittiği en kötü yerlerde bile mutlu olabilirdi.

Şimdi aradan geçen bunca zamandan sonra herşey çok farklı.

Şimdi artık bana ulaşabilir. Burada uzak bir ülkenin uzak kasabasına giderken herkesle konuşabilirim. Tabii ben istersem.

Cep telefonum yanımda ama kapalı.

Orada bu tuhaf yolculuğun sonunda yalnız olmalıyım.

Bu kararı kimseye sormadan verdim. Onun için kimseden yanımda olmasını isteyemem.

Herkese birkaç günlüğüne arınma merkezine gittiğimi, biraz yalnız kalmak istediğimi söyledim.

Şimdi biraz pişman mıyım? Evet. Ama hala zamanım var.

Galiba bu, trene ikinci binişim. Zar zor hatırladığım ilk keresinde İstanbul'dan Ankara'ya gitmiştik. Annem, babam, ben. Bir akrabanın düğününe mi? Cenazesine mi? Hatırlamıyorum.

Biri gelip yatakları açmıştı. O küçük kompartımanda sallanan vagonda dolap gibi yatağın içinde uyumak heyecan vericiydi.

Pencereden hiç bilmediğim, tanımadığım yerlere, evlere, gazete isteyen yoksul çocuklara, uçsuz bucaksız çayırlara, tarlalara, tek tük evlere, geçip giden telefon direklerine bakmıştım saatlerce büyülenmiş gibi...

Kucağımda yine Puska vardı.

Babam gazetelerini okuyordu. Annem kah uyukluyor kah bana birşeyler soruyordu. Bense hayatımın bu ilk garip macerasında bambaşka bir dünyadaydım.

Tren durduğunda gazete isteyen çocukların yoksulluğunun da, bu köylerin, kasabaların yalnızlığının da, hayatın aslında nasıl farklı, nasıl akıl almaz biçimlerde yaşandığının da farkında değildim...

Yalnızca toprağın (yağmur yağıyordu) kokusunu duyuyordum. Ve biz bütün bu hayatların, bütün bu unutulmuşluğun, bütün bu çilenin içinden öylesine geçip gidiyorduk.

Ben tüm bunları masal sanacak bir yaştaydım ama aslında hiç birşey masallardaki gibi değildi.

Ne olmuştu bana birdenbire böyle?

Daha akşam onun geleceğini duyduğum an ne giyeceğimi düşünmeye başlamıştım.

Sanki önemli olan buymuş gibi...

E hani ben böyle şeyleri umursamazdım. Umursuyordum işte ne yapalım...

Zaten kışlıklar yazlıklar, Londra'ya gidecekler, annem bütün dolaplarımı altüst etmişti.

Tolga'yı aradım, çarşıya çıktık. Seda'yı bir iki gün görmesem daha iyiydi çünkü soracağı sorulara ne cevap vereceğimi kestiremiyordum.

Nişantaşı, Şişli bütün gün dolaştık. Sonunda çizgili renkli incecik bluzla pilili kısa bir etek aldım. Aslında bol dökümlü bir pantolon beğenmiştim ama Tolga itiraz etti.

"Ne bu erkek çocuğu gibi pantolon giyip duruyorsun," dedi.

Ne bileyim oldum olası etekle kendimi çıplak hissederim.

"Bizde zaten mini etek yastıkla moda oldu," diye güldü.

"Ne demek o?"

"Mini etek giyen kızlar otururken bacaklarının üstüne yastık koyuyor ya..."

Öyle bir kahkaha attım ki herkes dönüp bize baktı.

Dünkü Ebru'yla şu anki Ebru arasındaki fark beni öylesine şaşırtıyordu ki giysileri denerken aynaya bakıp bambaşka birini görüyordum.

Akşam onu göreceğim.

Aslında bundan başka birşey yoktu aklımda.

Mağazadan elimizde paketlerle çıktık, yürürken, birden,

"Birşey var ama," dedi, "nasıl söylesem..."

"Hayır," dedim, "söyleme, duymak istemiyorum..."

Çünkü ne söyleyeceğini biliyordum.

O kadar aptal değildim. Ama şu an o kadar aptal olmak istiyordum.

Ferhat'ın bunu bir tek benim için yaptığına inanmak istiyordum.

Ve başka ne yaptığı, neler yaşadığı, kaç sevgilisi olduğu, çapkının biri olup olmadığı umurumda bile değildi.

Bunu bir tek benim için yapmıştı.

Yapmasa da bundan sonra öyle olacaktı.

Dönüp baktım, eliyle ağzına fermuar yaptı, güldük.

Saçlarımı açık bıraktım. Giyindim. Annem geldi, bana baktı, anladım laf geliyor, "Üff bu etek de biraz garip oldu ama Tolga aldırdı zorla, son modaymış," dedim, "Biraz fazla olmuş," dedi, "Yabancı yere gitmiyorum anne," dedim. Bana şöyle bir baktı, "Yemek hazır," dedi sadece...

Anneannemin sofrasına oturmadan önce annemle yemek yerdim. Çünkü o aşağıya, kalabalık sofralara gelmezdi. Onun evde tek başına yemesini istemezdim.

Fırında tavukla püre vardı yemekte.

"Sanki bir günde büyüdün," dedi, "dün gece sana bakarken gurur duydum..."

Aslında benimle böyle konuşmazdı pek. Şaşırdım.

"Gurur mu duydun?"

"Evet, bütün olan bitenlere rağmen iyi dereceyle okulunu bitirdin, güzel bir gelecek için hazırsın ama daha önemlisi artık çocuk değilsin..." sonra durdu, "gerçi ne zaman çocuk oldun ki?.." dedi.

Lokmamı yuttum. Suyumdan bir yudum aldım. Böyleydi değil mi?

Ben hiç çocuk olamamıştım.

Herşey öyle istediğiniz gibi olmuyor ki hayatta. Tıpkı o geceki gibi, pırıl pırıl ay gözlerinizi mutluluğa boyuyor ama sonra birden bir bulut geliyor.

Kendime aynada baktım. Eteği giymeye cesaret edemedim. Yine pantolon giydim.

Aşağı indim. Çerkes tavuğu, vişneli yaprak sarma, patates salatası, enginar, pancar, közde patlıcan, domates dolması, pastırmalı humus, kavun, peynir, küçük tabaklarda istavrit, tarama, ançuez, fava, kabak çiçeği dolması... Saniye'ye masayı kurarken yardım ettim.

Kristal avizeler yanıyordu.

Misafirler yavaş yavaş gelmeye başladı.

Sohbet koyulaştı. Konuşmalar sürerken, o en sevdiğim şairin dizelerini dinlerken sanki anlatılanların hepsini üstüme alınıyordum.

"Gözlerine bakıp sanki mavi diyeceğim / sanki çocuk diyeceğim.."

Kapı her çalındığında yerimden fırlamak istiyordum.

Geç kalmıştı.

Kalın gözlüklü sinema eleştirmeni İtalyan filmlerinin yeni sinemamız üzerindeki etkisini anlatıyordu. Kimileri söylediklerine katılırken bazıları itiraz etti. İnsan film üzerine konuşurken bile en sıkıcı kısmıyla neden ilgilenir bilmem.

Benim aklımda o filmlerdeki mutlu sonlar vardı. Hep ayrılık için bir neden... Savaş... Yanlış anlamalar... Ya biri evlidir, ya biri çok yaşlıdır... Hep imkansız birşey vardır... Araya giren birileri... Sonra biri kaçar... Biri onu izler... Onlar da biz de doğrunun bu olmadığını düşünsek de yine de vazgeçmeyiz... Bir mucize bekler gibi bekleriz... Bekleyişler vardır hep... Aptalca rastlantılar yüzünden birbirinin yanından geçip giden insanlar... Bir an gelip ikisi de vazgeçer ve seyirci hayal kırıklığına uğrar...

Ama sonunda tam adam trene binip giderken kadın koşarak gelir, peronda yüzlerce insanın arasında tedirgin halde onu görmeye çalışır... Adam bavullarını yerleştirmektedir, pencereden dışarı bakmaz. Tren kapılarını kapatır, ilerlemeye başlar, kadın koşmaktadır çaresizce, fonda birbirlerine ilk rastladıkları salaş meyhanedeki müzik çalmaktadır, kadın çaresizlikle trenin gidişine bakar, ağlamaktadır, adamın onu görüp görmediğini bilemeyiz, sonra tren giderken kadın tek başına peronda öylece durur, trenin son vagonu da geçer ve karşıda elinde bavuluyla adamın trenden indiğini görürüz.

Evet, ben böyle sonları severim.

Ünlü şairin "Sen bu şiiri biliyor musun küçük hanım," demesiyle kendime geldim. "Benim şiirlerim okullarda okutulmaz pek..."

"Evet," dedim, "daha çok kafiyeli şeyler okutuluyor ama ben biliyorum..."

"İşte buna memnun oldum," dedi, "peki sevdiğin bir şiir mi?"

"Evet," dedim, biraz utanarak, "*insan kendisine rağmen yaşayamaz / kalbimiz siyah derken biz beyaz diyemeyiz...*"

Güldü...

"Tebrikler... Ama şöyle olacak, kalbimiz beyaz derken biz siyah diyemeyiz.."

Kıpkırmızı oldum. Elbette ezbere biliyordum ama heyecandan onun karşısında yanlış okumuştum.

Sonra kadeh kaldırdı, "İşte buna içerim, gençler şiir okuyorsa gelecekten korkmaya gerek yoktur..."

Ve tabii bu söz üzerine yeni bir tartışma başladı. O sıralar, kimse şiir okumuyor, roman bitti gibi laflar dolaşıyordu ortalarda. Dergiler bu konularda dosyalar hazırlıyordu.

Ama aklım orada değildi ki... Hatta ben bu masada bile değildim.

Gelmedi.

Bir ara anneannem, "Ferhat gelecekti ama gelmedi," dedi.

Nazlı Hanım, "Canım genç, yakışıklı adam, kimbilir nerededir, söylenenlere göre pek çapkınmış..."

Bir bardak soğuk suyu kafama diktim.

"Yahu bizimle oturup ne yapsın, bekar adamın çapkın olmasında beis yok, nasılsa bizim yaşımıza gelince böyle oturup masada çene çalacak..."

Gelmedi.

Sanki ben o trenin peşinden koşan kadınmışım gibi kalbim çarpıyordu, içimde tarif edemeyeceğim bir kasılma, sanki midem yukarı doğru yükselirmiş gibi garip bir his, tren yavaş yavaş gidiyordu, gece geç saatlere geliyordu artık, ben trenin peşinden koşmuyordum, olduğum yerde duruyordum ama gelmedi.

Saat geç oldu.

Herkes yavaş yavaş kalktı.

Gecenin başında şölen sofrası gibi parlayan masa dağınık, yorgun, terkedilmiş bir hale döndü.

Sare Hanım koltuğuna oturdu, kahvesini istedi, ben de yanına geçtim.

"Bak görüyor musun," dedi, "Selim yine çok güzel çiçekler getirmiş, ne zarif çocuk, getirsene, bak şurada…"

Getirdim.

"Biliyor musun ismini?"

"Hayır," dedim "ama çok güzeller…"

"Unutmabeni bunlar, eh romancıya da böyle çiçekler yakışır…"

Unutma beni…

Gelmemişti.

Belki de yalnızca basit bir rastlantı olmuştu. Belki bir yere gitmiş ve oradan çıkamamıştı. Belki bir resme dalmıştı.

Ama ya dün geceden sonra benimle karşılaşmak istemediyse?

Kimbilir, belki de düşününce pişman olmuştu yaptığına...

Bana ümit vermekten korkmuş ya da olanların anlaşılacağından çekinmişti.

Tanımıyor ki seni, dedim kendi kendime yatakta dönüp dururken...

Nereden bilsin ne yapacağını, ya herkesin ortasında olmadık birşey söylersen?

Ya dün geceden bahsettiysen?

İyi ama onu ben çağırmamıştım ki? Neden geleceğini söylemişti o zaman?

Anneanneme hayır diyemediği için mi?

Olabilir.

Belki de birdenbire böyle davranacağımı düşünmemişti. Çok mu hızlı gelmişti ona olanlar?

Yalnızken, ayışığında, denizin ortasında, sallanıp duran bir teknede öpüşmek güzeldir ama sonra herkesin içinde kimlikler değişir değil mi?

Ben dün gece başka biriydim.

Bunları sahiden düşünmüş olabilir miydi yoksa hiç umurunda bile değil miydi? Nazlı Hanım'ın söylediği gibi bu gece de başka bir heyecanın peşinden mi gitmişti?

Ben de onu tanımıyordum ama her nedense böyle yapmadığına inanıyordum.

Hatta emindim.

Belki de bütün gece karşımda rol yapmak istemedi. Hiç birşey olmamış gibi davranmak belki ona göre değil.

Zaten gelse de karşılıklı konuşamayacaktık ki... Ama ben gözlerine bakacaktım kaçamak... Belki bir gülümseme yakalayacaktım belli belirsiz. Belki ben o dizeleri okurken ne düşündüğü belli olacaktı.

Sonuçta ben kendimi çok büyümüş saysam da onsekiz yaşındaki kızla, kendisinden çok küçük bir kızla, hem de tanıdığı bir ailenin kızıyla, üstelik hakkında bunca dedikodu varken....

Evet evet... Bence onu öpeceğimi, böyle birdenbire aklıma estiği gibi davranacağımı düşünmemişti. Şimdi de ona kapıldığımdan, aşık olduğumdan ve başına bela olacağımdan korkuyordu.

Asıl korkması gereken ben değil miydim? Garip ama ben korkmuyordum.

Şimdi burada yatağın içinde kuşkular içimi kemirirken, binbir soruyla uğraşıp dururken bir günde nasıl bu hale geldiğimi anlamaya çalışıyordum aynı zamanda.

Gelmediyse gelmedi.

Ne olmuş seni öptüyse? Evlilik teklif etmedi ya... Sen de kalktın koşa koşa gittin peşinden. İnsan, üzerinde mezuniyet elbisesi, topuklu ayakkabılarla bu balıkçı sandalında gece vakti ne sallanıyorum diye sormaz mı?

Sormadın.

Üstelik hayatında ilk kez sarhoş olmuşken...

Yok öyle kendimi kullanılmış, kandırılmış filan hissetmiyordum. Yalnızca anlamaya çalışıyordum çünkü eğer içimdeki duygu bu kadar büyükse ondan gelenin bu kadar farklı olması mümkün değildi bence.

Ama eğer öyleyse de bir daha görüşmezdik olur biterdi. Madem pişman olmuştu ben de onu arayacak değildim.

Sonuçta okulun yakışıklılarından biriyle de öpüşmüş olabilirdim karanlık bir köşede dansederken ve o da beni bugün aramayabilirdi...

Ne yapalım ki, herşey her zaman bizim anladığımız gibi olmuyor.

Bir oraya bir buraya dönüp uykuya dalmadan önce verdiğim cevaplar beni hiç mutlu etmemişti.

Tren gitmişti ve peronda kimse yoktu.

Pazartesi, salı, çarşamba, perşembe...

Geçti.

Gerçi artık günlerin fazla anlamı yoktu çünkü tatildeydik. Bitmek bilmeyen pazartesi, sıkıcı salı, dilbilgisi çarşambası değildi.

Ondan ses çıkmadı.

İki duygu arasında gidip geliyordum aslında. Kapısını çalıp neler oluyor diye sormakla beni öpüp sonra ortadan kaybolan adamı bir daha aramamak arasında kalmıştım.

Tolga, "Adam korktu, biliyorum ben, başına iş açılacak diye düşünüyor, ama şunu da söylemeliyim ki bu iş zaten yürümez..." diye konuşup duruyordu.

"Bu konuyu kapatalım ve artık konuşmayalım olur mu?" dedim.

"Tamam," dedi, "ben yalnızca senin üzülmenden korkarım..."

Seda, Tolga, Gülgün, Tolgaların teknesiyle tatile gitmeye karar verdik.

Tabii benim yanımda ne düşünsem de kafamdan atamadığım biri daha vardı ama onu kimse görmüyordu.

Bodrum o sıralar henüz bir cehenneme dönüşmemişti. Tatilin bu ilk günlerinde çok kalabalık değildi.

Su beni her zaman mutlu eder. Ilık çarşaf gibi suda yüzerken, güneşe yüzümü dönüp kendimi bırakırken, mutluydum. Gülgün bir öne bir arkaya dönüp bütün gün güneşlendiği için hemen kapkara oldu. Okul günleri, gelecekte yapılacaklar, çoktan unutulmuş sandığımız anılar, öyle çok gülüyorduk ki...

İlk kez o ıssız, sakin koylarda kendi başımızaydık. Oraya gitme, fazla açılma, dikkat et, erken yat diyen yoktu.

Tolga teknenin kaptanı gibi herşeyi idare etmekle uğraşıyordu. Kahvaltı, yemek, akşamüstü meyvaları, kendi hazırladığı kokteyller... Emektar kaptan da arada sohbete katılıyor, sonra birden ortadan kaybolup bizi yalnız bırakıyordu.

Akşamüzeri gün batarken sudan çıkıyor, hazırlanıyorduk. Onun mutlaka bir planı vardı. Sanki dört arkadaş, ıssız adaya düşmüştük ve ne istersek yapmakta özgürdük.

Gülgün'ün hazırlanması biraz uzun sürüyordu. O kokoş haliyle sahilde yürüdüğümüz zaman hemen kendimizi bir yere atmak istiyorduk çünkü herkes ona bakıyordu.

Tolga hem kendi derdindeydi hem de bize sahip çıkması gerektiğini hissediyor, yanımıza gelenleri püskürtmek için elinden geleni yapıyordu.

Ama bunu söylemeliyim ki, Gülgün'den beklerken asıl hareket Seda'dan geldi bir akşam.

Bir köşede durup kendi kendimize eğleniyorduk.

Gecenin ilerleyen saatlerinde artık tekneye dönecekken bir ara Seda'nın ortadan kaybolduğunu farkettik.

Tolga gidip onu aramaya koyuldu.

Sonra telaş içinde yanımıza döndü. Kaygılı bir halde, "Kumsaldaki şezlongların birinde oğlanın biriyle oturuyor," dedi, "hem de elele..."

"Ee gitmedin mi yanlarına?"

"Gittim, gitmez olur muyum, siz gidin ben sonra gelirim," dedi...

"Nasıl gelecek ki sonra?"

"Soramadım ki..."

"Olmaz öyle şey," dedi Gülgün, "onu bırakıp gidemeyiz, kimdir, nedir bilmediğimiz adamla..."

Gülmeye başladım. Bunu söyleyen Gülgün müydü?

"Ne olacak adam seri katil mi çıkacak?"

"İyi ama tekneye dönemez ki sonra..." dedi Tolga...

"Döner döner," dedim, "tabii isterse, şurada sandallar var, biriyle konuş, istediği zaman ona biner gelir..."

Ertesi sabah uyandığımızda Seda yoktu. Önce biraz meraklandık ama öğlene doğru geldi.

Söylediğine göre çocuğun arkadaşları gelmiş, hep birlikte sessiz bir kumsala gitmişler, orada gitar çalıp şarkılar söylemişler sonra da uyuyakalmışlardı.

Gözlerine baktım. Belki de onu tanıdığımdan beri ilk kez mutlu ve sakin görünüyordu.

Ötesini sormadım.

Kaptan karpuz, peynir, üzüm getirdi. Tombalak pembemsi üzümler buzların içinde parlıyordu.

Ben suya atladım.

Dibe, daha koyu bir yeşile doğru giderken hayat aslında hep böyle olsa diye düşündüm.

Derinleştikçe güzelleşse...

Dört, beş günlük tatil bana çok iyi gelmişti. Tabii ki Ferhat hiç aklımdan çıkmamıştı ama şimdi ne yapacağımı biliyordum. Üç ay sonra gitmiş olacaktım. Benim zamanım azdı. Öyle mi oldu, böyle mi dedi, ne düşündülerle geçirecek vaktim yoktu.

En başta kalkıp ona giderken nasıl kendim karar verdiysem şimdi de öyle yapacaktım.

Sonra?

Sonrasını hiç düşünmek istemiyordum.

Kendi kendine hayaller kurmazsan onlar gerçekleşmeyince üzülmezsin.

Ama aradan zaman geçmişti. Belki o da benim yaptığıma pişman olduğumu ya da vazgeçtiğimi düşünmüştü. Hem o da bir yerlere gitmiş olabilirdi.

Eski otelin salonunda yine aynı köşede aynı saatte onu elimle koymuş gibi buldum.

Üç beş turist uzun, şemsiyeli bardaklarda renkli koteyller içiyordu.

Garson beni tanıdı. "Hoşgeldiniz, beyefendi burada, buyurun," diye bana yol gösterdi. Şaşırdım ama ses çıkarmadan onu izledim.

Beni gördü. Başını kaldırdı, gülümsedi. Önündeki defteri kapatıp ayağa kalktı.

"Tatil yaramış," dedi.

"Demek buralardasın," dedim, "tatilde olduğumu nasıl anladın o kadar mı yanmışım?"

"Biraz ama aslında Sare Hanım'dan öğrendim," dedi.

Demek aramıştı.

"Oturmaz mısın?"

"Evet kahve içebilirim, zamanım var," dedim. Sanki buraya onun için geldiğim belli değilmiş gibi...

Olsun bozmayalım.

"Çalışıyorsan..."

"Yok yok her zamanki gibi karalıyorum sadece..."

Öylece bana bakıyordu. Gözlerimi kaçırdım, turistlere baktım. Yüksek sesle gülüp konuşuyorlardı.

"Ve," dedi, "seni gördüğüme çok sevindim..."

Hayır, bu sefer biraz mesafe olacaktı.

Hiç duymamış gibi, "Eee, neler çiziyorsun, bakabilir miyim?" dedim.

"Bazen yalnızca eşyaların farklı hallerini çizerim, farklı açılardan nasıl göründüklerini, bir tür el alıştırması..."

Defteri açtı. Aslında bu bir defter değildi, içinde kalınca kağıtlar olan büyük bir dosyaydı. Sandalye, şamdan, avize, salondaki akvaryum, bunları çizmişti, o sırada garson kahvelerimizi getirdi, ama alırken eline çarptı ve kahve dökülmesin diye dosyayı hızla çekti, çekince içinden birkaç sayfa düştü, yere eğilip aldım.

Garson özür dileyerek kahveleri bırakıp gitti.

Ben elimdeki kağıda bakıyordum.

"Eyvah fena yakalandım," dedi...

Benim resimlerimdi. Büyükçe bir sayfada beş, altı resim vardı. Hepsi farklı açılardan çizilmiş ama gözlerim nedense hep çok büyük.

"Ben miyim bu?" dedim, başka laf bulamayıp.

"Aklımda kalan sen..."

"Ben böyle mi bakıyorum?"

"Hayır," dedi, "aklımdaki sen böyle bakıyor.."

"Biri ilk kez resmimi çiziyor da," dedim "şaşırdım biraz.."

"Bunların arasındaki farkı görebildin mi?" dedi.

Yeniden baktım.

"Sanki ayrı zamanlarda çizilmiş gibi..."

"Çünkü seni gördüğüm ayrı zamanları çizmeye çalıştım..."

Şu yandan çizilmiş olan Tolga'yla evine ilk gittiğimiz gün... Şu biraz daha gülümsermiş gibi ve şaşkın bakışlı ikinci gün... Biri burada karşılaştığımız öğledensonra ve son ikisi teknedeki gece...

"Evet," dedim, "ne garip insan baktıkça başka şeyler farkediyor..."

Ben onun beni hiç aklına getirip getirmediğini düşünürken o her günü unutulmaz kılmıştı bile...

Utandım, ürperdim, şaşırdım, ne düşüneceğimi, ne söyleyeceğimi bilemedim.

"Peki ama," dedim, "bunda neden gözlerim görünmüyor..."

Baktı, "Çünkü o akşamüzeri yukarı çıkmıştık ve güneş gözlerini kamaştırmıştı, gözünde yalnızca parlak bir ışık vardı..." dedi.

Ne garip, güneşe bakıp gözlerim kamaşmıştı ve gerçekten de gözlerimde o ışık kalmıştı ama bu, dışarıdan görünen birşey olamaz değil mi?

"Her zaman yapar mısın bunu?" diye sordum.

"Neyi?"
"Yani böyle günleri, anları hep çizer misin?"
Biraz ileride oturan turistler eşyaların, akvaryumun, avizelerin hatta tavanların bile fotoğraflarını çekiyordu.
Kahkaha attı, "Onlar gibi mi? Hayır..."
Ya, demek öyle. Demek bardaki içki şişeleri, şamdan, avize, sandalye gibi değil.
"Ama anları çizmek sözünü çok sevdim. Belki de gerçekte yapmak istediğim budur. O an'ı ölümsüzleştirmek ama benim gözümdeki haliyle..."
"Peki bugünü de çizecek misin?"
"Hayır ama eğer yarın bana gelirsen aklımdakini değil de karşımdakini çizerim istersen..."
Onun aklındakini bilmem de benim aklımdakini okuduğuna kuşku yoktu.
Yine de bazen biraz durmak gerekebilir... Kızlar böyle yapar değil mi? Niyeyse?
"Olabilir ama yarın değil. Yarın biraz işim var. Belki öbürgün eğer sana da uygunsa..."
"Evet," dedi, "bana da uygun... Bir de telefonumu al istersen çünkü ben seni arayamıyorum, belki aramak istersin..."
Kahvemden bir yudum aldım. Arkama yaslandım. İçimden güldüm. Evet artık sohbete başlayabiliriz Ferhat Bey...
Tatil nasıl geçti diye mi sormuştu az önce?

Evet böyleydi. Bazı şeyleri konuşmaya gerek yoktu. Akşam olurken kalktım, resmi istemeye utandığım için biraz kızdım sonra kendime... Aslında kalkmaya niyetim de yoktu ama Seda bana gelecekti.

Tabii ki Bodrum'daki o geceyi dinlemek zorunda kalacaktım. Neler söyleyeceğini, soracağını şimdiden biliyordum ama çare yoktu.

Aynı beklediğim gibi oldu. Annemle yemek yedik. Sonra benim odaya geçtik.

Bana müzik açtırdı annem belki duyar diye.

Fısıltıyla konuşmaya başladı.

"N'apıyorsun?" dedim, "annemin işi gücü yok kapıyı mı dinleyecek? Ne yaptın birini mi öldürdün?"

"Aman sana göre kolay. Bilmiyorsun neler olduğunu..."

Biliyorum. Hatta adım gibi eminim. Öpüştünüz, çocuk biraz üstündekileri sıyırıp oranı buranı karıştırdı sen izin vermedin, bu böyle sabaha kadar sürdü ve sen çocuğun sana aşık olduğunu sanıyorsun.

Bunları söylemedim tabii...

"Oğlanın arkadaşlarının filan gelmediğini biliyorum en azından..."

"Off tamam n'apiym, yalan attım."

"Emin ol kaptan bile inanmadı..."

Şu an o havadaydım ki aslında sıkılacağım bu konuşma beni eğlendiriyordu.

Aynen dediğim gibi olmuştu. Tabii oğlan arada bizimkinin uzun konuşmalarını dinlemek zorunda kalmıştı. Şimdi ben de aynı durumdaydım. Ve ona, "Hayatında tanımadığın biriyle sabaha kadar öpüşmek hem saçma hem de sıradan, bunun için kendini suçlamana gerek yok, bunu süsleyip özel bir duruma çevirmene de gerek yok, oldu bitti, geçti," diyemezdim.

Döneli çok olmamıştı.

"Geldiğimden beri aramadı," dedi.

"Arayacak mıydı?"

"Evet telefonumu aldı. Gelince görüşürüz dedik. Teknik üniversitede okuyormuş. Benden üç yaş büyük. Yeşilköy'de doğup büyümüş. Hala da orada oturuyorlarmış. Biliyor musun çok akıllı çocuk. Hem de efendi. Yani öyle zorla üstüme filan saldırmadı."

Tolga'yı özledim. Şimdi burada olsa, "Niye ki? Sen saldırsaydın?" deyiverirdi.

Ne garip. Aslında belki de çok farklı durumda değildik. En azından ikimizin de aklında biri vardı ve ikimiz de aklımızdakini pek fazla tanımıyorduk.

"Sence birlikte olacağın biri mi yoksa o gece biraz da oradaki durumun etkisiyle fazla abartıyor olabilir misin?"

"Bilmiyorum," dedi, "ilk kez geliyor başıma sen de biliyorsun..."

"Neden onu tekneye getirmedin?" diye sordum.

"Çekindim.. Aklıma gelmedi değil ama Tolga'yla Gülgün ne yapar bilemedim..."

Aslında öyle değil. Onunla yalnız olmak istedin. Onun seni, olduğun gibi değil, senin istediğin gibi tanımasını istedin. Ona hayat hikayeni, nasıl biri olduğunu belki bizim bilemeyeceğimiz biçimde anlattın. Ve bundan utanmana gerek yok.

Üstelik bunu yapmanın nedeni, hepimizin bildiği gibi, yıllardır ayılıp bayıldığın ama asla senin farkında olmayan Can'ın, mezuniyet gecesi her nedense seninle danslar edip sonra da ortadan kaybolmasından duyduğun öfke, hayal kırıklığı ya da her neyse oydu.

Tabii ki bunları da söylemedim.

"Aman canım," dedim, "o aramadıysa sen ara, ne var bunda?"

"Yani sen şaşırmadın mı?" dedi.

Ben sen miyim Seda? Ben sana anlatsam kimbilir şimdi bana neler söylersin. Ama işte beklenmeyen şey senin başına geldi.

"Biraz şaşırdım doğrusunu istersen ama bu bizim okul yıllarından beri ilk tatilimiz, başımızda kimse olmadan... Hem galiba biraz sarhoş olmuştun..."

"Hayır, hayır," dedi, "yani çok az..."

"Bence," dedim, "üstünde çok fazla düşünme, oluruna bırak, ya da bir iki gün sonra sen ara, sonuçta tanımadığın biri, hakkında ne düşüneceğinden sana ne...."

"Ama," dedi, "o kadar güzel bir geceden sonra hiç ses çıkmaması garip değil mi? Sence ne düşünüyordur?"

Biliyordum başıma geleceği... Şimdi bu soruları hiç durmadan sorup duracak, aldığı cevapları da beğenmeyecek, böyle günlerce uğraşacaktı.

Birden kızardım. Benim durumum sanki çok mu farklıydı? Ben de bana her zaman komik gelen bu hale düşmemiş miydim?

Aradı mı, aramadı mı, geldi mi gelecek mi, ne düşünüyor, ne hissediyor diye yatakta habire dönüp durmuyor muydum?

Kendime kızdım.

Hayır, ben bütün hayatım boyunca bu saçmalıklarla uğraşmayacaktım.

"Ne düşünürse düşünsün herhalde hayatında bir kere gördüğün adama birdenbire deli gibi aşık olmadın."

Aslında onun ne duymak istediğini biliyordum.

"Hem," dedim, "belki o tatiline devam ediyordur, dönünce arar, yaptığından utanmayı da bırak, çocuk değilsin, eğer saçmalık yaptığını düşünseydim gelip seni oradan kaldırırdım..."

Bir gün sonra sözleştiğimiz gibi kapısını çaldım. Sanki tüm bunlar olmamış gibi, her zaman buluşan iki dost gibi yine karşılıklı oturup sohbete daldık. Burası her nedense bütün bu karmaşasına, benim yaşadığım yerlerden tümüyle farklı olmasına rağmen bana huzur veriyordu.

Her keresinde yeni keşfettiğim şeyler, minicik biblolar, neye yaradığını anlamadığım garip eski makinalar, kurgulu oyuncaklar, yokolup gitmiş geçmiş zaman parçaları...

Sanki o dünyanın her yerinden ve zamanın farklı dönemlerinden öyküleri toplamış ve burada kendine özel bir gezegen kurmuştu.

Hem de kapının hemen önünde sıradan mahalle hayatı sürerken...

İnsan yalnızca bir kapıyı açıp birdenbire başka bir evrene geçebilir mi?

Bahçeden çiçeklerin kokusu geliyordu. Serin ve loş. Hep o güzel, uzaklardan gelen müzikler çalıyordu. Sanki kentin dışında, bambaşka bir yere, belki bir tatil kasabasına gelmiş gibi hissediyordum kendimi.

Deniz yakınlardaydı, martıların bağırışması hiç kesilmiyordu.

Ve o her seferinde utangaç bir çocuk gibi karşımda oturuyor, yanıma gelip beni öpmeye bile çekiniyordu.

Oysa ikimiz de biliyorduk buraya neden geldiğimi...

Mavili, yeşilli neredeyse şeffaf, incecik bir bluz vardı üstümde... Kısacık etek ve annemin gençlik yıllarından kalma mantar topuklu ayakkabılar. Bir de yine ondan yürüttüğüm hippi dönemi kocaman taşlı bir kolye... Biliyorum bunların zamanı çoktan geçmişti ama benim hoşuma gidiyordu. Zaten artık benden başka kimse o uzun saçlı dört adamın çaldığı aşk şarkılarına, gökyüzünde elmaslarla uçan kıza da bayılmıyordu.

Bu an'ı düşünerek sabahı ettiğim için sersem gibiydim. Hatta sabah aynada yüzüme tokat attım ki beyazlığım gitsin... Saçlarımı toplamıştım ama öylesine... Neden bilmem, biraz dağınık görünmek hep hoşuma gider...

Nelerden sözediyorduk hatırlamıyorum, çünkü aslında dinlemiyordum... Bir ara içecek birşeyler getirdi ve sonra elimden tuttu. Ayağa kalktım. Yürüdü. Yalnızca elimi tuttu ve ben de peşinden gittim.

Perdeleri kapalı, karanlık odada, kocaman yatak, duvarlarda pek göremediğim resimler, köşede üzerine giysiler atılmış bir koltuk... Yatağın hemen yanında sehpanın üzerinde büyükçe bir abajur.

Bir an kapıda durdum. Ben onu ellerinden çektim ve yere yatağın yanına oturdum. Karşımda diz çöktü. Ya sıcaktan ya çarpıntıdan bayılacağımı sandım. Hem bu anın durmasını istiyordum hem devamını görmek.

Ama bu durdurup sonra izleyeceğiniz bir film ya da masaya bırakıp sonra devamını okuyacağınız bir roman değildi.

Bu hayattı.

Beni öperken gözlerimi kapadım ve ona sarıldım.

Sanırım ilk hissettiğim gitme duygusuydu. Hayır buradan gitmek, kaçmak değil, onunla birlikte gitmek... Sanki o an birlikte yolculuğa çıkmışız gibi...

Bu bir ilkti. Ama belki de son. Belki birşeyin başlangıcı olduğu için böylesine güzeldi, belki hiç bitmeyecek birşeydi.

Derine dalmış gibi dingin ve herşeyden uzak... yüksekten atlayıp uçarmış gibi hafif, heyecanlı... rüyanın en güzel anında sebepsiz yere korkmak gibi telaşlı... gizemli bir mağaraya girmiş gibi ürkütücü...

Arkadaki aynada görüntülerimizin çoğalması gibi birbirimize dokundukça o tanımlayamadığım şey, o benzersiz heyecan, o başka hiçbir yerde duymadığım zevk de çoğalıyordu.

Kendimi ona bırakmıştım aslında, çünkü zaten ne yapacağımı bilmiyordum ki, yalnızca onu öpmeye dokunmaya devam ediyordum.

Hayır gerçekten de bu kadar mutlu olacağımı düşünmemiştim.

Sanki bütün bedenim baştan aşağı dalgaya kapılmıştı ve onunla yükselip indikçe hani arabayla büyük kasislerden geçerken içimizde oluşan o garip duyguyla kasılıyordum.

Başım dönüyordu ama korkmuyordum.

Elinden tutmuştum ve şimdi benim gizli bahçemde birlikte dolaşıyorduk. Hayallerden bir bahçenin kapısı açılmıştı. Ben kendi bahçemde çok zaman geçirmiştim ama yanımda kimse yoktu. Orası benim en derin yalnızlığımdı. Bu dünyadan, istemediğim şeylerden, bütün o hastalıklardan, korkulardan, üzüntülerden kaçtığım yerdi.

Ve şimdi orada, içimde bir yerde bir başkası dolaşıyordu.

İnsan sevişirken böyle şeyler düşünür mü? Ben düşünüyordum işte.

Korkutucuydu aslında, içimde dolaşan bir canlı varmış gibi, kulağımda garip sesler, inlemeler...

Komikti bir yanıyla...

Ama aynı anda ne tuhaf, ağlamak da geliyordu içimden.

Gözlerimi açmıyordum, karanlıkta, içerden gelen müzikten başka ses yokmuş gibi ve o da konuşmuyordu...

İkimiz de o kadar sıcaktık ki sanki kumsalda kızgın kumların üzerinde sevişiyormuşuz gibiydi.

Uzun saçlarına yapışıp öperken dudaklarını ısırıyordum.

Yuvarlandığımızı, bir yerlere çarptığımızı hissediyordum, direnmiyordum sadece ona tutunmuştum, bu duyduğum her neyse öylesine yükseliyordu ki bağırmamak için zor tutuyordum kendimi, o zaman tırnaklarımı sırtına saplıyordum durması için ama durmadı, ben de bağırdım, titriyordum ve ne yapacağımı bilemiyordum, sonunda ona tümüyle yapışmış halde ağlarken durdu.

Gözlerimi açtım. Biraz şaşırmış, biraz korkmuş bana bakıyordu.

Titreyip hıçkırıyordum ama sonra gülmeye başladım.

Bu kendiliğinden olmuştu. Ağlamak ya da gülmekle, mutluluk ya da hüzünle ilgili değildi.

O an orada onun kucağındaydım, çıplak, sıcak, ürkek ama aslında aynı anda çok uzaklardaydım. Neredeyse bütün dünyayı yukarıdan görebileceğim kadar uzakta...

Titrerken renkler görmüştüm, hiç görmediğim güzellikte, parlaklıkta, birbirine karışmış, kendiliğinden desenler oluşturmuş renkler... Keşke bunları birine anlatabilsem, keşke ona anlatabilsem ve o da çizebilse diye düşünmüştüm.

Mutluluğun resmi işte böyleydi.

Anlamsız ama eşsiz.

İnsanın hayat boyu içinde kalmak isteyeceği bir an'dı.

O benim yazımdı.
Her iki anlamda da...

Evet ben onun yüzüne, gülüşüne, konuşmasına, sesine, bakışlarına, yakın gözlüğünü takıp çıkartmasına, sigarayı tutuşuna, içkisini yudumlamasına, kokusuna, saçlarını eliyle karıştırmasına, suratını astığı, dalıp gittiği anlara aşık olmuştum.

Heyecanla yeni yaptığı resmi anlatmasına, gözlerinin dolduğu dokunaklı anılara, bazen iki çocuk gibi bazen iki koca insan gibi konuşmalarımıza...

Küçücük bir salonda o güne kadar görmediğim filmler izlemeye giderdik. Sonra o film üstüne saatlerce konuşurduk. Çoğu zaman anlamadığım şeyler anlatırdı, bilmediğim kavramlar, tanımlamalar... Bazen sorardım, bazen utanırdım.

Ben ondan sıkılmamaya da aşık olmuştum.

Beni okşamasına, yüzümü iki eliyle tutup gözlerime bakıp susmasına, kucağında kendimi kaybetmeye, onunla buluşmaya giderken titremeye, onu düşündüğüm zamanlar olur olmaz gülümseyişime, onun için ne giyeceğimi düşünmeye, günlük konuşmaların içinde gizlice kendimi herkesten farklı hissetmeye de aşık olmuştum.

Ama aslında bütün bunların dışında, onun yaptıklarına, dışarıdan görmenin, anlatmanın mümkün olmadığı içinde gizlenmiş Ferhat'a aşıktım.

Onu tanıdıkça sanki karmaşık bir yapbozun parçalarını biraraya getirip yeni yeni resimler ortaya çıkartır gibi şaşırıyordum.

O aslında kocaman bir adamdı. Benden çok büyüktü. Ama bana öyle geliyordu ki hala küçük bir çocuktu.

Sanki o bu dünyaya yanlışlıkla gelmiş, kimsenin formülünü bilmediği incecik camdan yapılmış bir canlının tek örneğiydi ve bu yüzden onu tüm kötülüklerden korumak istiyordum.

Bu gerçek mi yoksa benim kurduğum, inandığım bir hayal mi diye düşünmekten kendimi alamıyordum.

Ve açık söylemem gerekirse çok da umurumda değildi.

Duygularla gerçeklerin birbirini tutmadığını söylerler.

Duygular gerçek midir diye çok düşündüm. Evet gerçek olduğunu biliyorum. Çünkü içimde hissettiğim böylesine güçlü birşeyin gerçek olmaması imkansız.

Ama o tümüyle bana ait olan gerçek.

Hayatın gerçeğiyle ilgisi yok.

Bir akşam yemek yiyorduk. O yine anlatıyordu ama dinlemiyordum. Onu o kadar çok öpmek istiyordum ki ne dediği umurumda bile değildi.

"Ellerimi yıkayıp geleceğim," dedim ve kalkıp gittim.

Girdim, ellerimi yıkadım. Biraz sonra kapı açıldı ve içeri girdi. Kabinlerden birine beni soktu ve öpüşmeye başladık. Sonra içeri bir kadın girdi. Bekledik. Bana eliyle sus işareti yaptı. Sonra ben çıktım. Gelip masaya oturdum. Biraz sonra yanıma geldi. Kaldığımız yerden konuşmaya devam ettik.

Kimsenin bilmediği bir dünyada gizemli bir mutluluk...

Küçük, benzersiz anlar...

O kadar güzeldi ki...

Olup bitenleri kimseye söylememeye karar vermiştim. Tolga'ya bile...

İlk kez herkesten birşey saklıyordum aslında.

O bana böyle birşey söylememişti. Bunu hiç konuşmamıştık.

Evet itiraf edeyim ki herkese anlatmak istiyordum. Ama yapmadım.

Bu benim gizli hayatımdı, gizli bahçemdi ve oraya başkalarının girmesini, bir budalanın bile düşünebileceği şeyleri söyleyip kafamı karıştırmasını, bu büyüyü bozmasını istemiyordum.

O kadar iyi biliyordum ki neler söyleyeceklerini...

Hayır, dinlemek istemiyordum.

Eğer onu ilk gördüğüm gün hissettiğim doğru çıktıysa herhalde bunda bir sihir vardı.

Ben o sihri kimsenin bozmasına izin vermeyecektim.

Galiba o yaz yalan söylemeyi öğrendim.

Annem, bütün bu giyinip kuşanıp ortadan kaybolmalarımı, mezuniyet gecesinden beri beni arayıp duran Murat'a bağlıyordu. Evet aslında dansetmiştik ve kulağıma beni çok beğendiğini, görüşmek istediğini söylemişti.

Hoşuma gitmedi desem yalan olur çünkü okulda bütün kızların bayıldığı, yüzme şampiyonu, yakışıklı, zengin, okula babasının son model arabasıyla gelen, öğretmenlerin gözdesi...

Tolga işleri bozmasa ve gecenin bir saati Ferhat çıkıp gelmese ne olurdu açıkçası emin değilim.

Bir de tabii dans ederken babasının mezuniyet için hediye ettiği saatin ne kadar pahalı olduğunu iki saat anlatmasa...

Ama ne olmuşsa olmuş, çocuk o geceden beri sürekli aramaya başlamıştı.

Ne garip, bunca yıl aynı okulda yüzüme bakmayan oğlan, o gece gözlükler çıkınca, kendi çizdiğim giysiyle, biraz makyajla birdenbire beni farketmişti... Küçük budala...

O akşam Ferhat'ın yanından eve döndüğümde tümüyle başka biriydim.

Ama kimse bunu bilmiyordu.

Yemekten sonra odama çıktım, o günü düşündüm, benim bir sırrım vardı, beni mutlu eden, bana istemediklerimi unutturan bir sır.

Ama kuşkuluydum. O ne düşünüyordu, ne hissediyordu, bilmiyordum.

Bütün akşam annemlerle otururken aklımda o vardı ama çaktırmadım.

Üstümü başımı çıkardım, aynada kendime baktım, değişiklik var mıydı, bence vardı...

Bu bir ilk ve son muydu?

Belki de artık beni hiç aramayacaktı.

Zaten hiç aramamıştı ki...

Omuz silktim kendi kendime. Aramazsa aramasın. Ben ne istiyorsam onu yaptım. Bundan sonra ne olacaksa olur...

Ceketimi asarken cebinden küçük, katlanmış bir kağıt parçası düştü.

"Yarın bir arkadaşım adaya davet etti, benimle gelir misin?"

Elimde olmadan gülümsedim.

Bu ilkti ama son değildi öyleyse...

Gider miyim?

Giderim...

Doğrusu yeniden görüşüp görüşmeyeceğimizi, tümüyle ortadan kaybolup kaybolmayacağını bilmiyordum.

Çünkü evden çıkmadan önce kahvelerimizi içerken yine her zamanki gibi konuşmuştuk. Hatta beni uğurlarken yine yanaklarımdan öpmüştü.

Ve eğer aramazsa, bugünün hayatımda özel bir gün olarak kalacağına, bundan asla pişman olmayacağıma ama o zaman onu asla aramayacağıma kendi kendime söz vermiştim.

Tabii ki içimden bir ses ondan birşey geleceğini söylüyordu.

Ve geldi de...

O yüzden yatağın üstünde yarı çıplak oturmuş elimde küçük kağıt parçası, onun kargacık burgacık yazısı, kendi kendime gülümsüyordum.

Bunun nereye varacağını bilmiyorum.

Bildiğim nereye çağırsa gideceğim...

Ama ona bunu söylemeyeceğim...

Korktuğunu biliyorum çünkü.

Evet, faytona binmek istiyorum, hem de arabacının yanına oturup çıngırağı çalmak...

Vapurun saati ve iskelenin adı vardı notun altında...

Kuşlara simit atıyorum.

Vapurun güvertesinde rüzgar saçlarımı savururken...

Bugün onunla dışarıda ilk günümüz.

Martılar bizi izliyor. Deniz durgun ama rüzgar esiyor.

Biraz ürperiyorum, bana yine ceketini veriyor.

İskeleye iniyoruz. Kimseler yok.

Faytonun yanında küçük tay bizimle yürüyor. Tepeye çıkıyoruz. Faytoncu çıngırağı çalıp duruyor.

Beyaz kocaman köşkün önünde duruyoruz.

Siyah büyük bir köpekle, saçlarını kalemle toplamış sarışın bir kadın kapıyı açıyor.

Büyük dağınık bahçedeki sofraya oturuyoruz.

Köpek beni kokluyor. "Meraklanma ısırmaz, cüssesine bakma," diyor kadın...

Sakallı, şişman bir adam geliyor. Onu tanıyorum. Ünlü bir oyuncu... Ferhat'la kucaklaşıyorlar. Bana ondan sözetmemişti...

Yan gözle beni süzdüklerini hissediyorum. Benden haberleri olmadığı belli. Buraya başka kadınlarla da geldi mi? Gelmiştir.

Ben de onlardan biri olmalıyım. Belki de onun için böyle bakıyorlar. Fazla mı küçüğüm onlar için?

Elimi ayağımı nereye koyacağımı bilemiyorum.

Sarışın kadın huzursuzluğumu anlamış gibi benimle konuşuyor, ne kadar eski arkadaş olduklarını anlatıyor.

Yeni sahneleyeceği oyundan sözediyor adam. Kadın rollerini erkeklerin, erkek rollerini kadınların oynayacağı bir oyun.

Bir rulo kağıt getiriyor. Üzerinde çizimler var. "Dekor için bana akıl vermen lazım," diyor Ferhat'a, "kendimce çiziktirdim ama istediğim gibi olmadı..."

Önümdeki peynirlerle oyalanıyorum onları dinlerken...

Sonra birden, "Biliyor musun," diyor Ferhat, "Ebru çok güzel kostümler çiziyor, bu yıl Londra'ya tasarım eğitimi görmeye gidecek..."

Kızarıyorum.

Adam piposunu yakıyor. O an'a kadar benimle hiç konuşmadı. Göz göze bile gelmedi.

"Öyle mi?" diyor bana dönüp, "tiyatroyu sever misiniz?"

"Evet," diyorum, "severim..."

"Peki piyes okur musunuz?"

Bütün ünlü oyuncular gibi etkileyici ama sahte bir sesi var.

Herkes bana bakıyor. Çayımdan bir yudum alacaktım, vazgeçiyorum, bardağı tabağa bırakıyorum.

"Aslında," diyorum, "piyes okumayı daha çok severim."

Piposunu çakmakla yeniden ateşliyor.

"Öyle mi? Niye?"

"Çünkü o zaman sahneyi, giysileri, dekoru, karakterleri gözümde istediğim gibi canlandırabiliyorum..."

Elindeki aletle tütünü bastırıyor..

"İşte bu hoşuma gitti, o zaman belki bizim oyunun kostümlerini de gözünüzde canlandırabilirsiniz...."

Ben aslında sarışın kadınla konuşurken onları dinliyordum. Bunu yalnızca nezaketen söylediğine emindim. O çok ünlü bir oyuncu ve yönetmen. Ama yine de dayanamadım.

"Buna cesaret edebilir miyim bilmem," dedim, "ama erkeklerin kadın, kadınların erkek rolü oynayacağı bir oyunun kostümlerini çizmek gerçekten de çok güzel olurdu..." durdum, kızardım, "Keşke yapabilseydim..."

Ferhat bana baktı. Gülümsedi.

"Neden olmasın," dedi, "en azından denemelisin..."

"Ama," dedim, "ben hiç böyle birşey yapmadım, nasıl olacağını da bilmiyorum..."

Adam piposunu tablaya bıraktı, gülerek, "Aslına bakarsanız, ben de ilk kez yapıyorum ve nasıl olacağını bilmiyorum..." dedi.

Şaşkın şaşkın baktım. Bu gerçek miydi?

Adam masadan kalktı, içeri gitti ve elinde şarapla geri döndü.

"Öyleyse," dedi, "kutlamalar için asla erken sayılmaz, değil mi Hümeyra Hanım..."

Kadın gidip içerden kadehleri getirdi.

"O zaman yeni kostüm tasarımcımıza kadeh kaldıralım..."

Akşamüstü yürüyüşe çıktığımızda artık ben de onlarla aynı yaştaydım. Geldiğimden beri yanımdan ayrılmayan Papi'yle beraber adanın en tepesinden aşağıya bakıyorduk.

Ben buraya Ferhat'la bir gün geçirmek için gelmiştim. Faytona binmek, elele gezmek, eski filmlerdeki gibi ağaçların arasında koşturmak için...

Komik mi?

Ama öyleydi.

Şimdiyse bambaşka bir yerde bulmuştum kendimi…

Bütün günü yeni sahnelenecek oyunla ilgili konuşurken…

Ve o oyunun giysilerini ben tasarlayacaktım.

İskeleye geldik. Yaşlı adam niyet çekiyordu. Küçük tavşanın gösterdiği kağıt parçasını alıp bize verdi. "Bir hazine var seni bekleyen/ uzaktan sana seslenen/ aç kulağını dinle/ içindeki sesi izle…"

"Aa ne güzelmiş," dedim.

"Unutma sakın bunu," dedi niyetçi.

"Unutmam," dedim.

Vapur karanlıkta geri dönerken başımı omuzuna koydum.

"Ne o?" dedi, "yoruldun mu? Yoksa hazineyi mi düşünüyorsun?"

Hayır, yorulmadım. Sana bütün bunlar gerçek mi diye sormak istiyorum ama sormayacağım.

Çünkü gerçek olmamasından çok korkuyorum.

Ve kimbilir belki de hazineyi bulmaktan çok onu aramak güzeldir…

Bu aslında beklenmedik birşey oldu. Çünkü bu sayede Ferhat'la rahatlıkla görüşebilecektim. O, oyunun dekorlarını yaparken ben de kostümlerini tasarlayacaktım.

Anneanneme, rastlantı eseri ünlü oyuncu ve karısıyla tanıştığımı, onların bana böyle bir teklif yaptığını, Ferhat'ın da işin içinde olduğunu söyledim.

"Selçuk Bey sana böyle bir teklifte mi bulundu? Bak şimdi gözüme iyice girdi, her zaman gençlerle çalışmak lazım derim..."

Sare Hanım buna sandığımdan çok sevindi. Onları eve de çağırdı ama adada oturdukları için fırsat bulup gelemediler.

Derken provalar başladı. Oyun, birbirini tanımayan iki çiftle ilgiliydi. Kayağa gittikleri küçük dağ kasabasındaki otelin barında karşılaşıyorlar. Geldikleri kentten, çocukluklarından, ortak tanıdıklardan sözederlerken sohbet derinleşiyor. İlişkiler, aldatma, evlilik üzerine zaman zaman tartışmanın şiddetlendiği, zaman zaman sırların ortaya saçıldığı bir konuşmaya dönüşüyor. Birlikte geçen uzun yılların içinde unutulmuş anılar, gizlenmiş kırgınlıklar, sırlar ortaya çıkıyor.

Oyundaki erkekler kadın giysileri giyiyor, kadınlarsa erkek...

Oyunu okuyup işin içine girince biraz paniğe kapıldım. Neyse ki Selçuk Bey'in kafasında herşey yerli yerindeydi. Benim işim aslında yepyeni kostümler çizmek değil de, oyunculara ne giydireceğimi bulmaktı.

Eh bunun için Tolga'dan iyi yardımcı olur mu? Gezmediğimiz yer kalmadı tabii... Tiyatronun deposundan Sare Hanım'ın gardırobuna kadar her yeri talan ettik.

Galiba birini tanımanın en iyi yollarından biri onunla çalışmakmış.

Kafamdakileri kağıtlara aktarıp, örnekler getirip heyecanla anlatırken Ferhat beni dinliyor, bu olmaz, o olmaz demiyor, ama saatler sonra bakıyordum ki ilk anlattıklarımla son geldiğimiz yer arasında dağlar kadar fark var.

Ama sanki o bunları söylememiş de hepsini ben bulmuşum gibi hissediyordum.

"Acaba" diyordu örneğin, "bu iki renk biraz fazla mı olur? Tabii özellikle seçmediysen..."

Birisi benimle konuşmasını görse, yıllardır bu işi yaptığıma inanabilirdi.

O kadar rahat ve sakindi ki, bütün gerginliğim on dakikada gidiveriyordu.

Bazen saatlerce orada oturup kitap karıştırıyordum.

"Bak ne buldum dün akşam, belki ilgini çeker," diye bir kitap getiriyordu.

Bazen kahvesini içerken başımı çeviriyordum ki öylece dalmış bana bakıyor.

Ama tabii ki her gidişimde ona söyleyeceklerimi filan unutuyor ve onu görür görmez üstüne atlıyordum.

Birdenbire bütün o yabancılık, ürkeklik, çekingenlik uçup gitmişti.

Sonra gün geldi ve şaşkınlıkla farkettim.

Eve dönmüştüm, yatağın üzerinde dergi karıştırıyordum. Dergide okuduğum yazıya güldüm ve dönüp sanki oradaymış gibi ona anlatmak istedim.

Bu kadar kısa sürede nasıl olduysa ona alışmıştım.

Konuşmasına, gülmesine, saçlarımı okşamasına, bana sarılmasına, öpmesine, yanımda öylece oturmasına, dalıp gitmesine, eliyle saçlarını geri atışına, uzun, ince, güzel parmaklarına...

Sanki yıllardır tanırmış gibi...

Oysa daha yeni başlamıştı. Hatta başlayan neydi ondan bile emin değildim ama o gece ilk kez "peki sonra ne olacak?" diye düşündüm, korktum.

Bunu bu kadar erken düşündüğüm için korktum.

Çünkü bazen biri sıradan bir rastlantıyla hayatınıza girer ama hayatınızdan çıktığı zaman geriye kalanın ne olacağını bilemezsiniz.

Yok canım bunu şimdi uyduruyorum. Yoksa o sıralar bunlar aklımın ucundan bile geçmiyordu.

Küçük kasabada duruyor tren. Çay söylüyorum kendime. Keşke tüm bunları yazabilseydim. Anlatılamayacak ayrıntıları, unutulmaz saatleri, rüyayla gerçeğin arasındaki gelgitlerimi...

Ama en çok da ne hissettiğimi... Galiba asıl imkansız olan bu...

Yalnızca birkaç durak kaldı.

Düşünmeyi unutmuşum. Belki de üzüleceğim için hep yaptığım gibi bütün bunları hatırlamayı bırakmışım.

Şimdi böyle hepsini yeniden hatırlamak, belki de gerçek kimliğimi bulmak için çok az zamanım var...

İnsan hayatında sevmediği, istemediği ayrıntıları gizleyerek, unutarak, belleğin tavanarasına tıkıştırarak mutlu olabilir mi?

Başkalarını belki ama bir hayat boyu kendini kandırabilir mi?

Ben öyle olacağını sanıyordum.

Şimdi böyle bir anda, bu dönüm noktasında ansızın bütün bu karşılaşmalar, yüzleşmeler yalnızca rastlantı olabilir mi?

Bu bir başlangıç mı? Yoksa son mu?

Çayımı içerken, evi, annemi, anneannemi ne çok özlediğimi anlıyorum. Bizim çaylara hiç benzemiyor.

Karşımda oturan adamın sorularına kısa cevaplar veriyorum. Benim yaşlarımda bir kızı olduğunu, evlenip uzak bir kente yerleştiğini, torunlarını görmek için bunca yolu geldiğini anlatıyor. Bütün hayatını birlikte geçirdiği eşini geçen yıl kaybetmiş. Onu, belki de yıllarca çalışıp edindiği, küçük, bahçeli evinde tek başına yemeğini hazırlarken, yerken, televizyon izlerken düşünüyorum. Yeni bir hayat kurması için çok mu geç?

"Karımın da senin gibi yeşil gözleri vardı ve sabahları ona bakınca işe gitmek bana hiç ağır gelmezdi..." diyor.

Neden mutluluk anları hep hüzünle gölgeleniyor?

Yaz sabahı parlayan güneşle kendimi denize atmak isterken birdenbire bulutun ışıkları kapatması gibi...

O anlatırken beni burada sanıyor ama değilim. Ben şu anda çok uzakta, bambaşka bir yerdeyim ve orada olmaktan mutluyum.

O yaza dönmek ve hep orada kalmak istiyorum.

Ferhat bir resim çizmişti. Cennet gibi bir yerde sayısız insan denize giriyor, çocuklar rengarenk deniz toplarıyla oynuyor, tam keşmeşkeş ama yukarıda kara bir bulut bütün ışığı değiştirmiş, herkesin mutlu olduğu an, kasvetli bir havaya bürünmüş.

Bana resmi gösterdiği zaman elimle bulutu kenara çekmek istediğimi söyledim.

Eline fırçayı alıp bulutu kenara çekti.

Sonra baktı ve güldü.

"Galiba bu benim en neşeli resmim oldu," dedi.

Yalnızca resimde değil gerçekte de o bulutu kenara çektiğini biliyor muydu benim için?

Ne tuhaf, onunla hiç ikimiz hakkında konuşmadık. Ne yaptığımızı, bunun nasıl bir ilişki olduğunu, nereye varacağını...

Bunları hiç konuşmadık. Herşey nasıl kendiliğinden olduysa öylece sürüp gidiyordu. Sanki incecik bir ipin üstünde yürür gibi... O da benim gibi her an düşünüyor muydu? Yanında olmadığım zamanlarda beni özlüyor muydu? Gözlerime baktığı zamanlar duyduklarımı her zaman hissediyor muydu?

Sormazdım.

Zaman geçiyordu ve belki hayatta en çok istediğim şey gerçekleşecekken, ben zamanı durdurmak, ertelemek, burada daha fazla kalmak istiyordum.

O zamana kadar hiç birşeye, hiç kimseye bağlandığımı hissetmediğim için başıma gelenin ne olduğunu anlamıyordum.

Bir arkadaşımın sevgilisi bir akşam ortadan kaybolmuştu. Kız onu her yerde aramış ama bulamamıştı. Ertesi gün çocuk ortaya çıktığında kıyametleri kopartmıştı. Tek düşündüğü oğlanın onu aldattığıydı.

Başına birşey gelmiş olabileceğini düşünmemişti bile.

Ferhat ortadan kaybolduğunda ben korkardım. Ona birşey olmasından, başına bir kötülük gelmesinden...

Hakkında söylenenler umurumda bile değildi.

Ve ona çok fazla şey söylemezdim. Çünkü o da benim gözlerime bakarken, beni öperken, ona yapışmışken ne hissettiğimi anlamıyorsa sözcükler daha fazlasını anlatamaz...

Benim şimdi gizli bir hayatım vardı. En yakın arkadaşlarımın bile bilmediği...

Tabii farkındaydım. Bu benim hayatımın en güzel zamanıydı ama o kimbilir kaç kadınla benzer şeyler yaşamıştı.

Bazen onun tümüyle bana ait olduğunu düşünürdüm bazen de bütün bunların yalnızca benim hayalim olduğunu.

Bir resmi vardı. Öyle bir boyayla boyamıştı ki zaman içinde resim yokolup gidecek belki yalnızca desenlerin izi kalacaktı.

Belki bizimki de böyleydi.

Uçup gidecek ve yalnızca izleri kalacak...

Onunla sevişmek...

Mutluluktu...

Beni oradan, şimdiye kadar yaşadığım yerden, bütün bağlılıklardan, yerçekiminden bile koparıp alan, uçan halının üstünde gidermiş gibi bambaşka ülkelere götüren birşeydi.

Öyle güzeldi ki manzara... Kimsenin ulaşamayacağı kadar yukarıdan herşey ne kadar da küçük, önemsiz görünüyordu.

Heyecandı...

Belki de hayatımda duymadığım kadar büyük bir heyecan. Daha evden ona gitmek üzere çıkarken ya da aynanın karşısında hazırlanırken başlayan o çarpıntı.

Korkuydu...
Dünyanın en güzel sevişmelerinin adı neden korku olsun ki?
Kaybedecek olmaktan mı?
Bunun bir gün biteceği korkusu mu?
Başkasıyla asla böyle olmayacağını düşünmenin korkusu mu?
Onun benim gibi hissetmediğini düşünmenin korkusu mu?
Belki de hepsi.

Huzurdu...
Ait olduğun, kimsenin sana dokunamayacağı, güvenli bir yatakta uyumak gibi... Bütün büyüklerin yanlarında olduğu bahçede, yaz akşamüstü öylesine dolaşan dertsiz çocuklar gibi...

Gizemdi...
Çünkü bilmediğim kapılardan geçerken sonra neler olacağını bilmiyordum. Bu biriyle değil de sanki orada olmayan birşeyle, tanımlanmaz, elle tutulmaz, görülmez bir varlıkla sevişmek gibiydi.

Oyundu...
Tümüyle yetişkinlere ait gibi görünse de, belki başka kimselere söylenmeyecek sözcükler içerse de, herkesten gizlediklerimizi ortaya döküversek de aslında çocukça, oyunsu bir yanı vardı bütün bu hareketlerin. Ve o kapılar açıldıkça merakla sonrakine ulaşmak için gitmekten kendimi alamıyordum.

Bağlılıktı...
Belki bazı erkekler içinize yalnızca girip çıkar. Bazense orada sonsuza dek kalır.
Ben o hep içimde kalsın istiyordum.

Yalnızlıktı...

Bütün o coşku anları, yükseliş, kopuş, çığlıklar, kendinden geçmeler, baş dönmesi, titremeler, kasılmalar bittiğinde gelen yalnızlık.

Özgürlüktü...

Belki yalnızca kendi hayatım boyunca değil, geçmişten, binlerce yıl ötesinden gelen kalıpların, yargıların, utancın, cezalandırılma korkusunun uçup gittiği anlardı çünkü. Kendinle tümüyle çıplak kaldığın ve beğensen de beğenmesen de kim olduğunu gördüğün bir aynaydı.

Oyunun ilk sahnelendiği gece kalbim yerinden fırlayacak gibiydi.

Son provayı izlediğim halde sanki ilk kez görüyormuş gibi nefesimi tutarak izledim oyunu.

Işıklar yandı ve alkış koptu.

Oyuncular tek tek ve birlikte gelip selam verdiler.

Sonra ismimi duydum. Ferhat elimden tutup kaldırmasa ne olduğunu anlamayacaktım.

Bizi de çağırıyorlardı sahneye...

Hayatımda ilk ve herhalde son kez sahnede alkışların arasında çiçek aldım.

Hem de yanımda Ferhat'la...

Oyuncularla birlikte selam verirken seyirci ayakta alkışlıyordu.

Elini sımsıkı tutuyordum.

Annem, anneannem, Yıldız Teyze, Saniye, tam karşımda en önde...

Niye ağladığımı bilmiyorum.

Ama onlar da ağlıyordu.

Eve elimde rengarenk çiçeklerle döndüm.
Neredeyse herkes bizimle gelmişti.
Tabii ki kutlama anneannemde yapılacaktı.
Ferhat'a bakıyordum ve gidip ona sarılıp öpmek istiyordum.
Bunu o kadar çok istiyordum ki anlatamam.
Ama yapamadım. Annem, anneannem, Tolga herkes oradaydı.
Sakallı, gözlüklü bir adam gitar çalıp şarkı söylüyordu.
Yıllar sonra ünlü olacak bir şarkı. Kimsenin bilmediği bir şarkı.
Ben hala büyünün içindeydim.
"Ne güzelmiş, adı ne bu şarkının?" diye sordu biri...
Kimse bilmiyordu.
Yalnız ikimiz biliyorduk.
Bütün o konuşmaların, bütün o bakışların içinde kimse farketmeden gözgöze geldiğimizde ne olduğunu biliyorduk.
İlk kez herkesin içinde sabaha kadar birlikteydik.
Birlikte birşey yapmıştık. Elele sahneye çıkıp selam vermiştik. Birlikte alkışlanmıştık.
Hayatın içinde, beklenmedik bir anda sizi mutlu eden ve hiç unutulmayacak o yaz esintilerinden biriydi.
O esintiyle içimden birşey uçuyormuş gibi geldi bana o gece.

Tam da o eski filmlerdeki dış sesin söylediği gibi "günler günleri kovaladı..."

Bütün yerlere yaz bir gün gibi geçip gitti gerçekten de...

Hiç bilmediğim yerlere, geleceğe doğru yola çıkıyordum ama aynı zamanda içimde bir burukluk vardı.

Onunla ilgili düşündüklerimi ona hiç söylemedim. Aklıma eseni anlatırken yüzüne bakışımı kim görse anlamaz mıydı?

Ama ben yine de belli etmemek için elimden geleni yapmıştım.

O son buluşmamızda, yola çıkmadan önce birdenbire neredeyse herşeyi anlatacaktım ama yapmadım.

Bunun bir yaz aşkı olmadığını biliyordum. Ama onun ne düşündüğünü bilmiyordum. Çünkü o da söylemezdi. Sanki ne varsa böyle kendiliğinden olmuş, kendiliğinden bu yola girmiş, anlatmaya, konuşmaya gerek kalmamış gibiydi.

Zaten bilmezdim ki bunları. Ne yapmak gerekir, ne söylemek gerekir, nasıl davranmak gerekir...

Yalnızca içimden geldiği gibi davranmıştım.

Belki de çok hızlı olmuştu. Araya zaman ve uzaklık girince tüm bunlar değişecekti belki.

O gün daha çok orada neler yapacağımdan, yeni hayatımdan sözettik. Ben aslında fazla konuşmadım. Daha çok ona bakıyordum. Sanki bu anları belleğime yerleştirmek ister gibi.

Her nedense o gün bütün terslikler üstüste gelmiş, iki ayağımız her zaman olduğu gibi son gün bir pabuca girmiş ve yalnızca kısa süre görüşebilmiştik.

Eve geldiğimde herkes nereye kaybolduğumu soruyordu.

Ne garip, oysa gitmeden önce onunla bu son görüşmeyi çok farklı düşünmüştüm.

O da birşey söylemiyordu. Belki bu gizli kalmış aşk hikayesi, yıllar sonra hatırlayınca gülümseyeceği bir anı olarak kalacaktı.

Kimbilir belki o da benim gibi konuşmaya başlarsak bunun bir vedaya dönüşebileceğinden korkuyordu. Oysa şimdi herşey olduğu gibi kalmış olacaktı. Herhangi bir söz vermeden. Bir karar vermeden. Gelecek için plan yapmadan.

Ve biz bir gün, kısa süre sonra, ("Zaten konuşuruz, hem sen tatilde gelirsin," diyordu) kaldığımız yerden yeniden başlayabilirdik.

İçimdeki ses belki de böyle olmayacağını, gider gitmez beni unutacağını, kısa süre içinde başkasını bulacağını söylüyor ama ben o sesi o an hiç duymak istemiyordum.

Zaten o aptal filmlerde günler günleri kovalayınca ondan sonra hiç de iyi şeyler olmazdı.

Kapıdan çıkarken sarılıp öptü ve bana küçük, kadife bir kese verdi.

"Bunu yanından ayırma, seni koruyacak küçük bir tılsım..."

O minicik çok eski bir heykelcikti. Yeşim taşından çok güzel küçücük bir kedi. Gözlerinde iki parlak taş vardı.

"Demek bu benim küçük muhafızım..." dedim gülerek.

"Evet, zamanında bir prensesi korumuş, seni de koruyacak..."

"Peki," dedim, "onu yanımdan ayırmayacağım..." Tam giderken döndüm, "eğer onu ovalarsam, çıkıp gelir misin yanıma?"

"Eğer çok istersen, gelirim," dedi.

Taksiye bindim. Kediciği okşadım, gülümsedim.

Hayır ağlamayacağım.

Bazı şeyleri ille de söylemek gerekmez.

Biliyorum ben.

Sabahın erken saatinde evden çıkışımız bile tam hengameydi. Neredeyse üç gündür bavul yapmakla uğraşan annem yine de son anda ne unuttum acaba diye söylenip dolaştıkça anneannem de sinirleniyordu.

Tolga gelip bizi aldı, tabii ki hepimiz ağlıyorduk, Saniye arkamızdan su dökmeyi unutmadı.

Tolga'nın annesiyle babası havaalanına geldi.

Birşeyleri geride bırakmak nedense beni hep korkutur. O yüzden tatile gitmeyi, uzak yerleri sevmem.

Tolga yerinde duramıyordu ama ben uçağın penceresinden aşağıda giderek küçülen evlere bakarken ağlamak istiyordum.

Annem de bizimle geldi.

Kimse bunu söylemiyordu ama ben onun neden geldiğini, aslında neden korktuğunu biliyordum.

Uzun süredir daha doğrusu yaz boyunca hastalığım nüksetmemişti. Yine birkaç kez gece ter içinde uyanmıştım. Yine ayaklarım, başım, ellerim ağrıyordu ama ben bunlara artık alışmıştım. Ve kulağımda hiç bitmeyen o derin uğultu...

Güneşli bir İstanbul gününden karanlık Londra akşamüstüne geldik.

Daha yaz yeni bitiyordu ama hava karanlık ve yağmurluydu.

Eve girerken güldüm. İngilizce kitaplarımızdaki merdivenle çıkılan, küçük, iki katlı, kırmızı tuğladan yapılmış eski evlerden biriydi.

Sanki Mrs. Brown kapıyı açıp bize merhaba diyecek gibiydi.

Biraz daha küçük olsak tavanarasında kimbilir ne oyunlar kurardık.

Eşyalarımızı yerleştirip dolaşmaya çıktık.

Ev eski ve küçüktü ama hem okula hem de merkeze çok yakındı.

Şimdi birdenbire bambaşka bir dünyadaydım.

İlk kez başka bir ülkede, yağmurun ışıkları bozduğu bu akşamda, kentin kalabalığında, içimde ayrılık, hüzün, mutluluk, yeniden başlamanın heyecanı, karmakarışık duygular içinde yürüyordum.

Meydandaki atlıkarınca koca kente çocuksu bir görünüm veriyordu.

Çok uzun zaman sonra ilk kez annemi de heyecanlı gördüm. Sanki o çocukluk yıllarımdaki hali birden geri gelmiş gibiydi.

Yemek boyunca ertesi gün neler yapılması gerektiğini, neler alınacağını anlatıp durdu.

Elindeki küçük fotoğraf makinesiyle habire fotoğraf çekiyor, bize de poz verdiriyordu.

Tolga, babasının tüm söylenmelerine karşın edebiyat sosyolojisi diye ne olduğunu bilmediğimiz bir bölüme kaydını yaptırmıştı.

"Hem içinde edebiyat var hem de havalı, tam benlik," diye gülüyordu.

Tabii ki babası onun işletme, ekonomi gibi bir bölüm okuyup geri döndüğünde işlerin başına geçmesini istiyordu ama Tolga'nın bunu yapmayacağını hepimiz bilyorduk.

Daha birkaç yıl önce, bana, "Babamın bütün hesaplarını, yatırımlarını buldum, eğer o ölünce bütün işleri batırsam bile hayatımın sonuna kadar bir elim yağda bir elim balda yaşayabilirim..." demişti.

"Seni evlatlıktan reddederse görürsün," diye dalga geçtim.

"O ancak filmlerde oluyor, Hulusi Kentmen Tarık Akan'ı evlatlıktan reddediyor ama onu da öğrendim bizde öyle bir yasa yokmuş..."

Tabii o sırada buna gülüp geçmiştim. İnsan lise yıllarında böyle planlar yapar da hayat bunlara pek izin vermez. Bir anda kendini bambaşka bir yerde buluverirsin. Ama Tolga'nın fikri pek değişmiş gibi değildi. Asıl derdi burada özgür olmak, yazılarını yazmak, müzelere, sergilere, konserlere gitmekti.

Aklım İstanbul'da, Ferhat'ta olsa da bu yabancı kentin sokaklarında yürürken keyfim yerine gelmişti. Çocukken ikimize ait evimiz olsa, keşke kardeş olsak ve aynı evde otursak diye konuşurduk. Belki artık çocuk değildik ama hayalimiz gerçekleşmişti işte.

Yeni insanlar tanıyacaktık, yeni yerler keşfedecektik, belki kendimizle ilgili bilmediğimiz şeyler öğrenecektik...

Tolga'nın daha önce kitaplardan gösterdiği görkemli eski yapıların, sarayın, müzelerin, heykellerin arasından yürürken yeni hayatın ilk gününe adım attığımı biliyordum.

İçimde tuhaf bir duygu vardı.

Tolga'ya sarıldım yolun ortasında.

"Evet," dedim, "işte yaptık... Buradayız..."

Annem şaşkın şaşkın biz birbirimize sarılmış dönerken şemsiyeyi üstümüze tutmaya çalışıyordu.

Henüz bilmiyordum ama galiba bu kentten en çok hatırlayacağım şey yağmur olacaktı.

İnsan ne zaman geçmişi düşünür?

Geleceği düşünmek istemediği zaman mı?

An'da olmak acı verdiği zaman mı?

Belki de onun için şimdi bütün bunları yeniden sanki roman yazar gibi hatırlamaya çalışıyorum.

Korktuğumu biliyorum ama korkmamış gibi yapıyorum.

Hep böyle yaptım. Hayatım boyunca.

Ferhat'la yeni tanıştığım, evine gittiğim ilk günlerde rüyamda çok garip bir yer görmüştüm. Tümüyle biçimsiz, bildiklerimize benzemeyen bir evdi.

Birbirine tam bağlanmayan katlardan oluşan, duvarları olmayan bir ev.

Hiç tanımadığım garip bir adam oturuyordu orada. Niye orada olduğumu bilmiyorum. Bazı insanlar yemek yiyor, bazıları oyun oynuyor, ev sahibi herkese emirler yağdırıyordu. Canlı köpekler, oyuncak trenler sanki yerçekimi yokmuş gibi havada uçuyordu.

O adamdan da o evden de korkup gitmek istedim ama yapamadım. Onun üst kattaki odasını görmek istiyordum. O başkalarıyla ilgilenirken oraya girdim.

Büyük ağaçlar vardı odada. Aynı zamanda sanki akvaryumdaymışız, suyun içindeymişiz gibi ama su yoktu. Yalnızca suyu hissediyordum.

Gerçeküstü bir resmin içinde gibiydim ama gerçekti. Şaşkınlıkla eşyaların arasında dolaşırken ev sahibi zorla sürüklediği kocaman, eski bir bavulla geldi. "Ben de sizi arıyordum, bavulunuzu getirdim, bundan sonra burada kalacaksınız..." dedi ve nefes nefese çıkıp gitti.

Kapıları, duvarları olmayan bir ev. Sanki sonsuz boşluktaki uzay istasyonu gibi... Burada ne işim var, bu tanımadığım adam kim, neden burada kalmam gerekiyor diye düşünüyordum ama öte yandan da tüy gibi hafif hissediyordum kendimi. Bütün bunları düşünmek, kaygılanmak istemiyordum.

Tanıdık birşeyler, tanıdık birilerini arıyordum ama yoktu.

Burada tek başımaydım.

Bir an öldüğümü düşündüm.

Rüyamın içinde öldüğümü...

Öldüğümü ve yanımda tanıdığım kimse olmadığını...

Uyandığımda uzun süre bu rüyanın etkisinden kurtulamadım. Ama korkmamıştım. Aksine yeniden uykuya dalıp neler olacağını görmek istiyordum ama tabii ki yapamadım.

Garip olan şu ki, Londra'ya gittiğimiz o gece biraz yorgun uykuya daldığımda aynı evi yine gördüm.

Ama o rüyayı daha önce gördüğümü hatırlamadım. Yalnızca bu evi nereden tanıyorum diye düşündüm.

Tren ilerliyor. Biraz uykum var. O, kimseye, doktorlara bile anlatamadığım uyuşma başladı yine her yerimde. Başımdan ayaklarıma kadar. Kulağımı sanki incecik bir matkapla deliyorlarmış gibi ince bir sızı ve kesilmeyen ses...

Bileklerimde yine o morluklar var.

Birkaç ilacın saati geldi, onları içiyorum.

Hepsi gerçekten geçecek mi?

Buraya gelme kararını verirken çok kısa süre içinde hiç beklenmedik şeyler olacağını bilmiyordum. Onun için de kendi kendime ya hepsi geçecek ya da o garip ev gibi yerler göreceğim uzun, sonsuz bir uykuya dalacağım, diyordum.

Ama şimdi...

Yolun sonuna geliyoruz ama ben bu yolculuğun bitmesini istemiyorum.

Tıpkı o rüyanın bitmesini istemediğim gibi...

Yapamaz mıyım? Son istasyonda inip başka bir trene binip tüm bunları unutup geri dönemez miyim?

O yalnızca birkaç saat uzakta... Nereye gittiğimi bilmiyor.

Yeniden yanına dönmek, yeniden yıllar öncesine, o ilk tanıştığımız günlere dönmek istiyorum. Bir zaman hatasını geriye almak neden imkansız olsun?

Sarışın, tulum giymiş çocuk bahçeli küçük bir evin önünde bisikletine binmiş bize el sallıyor.

Kimbilir kaç kez önünden geçip giden tanımadığı hayatlara böyle el salladı, sallayacak.

Ama sonra nereye gittiğini, ne yaptığını bilmediği o insanları unutup yoksul, eski evine geri dönecek.

Küçük çocuk hızla küçülüyor, kaybolup gidiyor.

Gözümü kapıyorum ve yalnızca üzerindeki lacivert tulumu görüyorum.

Neden korkuyorum, ölümden mi?

Aslında hayattan da hep korkmadım mı?

İnsanın başına gelecek en güzel şey ne olabilir?

Belki bir hastalıktan kurtulmak...

Tabii bir süreliğine...

Bir sabah uyanamayacağınızı bilirsiniz. Ama bir sabah birdenbire yirmi yaş genç uyanacağınızı düşünemezsiniz.

Herkes günün birinde deprem olacağını, kaza geçirebileceğini, ya da aklını kaybedebileceğini bilir ve aynı zamanda mucizeler olmayacağını da...

Ama dünya tıpkı benim rüyamdaki gibi öylesine renkli ve bilinmezlerle dolu ki herkes hayatın sonu olduğunu bilmiyormuş gibi yaşıyor.

Zamanın içinden geçiyorum. Hayatların içinden.

Mutluluk ancak anlarda var diye düşünüyorum. Kısa, geçip giden zamanlarda...

Hep öyle düşündüm.

Hayat, güneşin doğuşuyla başlayıp batışıyla biten, yorucu, zor, çileli bir uğraşın sonunda toplanan küçücük çiçeklerin kokusunu aldığında hissettiğin kadar aslında...

Hepsi bu.

Rüyamdaki o ev belki asla gerçek bir ev kuramayacağımızı anlatıyordu. O adam Ferhat'a hiç benzemese de belki o ev onun eviydi.

Onu düşünüyorum.

Olmak istediğim tek yer onun yanı şu an.

Neden söylemedim peki?
Bunca yıl sonra bütün bunlar sıradan rastlantılar olabilir mi?

Doktor, "Yanınızda kimse olacak mı?" diye sormuştu. "Hayır", dedim. Bütün belgeleri imzaladım.

Bu benim hayatım.

Benim ölümüm.

Belki de uzaklıklar aşkı daha yakına getirir.

Yeni bir hayatın içinde, tanımadığım bu kentte yabancıyken kimi zaman çok neşeli kimi zaman hüzünlü dolaşırken, olur olmaz yerlerde aklıma o gelince gözlerim dolarken kendi kendime dedim ki, bunda üzülecek ne var, pek çok insan yanında biri varken bile böyle bir çarpıntı hissetmiyor, içinde bu duygu varken o uzakta olmuş olmamış ne farkeder?

Bazı insanların gözlerinde tam olarak adlandıramadığınız birşey vardır. Farklı birşey. Sanki içinizi görüyormuş gibi bir bakış. Sanki gözlerinizin içine bakarken o an ne düşündüğünüzü hissedermiş gibi... Sizi bazen üzebilen, bazen ne olursa olsun mutlu eden, bazen kuşkuya sürükleyen... Sizinle ilgili sizin bile bilmediklerimizi bilen...

Bazen sizi kendine çeken bir erkek gibi, bazen kendi içine kapanıp uzaklara gitmiş biri gibi, bazen şaşkın, küçük bir çocuk gibi...

Ama her zaman anlamı olan bir bakış.

Bir keresinde heyecanla konuşurken birden durdu ve "Beni dinlemiyorsun değil mi, ne oldu?" diye sordu.

Evet dinlemiyordum. Daha doğrusu dinlediğimi sanıyordum ama ne söylediğinin farkında bile değildim.

Dedim ki: "Gözlerinin içine girdim ve sanki içindeki gizli geçitlerde kayboldum."

Bu kez düşünceli, ürkek baktı.

"Hayır hayır, öyle değil, orada kaybolmaktan çok memnunum..." durdum, daha alçak sesle içimden geleni söyledim: "hatta galiba orası kendimi en iyi hissettiğim yer..."

Böyle konuştuğum zaman yüzümü okşar ya da bana sarılırdı.

Şimdi düşünüyorum da bana bildik sevgi sözleri söyler miydi, iltifat eder miydi, ara sıra cesaret edip bunları söylediğimde cevap verir miydi?

Hayır, pek sanmıyorum.

Ama sanki o konuşmadan da bana herşeyi anlatırdı. Kimbilir belki de bana öyle gelirdi.

Ama ne önemi var ki?

Asıl olan birinin size söylediklerinden çok hissettirdiği değil midir?

Hem doğrusunu söylemek gerekirse, daha önce güya bana güzel sözler söylemeye çalışan hatta bunu abartan insanlar da tanımıştım ve bazen gerçekten boğazım sıkılıyormuş gibi olup nasıl kaçsam diye düşünmüştüm.

Bazen derler ya sevgi emektir diye...

Hangi sevgi? Belki çocuk sevgisi, anne sevgisi...

Aşk emek filan değildir.

İnsan birine aşık değilse sırf size çok iyi davranıyor diye ona aşık olamazsınız. Evet belki seversiniz, o kadar.

Adamın biri beni el üstünde tutuyor diye ona kalbim çarpacak değil.

En azından benim için bu böyle.

Onun yanında hiç, aşkıma karşılık veriyor mu, benim gibi mi hissediyor, benim gibi her an görmek istiyor mu diye düşünmedim.

Yok yalan söylemeyeyim, tabii düşündüm ama bu pek umurumda olmadı.

Bunları kurup üzülmedim.

Bazen uzun zaman ortadan kaybolduğunda kaygılandım, bazen söylediklerinden, anlattıklarından kendime pay çıkartıp gitmemi mi istiyor diye üzüldüm, kimi zaman artık gitmem gerektiğini düşündüm ama bunlar hep anlık şeylerdi.

Yeniden görüştüğümüzde aklımdaki kuşkuların hepsi o an uçup giderdi.

Genç bir kızın duygularından, ona olan aşkından çok mu gururlanıyordu?

E n'olmuş? Suç muydu bu?

Hatta denilebilir ki onu ayartan bendim.

Bana söz vermiş miydi, bana yalanlar mı uydurmuştu, gitmek istemiştim de gitme diye yalvarmış mıydı? Hayır.

Onun kendine göre hayatı vardı, nasıl istiyorsa öyle yaşıyordu. Ama daha önemlisi, bazıları gibi, herkesin onun düşüncelerine, hayat biçimine uymasını, öyle davranmasını beklemiyordu.

O gözlerde ne vardı? Belki kimsenin belki kendisinin bile bilmediği birşey. Kendi gözlerini görmemişti ki zaten... Benim için böyleydi. Başka bir yerden gelmiş gibi... Uzaktan, hiç görmediğimiz yerlerden... Çok eskiden, belki hayatlarımızdan daha uzun zaman öncesinden...

Evinde olduğumuz bir gün ellerim titremeye başladığında ve anlayacak, hastalığımı farkedecek diye korku içinde bir an önce oradan gitmek istediğimde beni yatağa yüzüstü yatırdı.

Gözlerimi kapatmamı istedi.

Yanıma oturdu. Bana dokunmuyordu ama ellerini üzerimde gezdirdiğini hissediyordum. Başıma doğru geldiğinde sıcaklık arttı. Şaşırdım. Şaşırdım ama gözlerimi açıp bakamadım. Bir süre hiç kıpırdamadan öylece elleri başımın üzerinde durdu. Oradaydı elleri çünkü giderek artan sıcaklığı hissediyordum. Ama dokunmuyordu. Derin derin nefes aldı yalnızca.

Çok kısa sürdü, belki beş, belki on dakika...

Sonra durdu.

"Yavaşça kalkabilirsin," dedi.

Sanki doktorun söylediklerini dinler gibi dediğini yaptım şaşkın şaşkın.

Yatağın kenarına oturdum.

"Bu senin için çok büyük ağırlık," dedi, "en azından şimdilik ondan kurtuldun..."

Ne dediğini anlamadım.

Ayağa kalktım. Koltuğa geçip oturdum. Başım ağrımıyordu ve ellerim de titremiyordu.

Ürpererek ona baktım. Gözlerinde yine o uzaktan, derinlerden gelen bakış vardı.

Bu neydi?

"Ne yaptın?" dedim.

Birden bakışları değişti, gülümsedi, "Birşey yapmadım," dedi, "şimdi başının ağrısı geçti mi?"

Başka yerlerden gelen enerjiler, bilinmeyen boyuta geçebilen insanlar, kozmik bağlar, bilinmeyenden alınan haberler...

Hayır bunlara asla inanmadım.

Yalnız bir keresinde anneannem, "Biz hayatı çok iyi bildiğimizi sanırız ama küçük beynimiz ancak birkaç sözcükle kurabildiğimiz cümleleri anlayacak kadardır, geri kalanları asla bilemeyiz," demişti.

Başımın ağrısının aniden geçmesini anlayamadığım o gün birşey daha oldu. Köşede duran bir teknenin yanına götürdü beni. "Bak," dedi, "sana ismine uygun bir uğraş buldum.." Baktım ama anlamadım. "Bu bir ebru teknesi, bunu sana göndereceğim, annenlere kendin aldığını söylersin, şurada biraz daha büyüğü var, bir dahaki gelişinde sana nasıl yapıldığını gösteririm, çok hoşuna gideceğini ve sana çok iyi geleceğini düşünüyorum..."

Eve döndüğüm zaman başımın yeniden ağrıyacağını düşündüm ama ağrımadı. Huzurlu, gülümsediğim bir uykuya daldım.

Evet, hayatımda ilk kez beni rüyamda bile gülümseten biri vardı.

Önceleri ilk başladığımda ne yaptığımın farkında değildim. Öylesine suyun içine boyaları bırakıyor ve kendiliğinden biçim kazanmalarını sonra da bozulmalarını izliyordum.

Sonra yavaş yavaş renklerin içiçe geçip oluşturduğu ve küçük dokunuşlarınıza direndiği, sanki sizin değil de doğanın istediği biçimlerin ortaya çıkmasını, anların, saniyelerin bile yakalamaya çalıştığınız deseni birdenbire bambaşka birşeye dönüştürdüğü ya da bozup yokettiği inanılmaz bir süreçle karşılaştım.

Resim yapmak gibi değildi. Sürekli devinim, sürekli bir değişim, küçük teknenin içinde sonsuz formlar yaratmak. Ve zamanla orada canlı bir organizmanın farklı biçimlerle bana kendini gösterdiğini benimse yalnızca ona aracılık ettiğimi farkettim.

Bazen yaptıklarım, çiçeğe, göze, kuşa benziyordu bazense varolmayan, yalnızca orada o an için bana kendini gösteren sanki neşeyle göz kırpıp ortadan kaybolan canlılara...

Tıpkı hayata benziyordu. Siz hayal kuruyordunuz ve düzen oluşturmaya çalışıyordunuz ama su canlı gibi kımıldıyor, o mükemmel biçim bozuluyor, kayboluyor, yakalayamıyordunuz yeniden, belki yalnızca o an görüyordunuz ve değişiyordu.

Böylece aslında aynı resmin içinde binlerce resim görüyordunuz.

Zamanla anladım ki bunu bana yalnızca ismim yüzünden vermemişti. O suyun içindeki resimlerle uğraşırken istemediğim şeyleri unutacağımı ya da aksine hatırlayacağımı ve kimi zaman gözyaşıyla, kimi zaman neşeyle o teknenin başında saatler geçireceğimi çok iyi biliyordu.

Aklımdaki deseni çalışıyordum ve az sonra bakıyordum ki bambaşka renkler çıkmış ortaya ve gerçekte akıl edemeyeceğim kadar mükemmel figürler oluşmuş.

Bazen öyle hissederim ki uzaktan bir el dokunuyor bana, o anları yeniden yaratıyor, zamanın geçişini benimle birlikte anlamlandırıyor.

Sonra onları kağıtların üzerine alıyordum ve ertesi gün yeniden baktığımda şaşırıp kalıyordum çünkü çoğunu hatırlamıyordum bile...

Bir keresinde biri bana bunun nasıl bir süreç olduğunu sordu. Tabii ona söyleyemedim ama bence Ferhat'la seviştiğimde hissettiğim şeyle aynıydı. Kaybolmak, unutmak, buradan sonsuzluğa gittiğini, belki de varolmayan birine ait olduğunu hissetmek ve yalnızca mutlu olmak.

Onun için ilk açtığım serginin adını da "Benim Gizli Rüyalarım" koymuştum.

Ama bunlar çok sonra oldu.

Bütün bunların olması için zamanın geçmesi, benim büyümem (büyüdüm mü gerçekten?) pek çok şeyi unutmak ve bazılarını yeniden ilk günkü gibi hatırlamak istemem gerekiyordu belki de...

Kokular, renkler ve desenler çocukluğumdan beri hayatımdı belki ama günün birinde tüm bunların biraraya geleceğini, benim için bambaşka bir dünya oluşturacağını o zamanlar hiç düşünmemiştim.

O küçük teknenin zamanla büyüyeceğini, desenlerin artık kağıtlara değil kumaşlara basılacağını, dünyanın dört bir yanında ipek fularlara, şallara, eşarplara, mendillere hatta elbiselere hayat vereceğini kim bilebilirdi ki?

Oldu işte.

Londra'daki okul benim bildiğim okullara benzemiyordu. Daha çok atölyede öğretmenlerin gözetiminde çalışıyorduk ve kimse bizden kendi söylediklerini yapmamızı istemiyordu. Yalnızca arada gelip düzeltmeler yapıyor ya da önerilerde bulunuyorlardı. Bazen de pek fazla konuşmadan çizdiklerinizi buruşturup atıyorlardı.

Zaman zaman ünlü modacıların, terzilerin atölyelerine gidiyor ve işlerin nasıl yürüdüğünü öğrenmeye çalışıyorduk.

Herkes şimdiden birbirine rakipmiş gibi görünüyordu ama bir yandan da birbirimizin yaptıklarını izliyor ya da aramızda tartışıyorduk.

Farklı yerlerden gelen genç insanların farklı fikirleri, farklı yetenekleri, farklı renkleri, desenleri vardı. Adeta bütün dünya orada ülkelerinin tınılarını, duygularını getiren müzisyenlerden oluşan bir orkestra gibiydik ama aynı zamanda hepimiz yalnızdık.

Temel derslerin dışında eğlenceli görünüyordu ama aynı zamanda kimse size ne yapacağınızı söylemediği için tek başınıza kalakalıyordunuz. Belki de biz böyle alışmadığımız için bu beni biraz zorluyordu.

Bulabildiğim bütün kitapları alıyor, alamazsam kütüphanede onları inceliyor, müzeleri geziyor ve her geçen gün ne kadar az şey bildiğimin ama çok bildiğimi sandığımın farkına varıyordum.

Annem tabii ki evi hemen düzene sokmuş, her gün nereden buluyorsa alıştığımız yemekleri pişiriyor, bazen gündüz gezse de akşam mutlaka bizi evde karşılıyordu.

Sonra bir akşam birdenbire artık geri dönmeye karar verdiğini söyledi.

Tolga'nın buna benden çok sevindiğine eminim. Artık kendi başımıza kalacaktık. Onun için neden böyle ani bir kararla geri döndüğünü sorgulamadım. Geldiğimizden beri hastalanmamıştım, nöbet geçirmemiştim, keyfim yerindeydi, herşey tam da düşündüğümüz gibi gidiyordu. Herhalde artık beni yalnız bırakmasının zamanı geldiğini anladı diye düşündüm.

Tolga doğrusu biraz dağıtmıştı. Annem gittikten sonra bunun daha da kötüye gideceğini biliyordum. Öyle de oldu. Okula gidiyor, derslerine çalışıyordu ama aklı fikri gezmekteydi.

Yıllar sonra ilk kez kimsenin onu yargılamayacağı bir yerdeydi ve üstündeki o büyük baskı ortadan kalkmıştı.

Ama belki de şimdi buradan, uzaktan bakınca, bu yılların getirdiği sınırlamanın kalkması onun için taşınması ağır bir yük olmuştu.

Ferhat'la birkaç kez telefonla konuştuk. Ben ona mektuplar yazdım ama ondan küçük kartlar üzerine çizilmiş resimler ve birkaç satır dışında pek birşey gelmedi.

Aslında yeni şeyler öğrenirken, yeni insanlarla tanışırken, alışamadığım bir kentte hala konuşmakta zorlanırken (trafik bile tersten akıyordu) çok düşünecek zaman kalmıyordu.

Akşamları bütün gün okulda anlatılanları, gösterilenleri yeniden gözden geçiriyor, anlamadıklarımı başka kitaplardan bulmaya çalışıyordum.

Bu benim için büyük şanstı ve yalnızca okula gidip gelerek birkaç yıl geçirmek, sonra elimde diplomayla İstanbul'a dönüp modaevi açmak gibi bir niyetim yoktu. Bu okuldan mezun olan ve ara sokaklarda küçücük, ancak meraklıların geldiği dükkanlar açan genç kadınlara hayrandım. Bambaşka, alışılmamış şeyler tasarlıyorlardı. O yılın moda kumaşlarını, renklerini filan umursamadan... Tümüyle kendi istedikleri gibi...

Zaman buldukça oralara gidiyor, onlarla tanışıyor, yaptıklarını anlamaya çalışıyordum..

Ve tabii haftasonları Tolga'yla küçük eski sinemada izlediğimiz filmler...

Kimi olağanüstü fotoğraflardan oluşan, kimi yalnızca bir kadının bilinç akışını anlatan, kimi karmakarışık bir kentte sizi anlaşılması güç maceralara sürükleyen özel filmlerdi bunlar.

Sanki insan belleğinin sınırlarını zorlayan, onun kısıtlanmış çılgınlığını göstermeye çalışan, belki hepimizin gördüğü yaşadığı şeyleri bambaşka bir biçime sokup sizi şaşırtan acayip filmler.

Aslında tüm bunlar bana heyecan veriyordu. Sinema, konserler, ben fazla içmesem de kalabalık, soğuk barlar... Sergilere gidiyordum ve Ferhat'ı düşünüyordum. Acaba günün birinde o da böylesine ünlü olacak mıydı? Buralarda sergileri açılacak mıydı? Hatta kimbilir eserleri müzelere konulacak mıydı?

Kimi zaman yolda yürürken, kimi zaman uykuya dalarken tabii ki hep aklımdaydı.

Bazen kalkıp ona mektup yazmaya koyuluyor sonra okuyunca yollamaktan vazgeçiyordum. "Bize ne olacak şimdi, biz birlikte miyiz, sen benim sevgilim misin?" gibi şeyler vardı aklımda ama bunları yazınca kendime kızıyor, yırtıp atıyordum.

Bir iki kez telefonlaştık ama telefonda konuşmayı bilmez. Sanki herhangi bir arkadaşımı aramışım gibi okulu, dersleri, neler yaptığımı, hangi sergiye gittiğimi soruyordu. Birden yalnızca gerçek anlamda değil ikimizin arasında da bir mesafe belirmişti.

İnsan bazı şeyleri düşünmek istemese de aklına gelmesini engelleyemiyor. O da böyle sanki gittiğim her yerde bir biçimde, yanımdan hiç ayırmadığım o küçük kediciğin içindeymiş gibi benimleydi.

Göz görmeyince gönül unutur derler.

Hayır unutmuyor aslında. Ama araya başka görüntüler giriyor.

Tolga kısa süre sonra sanatçıların gittiği bir pub'a takılmaya başladı. Ve sonra da genç, çok yakışıklı bir bale öğrencisiyle tanıştı.

Artık birbirimizden gizleyecek birşeyimiz yoktu.

Kıskançlığın ne olduğunu gerçekte ilk kez onlardan öğrenecektim.

Bir gece birlikte gittikleri davetten çıkınca kıyametler kopmuş, Tolga başka biriyle biraz samimi olduğu için yolda kavgaya tutuşmuşlar ve karakolluk olmuşlardı.

Çocuk da onu terkedip gitmişti.

Geç kalmasına alışıktım ama içime doğmuş gibi o gece uyuyamadım. Sabaha karşı geldiğinde hala sarhoştu ve deliler gibi ağlıyordu. Sakinleştirip uyutmam epey zaman aldı.

O hafta evden çıkmayıp yazılar yazdı, ağladı, müzik dinledi.

Neyse ki sonunda cumartesi sabahı çocuk kapıda belirdi.

Onu içeri alırken Tolga, "Hayır, defolup gitsin, onu görmek istemiyorum," diye bağırıyordu. Hemen üstüme yağmurluğumu geçirip kendimi dışarı attım.

Niye hepimiz gerçekte o anda ondan başkasını görmek istemediğimiz halde böyle yaparız?

Yolda yürürken bile bağırışları geliyordu.

Ben kimseyle kavga edemem. Birbirine bağıran insanların yanında durmak istemem. Şuralarda bir yerde tahta var mı diye baktım, benim başıma bunlar gelmesin diye tahtaya vurdum.

Neyse ki işler tatlıya bağlandı ve ertesi cumartesi kendimizi kentin iki saat uzağında harika bir eski zaman kasabasında bulduk. Andrew'nun ailesinden kalma evde onun özenle hazırladığı yemekleri yiyip uçsuz bucaksız kırlarda dolaştık. "Dikkatli basın bu gördüğünüz yeşillikler, dağlar, tepeler hep kraliçenin mülküdür," diye dalga geçiyordu.

Yıllar sonra onu dünyaca ünlü bir balenin ilk gösteriminde alkışlarken bu haftasonunu hatırlayacağımı bilmiyordum tabii.

Nedenini bilmiyorum, belki de o ikisinin ben uzun koltukta uyuklarken klasik müzik eşliğinde şaraplarını içip uzun uzun kitaplardan, şiirden sözetmelerini, kalkıp dans etmelerini görünce, Ferhat'a mektup yazdım.

Ama bu kez bu haftasonunu, evi ama daha önemlisi bütün duvarları süsleyen yüzlerce yıllık tabloları anlatırken birdenbire, ona biriyle tanıştığımı yazdım. Evet benden hoşlanan ve ara sıra buluştuğumuz bir çocuk vardı ama öyle ciddiye alınacak türden değildi. Bunu neden ona yazdım bilmiyorum.

Belki de biliyorum da söylemek istemiyorum.

Bu mektuptan sonra ondan uzun süre ses çıkmadı. Telefon etmeye de çekindim. Kızmış mıydı? Bunları duyunca artık görüşmemenin daha doğru olacağını, ona bunu ima ettiğimi mi düşünmüştü?

Yoksa zaten istediği buydu da bana söyleyememiş, şimdi hazır bahane bulmuşken rahata mı ermişti?

Ne diye durup dururken böyle bir saçmalık yaptım diye kendime kızıyordum tabii.

Kendim yapıp sonra giderek ona kızmaya başladım. İnsan en azından arayıp sormaz mıydı? "Sen ne biçim kızsın, gider gitmez birini mi buldun?" demez miydi?

Ah tabii kendi yeni sevgili bulmadıysa!

Aklıma bunlar geliyor, iyice deliriyordum. Her gün telefon çalacak mı, mektup gelecek mi diye beklemeye başladım. Kendime inanamıyordum. Aklımca onu denemeye mi kalkışmıştım? Biriyle tanıştım diye deliye dönüp koşa koşa buraya gelecek filan mı sanıyordum acaba?

Ne budalayım!

Dayanamayıp Tolga'ya ne yaptığımı anlattım.

"Erkek milleti değil mi hepsi aynı," diye beni güldürdü ama aynı zamanda kızdı. "Deli misin kızım sen, koskoca adama böyle şey söylersen ne yapacak, emin ol karalar bağlamış oturuyordur evinde... Genç aşık iki ay geçmeden yenisini bulmuş! Sence ne düşünüyordur?"

"Zaten sana söyleyende kabahat..."

"Tabii adamı durup dururken kıskandırmaya çalışacak kadar ezik olanda hiç kabahat yok," diye beni iyice çıldırttı.

Şimdi yeniden yazıp durumu düzeltebilir miydim?

Yok ona da elim gitmiyordu.

Anlaşılmaz biçimde tam kendime kızmışken birden ona kızmaya başlıyordum çünkü.

Böyle epey zaman geçti. Sessizlik uzadıkça uzadı. Ne kart, ne mektup, ne telefon...

Demek böyle bitecekmiş dedim kendi kendime yolda yürürken, ağlıyordum ama inadım tutmuştu. Eve gelince kediyi aldım, tam çekmeceye kaldıracaktım ki aklıma geldi. Komik ama ovaladım.

Sihirli lambadan çıkan cin gibi gerçekten gelecek miydi?

Bana öyle söz vermemiş miydi?

Kıyamadım yine çantama koydum.

O yılbaşı kendimi hiç iyi hissetmiyordum. Tolga beni neşelendirmek için evde parti vermek niyetindeydi. Andrew'yla oturup kostüm partisi mi yapsalar dönem partisi mi yapsalar tartışırken bile kavga çıkmış, çocuk yine evden kovulmuştu.

Artık onların bu haline alışmıştım. Çünkü pek neşeli, güzel başlayan akşam birden bir sözle değişiyor, kıyametler kopuyor, bardaklar havada uçuşuyor ve sonunda her zaman Andrew evden çıkıp gidiyordu.

Ama bu fazla uzun sürmüyor, birkaç güne kalmadan yine buluşuyorlar, hiçbirşey olmamış gibi kaldıkları yerden yeniden başlıyorlardı.

Ben hiç yeni yıl havasına girememiştim. Zaten burada kar da yağmıyordu ki...

Mağazaların vitrinleri, sokak ışıklandırmaları, meydanlarda dolaşan Noel Babalar beni pek etkilememişti.

Kendime itiraf edemiyordum ama uzakta da olsa Ferhat'ın varlığı bana neşe veriyordu. Şimdi durup dururken yaptığım saçmalık yüzünden onu kaybettiğime hem inanamıyordum hem de hala ona dargındım.

Hem ona hem kendime...

Tolga iki gün öncesinden evi süslemeye başladı. Sonunda 70'li yıllar partisi yapmaya karar vermişlerdi. Müzikler, giysiler ayarlandı, yemek ve içki alındı... Hatta nereden bulmuşlarsa garip bir alet almışlardı, karanlıkta duvarda dönüp duran renkli desenler oluşturuyordu.

Bir gece önce Andrew'yla ikisi sabaha kadar uğraştılar. Ben yatıp uyudum.

Sabah erken kalktım. İkisi yeniden geri kalan ufak tefek şeyleri almak için alışverişe gittiler. Ben de köşedeki kafede kahvaltı ettim. Sonra da onlara hediye almaya gittim.

Zaten benim çağırdığım okuldan üç beş kişi ve bir öğretmenle eşiydi. Onların da geleceğine emin değildim.

Yağmurlu, karanlık bir gündü. Bu havada bile çiçekçiler yerindeydi. Dönerken çiçek almayı unutmayayım dedim. Birkaç mağaza dolaştım. İkinci el dükkanlarından birinde istemediğim kadar çok şey vardı.

Sanki gerçekten 70'lere dönmüş gibiydim. Mağazada çalışanlar bile o günlerden kalmıştı sanki. İçeride deli gibi rock çalıyor, gelenler üstüste atılmış yüzlerce elbisenin, pantolonun, gömleğin içinden birini çekiştirip duruyordu.

Tolga'ya rengarenk kocaman bir şapka beğendim. Satıcı kadın bunun ünlü zenci şarkıcının şapkası olduğunu söyledi ve hatta fotoğraf gösterdi ama adamı tanımıyordum.

Andrew için de kocaman, ağır tokası olan yılan derisi bir kemer aldım. Bu akşam giyeceği üstüne yapışan kırmızı pantolonla güzel duracaktı.

Sonra çiçekleri aldım ama taksi bulamadığım için epeyce yürüyüp epeyce ıslandım.

Eve geldiğimde her yerimden sular akıyordu. Neyse ki çiçeklerle hediyeleri iyi sarmalamıştım.

Titriyordum soğuktan.

Kapının önünde rüzgar yağmur damlalarını yüzüme öyle sert vuruyordu ki çantamdan anahtarı çıkartamıyordum.

Tek istediğim hemen eve girmek ve kendimi sıcak suya atmaktı. Ayaklarım donmuş gibiydi çünkü.

Anahtarı çıkartmak için elimdekileri merdivene bırakırken kafamı kaldırdım.

Ve öylece kalakaldım.

Merdivene oturmuş, sigara içiyordu.

Başında eski moda kasket, üstünde yakalarını kaldırdığı uzun balıksırtı palto, sigarayı avucunun içinde tutmuş bana bakıyordu gülerek...

Bazı anlar vardır ya ağlamakla gülmek arasında kalırsınız. Aslında mutlusunuzdur ama aynı zamanda içinizden ağlamak gelir. Hani çok güzel filmlerin acıklı biteceğini düşünürken beklenmedik bir rastlantı olur ve aslında herşey yoluna girdiği halde ağlarsınız ya işte onun gibi...

Ama tuhaf olan bu benim için yalnızca o an değil orada onunla geçirdiğimiz üç gün boyunca böyle oldu. Yüzüne bakıyordum ve gülerken birden gözlerim doluyordu.

Sanki hayatta en çok istediğini bulmak ama onu kaybedeceğini bilmek gibiydi bu.

Londra'nın hiç gitmediğim çok güzel, sakin bir semtinde, kısa süreliğine Paris'e giden bir ressam arkadaşının evini ayarlamıştı.

Tabii ki yılbaşı partisine katılamadım. Üstümüzü başımızı kurulayıp eşyaları bıraktıktan sonra yanıma birkaç şey aldım ve Tolga'ya not bıraktım. Hayır, bunca zaman sonra kalkıp gelmişken onu tanımadığı insanlarla paylaşmaya, belki de hayatımın en özel yılbaşı gecesini, ilerleyen saatlerde tamamen kafayı bulup saçmalayacaklarına emin olduğum bir sürü deliyle mahvetmeye hiç niyetim yoktu.

Yağmurun altında sarılıp yürüdük. Bir yılbaşı akşamüstüydü. İnsanlar evlerine yetişmeye çalışıyordu. Bütün taksiler doluydu. Her yer ışıl ışıldı. Sanki benim için özel bir kutlama yapılıyormuş gibiydi. Dağılıyordu ışıklar yağmurda. Ne kalabalık, ne yağmur, ne birbirine çarpan telaşlı insanlar umurumdaydı. Ben kendimi benim için bu geceye özel hazırlanmış kentte onunla yalnız hissediyordum.

Sonunda taksi bulup eve geldik.

Ama içimde bir tedirginlik vardı. Ne zamandır görüşmüyorduk. Üstelik son yazdığım mektuptan sonra bana kızdığını, kırıldığını düşünüyordum. Şimdi ne olacağını, herşeyin istediğim gibi olup olmayacağını bilemiyordum. Burada ilk kez onunla gerçekten yalnızdık. Onun evinde değil. Kendi şehrimizde değil. Üç günlüğüne gelmişti.

Yalnızca o ve ben.

Ev soğuktu.

Şömineye birkaç odun atıp tutuşturdu.

"Bu gerçek mi?'" diye sordum, "Yani burada olman..."

Daha bu akşamüzeri ansızın kendimi hiç bilmediğim bu semtte hiç bilmediğim bir evde onunla şöminenin önünde bulacağım aklımın ucundan bile geçmemişti.

"Umarım geldiğime sevinmişsindir, belki de sormam gerekirdi ama bir anda karar verdim..."

Sevinmek mi?

Delirmiş.

İçimdeki duygunun adı sevinçle, mutlulukla, böyle tek bir sözcükle tanımlanamazdı. Eğer bir yazar ya da şair böyle bir sözcük bulmuşsa da ben onu bilmiyordum.

"İyi ki geldin," dedim yalnızca.

Öpüşürken ağlamak üzereydim ve kendimi tutmaya çalışıyordum.

Ama o böyle duygusal konuşmaları sürdüremez. Hemen bana komik hikayeler anlatmaya başladı. Yalnızca yarım saat sonra sanki hep buradaymış, daha dün birlikteymişiz gibi çene çalıyorduk.

Bana sormasından korkuyordum ama bir yandan da yaptığım saçmalığı anlatmak, aslında böyle birşey olmadığını söylemek istiyordum ama sanki o mektubu okumamış gibiydi.

Bu hep böyle olmamış mıydı? Bana dokunduğunda, beni öptüğünde kendimi ona bırakmak isterken birden öylesine anlatmaya başlar, ben de ne yapacağımı şaşırırdım...

"Hadi kalk bakalım,"dedi, "bu gece yılbaşı..."

Camları, kapıları ışıklarla süslenmiş evlerin önünden geçip eski, küçük pub'a geldik. Arkadaşının adını söyleyince hemen yer buldular. Geçmiş zamandan kalma bir yer gibiydi. Gibi değil de bence zaten öyleydi. Sanki burada zaman donmuş, dışarıdaki dünyadan farklı bir biçimde birileri burada kendi istedikleri zamanı yaşamaya devam ediyordu.

Biz atıştırırken içerisi yavaş yavaş dolmaya başladı. Zaten gelenlerin hepsi birbirini tanıyor gibiydi. Şu para atıp istediğiniz şarkıyı çaldığınız müzik kutularından vardı. Epeyce bozukluk aldık ve aklımıza gelen bütün şarkıları üstüste çalmaya başladık.

Önceleri belki aslında yalnızca meraktı. O güne dek hiç tanımadığım, rastlamadığım bir dünyaydı çünkü. Dünya derken gülümserdim kendi kendime... Bir odanın içinde nasıl bir dünya olabilirdi ki?

Ama olmuştu işte.

O atölyeye gittiğim ilk günden sonra hep sanki gizemli bir masalı okurken birdenbire kendimi masalın içinde bulmuş gibi hissetmiştim.

Her yerde sanki antika dükkanındaymışsınız gibi garip eşyalar vardı. Bunları nereden bulmuş, neden almış bilmek zordu. Çünkü hemen hemen hepsi işlevsizdi.

Çalışmayan radyolardan eski daktilolara, kırık dökük kristal takımlardan kurmalı oyuncaklara kadar binlerce irili ufaklı eşya vardı her yerde.

Tıpkı resimleri gibi...

Sanatçılar kendilerine bu dünyanın içinde yeni bir dünya yaratabilirler ama o bence bütün bu resimlerle heykellerle uğraşırken aslında kendisini yeniden yaratmaya çalışmıştı. Tıpkı mermer bloktan bir insan figürü yapıp sonra onun canlanmasını beklemek gibi...

Bu mümkün müydü?

Neden kimi zaman çok güzel yüzler, figürler çizdiği halde daha çok karmakarışık, çirkin insanları, açılmış yaraları, bir yerinde bir sakatlık olanları, cüceleri, garip kılıklara bürünmüş kadın mı erkek mi belirsiz insanları çizdiğini anlamak zordu.

İnatla bunları çizmesinin ve bu nedenle de insanların bu resimlere bakmak bile istememesinin nedenini uzun zaman anlamamıştım.

Şimdi bunca zaman sonra belki anlayabiliyorum...

O, insanların birbirine olan düşmanlığını, başkalarına olan öfkemizi, bize benzemeyenleri nasıl sevmediğimizi anlatmaya çalışmıştı belki de...

Ve neden en küçük kağıt parçalarına, yanından ayırmadığı defterinin sayfalarına bile onca insan yüzü çizerdi?

İçiçe geçmiş bu yüzler farklı açılardan baktığınızda farklı biçimlere dönüşürdü.

Önce hep küçük bir kağıtla başlar sonra giderek büyütür ve bazıları dev birer yağlıboya tabloya dönüşürdü.

Aynı şeyi o tahta top için de yapmıştı. Önce küçük misket kadar olanlarıyla başlamış sonra giderek büyütmüştü.

Hem çok gerçekti bütün bu insanlar, yüzler, çocuklar, hayvanlar hem de sanki bir hayalin içinde silinip gidecekmiş gibi görünüyordu.

Farklı zamanlardan eşyaların, olur olmaz bitkilerin, meyvelerin ne olduğunu ancak şimdi yıllar sonra anlayabiliyorum.

Evet o aslında insan belleğini çiziyordu. Farklı zamanlardan, karmakarışık anılarla, bilgilerle, görüntülerle dolu belleğin o inanılmaz eriyiğini resmediyordu. Ve öylesine deliceydi ki bakarken huzursuz oluyordu insan.

Birdenbire onca insanın, onca eşyanın, renklerin arasından zincirinden kopmuş bir atlıkarıncanın atları üzerinize geliyordu örneğin.

Belki de rüyalarıydı bunlar onun ya da bir eleştirmenin yazdığı gibi bilinçaltına yapılan yolculuk...

Sayısız kez baktığınız bir resimde bile bir gün o ana kadar göremediğiniz bir ayrıntıyla karşılaşabilirdiniz.

Kimileri resmin içindeki bütün bu parçaları birbirine bağlamaya, bundan öyküler çıkartmaya uğraşmışlardı. Ama eski zamanlardan kalma bir çalgıyla bir konser biletinin, küçük böceklerle Bremen Mızıkacılarının, kurşuna dizilen bir adamla birbirine geçmiş sevişen insanların, yüzü yaşlı kırışık bebekle yarım yamalak bir aşk mektubunun ve buna benzer sayısız şeyin biraraya geldiği tablodan nasıl bir öykü çıkartılabilirdi ki...

Kimbilir belki de herkes kendi öyküsünü çıkartıyordu...

Ama o bunları konuşmayı sevmezdi. Resimleri hakkında hiç konuşmazdı.

O hayatın tümüyle bir rastlantılar zincirinden oluştuğuna inanırdı. Belki de resimlerindeki bu birbiriyle ilgisiz görünen ayrıntıların nedeni buydu.

Elbette o gece, o eski püskü tavernada otururken bütün bunları düşünmüyordum. Ona söylemesem de aklıma gelen tek şey hayatımda nedensiz biçimde kendimi ondan başka kimseye ait hissetmediğimdi.

Oturduğumuz duvarın önünde çok eski büyükçe bir duvar saati vardı. Şu sarkaçlı olanlardan. Kurt yenikleriyle dolu, antika, anneannemin evindekine benzer bir saat. Ben ona pencereli saat derdim. Çünkü camını açıp kurma görevi benimdi.

Eğer saatin kadranını ayarlayabildiğimiz gibi gerçek zamanı da ayarlayabilsek, ileri, geri alabilsek ya da durdurabilsek hayat ne kadar başka olurdu.

O üç gün biterken bana bıraktığı mektup hala yanımda. Sabah uyandığım zaman başucumda bulduğum mektup.

"Biliyorum birlikte çok az zaman geçirdik. Birbirimizi tanıdığımızı bile söyleyemeyiz değil mi? Tıpkı isminle anılan o sanattaki gibi seni düşününce değişen renkler, biçimler, elle tutulamayan şeyler geliyor aklıma. Çok güzel ama belirsiz. Belki senin için de böyledir. Heyecan verici ama aynı zamanda kaybolup gideceği için ürkütücü...

Gerçek mi hayal mi belli olmayan birşey.

Kimbilir belki asıl güzel olan, bütün bu kısa anları benzersiz kılan, içimde yıllar sonra ilk kez böyle bir duygu uyandıran da bu.

Senin o güzel yüzünü tutmak sanki suya renk bırakmak gibi... Onun gözlerinde dağılışını izlemek... Bakışlarındaki derin ama bilinmez düşünceleri okumaya çalışmak... Başka dünyada büyümüş bir kız... Başka bir dünyadan gelmiş koskoca bir adam... Hala rüyasının içinde kalmayı başarmış küçük bir çocuk...

Benim için başından beri sevmekle korku birarada oldu. Seni incitmek mi? Üzmek mi? Hayatının daha başında canını yakmak mı? Bilmiyorum.

Sen bana bunları hiç söylemedin. Hatta umursamazmış gibi davrandın.

Ama biliyor musun, insan büyüdükçe, yaşlandıkça, birinin hayatına girmenin çok kolay ama çıkmanın çok zor olduğunu anlıyor. Eğer ilişkiye başlarken yıllar sonrasını görebilseydik belki de çoğumuz daha en baştan vazgeçerdik.

Ama kimbilir belki de en iyisi geleceği hiç düşünmemektir.

İlişki dedim ve derken bile birdenbire elim durdu. Bizimkine ilişki denebilir mi? İkimiz de birbirimizin hayatından ancak anlattığımız kadar haberdarız. Ne kadar yalan ne kadar doğru söylediğimiz, yaşadıklarımızı nasıl değiştirdiğimiz, anıları bile nasıl anlattığımız belli değil.

Sen şimdi hayatının başındasın. Yapacağın çok şey var ve eminim en güzelini yapacaksın. Bense şimdiden çok yorgunum. Yapmak istediklerimi yapabilecek miyim onu bile bilmiyorum.

Seni görmek inan ki uzun zamandır bana en iyi gelen şeydi. Hatta belki de hep aklımda olan ama bir türlü başlayamadığım resimleri yapmam için bana yeniden ilham verdi.

Biz hiç bundan sonra ne olacak demedik birbirimize... Aslında galiba ben kendi hayatımda da bundan sonra ne olacak, hiç bilemedim. Şimdi de bilmiyorum.

Uzakta olduğunda da seni düşündüğüm zaman hep gülümsüyorum. Bazı sabahlar uyandığımda aklımda senin yüzün oluyor. Garip bir biçimde senin yüzünü, bakışlarını, dalmış, uzaklara gitmiş halini, içtenlikle gülümsemeni, saçların yüzüne dökülmüş hüzünlü duruşunu çizmek istiyorum. Çiziyorum da...

Bazı şeyleri konuşmamamızın nedeni galiba gerçek olmasa da ikimizin arasında bir dünyada buluşuyor olmamız. Belki de söylemediklerim söylediklerimden, söyleyebildiklerimden daha çok.

O bazı şeyler bu dünyayı bozacak ve aniden renkleri, ışığı, eşyayı sıradanlaştırıp bizim onlara yüklediğimiz anlamdan, verdiğimiz biçimden uzaklaştıracak gibi geldi belki de ...

Sabah uyandığımda Londra'nın puslu ışığında uzun uzun seni seyrettim. Rüyanda nerelerde olduğunu düşündüm. İstediğim, böyle tanımadığımız bir evde, uzak bir kentte, kimseler yokken yanında uyumaya devam etmek ve günleri hep böyle aldırışsız, dışarıda dünya yokmuş gibi geçirebilmekti.

Yazık ki hayat buna izin vermez.

Onun için çalınmış zamanlarımız çok güzeldi.

Dışarısı soğuk, yağmurlu, karanlık... Bu satırları yazıp kalın kazağımı, yağmurluğumu giyip havaalanına doğru yola çıkıyorum.

Seni uyandırmadım.

Vedaları sevmem.

Kucağımda kulağıma fısıldadığın son sözcüklerin güzelliğinde, mutluluğunda, huzurunda kalmanı istedim.

Hep böyle kal."

Sonraları çok düşündüm. Herşey bir zaman sorunu mu? Bir arkadaşım üç yıllık ilişkisi sürerken ama o ilişkiden aslında çok mutsuzken biriyle tanışmıştı. Gizli saklı onunla birlikte olmuştu.

Ama nişanlısı ondan ayrılmak istemiyordu ve o da kızı üzmemek için mi yoksa söz verdiği için mi bilmem bu ilişkiye son veremiyordu. Öte yandan gizli ilişkisi onu mutlu ettiği için de hayatına devam ediyordu.

Belki onunla tanışmasa nişanlısından ayrılacaktı. Belki de evlenecekti. Sonunda bir gün kıza herşeyi anlatıp ayrılmaya karar verdi. Ama bu konuşmalar biraz uzun sürdü ve o arada gizli sevgilisiyle görüşmedi. İlişkisini bitirip sonra onunla konuşmayı ve artık onunla birlikte olmayı hatta evlenmeyi düşünüyordu.

Gözyaşları, kavgalar uzayıp gitti ama sonunda kızcağız durumu kabullendi ve herşey bitti.

Ama bilmediği şuydu. Gizli sevgili bu arada başkasıyla tanışmış ve onunla bir yola girmişti. Aradığı zaman artık bu ilişkinin onu mutlu etmediğini ve bitirmeleri gerektiğini söyledi.

Ne yaptıysa, ona ilişkisini bitirdiğini ve artık yalnızca onu istediğini söylese de geç kalmıştı. Belki yalnızca birkaç hafta...

O mektubu yazdığı gece dışarda biraz üşümüş kahve içerken ellerimi tutup bana baktı. Önemli birşey söyleyeceğini düşündüm. Yoksa ona yazdığım mektubu, uydurma sevgilimi mi soracaktı? Sormadı. Her ne söyleyecekse dilinin ucuna kadar gelmişti ama söylemedi.

"Hadi eve gidelim, üşüdün sen, burnun kızarmış," dedi yalnızca.

Sabah yüzümde gülümsemeyle uyandım ama sonra yanımda olmadığını farkettim. Seslendim, yoktu. Belki de yiyecek birşey almaya gitti kahvaltı için diye düşündüm. Ama kalkıp biraz kendime gelince farkettim ki eşyaları yok.

Sonra masanın üzerinde mektubu buldum.

Evet vedaları sevmezsin biliyorum. Ama keşke izin verseydin de en azından havaalanına kadar yanında kalsaydım.

Okudum, yeniden okudum, pek anlamadım aslında. Bu veda mektubu muydu? Öylesine yazılmış bir mektup muydu? Yoksa böylece devam edeceğimizi mi anlatıyordu?

Bir tek uyanıp yüzüme baktığı cümlesi kaldı aklımda. Çünkü sabah uyanıp yanınızdaki insana bakarken mutlu olmaktır aşk.

Başından beri olduğu gibi yaşananlar sis bulutunun ardındaydı. Tam elle tutacağınızı sandığınız an kaybolan tanımlanamaz birşey gibiydi.

Hem çok mutluydum hem de hüzünlü.

Eşyaları topladım, mektubun sonunda yazdığı gibi her tarafı kilitleyip anahtarı söylediği yere gizledim.

Keskin hava insanın yüzüne çarpıyordu ama bana iyi geldi. Biraz yürüdüm. En azından bu sokakları, bu evleri, bu güzel semti o günkü haliyle belleğime kazımak için.

Tıpkı yılbaşı akşamüstü merdivenlerde belirdiği gibi üç gün sonra aynı biçimde kaybolup gitmişti.

Kediyi ovalamıştım değil mi?

Öyle anlar, o anlara ait duygular, renkler, akılda kalan resimler, kokular var ki hayatın içinden onları çıkartmak, tıpkı bir tablodaki gibi dondurmak ve sonsuza dek korumak istiyor insan.

Ama olmuyor.

Bir keresinde Ferhat benim fotoğrafımı çekerken, "Yazık ki bazı şeyler fotoğrafa çıkmıyor, bazı insanlar da..." demişti. Buna çok gülmüştüm.

"Ben fotoğrafa çıkmıyor muyum?"

"Evet," dedi, "bazen gördüğün derinlik, gördüğün şeyin arkasındakiler, belki de ona bakarken içinden gelenler fotoğrafa çıkmıyor, yalnızca herkesin görebildiği suret beliriyor, galiba bu nedenle resim çiziyorum..."

Ama resimler de fotoğraflar gibi o anların bellekteki algısını tam olarak yansıtamaz.

Ben o sabah yolda yürürken, yağmur yüzüme çarparken, o üç günün içindeki anları, kokuyu, dokunuşları, onun sesini, kendine özgü vurgularını, bakışını kaçırmasını, elinin üzerindeki damarları, kulağıma karanlıkta fısıldayışını, yerçekimsiz bir ortamdaymış gibi kucağında yuvarlanışımı, titreyişleri, sıcaklığı, kendi içimden çıkıp uzaktan kendime bakarmış gibi hafiflediğimi, ayak parmaklarımın bile uyuşmasını, gülmekle ağlamak arasında gidip gelişimi, ürpertiyi, korkuyu, direnmeyi ve kendini tümüyle bırakışı, öpmek sevmek ve canını yakmanın aynı anda nasıl istenebileceğini, bilincimden geçen ve hiç anlam veremediğim sayısız düşüncenin, görüntünün biraz sonra yalnızca kendi başıma dolaştığım kişisel bir sirke dönüşmesini, orada bulduğum şeylerle yaşadığım anın karışmasındaki inanılmaz uyumu belleğimde taşıyordum.

Ama onu resmetmek hatta sözcüklere dökmek imkansızdı.

İşte deniyorum ama olmuyor.

Kimbilir belki de asıl önemli olan yaşananlar değil yaşadıklarımızı nasıl algıladığımızdır.

Hepimiz annemizin kucağındaydık ama hiçbirimiz aynı kokuyu duymadık ve sorsak hiçbirimiz o kokuyu anlatamayız.

Onun bir resmi vardı.

Yukarıda, kağıttan kesilmiş yüzlerce küçük beyaz kuş uçuyor, aşağıda insanlar panayırda geziniyorlardı. Ayrıntılara bakarsanız kimileri oyuncak ayı için atış yapıyor, kimileri hilkat garibesini izliyor, kimileri halka atıyor, kimi yalnızca dondurma yiyerek dolaşıyordu. Küçücük insanların yüzlerine yakından bakınca güldüklerini, öylesine bir yerlere baktıklarını, yorgun olduklarını bile görebilirdiniz.

Resmin üstünde bir ışık vardı. O ışıkta kuşlar dalgalanıyor ve uçuyormuş gibi görünüyorlardı.

Sonra tabloyu kenara çekince bir başka resim ortaya çıkıyordu. Aslında ilk anda aynı tablo gibiydi. Ama bu kez kuşlar savaş uçaklarına, aşağıdakiler de kaçışan, çocuklarını kurtarmaya çalışan, yerlerde sürüklenen, kanlar içinde yatan insanlara dönüşüyordu.

İkinci resim açılıp da bunları görünce irkildim. Çok etkileyiciydi ama aynı zamanda çok üzücü…

Dayanamayıp, "Neden bunun tersini yapmadın?" diye sordum.

"Çünkü hep böyle olur…" dedi.

Nedense yolda yürürken aklıma o tablo geldi yine. Sonra unuttum. Şimdi uçakta olmalıydı. Acaba neler düşünüyordu? Benim gibi mutlu muydu? Kuşkulu muydu? Uçakta yine bu üç günün resimlerini çiziyor muydu?

İnsanların pardesülerine, yağmurluklarına sarılıp üşüyerek hızlı hızlı yürüdüğü soğuk, puslu Londra sabahı… Neredeyse önümü zor görüyordum.

Ve o çocuk müzikallerinden birindeymiş gibi neredeyse zıplayarak yürüyordum.

Gerçekten hep öyle mi olur?

Neden sonra donmak üzere olduğumu farkettim ve kendimi taksiye zor attım.

Şimdi gel de olup bitenleri Tolga'ya anlat.

Herhalde meraktan delirmiş halde beni bekliyordu. Üstüste sorularla beni delirtecekti.

Yok tabii ki anlatmayacaktım. Ki anlatmak için de delirmiyor değildim. Taksi de inadına her kırmızı ışığa yakalanıyordu.

Ama zaten o değil herhangi biri yüzüme baksa ne hissettiğimi, neler olup bittiğini anlayabilirdi.

Herhalde buraya geldiğimden beri beni ilk kez böyle sıçrayarak yürürken görecekti.

Tıpkı eski günlerdeki gibi hemen onun yanına gitmek istiyordum.

Tabii okula gitmeye kalkmadıysa... Yok benim bu sabah eve geleceğimi biliyorken kesinlikle gitmemiştir.

Bir yandan da saate bakıyordum. Ferhat ne zaman varacaktı İstanbul'a? Hesabım da o kadar kötüdür ki saat farkını bile tutturamıyordum. Bu akşam beni arayacak mıydı? Aramazsa ben aramalı mıydım?

Aman neyse, şimdi gidip sıcak suya girecektim ve uzun uzun orada kalacaktım. Sonra sandviç ve çay alıp meraktan çıldırmış arkadaşımla sohbete dalacaktım. Bugünü tembelliğe ayırdım. Kulağımdaki ağrı bile şu an umurumda değil.

Eski Londra taksisi büyük sarayın önünden geçiyor, sincapların dolaştığı parkın, heykellerin, turistlerin, yağmurda hızlı hızlı yürüyen insanların, şemsiyelerin arasından geçiyor.

Şoför dikkatle radyodaki maçı dinliyor. Arkada ayaklarımı uzatmış etrafı seyrediyorum.

Parkta şık giysileriyle iki genç kız at biniyor. Yaşlı çöpçü imkansız bir çabayla yerdeki sarı yaprakları süpürmeye çalışıyor. Kendi kendime o şarkıyı mırıldanıyorum, "Sonbahar Yaprakları"...

Galiba buraya geldiğim günden beri ilk kez kenti böyle turist gibi geziyorum.

Öyle puslu ki, gerçeküstü bir resim gibi.

Sanki az sonra her yer sisin içine gömülecek ve biz kentin dolambacında kaybolacağız.

Dickens romanları gibi...

Yolu kaçırmamak için dikkat kesiliyorum.

"Evet, buradan sağa lütfen."

İlk kez başını çevirip bana bakıyor, gülümsüyor, "Biliyorum," diyor. "Meraklanma biz alışığız," der gibi.

Eski otelin önündeki kapıcı melon şapkasını çıkartıp büyük, lüks arabadan inen şık hanımı karşılıyor. Çinçilla kürkünün içindeki kadın da ona selam veriyor.

Geçtik.

Rüzgarda uçuşan eteklerini kapatmaya çalışan kız şemsiyesini düşürüyor.

Geçtik.

Bastonuyla aniden kendini yola atan yaşlı beyefendi yüzünden fren yapıyoruz. Adam yalnızca dönüp bize şöyle bir bakıyor ve istifini bozmadan ağır adımlarla karşıya geçiyor. Şoför garip bir aksanla küfrediyor ama anlamıyorum.

Geçtik.

Silecekler daha hızlı çalışıyor.

Camları silmeye çalışan, kırmızı ışıkta durunca dilenen çocuklar yok henüz.

Belki de bizim göremediğimiz yerlerdeler.

Yüksek topuklu ayakkabıları, kırmızı paltosu, kocaman şapkasıyla bir kadın minik, tüylü köpeğini gezdirirken yağmurun altında iskeleye çelik borular taşıyan mavi tulumlu iki işçi ona ıslık çalıp gülüşüyor.

Geçtik.

Bir kenti yalnızca böyle taksinin içinde geçerek izlemek bile bir film gibi. Elimde kamera olsa, sislerin içinde olup bitenleri, sanki bir hayalin içinde geçen sıradan bir günün sıradan hikayeleri gibi çekebilsem...

Çünkü tüm bunlar hayalle gerçek arasında...

Hayatımda gördüğüm en büyük atın üstündeki polis etrafı izliyor. Bir an gözgöze geliyoruz.

Geçtik.

Şoför birden çığlık atıyor. Dalgınlığımdan uyanıyorum korkarak. Herhalde takımı gol attı.

Gülümsüyorum sadece.

Köşeyi dönüyoruz ve evin önünde duruyor.

Evet tam da düşündüğüm gibi. Ev hep loş olduğundan sabah bile ışık yaktığı için Tolga'nın evde olduğunu anlıyorum ve seviniyorum.

Şimdi hem zaman hem de mekan olarak çok uzakta, o unutulmaz günün yıllar sonrasında, böyle trende giderken bir kentin değil, kasabaların, uçsuz bucaksız ormanların, insanın burada ne işi var diyeceği ıssız yerlerdeki tek tük evlerin, soğuk istasyonların –ellerinde bavullarıyla yolcular biniyor, yolcular iniyor– arasından geçerken o puslu Londra sabahını hatırlıyorum.

Hayatınızın bir sabahı herşeyi değiştirebilir.

Burada puslu bir hava yok. Aksine herşey özel bir gözlük takmışım gibi parlak.

Tren yavaşlıyor.

Karşımdaki adam kalkıp bavulunu alıyor, "Size iyi yolculuklar," diyor ve koridora çıkıyor. Tren sallanarak duruyor.

Burada mıyım şimdi yoksa o Londra sabahında mı?

Tolga kapıyı açtı. Heyecanla sarılıp öptüm.

Küçük bavulumu içeriye atıp hemen banyoya gireceğimi, bana sandviç yapmasını, sonra olanları anlatacağımı söyledim. Bütün bunları anlatırken onun hiç konuşmadığını farkettim.

Döndüm.

Yüzünde garip bir ifade vardı.

Eyvah, dedim, mutlaka kavga çıktı, yine ayrıldılar, bizimki bozuk...

"Dur, dinlemeden önce bana on dakika ver," dedim.

"Birşey oldu," dedi.

Dışarıya bakan pencerelerden yağmur süzülüyordu.

Yüzüne baktım ve sevgilisiyle kavga çıkmadığını o an anladım.

"Ne oldu?" dedim.

"Gel şuraya otur, anlatacağım," dedi.

Oturdum.

"Az önce annen aradı, okula gittiğini söyledim, akşamüstü yeniden arayacak ama istersen sen şimdi ara..."

Yılbaşı akşamı annemi aramıştım. Tolga ve arkadaşlarımızla beraber olduğumuzu söylemiştim.

Gülmüyordu.

Garip, tedirgin bir hali vardı.

"Kahve yapmıştım, üşümüşsündür, dur sana da getireyim," dedi.

"Ne oluyor Tolga?" dedim.

Onu o kadar iyi tanıyorum ki...

Yüzünden bile belli...

"Ne oldu, çabuk söyle..."

Geri döndü, yanıma oturdu.

"Dün gece anneannen rahatsızlanmış, telaşlanmışlar, e ben de okula gitti dedim, sen şimdi ararsın, herhalde önemli değildir..."

Biri size boş boş bakıp, önemli değildir diyorsa önemlidir.

Bunu bilecek kadar büyüğüm.

Babam o kapıdan çıkıp gittiğinde anneme ne olduğunu sorduğumda da "Birşey yok," demişti.

Koltuğa yığıldım.
"Bana doğru söyle," dedim, "ne oldu?"
"Söylüyorum ya canım, herhalde fenalık geçirmiş, doktor gelmiş, annen de seni aramak istemiş..."
Zaman...
Daha demin mutluluktan uçarken... Ayaklarım yerden kesilmişken... Belki de hayatımın en güzel günlerinden birini, bu puslu kentte masal alemindeymiş gibi yaşarken...
Bir bıçak saplandı.
Ne olur, dedim, ne olur, bu kez, hiç değilse bu kez kötü birşey olmasın. Hiç değilse bu sabah olmasın.
Ama oldu.
Öyle dememiş miydi Ferhat, "Çünkü hep böyle olur."

Yılbaşı akşamı tabii ki anneannemin evinde yine herkes toplanmıştı. Sabaha kadar süren sohbetlerden, şarkılardan sonra ertesi gün Sare Hanım biraz geç kalkmıştı. Başı ağrıyordu, çarpıntısı vardı. Pek umursamamıştı. Annemin ısrarına rağmen doktor çağırmak da istememişti.

"E sabaha kadar oturduk, bu yaşta bunlar olacak tabii, siz de herşeyi izam ediyorsunuz, başım ağrıdı doktor, sırtım kasıldı doktor, böyle hayat geçmez, akşama kalmaz toparlarım," demiş ama akşama doğru odasına çekilip uyumuştu.

Öyle gün içinde pek uyumazdı.

Ertesi gün daha iyi hissetmiş, yine kahvesini, sigarasını içmiş ama pek keyfi yokmuş.

Hiç adeti olmasa da hasta çorbası dediği tavuksuyu çorba istemiş, başına, "Sanki başım kaşınıyor, gıdıklanıyor, anlayamadım," diyerek buz torbası koydurmuş.

Annem bütün bunlardan hoşlanmadığı için doktor çağırmış. Anneannem her ne kadar buna kızsa da tansiyonu biraz yüksek çıkmış, çarpıntısı varmış, yatıştırıcı vermiş doktor, çok yorulduğunu, dinlenmesi gerektiğini söyleyip gitmiş.

Gece vakti Saniye, garip bir sesle yerinden fırlamış. Yanına gelince onun kendinde olmadığını, hırıldadığını, yüzünün bir yarısının kaydığını farketmiş.

"Rabbim affetsin, bir gözü başka yere bakıyordu," diye ağlamış sonra.

Bulabildiğim ilk uçakla İstanbul'a geldim.

Yol boyunca mucize olacak ve ben eve gittiğimde anneannem yine beni her zamanki gibi karşılayıp şaka yaptığını söyleyecek diye düşünüyordum. Böyle düşünüyordum ama ağlıyordum.

Elimde, okurmuş gibi yaptığım ama aslında tek satırını bile anlamadığım bir kitap vardı. Yanımda oturan kadın, "Çok mu acıklı kitap? Okumayın kızım, ben acıklı kitapları sevmem, zaten hayat yeterince acıklı," dedi.

Yalan mı?

Eve gelirken kendi kendime dedim ki, bu ne acayip yolculuk, daha dün bambaşka bir yerde, sisler içindeki eski zaman kentinde kendini masal kahramanı sanıyordun, şimdi yine bir eski zaman kentinde taksinin içinde bambaşka duygudasın.

Bangır bangır arabesk şarkı çalıyordu. Taksinin naylonla kaplanmış arka koltuğunda sallanıyordum, benimle birlikte arka camdaki oyuncak köpek de başını sallıyordu.

Yıkık dökük binlerce yıllık surların önünden geçiyorduk. Çok yaşlı, kambur bir adam sırtındaki çuvalla topladığı çöpleri arkasından sürüklemeye çalışıyordu.

Binlerce yıllık surlar... Dünyanın en büyük imparatorluklarından birinin meydan okumasının simgesi olarak yapılmış... Hemen önünde çöpleri taşıyarak yaşamaya çalışan yaşlı bir adam...

Sanki bütün bu imparatorlukların çöplüğünü taşırmış gibi bir ifade var yüzünde.

Dün hiç bilmeden geçtiğim sokaklarla, hayatımı geçirdiğimi sandığım ama aslında farkında bile olmadığım ülkemin sokakları arasında gerçekle rüya arasında incecik bir çatlak bulmuş gibi dolaşıyorum.

Yanımızda çalan çıngırakla kendime geliyorum, sebze yüklenmiş bir atlı araba yanımızdan geçiyor.

Aynı anda gürültüyle solumuzda dev gemiler...

Sağımızda kırık dökük evler... Pencerelere asılmış çamaşırlar... Neredeyse çökmek üzere olan ahşap eski zaman konakları...

Deniz fenerinin yanından geçiyoruz.

Ve bir tren geçiyor o eski mahallelerin arasından...

Trenler, gemiler, arabalar, faytonlar, uçaklar...

Hep bir yere mi gitmek istiyoruz?

Ne bulacağımızı düşündüysek...

Rengarenk çamaşırlar uçuşuyor, çocuklar küçük kağıttan topun peşinde koşuşuyor, gemilerin ne olduğunu anlamadığım düdükleri, martıların sanki çok ciddi şeyler anlatırmış gibi bağırışları...

Eski takside sallanarak gidiyorum ve dünyalar birbirine karışıyor...

Ben kimim?

Dün neredeydim? Şimdi neredeyim?

Puslu bir günün içinden çıkıp geldim.

Kimbilir ne zaman burayı korumak için yapılan surların önünden gidiyoruz. Eskiden düşmanı korkutsa da şimdi yıkık dökük, yosun tutmuş perişan taş parçaları...

Herşeye rağmen koruyamamışlar.

Ve koku...

Kömür kokusu, deri kokusu, çöplerin kokusu, lodosla gelen yosun kokusu, kentin atıklarının kokusu, taksideki keskin vanilya kokusu, şoförden gelen tütün kokusu, balık kokusu...

Yoksulluğun kokusu...

Buradayım.

Kendi ülkemde.

Evet, bu benim ülkemin kokusu, benim kokum.

Nereye gidersem gideyim benimle gelecek.

Benim evim burası.

Aslında neyle karşılaşacağımı bilmiyordum. Annem telefonda gevelemişti ama ona inanmıyordum. Beni evde Saniye'yle Seda karşıladı.

Doğruca hastaneye gittik. Sare Hanım yoğunbakımdaydı. Beynine pıhtı gitmiş ama doktorlar henüz ne yapacaklarına karar verememişler.

Seda kem küm anlatıyordu...

"Hayır, ona birşey olmaz, o atlatır," diyordum ağlamamak için takside.

Ama annem beni görür görmez ağlamaya başladı. Bekleme odası kalabalıktı. Daha birkaç akşam önce her zamanki gibi gülüp eğlenirken şimdi burada kaygılı, asık yüzlerle bekliyor, alçak sesle konuşuyorlardı.

Yanına girmeme izin verdiler. Her yerine borular bağlanmış, yanında garip sesler çıkartan makinalar, oksijen maskesi, öylece yatıyordu. Gözleri kapalı. Uyur gibi...

İncelmiş damarlarına iğne takılmış. Elini tuttum. Sanki elimi sıktığını hissettim.

"Ben geldim," dedim.

Kopmak üzere olan gergin bir tel gibi hissediyordum kendimi.

Sakın ağlama.

Bir keresinde ben fenalaştığımda yanıma gelmişti. "Ölecek miyim anneanne?" diye sormuştum. "Kimse ölmüyor, daha uzun zaman buralarda olmanı istiyoruz, hem insan öyle kolay kolay ölmez merak etme, olsa olsa çile çeker, hem dur bakalım ben dururken sen nereye gidiyorsun," diye güldürmüştü beni.

"Hatırladın mı anneanne," dedim, "daha uzun süre buralarda olmanı istiyoruz, uzun, güzel bir uyku çekip sonra yanımıza geleceksin..."

Çıktım, insanlarla konuşuyordum, annemle konuşuyordum ama sanki hala o sisin içinde gibiydim. Sürekli birileri gelip gidiyordu. Ne konuşmaları tam anlıyordum ne de elimden birşey geliyordu. Kulağımdaki ağrı dayanılmaz hale gelmişti.

Yürürken bir ara ayağımı boşa atıyormuşum gibi oldu, az daha düşüyordum, duvara tutundum belli etmeden, su alıp bir yere oturdum.

Sonra Taner Amca geldi. "Şu anda yapabileceğimiz hiçbir şey yok, doktoruyla konuştum, beklemek zorundayız, Sare Hanım güçlüdür, siz de güçlü olacaksınız," dedi.

Evet o güçlüdür. Her zaman herşeyin üstesinden gelir. Ama şimdi kıpırdamadan yatıyor. Çaresiz. Aklından birşey geçiyor da söyleyemiyor mu? Neler olduğunun farkında mı? Yoksa yalnızca derin, sessiz bir uykuda mı?

Hayır ben değilim. Ben güçlü filan değilim. Olmak da istemiyorum artık. Bunca zaman yalnızca güçlü olmayı oynadım.

Yıllardır en yorgun olduğum zamanlarda bile kulağımdaki o ağrıyla, derinlerden, çok uzaktan gelen sesle yaşamaya alıştım. Çocukken kendi kendime bunu geçirmenin mutlaka bir yolu olduğuna inanırdım. Kafamı sıkmak, ellerimle alnımı ovuşturmak, kulaklarımı kapamak, yastığın altına girmek, soğuk suyun altında durmak, dua etmek...

Ama öyle olmuyor.

Taner Amca yanıma geldi, oturdu, "Sen iyi misin?" dedi.

O benim yalnızca doktorum değil. Benim şansım. Ona hep güvendim. Ne söylerse yaptım. Acıdan ağlarken, artık düşünemezken, herşeyden vazgeçerken beni azarlamasına bile alışığım. Ama şimdi o da çaresiz görünüyor.

Boş boş yüzüne baktım. İyi miyim? Düne kadar o kadar iyiydim ki... Yollarda çizgi film kahramanları gibi sıçrayarak yürüyordum.

"Yarını bekleyeceğiz. Sabah yeniden gelirim. Seni içeri alacaklar. Yanına gidip elini tut. Onunla konuş. Seni duyacağını biliyorum."

Neden ağlamamaya çalışıyorum?

Binlerce yıldır varoluşla yokoluşu kimse çözebildi mi?

O eski uygarlıkların, ölüm ülkesine giderken neler yapmamız gerektiğini anlatan kitaplarını hatırlıyorum burada, ayaklarını sürüyerek dolaşan, artık gerçek hayatlarındaki alışkanlıklarını umursamayan, bıkkın, asık yüzlü insanların arasında...

İşte şimdi oradayız. Yaşamla ölüm arasında.

Asla çözemediğimiz o incecik sınırda.

Hep biri öldüğünde ne derdi gülerek, "E canım buraya kazık kakacak halimiz yok ya, elbet bir gün uykuya dalacağız ve kimbilir belki de bu en güzel uykumuz olacak..."

Aklımda daha birkaç gece önce dinlediğimiz o güzel şarkı var.

Ferhat geçiyor aklımdan, neden burada olmadığını hatırlıyorum. Londra dönüşü Van'a gideceğini, orada çocuklarla çalışma yapacağını...

Yoğunbakımın bekleme odası geceyarısı bile dolu. "Ne çok seveni varmış," diyorlar. Gidip pencereden bakıyorum. Başka hastalarla birlikte öylece yatıyor. Onların yakınları da kaygılı...

"Elini tuttum ve o da elimi sıktı," diyorum doktora, "Bazen istemsizce yaparlar, şu an bilincinin açık olduğunu söyleyemem," diyor ve işine geri dönüyor.

Onun için, hayatla ölüm, bilinenle bilinmeyen arasındaki sınır sıradan... Kimbilir kaç kişinin oradan oraya geçtiğini görüyor her gün.

Ama ben elini tuttum. Eli sıcaktı. Elimi sıktı.

Ben biliyorum.

En azından...

Bilmek istiyorum.

Neden hiçbirimiz, her gün herkesin başına gelenlerin sonunda bizim de başımıza geleceğini düşünmeyiz?

O benim bütün hayatımı değiştiren kadın.

Belki bana hayatı öğreten kadın.

Doktorların söylediklerini hiç dinlemedi ki... Hep gülüp geçti.

"İnsan ya kendisine hayatı yasaklar ya da hayatını yaşar," derdi hep.

Çünkü uzun yıllar o yasaklarla yaşamıştı. Doğru olanı yapmaya, yapılması gerekenleri düşünmeye çalışmıştı.

"Hayatın bütün bilgisine sahip olduğuna inanan ve bize ne yapmamız gerektiğini söyleyip duranlardan kaçı sonsuza dek yaşadı, var mı etrafta öyle bir tanıdığınız?" diye kahkahayı patlatmıştı bir keresinde.

Bunca yılda onu nadiren başında buz torbasıyla yatarken görmüştüm.

Hastalık sözünü bile sevmezdi.

Bir kış, ciğerleri sökülür gibi öksürürken doktor ona sigarayı tamamen yasaklamıştı. O gider gitmez, ünlü bir yazarın hediye ettiği uzun ağızlığı çekmeceden çıkarttı, "Ne yapalım bundan sonra bununla içeceğiz," deyip yaktı.

Sabaha karşı hastanede, kirli, yer yer döşemesi sökülmüş kanepede oturuyorum. Annem ağlamaktan bitap düşmüş kucağıma uzanıyor. Yorgun. Saçlarını okşuyorum ve ona acıyorum.

Neden bu inanılmaz insanın, torunuyla kurduğu ilişkiyi kızıyla kuramadığını düşünüyorum.

Hiç konuşmadık bunları.

Her zaman annesinden uzak durduğunu, ondan çekindiğini, ona içten içe gizli bir öfke duyduğunu ama onu çok sevdiğini biliyorum.

Saniye sanki evdeymişiz gibi hastaneyi ezber etmiş, bize yiyecek içecek getiriyor, hastabakıcılar etrafımızda pervane olmuş, onlara emirler yağdırıyor.

Seda şaşkın, ne yapacağını bilmez halde beni rahatlatmak için durmadan konuşuyor.

Dinlemiyorum.

Çok yorgunum.

Yine rüyayla gerçek arasındaki o buğulu alandayım.

Daha birkaç gün önce tümüyle kaybettiğimi sandığım insanı yeniden bulmuştum.

Bütün kenti kaplayan sis onu görünce silinip gitti.

İnsanın içindeki duygunun, gerçek bir duygunun, siz istediniz diye öylesine kaybolup gitmeyeceğini anladım.

Mutsuzluktan mutluluğa geçiş yalnızca bir andı.

Ve birkaç gün sonra tam tersi de yalnızca bir an...

Artık biliyorum, mutluluk sürüp giden birşey değil.

Mutsuzluk da öyle.

Ara ara kapalı kapının camından içeri bakıyorum. Öylece yatıyor. Uzun, derin bir rüyada gibi...

Eğer konuşabilseydi, "Şu kordonları sök ve beni buradan çıkarıp eve götür," derdi. Onun tonlamasıyla...

Garip ama gülümsüyorum.

Dedim ya rüyayla gerçek arasındaki buğulu alandayım diye...

Peki gerçeklerle yüzleşmeye hazır mıyım?

Tabii ki hayır.

Galiba sabaha karşı uyuyakalmışım. Saniye, çayla simit getirip beni uyandırdı. Doktor gelmişti ama değişiklik yoktu.

Bir iki saat sonra birkaç doktor biraraya gelip ne yapacaklarına karar vereceklerdi.

Anladığım kadarıyla ameliyat yapmak istiyorlar ama yaşı nedeniyle buna cesaret edemiyorlardı.

Rüyamda Ferhat'ın, bir şiirin dizelerini dev bir tuvale resmettiğini görmüştüm. Yere yaydığı kocaman tuvalin üzerinde harflerle oynuyordu.

Sonra kendimi uzaklarda, deniz kıyısında görüyorum, neden anneannemin yanında değilim diye suçluluk duyuyorum, birilerine geri dönmek istediğimi anlatıyorum ama yanımda kimliğim yok ve nerede olduğumu bilmiyorum. Size yardım edemeyiz diyorlar. Dillerini bilmediğim insanların arasındayım, neden orada olduğumu, ne yapacağımı bilmiyorum ve paniğe kapılıyorum.

Uyandım ama rüyanın etkisi hala üzerimde.

Bir türlü kendime gelemiyorum.

Başımda garip bir uyuşukluk, kulağımda yine o uğultu...

Kendini topla.

Çayımı içerken birden kapı açıldı ve o içeri girdi.

Üzerinde yine o eski balıksırtı palto, saçlar dağınık, sakalları biraz uzamış...

Bu şimdi gerçek mi?

Gelip bana sarılınca gerçek olduğunu anlıyorum.

"Sen... Van'da değil miydin?"

"Bir arkadaşım aradı, atlayıp geldim," diyor.

Annem, Seda, herkes bize bakıyor.

Bu adamın kim olduğunu biliyorlar ama neden buraya geldiğini, neden bana böyle sarıldığını kimse bilmiyor.

Daha neye uğradığımı şaşırmışken hemşire içeriden çıkıp doktora sesleniyor. Genç doktor koşarak yoğunbakıma giriyor.

Birşeyler oluyor.

Hepimiz yoğunbakımın kapısına gidiyoruz.

Sare Hanım yüzündeki oksijen maskesini çıkarıp atmış, damarlarındaki iğneleri sökmeye çalışıyor.

Rüyadan uyanıyorum.

İçeri girmek istiyorum, bırakmıyorlar.

Son durağa geliyoruz. Az kaldı. Aslında çok da uzun olmayan bir yolculukta bugüne kadar sanki vakit bulamamışım gibi bütün hayatımı yeniden düşünüyorum.

Ne garip, unutulmuş anılar çıkıp geliyor, hiç üstünde durmadığım ayrıntılar beliriyor, bazı şeylerin hatırladığım gibi olmadığını anlıyorum, bazılarını ne kadar zorlasam da hatırlamakta güçlük çekiyorum.

Belki de bazılarını şimdi böyle geriye bakarken yeniden anlamlandırıyorum.

Belki de onlara olmayan anlamlar yüklüyorum.

Ama öyle olmamış mıydı?

O sabah daha tam uyanamamışken, hiç aklımda yokken o kapıdan girmiş ve aynı anda anneannem kendine gelmişti.

Yalnızca rastlantı mı?

O zamana kadar kendimi tutmuştum ama artık daha fazla dayanamadım ve Ferhat'a sarılıp deli gibi ağlamaya başladım.

Yaşlı doktor geldi, içeri girdi. Annemle Saniye dualar okuyordu.

"Geri döndü," dedim Ferhat'a, "döndü değil mi?"

"Buraya gelirken içimden geçtiği gibi..." dedi.

Bir keresinde Taner Amca'yla benim hastalığımdan konuşurken, "Belki gökyüzü hakkında bile çok şey biliyoruz ama kendi beynimiz hakkında pek az şey..." demişti.

Şimdi yaşlı doktor da benzer şeyler söylüyordu. O bilinçsizlik hali geçmişti ama ne zaman ne olacağını bilmiyorlardı. Bir tarafı tutmuyordu. Yüzü kaymış gibi, ağzı uyuşuk, güçlükle konuşuyor, dediklerinin ancak bir kısmı anlaşılıyordu.

Bunun da kalıcı olup olmadığı belli değildi.

Yine de hepimiz mutluyduk. En azından geri gelmişti. Eve gitmek istiyordu ama doktor izin vermedi. "Biraz daha elimizin altında olsun, her an müdahale etmek gerekebilir, böyle zamanlarda dakikalar bile çok önemli," dedi.

Tabii onu ikna etmek de bana düştü.

Ertesi gün odaya çıkartma sözü verdik. O soğuk odada, iki dünya arasındaki bekleme odasında öylece kıpırdamadan yatmak istemiyordu.

Sonra Taner Amca geldi, doktoruyla birlikte yeniden yanına girdiler. "Bu gece bizim için önemli," dedi sonra, "bu geceyi yoğunbakımda geçirsin, ani birşey olmasını istemiyoruz, bazı ilaçlar veriyoruz, heyecan ya da panik yeni bir duruma yol açabilir, yanına girebilirsiniz ama fazla kalmayın ve mümkünse ağlamayın. Ben yarın daha iyi haberler vereceğimi düşünüyorum..."

"Durumunun farkında mı?" diye sordum.

"Az çok," dedi, "şu anda aslında yarı uyur durumda, kriz geçirdiğini ve düzeleceğini, kontrol altında olduğunu söylüyoruz, bu gece uyuyacak, konuşurken saçmalarsa korkmayın..."

Üşüdüm. Akşam oluyor. Çayla kurabiye yiyorum. Neden bütün bunları yazmadım diye kızıyorum kendime.

Sanki yazmak hayatı saklamaya yetermiş gibi...

Sanki hayatımın romanını yazarmış gibi yolculuk bitmeden tüm bunları hatırlamaya çalışıyorum.

Neden?

Bir anlam bulmak için mi?

Gerçekten de bir anlamı var mı?

Bütün bu görüntülerin, rüyaların, bunca yılda yaşanan, hiç nedensiz biçimde kimileri unutulmazken kimileri yitip giden anların, beklenmedik bir karşılaşmayla bütün hayatımızı değiştiren insanların, onca çalışmanın, mutluluğun, ilk karşılaşmadan sonra bizi hep kaygılandıran korkuların, hastalıkların, ölümlerin, ölümü unutabilmek için bunca çabalamanın, taşınılan evlerin, kurulan hayatların, bütün bu eşyanın, uzaklara gitmenin, geri dönmenin, aşkların, sevgilerin, ayrılıkların, kavgaların, peşinden gidilen sözlerin, tutmaktan vazgeçilen sözlerin, bizim yalnızca kısa bir zaman diliminde içinden geçip gittiğimiz ama yine de değiştireceğimize inandığımız hayatın gerçekten anlamı var mı?

O gün Ferhat'ın telaşlı ve düşünceli bir hali olduğunu sanırım farketmedim. Zaten o anda neyin farkındaydım ki...

Gitmesi gerektiğini söyledi.

"Senin gelmeni hiç beklemiyordum," dediğimde, yüzüme gülümseyerek bakıp, "Hayır, bekliyordun..." dedi.

Sonra bana sıkıca sarıldı.

Vedalaştık.

Anneannem görmese de yoğunbakımın penceresinden içeri baktı ve ona el salladı.

Birkaç gün sonra eve döndük.

Sonunda kurtulduğu için mutluyduk. Ama artık eskisi gibi değildi.

İşte bir bulut gelmiş ve bütün resmi, renkleri, ışığı, müziği değiştirmişti.

Sare Hanım büyük koltuğunda oturuyor, boşluğa bakıyor, yüzünde bambaşka bir ifade var artık. Bir yanı tutmuyor. Artık istediğini yapamıyor. Aslında yapmak da istemiyor.

İstekleri dışında pek konuşmuyor. Her gün alması gereken sürüyle ilaç var.

Biz sanki hayat eskisi gibi oyunu oynuyoruz ama tabii ki beceremiyoruz.

İlk günler gelen giden eksik olmuyor.

Ama sonra onlar da yavaş yavaş azalıyor. Zaten onların gelmesinden çok memnun görünmüyor. Çoğu zaman konuşan insanlara değil de uzaktaki bir noktaya bakıyor.

Çocukken anneme kızdığım zaman kendimce böyle bir oyun oynardım. Saatlerce dalıp gider, hiç konuşmazdım. Deli olurdu annem.

Şimdi o da sanki böyle yapıyor. Küsmüş çocuk gibi...

Sanki bir yanı o hiçbirimizin bilmediği ama onun gördüğü dünyada kalmış gibi...

Eve ilk geldiğimizde ayna istedi. Eski el aynasını getirdim. Kendine baktı, baktı, iç geçirdi. Bir daha da istemedi.

Onu böylece bırakıp gidemezdim. Neredeyse gittiğim için kendimi suçluyordum zaten.

Kaydımı dondurmaya karar verdim.

Taner Amca, ona her gün çeşitli hareketler yaptıracak birini buldu. O ne yaparsa yapsın eskisi gibi davranmamızı, konuşmamızı istedi.

"Şu andaki durumu aslında beynindeki sıkıntıdan çok kendisini bu durumda görmek istememekten kaynaklanan bir depresyon ama ağır bir depresyon... Bunun için de bir doktor arkadaşımı göndereceğim. Durumunu kabullenmesi ve yeniden yaşamaya başlaması lazım. Şu an yaşamayı durdurmuş halde."

Yaşamayı durdurmak...

Öyle iyi biliyordum ki bu duyguyu...

Kimbilir kaç gece artık vazgeçmek, durdurmak değil, sonlandırmak bile istememiş miydim?

Şimdi tıpkı onun yaptığı gibi sürekli uyumak, karanlıkta kalmak, yorganın içinden çıkmamak...

O bir sürü ilacı artık içmemek...

Taner Amca'yı geçirirken kolumu tuttu, "Bence okuluna dönsen daha iyi edersin ama senin kararın yine de... Pek çok hasta bu durumda böyle tepki verir ama zamanla geçer. En azından sizinle burada... Sen kendini çok üzme, çok fazla düşünme, bunların geçeceğine inan. Bu arada seninle konuşmam gerekenler var ama yalnız. Bir ara bana uğra..." dedi.

Meraklandım ama çok üstünde durmadım.

O ışıltılı geceler, o güzel sabahlar, o evin neşesi kaybolup gitti. Sessizlik, hüzün, sıkıntı geldi yerine. Alışmadığımız, bilmediğimiz bir hayat başladı.

Eskiden buraya nadiren inen annem artık hep aşağıdaydı ve annesine bakmaktan sanki memnun gibiydi. Bunca yıl sonra Sare Hanım ilk kez ona muhtaçtı.

Ne demişti bana bir akşam:

"Çok şey bilince hiç birşey bilmiyormuş gibi olursun... çok şey yaşayınca hiç yaşamamış gibi olursun... çok yaşlanırsan çocuk gibi olursun..."

Şimdi o çocuk gibiydi ve annem de onun annesi gibi...

Yalnızca birkaç ay önce buradan giderken "yeni bir hayat" demiştim.

Çok kısa süre sonra böyle geri döneceğim ve yeni hayatın bambaşka bir biçim alacağı aklımın ucundan bile geçmemişti.

Hastaneye geldiği o sabahtan sonra Ferhat'tan ses çıkmamıştı. Birkaç kez telefon ettim ama telefon açılmıyordu.

Yeniden Van'a döndüğünü düşündüm.

Ama dönmemişti.

Herhalde birkaç hafta sonraydı. Anneannemi ziyarete gelen yaşlı gazeteci onun yurtdışına kaçtığını söyledi.

Kaçmak mı?

Şaşkın şaşkın baktım.

O kadar habersizdim ki olup bitenlerden.

Londra'ya geldiğinde bana Van'da çocuklar için yapacağı atölye çalışmasını uzun uzun anlatmıştı. İnanılmaz heyecan içindeydi.

İstanbul'da bunca konuşulan bir ressamken yeni sergi açmak yerine oraya gitmesi beni çok etkilemişti. Sergileri çok konuşuluyor ama resimleri satılmıyordu.

Galericiler ondan, daha küçük boyutta, evlere, işyerlerine asılacak, "karamsar olmayan" resimler çizmesini istiyorlardı.

"İçimden gelmeyenleri nasıl çizebilirim ki?" diyordu.

Sanırım uzun zaman yapmak istediğiyle yapması gerekenler arasında kalmaktan çok sıkılmıştı. Öte yandan para kazanması gerekiyordu. Sonra ünlü bir galericiyle anlaşmış, ona sergi sözü vermiş ve çocuklarla yapacağı bu çalışma için para almış.

Londra'ya da o parayla gelmiş olmalıydı. Gözlerinin parladığını farketmiştim yapacaklarını anlatırken... Sanki kendi doğup büyüdüğü topraklara geri dönerek aslında yaptıklarının anlamını yeniden bulmaya çalışıyordu. Bütün bu para konuşmalarının, pazarlama çabalarının, onu biçimlendirme isteklerinin dışına çıkmak istiyordu belki de...

Ama onbeş günlük kamp sırasında gözaltına alınmış, terör örgütüyle ilişkisi olduğu, çocukları buna alet ettiği gibi suçlamalarla sorgulanmıştı.

Gazeteci bunları anlatırken ne hissettiğimi bugün gibi hatırlıyorum.

Korku, büyük bir çarpıntı, şaşkınlık...

Böyle birşey olmadığına, asla olamayacağına emindim ama onun o kapalı hayatı nedeniyle daha önce başka konularda hakkında ne kadar çok söylenti varsa şimdi bundan da pek çoklarının kuşkulanacağını hatta inanacağını biliyordum.

Öyle bir zamandı ki akla gelmedik insanlara akla gelmedik suçlar atılıyor ve onlar kendilerini savunamadan birileri televizyonda, gazetelerde onları hemen mahkum ediveriyor, geçmişe dönüp, söylediklerinden, yazdıklarından kendilerince deliller buluyor, daha sorguları bile bitmeden cezayı kesiyorlardı.

Kimse tam olarak neler olduğunu anlamıyordu.

Herkes komplodan, kumpastan sözediyordu ama kimin kime komplo yaptığını, hangisinin doğru olduğunu kimse tam olarak anlayamıyordu.

Öyle çok ses çıkıyordu ki sesiniz o seslerin içinde boğulup gidiyor, aylar, yıllar süren davalar sırasında hapislere atılan insanların söyledikleri artık duyulmaz oluyordu.

Üstelik bu duruma herkes alışmaya başlamış, artık en olmadık insanlar hakkındaki en garip suçlamalar bile normal hale gelmişti.

Kimse kimseye inanmıyor, insanlar yakından tanıdıkları hakkında söylenenlere bile itiraz etmek yerine "acaba olabilir mi" diye düşünmeye başlıyordu.

Belki de asıl korkunç olan buydu.

En yakınlarından, yıllarca tanıdığın insanlardan hatta en sonunda kendinden bile kuşkuya düşmek...

Sare Hanım bunları dinlerken baktığı o boşluktan gözlerini çevirdi, bize döndü, "Nerede?" diye sordu.

Uzun zaman sonra ilk kez bir konuşmayla ilgilenmişti.

Gazeteci, "Gözaltında epeyce eziyet görmüş ama sonra bırakmışlar, galiba izlendiğini ve yeniden tutuklanacağını anlamış, yurtdışına kaçmış, şimdi nerede olduğunu kimse bilmiyor..." dedi.

Sıradan bir haberi anlatır gibiydi.

Birden o sabaha döndüm.

Yüzündeki o garip, düşünceli, kaygılı, yorgun ifade buydu demek ki...

Yine de oraya gelmişti.

Veda etmeye mi?

Belki de telaşla gitmesinin nedeni buydu.

Belki de oradan çıkıp bilinmeyen bir yere gidiyordu.

Belki de bana söylemek isteyip de söyleyemediğini düşündüğüm buydu.

"İşin kötüsü," diye devam etti gazeteci, "yakalama kararı çıkartmışlar, kaçmasaydı şu anda hapiste olacaktı..."

Kalktım. İçeri gittim. Karanlıkta duvara yaslanıp yere oturdum. Kulaklarımdaki çınlama neredeyse çığlığa dönüştü. Ellerimle kulaklarımı kapadım.

Ama işe yaramadı.

Çığlık dışarıdan gelmiyordu çünkü.

Çığlık benim içimdeydi.

Belki ancak şimdi aradan zaman geçince anlayabiliyorum bazı şeyleri.

Anneannemin hep güçlü, canlı, neşeli görünmesi aslında onun en büyük korkusuna karşı oluşturduğu bir kalkandı.

Ölüm.

Dedemin uzun ve acılı ölüm sürecini gün gün yaşamıştı. Onun artık bedeninin neredeyse tükendiği, her yerinde yaralar açıldığı günlerin ardından bilincini kaybetmesi, olur olmaz konuşması, kimseyi tanımaması Sare Hanım'da büyük bir korku yaratmıştı.

Ama sonuna kadar ona bakmış, her zaman başkalarının onu görmek istediği gibi güçlü, dirayetli, cesur bir kadın olmanın ağırlığını taşımak zorunda kalmıştı.

Onu kaybettikten sonra bambaşka bir hayat kurması, sürekli ışıkları yanan evde hiç yalnız kalmak istememesi, her akşam toplanan insanlar, eğlenceler, müzik aslında hepsi bu korkuyla ilgiliydi.

Doktorların tüm uyarılarına rağmen ne en küçük bir hastalığı ne de yaşlandığını kabul etmişti.

"İlaçlarımı alıyorum işte daha ne istiyorlar, sigara yok, kahve yok, o yok, bu yok, böyle de yaşanmaz ki canım," diye kestirip atardı.

Benim hastalığımı kabullenmeyişi, neredeyse görmezden gelmesi, beni de hep güçlü durmaya, olup bitenlerle başa çıkmaya zorlaması da bundandı.

Oysa aslında birçok doktorla konuşmuş, neler olup bittiğini ayrıntılarıyla öğrenmişti.

Belki de sonunda onların da gerçekte ne yapacaklarını bilmediğini, bir çare olmadığını anlayıp yapılacak tek şeyin bu hastalıkla yaşamak olduğunu düşünmüştü.

Ya da hep yaptığı gibi kötü şeyleri kapının dışında tutmak istemişti. Hep kızmaz mıydı bize, "Ölümden sözetmeyin çünkü o hep buralarda bir yerlerdedir, duyar, gelir," diye...

Annemle ilişkisinin bozulmasına, son yıllarında bütün enerjisini dedeme vermek zorunda kalıp kızıyla yeterince ilgilenemeyişinin neden olduğunu (bunu hiç söylemese de) bence biliyordu.

Hatta babamı seçmesine karşı çıktığı halde annemin onu dinlemeyişinde bile kendisini suçluyordu. Belki de gerçekten bu annemin ondan öç alma yoluydu.

Üstüne üstlük babamın gitmesinden sonra bir de bizimle ilgilenmesi gerekmişti.

Hayır, bundan şikayetçi değildi. Aksine bizim burada olmamızdan çok memnundu. Beni her gördüğünde "İşte benim küçük mutluluğum, neşem," derdi.

Bazen onun hayatını düşünürken, belki de ölümün bir gün birdenbire çıkageleceğini ve o zamana kadar istediği gibi yaşaması gerektiğini düşünüyordum.

Sanırım, bizlerin, çevresindeki insanların onunla ilgili algısına, sanki her zaman burada kalacağı, başına birşey gelmeyeceği yanılsamasına bir zaman sonra kendisi de inanmıştı.

Ve sonra en büyük korkusuyla yüzleşmişti.

O bekleme odasında yatarken aslında uzak ve geri dönülmez ülkenin kapısındaydı.

Ama eğer böyleyse ve o korkuyu yaşayıp geri geldikten sonra neden kaldığı yerden devam edemiyordu?

Başımı okşarken ona bakıyordum. Onu böyle görmek beni çok üzüyordu. Sanki gerçekten de çok uzaklardan gelmiş gibi yorgundu. Sanki artık o sırrı öğrenmiş ama söyleyemiyor gibi bir hali vardı.

Hayır, kötü düşünmeyecektim. Zaman geçecek ve o yeniden eski Sare Hanım olacaktı. Yine buraya insanlar gelecek, yine müzik çalacak, danslar edilecek, kahkahalar geceyarısından sonra bile etraftan duyulacaktı.

"Sen ne zaman okuluna dönüyorsun?" diye sordu bir akşam.

Onunla kalmak ve onu yeniden eski haliyle görmek istiyordum. O anda tek istediğim buydu.

"Ben o okulu sevmedim, burada okuyacağım," dedim.

İnanacak sanki...

Yüzümü okşadı, gülümsemeye çalıştı.

İlk kez bu evde dört kadın yalnız başımızaydık. Saniye sanki bu sayede tüm bunlar düzelecekmiş gibi durmadan yiyecek birşeyler getiriyordu. Şimdi de onun çok sevdiği meyve şekerlemelerinden getirmişti.

Annem her nedense vazgeçemediği Barbara Cartland romanlarından birini okuyordu.

Kalktım, ışıkların hepsini yaktım. Müzik dolabından onun sevdiği plaklardan birini alıp çalmaya başladım.

"Kimse bir yere gitmiyor Sare Hanım," dedim, "hepimiz burada yanındayız..."

Zoraki gülümsedi.

Hepimiz...

Ama sanki o artık burada değildi.

Belki de hayatımızın en sessiz, en uzun kışıydı. Kendimi içinde bulunduğum garip ruh halinden kurtarmak için ne yapacağımı bulmaya çalışıyordum. En çok da ebru. Neredeyse her gün...

Kağıdın üzerine aldıktan ve kuruttuktan sonra getirip anneanneme gösteriyordum. Bu ona çok iyi geldi. Garip bir biçimde onları görünce heyecanlanıyor, biraz geciksem sesleniyor, bitmedi mi hala diye soruyordu.

Ara sıra Seda'yla dışarı çıkıyor, dertleşiyorduk.

Belli etmiyordum ama başımdaki uyuşukluk, kulağımdaki ağrı ve sesler giderek artıyordu.

Birşeyin geldiğini biliyor ve çok korkuyordum.

Hiç sırası değildi.

Ne olur şimdi olmasın diye dua ediyordum her gece.

Yürürken sarhoş gibi birden ayağım boşluğa basıyor, bir yerlere, birine tutunmak zorunda kalıyordum ve bu giderek daha da sıklaşmıştı.

Bir yere uzun süre bakınca orada sanki boşluktaki ekranda film izler gibi başka görüntüler beliriyordu. Uyanıkken rüya görüyordum.

Sabahları erken saatte çarpıntıyla uyanıyor, yeniden uyumaya çalışırken başımdaki uyuşma yüzünden bir türlü dalamıyor ve böyle saatler geçiriyordum.

O kış ne çok kar yağdı.

Sare Hanım koltuğunu pencerenin önüne aldırdı. Oradan lapa lapa yağan kara bakar ve gülümserdi.

Denizin üstüne yağan kar, her iki kıyıdaki koruları kaplayan beyazlık, çok üşümemize rağmen iyi geldi bize.

Fazla iyileşme yoktu ama aylar geçtikçe daha çok konuşmaya başladı. Söylediklerini biz alıştığımız için anlıyorduk ama misafirler zorlanıyordu. Bu da onun canını sıkıyor, sonra yorulduğunu söyleyip başka kimseyi istemiyordu. Tek elini kullanmaya alıştı. Önceleri kahvesini eli titrediği için dökerken hemen her gün gelen terapist sayesinde güçlendi.

Hatta en baştan kesinlikle reddettiği tekerlekli iskemleyle onu birkaç kez dışarı da çıkardık. Çok sevdiği köşedeki balıkçıda Yorgo Amca ona harika bir buğulama yaptı.

Ferhat'tan hiç ses yoktu. Nereye gittiğini, ne yaptığını kimse bilmiyordu. Hakkındaki dava devam ediyor, herkes iddiaların çok kötü olduğunu, çok büyük bir ceza geleceğini söylüyordu. Onunla bağlantılı tanıdığım kimse yoktu. Mecbur kalmasa böyle yapmayacağını, en azından bana haber ulaştıracağını düşünüyordum ama yine de kızıyordum ona.

Selçuk Bey'i aradım, başkalarını buldum ama sanki herkes bir sırrı saklar gibi suspus olmuştu.

Sonra biri geldi ve onun Almanya'ya gittiğini, orada eski sevgilisinin evine yerleştiğini söyledi.

Boğazımda birşey düğümlendi. Başım döndü. Daha fazla soramadım. Doğru mu, yalan mı? Bilemedim. Ama öyledir ya, insan hep kötüsüne inanır.

Bu kader mi? Babam gibi aynı ülkeye mi gitti?

Kırgındım.

Ona, hayata hatta anneanneme bile...

Ne yapalım ki benimki de böyle bir hayattı.

Bir gün Seniha Teyze yaptığım ebrulara bakarken, "Bak aklıma ne geldi," dedi, "bunları kumaşlara basalım... İpek fularlar, eşarplar yapalım."

"Olur mu ki?" dedim.

"Neden olmasın, pek güzel olur ama önce küçük bir sergi açalım, herkes görsün, basında çıksın, ne yapacağımızı anlatalım..."

Tam da artık karların hemen ardından beyaz bahar çiçekleri açmaya başlamıştı.

Daha çok çalışmaya başladım. Artık kocaman bir teknem vardı. Küçük kağıtlar yerine büyük kartonlara alıyordum ebruları.

Ne tuhaf! Beni bırakıp gitmişti. Ama bana birşey bırakmıştı ve o benim bütün hayatımı belirleyecekti. Suyun içinde küçük dokunuşlarla değişen renklerle oluşan bir dünya.

Elinizden kayıp giden rüyalar gibi.

Demişti ki, "Ressam, her zaman yaptığı esere hakimdir, istediğini değiştirir, istediği rengi bozar, yeniden yapar, ama ebru sanatçısı görünmez bir elle birliktedir, bazen yakaladığı deseni, rengi yeniden bulamaz, bazen aklından geçeni yaparken hiç beklenmedik bambaşka bir desenle karşılaşır. Ve belki de asıl yapması gereken odur..."

Kayıp giden rüyalar.

Evet, renklere bakıyordum, desenlere ve onu düşünüyordum aslında, o benim kayıp giden rüyamdı.

Ve evet doğru, benim elimi tutan görünmez bir el vardı.

İşte öyle garip birşey.

Onu hatırlıyordum. Hep içimde bir yerde. Burukluk mu? Mutluluk mu? Özlem mi? Umut mu?

Çünkü günün birinde sanki onu yeniden bulacakmışım gibi, bir yerlerden çıkıp gelecekmiş gibi...

Yapmamış mıydı?

Ama gün günden yaşananlar siliniyor. Unutuluyor. Belki öyle istediğimiz için... Ara sıra kış ortasında yazdan kalma bir gün gibi bulutların arasından güneş parlayıp sönüyor.

Saklambaç oynar gibi...

Tam da öyle değil miydi?

Gözlerimi kapatıp sayarken ortadan yokolmuştu ve onu bulamıyordum.

Aylardan nisan mı? Mayıs mı?

Bilmiyorum.

Çünkü günler bizim için artık başkaları için olduğundan farklıydı. Günler, bu evin içinde yaşananlardı. Perşembe mi, pazartesi mi çok da umurumuzda değildi.

Birşeylerin yeniden değiştiği bir gün olduğunu biliyorum yalnızca.

O eski kulenin yanında daracık arnavut kaldırımı yokuşun üzerindeki galeride sergim açılıyor.

Ebrular çerçevelendi. Hepsine isimler verildi.

Son gece sabaha kadar onları asmakla uğraşırken bakıyorum ve kendi kendime "Bunları ben mi yaptım," diyorum. Yoksa gizemli bir el mi yaptırdı hepsini?

Kapıda fotoğrafım var. Turuncu, yeşil, mavi renklerle dolu bir ebrunun önünde boşluğa bakar gibi duruyorum.

Ben.

Ebru.

Sare Hanım herkesten önce sergiyi geziyor tekerlekli iskemlesinde. Elimi sıkıyor, ağlıyor. Sonra insanlar geliyor. Kalabalık. Gazeteciler sorular soruyor. Cevaplamaya çalışıyorum. Nasıl başladım? Neden başladım? Bundan sonra ne yapacağım?

Kem küm ediyorum. Neyse ki Seniha Teyze var yanımda. Ne söylenmesi gerekiyorsa söylüyor.

Tanıdıklar var, yazarlar, ressamlar, yönetmenler, akşam yemeklerinde birlikte olduğumuz pek çok insan...

Fotoğraflar çekiliyor. Gülümsüyorum.

Tolga, rengarenk çiçekler yollamış, "Sen herşeyin en güzelini yaparsın, orada olamadığım için deliriyorum ama yaza az kaldı, bu ilk sergin ama son olmayacak, sakın hepsini satma, en güzeli benim..." yazmış.

Aklıma mezuniyet gecesi geliyor.

Ferhat yine aniden çıkıp gelir mi?

Buradan, bu kalabalıktan beni çıkartıp nereye kaçtıysa beni de oraya götürür mü?

Hayır, gelmeyeceğini biliyorum.

Ama bu an'ı en çok onun görmesini isterdim.

İlk ebrunun ismi, "Gizli El".

Her neredeyse belki de neden o ismi koyduğumu bilir, hisseder.

Seniha Teyze çok mutlu. "Sana öyle bir koleksiyon yapacağım ki inanamayacaksın, bu fularlar, eşarplar efsane olacak," diye anlatıyor sürekli.

Annem bana sarılıyor. Sare Hanım'la kadeh kaldırıyoruz. Seda yanımdan ayrılmıyor.

Galiba bahar geldi.

Anneannem yoruldu. Annem onu eve götürdü.
İnsanlar içiyor, kendi aralarında konuşuyor ve artık sergiyle ilgilenmiyordu.

Genç kemancı eski çağlardan şarkılar çalıyordu. Başka çağlardan ama yine de bizi içine alıp hüzünlendiren, eski bir zamana taşıyan, yeniden buraya getiren...

Seda'yla bir köşede oturduk.

Ben de yorulmuştum.

Dün gece sabaha kadar düzenlemelerle uğraşmıştım ve heyecandan pek uyuyamamıştım.

Kısa, kırlaşmış saçlı, kirli sakallı, ince yünden çok şık koyu yeşil takım giymiş biri geldi yanımıza.

Seda ayaklandı.

Adam ona değil bana bakıyordu.

"Aaa, Onur Bey hoşgeldiniz," dedi.

Sonra benimle tanıştırdı.

Ünlü bir mimardı ama ben tanımıyordum.

"Sizi tebrik etmek istedim, ebrunun bu kadar ilgimi çekeceğini düşünmezdim, uzun zamandır bu kadar hoşuma giden eserler görmedim," dedi.

"Hangi ebrunun?" diye manasız bir espri yaptı Seda.

Zoraki gülümsedim.

Doğruyu söylemem gerekirse hayatımda gördüğüm en yakışıklı adamdı.

Espriyi duymamış gibi yaptı.

Belki şu sakallarını da kesse daha iyi olacaktı.

Yeni restore ettiği bir yalı için ebrulardan bazılarını almak istiyordu.

"Bu yalnızca sergi," dedim, "bunlar satılık değil.."

"Biliyorum,"dedi, "ama eğer gelip yalıyı görürseniz, bunların orada olmasını istersiniz bence, cumartesi sabah işiniz yoksa birlikte gidelim mi?"

Şaşkın şaşkın baktım.

Nereye?

Seda, "Boğazın en güzel yalılarından biri," dedi, "beraber gideriz, en azından görmen lazım çünkü Onur Bey çok güzel şeyler yaptı.."

Bir an gözgöze geldik, gözlerini kaçırdı.

Ne zamandır bana, "Artık biriyle tanışman lazım, bu adamı unutman lazım," deyip duruyordu.

"Aslında biliyor musunuz, evde bunlardan daha çok var, bir ara onları da görmeye gelin, sergi için aralarından zor seçtik," dedi.

O sırada bilmiyordum.

Seda'nın evli bir adamla birlikte olduğunu, Onur'un adamın en yakın arkadaşı olduğunu, bu nedenle tanıştıklarını ve onu o gece benimle tanıştırmak için çağırdığını...

Yalan söylemeyeceğim.

Çok yakışıklı, havalı, güzel konuşan, espriler yapan, etkileyici biriydi.

Sohbet devam ederken birdenbire kalktı, "Bu sizin geceniz, galiba fazla meşgul ettim, cumartesi sabah buluşuyoruz, yeniden tebrik ediyorum," dedi ve elimi sıkıp gitti.

Cumartesi sabah buluşuyor muyuz?

"Bu neydi böyle?" diye sordum Seda'ya.

Muzipçe gülümsedi, "Bilmem, sence?" dedi.

Gerçekten de hayatın bizi nereye sürükleyeceğini, hiç beklenmedik rastlantılarla dünyanın birdenbire değişebileceğini düşünmüyoruz.

Ama öyle oluyor.

Evet itiraf ediyorum ki o gece serginin heyecanıyla, yorgunluğuyla eve geldiğimde, belki de aylardır ilk kez güzel bir uykuya dalarken uzun zaman sonra birinin ilgimi çektiğini düşündüm.

Düşündüm ve bu yüzden utandım.

Öyle derin uyumuşum ki sabah beni uyandırmaya kıyamamışlar. Kendime geldiğimde neredeyse öğle olmuştu.

Sare Hanım bile bunca zaman sonra ilk kez keyifliydi.

Annem herkesin benim yaptıklarımla ilgili söylediklerini anlatıyordu heyecanla.

Kendime gelmek için kahvemi içerken annem, masanın üstüne dizdiği çiçekleri gösterdi.

Biri galeri sahibinden, biri Seniha Teyze'den gelmişti. Ve rengarenk lalelerden kocaman bir buket daha vardı. Küçük zarfın içindeki kartı çıkardım. "Laleler ebrulara yakışır diye düşündüm, görüşmek üzere, tebrikler... Onur..." yazıyordu.

Birden durdum.

Galiba Tolga'dan başka bir erkekten ilk kez çiçek alıyordum.

İyi ama adresi nereden bulmuştu? Galeriye mi bırakmıştı? Annem gözucuyla bana bakıyordu. Tabii ki sormadım.

İlk kez bir erkekten çiçek alıyordum, ilk kez bir erkeği aldattığımı düşünüyordum.

Ne saçmalıyorum ben? Belli ki çapkının biri. Benimle niye ilgilendi bilmem ama ilgilendiği belli. Hoş , zarif bir adam. Hepsi bu. Çok fazla düşünmeye, üstünde durmaya gerek yok.

Kendi kendime bunları söylerken cumartesi sabahını düşünüyor muydum?

Evet, düşünüyordum.

Bir iki gün sonra gazetelerde sergiyle ilgili yazılar çıktı. İlk kez kendi fotoğrafımı gazetede gördüm. Annem hepsini kesip dosyaladı.

Seniha Teyze'yle buluştuk ve neler yapacağımızı konuştuk. Doğrusu şaşkındım. O günlerde bunun yıllar sonra bambaşka birşeye dönüşeceğini, birçok ülkede tanınacağımı ve geçimimi böyle sağlayacağımı hiç düşünmüyordum.

Yalnızca o fularların, eşarpların üzerinde kendi desenlerimi, renklerimi, rüyalarımı görecek olmanın heyecanı içindeydim.

Seda bana herşeyi anlattı. Onun böyle bir ilişkiye girmesine çok şaşırdım. Gizli patikada yürüyordu ve sonuçlarına katlanacaktı. En azından çok uzun zaman sonra mutlu görünmesinin nedeni buydu ve bunu yargılamaya hiç niyetim yoktu. Bazen başkalarının hayatı için susmak en doğrusudur.

Adamın karısından ayrılacağını, zaten çok uzun zamandır mutsuz olduğunu, çok iyi biri olduğunu anlatıp duruyordu. Hem yaptığından utanıyor, hem de vazgeçemiyordu.

Şimdi olsa belki ona, kaçamak zamanların, çalınmış saatlerin, yalnızca keyifli geçirilen günlerin hep yarım kalacağını, sonunda hiç sandığı gibi olmayacağını söylerdim.

Yalnızca Onur'la beni tanıştırmak için planlar yapmasına kızdım. Ama biliyordum ki benim iyiliğimi düşünüyor, kayıp bir aşkın ardından gözyaşı dökmemi, boşu boşuna gelmeyecek birini beklememi istemiyor, içinde bulunduğum durumdan çıkmam için yeni heyecanlar yaşamam gerektiğine inanıyordu.

"O senin eserlerini istiyor, gerisi sana kalmış," dedi.

"Eserlerimi mi?" diye kahkaha attım.

Gece gitsem mi gitmesem mi diye düşünmekten uyuyamadım. Aslında galiba gideceğimi biliyordum ama her nedense içimdeki ses gitmemem gerektiğini söylüyordu.

Gittim.

Sabah Seda gelip beni aldı, bahar sabahı, denizin üstünde ışıklar titrerken sanırım hayatımda gördüğüm en güzel eve girdim.

Ev sahibesiyle Onur bizi kapıda karşıladı.

Zayıf, orta boylu, sade ama bakımlı bir kadın... Herhalde otuzlu yaşlarının sonunda. Yanındaki köpek bile özel seçilmiş. Kızıl kahve renkli uzun tüylü afgan tazısı. Bu ev ona büyük dedesinden kalmış. O zamandan kalan ağaçlarla dolu dev bir bahçe... İnsanın neredeyse bütün gününü yalnızca bakarak geçirebileceği bir manzara... Uzaktan geçen gemiler...

Onur'a baktım gözucuyla. Erkek için fazla şık ve bakımlı diye geçirdim aklımdan.

Öyleydi gerçekten de.

Fazla yakışıklı, fazla bakımlı, fazla düşünceli, fazla esprili. Belki de bazı insanlar için en başta hissettiğimiz doğrudur.

Garip ama Ferhat'ın neredeyse tam tersiydi.

Ferhat başkalarının ona bakışını ne kadar umursamıyorsa Onur tümüyle başkaları için yaşayan biriydi.

Ama aynı zamanda aralarında benzerlik de vardı. Onur da onun gibi kendisini yaratmış biriydi. Yani aslında kendi hayatının mimarıydı.

Elbette bütün bunları o gün değil, ardından gelen aylar içinde anlayacaktım.

Ama o aylar içinde bir biçimde ona alıştım. Hatta diyebilirim ki ben de ona uymaya başladım.

İnsanları alıp götürebilen, masadaki herkesin ilgi odağı olan, anlatacak pek çok hikayesi olan biriydi.

Belki asıl etkileyiciliği de bundandı.

İstanbul'da okumuş sonra yurtdışına gitmiş, ünlü bir mimarlık şirketinde çalıştıktan sonra geri dönünce yıldızı parlamıştı.

Hem işini iyi yapıyordu hem de gerçekten zevkliydi. Bir evi restore ederken öyle ayrıntılar buluyordu ki eve sihirli değnek girmiş gibi bambaşka bir hale getiriyordu.

O sabah bahçede dolaşırken ağaçların arasında duvar dibine dayanmış eski mermer çeşme dikkatimi çekti.

"Dayımların evinin bahçesindeydi. Erenköy'de küçük, orta halli, sobalı bir evdi. Şimdi tabii yıkıldı ve yerine apartman dikildi. Oradan ancak bu çeşmeyi kurtarabildim," dedi.

Onu dayısıyla yengesi büyütmüştü.

"Bana onlardan kalan tek şey bu. Onu görmek beni hem mutlu ediyor hem de üzüyor."

"O yüzden mi evinize değil de buraya koydunuz?" diye sordum. Bu bana biraz garip gelmişti aslında.

"Evet," dedi, "hani insan birini çok sever ama onun kendisine zarar verdiğini, üzdüğünü bilir, hem onu görmek hem de ayrılmak ister, aynı bunun gibi..."

Galiba ondan asıl etkilendiğim, bunu anlatırken gerçekten karşı kıyıya bakıp dalması olmuştu.

Her nedense aslında pek de önemli görünmeyen bu anı beni çok şaşırtmıştı. Belki onu anlatma biçimi...

Sanki o çeşmeye dokunurken benim bilmediğim gizemli bir geçmişe, çocukluğun karmaşık, üstüne tül örtülmüş dünyasına geri dönmüş ve yüzüne baktığımda hiç tanımadığım o küçük oğlanı bir an için gördüğümü sanmıştım.

O zaman onu ilk kez merak ettim. Bütün bu fazlalıkların içindeki adamı...

Ebruların nereye asılacağını gösterdi sonra bize... Üstelik tek tek anlatıyordu renkleriyle... Pırıl pırıl bir cumartesi sabahı. Seniha Teyze'ye sormam lazımdı.

"Ben sordum bile," dedi...

"Öyle mi?"

"Evet, o da sana sormamı söyledi..."

Ne diyeceğimi bilemedim ve "Peki o zaman," dedim.

"O zaman bunu kutlayalım," dedi Jülide Hanım.

Kendimizi bahçede özenle hazırlanmış masada bulduk. Üstelik yalnızca beş, on dakikalığına geldiğimiz bu evde, peynirlerle, kurutulmuş etler ve meyvelerle dolu masada saatlerce oturduk.

Bunca zaman sonra ilk kez birileriyle oturup konuşmak, neredeyse hayatın tek resmiymiş gibi belleğime kazınan koltuklardan, tablolardan, biblolardan başka bir yerde, uzun, üzücü, korkutucu kışın ardından ilk güzel bahar sabahında bana çok iyi geldi.

Kısa süre sonra sanki hepimiz eskiden beri tanışıyormuşuz gibi çene çalıyorduk.

İnsanın aklında, yüreğinde biri varken onu başkasıyla unutması imkansızdır.

Bunu biliyordum.

Ama Onur sanki bunu anlamış gibi, başlarda benimle yalnızca flört eder gibi göründü hatta arkadaşlarından biriymişim gibi davrandı.

Okulu bırakmıştım ama Seniha Teyze'nin yanına gidiyor, haftada birkaç gün oradaki ustalardan bilmediklerimi öğrenmeye çalışıyordum.

Ve tabii çizimlere de devam ediyordum.

Sare Hanım artık daha iyiydi. O da benim bir an önce okula dönmemi istiyor, onun yüzünden gidemediğimi düşünüp üzülüyordu.

Annem yeni biriyle tanışmamdan, dışarı çıkmamdan memnundu.

Seda bu sayede gizli sevgilisini benimle tanıştırabilmiş, hep birlikte bir yerlere gidebildiğimiz için de rahatlamıştı.

Ben Onur'u hep Ferhat'la kıyaslıyordum.

Aramızda mesafe vardı ve ne gariptir ki o mesafe hiç kapanmayacaktı.

Ben kendimi geri çekiyordum ama o da sanki tam yakınlaşacağımız zaman beni durduruyordu.

Yoksa fısıltılar başlamıştı.

Zaten hep birileriyle birlikteydik. Onun hayatı böyleydi. Evini bile ilk kez kalabalık bir partide görebilmiştim.

Camlar, aynalar, altın varaklar, modern tasarımlarla Osmanlı zevki birleşmiş ama bana kalırsa garip bir tarz çıkmıştı ortaya.

Yemek salonunun duvarları simsiyah boyanmış, büyük, ağır antika masa ve siyah kadife sandalyeler... Tavandaki süslemelerle, meyve resimleri biraz kırıyordu bu karanlığı...

Uzun koridor boyunca duvara eski bir savaş sahnesi resmedilmişti.

Bir odada yıpranmış, çatlamış kahverengi deri koltuklar ve büyük bir kütüphane vardı.

Belki binlerce kitap... Oraya girip ışığı yaktığınız anda hep aynı müzik çalmaya başlıyordu.

Uzak bir ülkeden ve eski zamandan gelen bir müzik.

Sonradan neden hep bu müzik çalıyor diye sormuştum.

Çok genç yaşta uyuşturucudan ölen bir arkadaşının bestesi olduğunu söylemişti.

İnsan başkalarından korkar.

Hepimiz en yakınlarımıza karşı bile zırha bürünürüz. Bizi yoran bir zırh. Büyümek belki de budur. Anne kucağından çıktıktan sonra, birileriyle karşılaşmaya başladığın anda, sonra okulda, sonra işte, sonra sokakta hep birilerinden korunmaya çalışmak...

Eğer Tolga'yı saymazsam bir tek Ferhat'ın yanında böyle hissetmemiştim. Garip bir biçimde onun yanında inanılmaz derecede rahattım. Oysa erkeklerin yanında kendimi hiç rahat hissetmem.

Nedenini bilmiyordum ama Onur'un yanında da rahat değildim. Çok bilmiş halinden mi? Kesin yargılarla konuşmasından, emir verir gibi cümleler kurmasından mı?

Çevresindekilere, çalışanlara, gittiğimiz yerlerdeki garsonlara sanki hepsi onun için dünyaya gelmiş ve istediğini anında yapmalıymış gibi davranmasından mı?

Bunları kabaca yapmıyordu. Aksine gördüğüm en nazik insanlardan biriydi ama yapıyordu işte.

Kızdığı zaman bile gülerek espriyle öyle bir cümle kurardı ki karşısındaki öylece kalırdı. Sonra sanki laf olsun diye söylemiş gibi başka bir konuyla devam ederdi.

Bazen söylediğini beğenmezse şöyle bakar ve konuyu değiştirirdi.

Galiba içinden tam olarak ne geçtiğini anlayamadığım o bakış beni rahatsız ediyordu.

Zaten o başkalarını dinleyen biri değildi.

Daha çok kendisi konuşurdu. Ağaçlardan oyuncaklara, kitaplardan müziğe, bilmemneredeki kayıp adadan türü tükenen böceklere kadar bilmediği yoktu. Bir konuşmada sıkılırsa öyle bir konu açardı ki kimse o konuda birşey bilmediği için dinlemek zorunda kalırdı.

İşin garip yanı bu durumdan kimse sıkılmıyordu. Her yere davet ediliyor, insanlar onunla olmak istiyor, çoğu zaman ondan hayranlıkla sözediliyordu.

Aslında belki de bütün bunları sonraları düşündüm. O günlerde pek üstünde durmuyordum. Yavaş yavaş onun haline tavrına alıştım. İki günlüğüne bir yere gitse özlemeye bile başladım.

Anneanneme onu tanıştırmadan önce anlatmıştım. Dinledi dinledi sonra elimi tuttu, "İyi biri mi?" diye sordu.

Bütün bu anlattıklarım ona birşey ifade etmemişti.

"Bilmem ki," dedim, "iyi biri bence..."

O yaz üç, dört günlüğüne kalabalık bir tatile gittik.

Ama teklifini kabul ederken birşeyler olacağını artık biliyordum.

Dans ettik, öpüştük, gece sabahlara kadar deniz kenarında konuştuk. Benim anlatacağım ne vardı ki? Her zamanki gibi o anlattı. Ben dinledim. Benim anlatacaklarım hiç de iç açıcı değildi çünkü.

Anlattıklarımı da biraz değiştirip biraz süsleyerek anlattım.

Herkes öyle yapmaz mı?

Odamda yalnız kaldığımda hala içimde suçluluk vardı.

Ya Ferhat zordaysa? Ya çıkar gelirse? O savaş filmlerindeki gibi hissediyordum. Öldü denilen asker geri döner ve sevgilisini evlenmiş bulur...

Ama neden suçluluk duyuyordum ki?

Asıl olan ne hissettiğim değil miydi?

Duyuyordum çünkü aslında hala onu seviyordum.

Onur'a aşık değildim.

Herhalde o da değildi.

Kendi kendime "O zaman fazla düşünmeye de gerek yok," dedim.

Çünkü çok yorgundum. Üzgündüm. Onun neşesi, beni getirdiği bu yeni hayat, yeni insanlar uzun zaman sonra kendimi iyi hissetmemi sağlamıştı.

O tatil bana iyi geldi.

Belki onun da herkesin üstünde taşıdığı zırhı biraz olsun çıkardığını farkettim.

Evden uzaklaşmak, bambaşka bir ortamda birkaç gün geçirmek, denize girmek güzeldi... Unutmak için... Yeniden başlamak için... Hayatın hep sıkıntıyla, kuşkularla, kaygılarla kurulmadığına inanmak için...

Belki de Seda haklıydı. "Adam sana deli oluyor, bütün kadınlar peşindeyken senden başkasıyla ilgilenmiyor, bunca zaman ne bekliyorsun anlamıyorum, fazla naz aşık usandırır benden söylemesi..."

Tatilden döndüğümüzde beni eve bırakırken sarılıp uzun uzun öptü beni.

Artık kafam karışık değildi.

Ya da öyle olduğuna inanmak istiyordum.

Ne yapalım ki böyle.

Biri seni elinden tutup bir yerlere taşıyor, biriniyse oturup bekliyorsun gelsin diye, gelmiyor.

Tatilden döndüm ve karşımda Tolga'yı buldum.

Anneannemin dizinin dibine oturmuş, ona Londra hikayeleri anlatıyor.

Büyük olasılıkla yarısını uyduruyor.

Sarıldık. Ne çok özlemişim onu.

"Arkadaşlarla" gittiğim tatili anlattım ben de...

Annem yüzüme renk geldiğini söylüyordu.

Tolga bir ara kulağıma, "Ben senin yüzüne niye renk geldiğini biliyorum merak etme tek tek anlatacaksın biraz sonra," diye kıkırdadı.

Hiç ona anlatmadan olur mu?

Birkaç kez telefonla konuşmuştuk ve ona şöyle hafiften sözetmiştim ama Seda'dan da ayrıntıları aldığına şüphem yoktu.

Ayağında leopar desenli ayakkabılar, daracık neredeyse üstüne yapışmış pantolon, üstünde rengarenk gömlek bir de karışık taşlardan kocaman kolye...

Her zamanki gibi farklı...

Yemeğe oturduk hep birlikte. Saniye bile Tolga'yı gördüğüne pek sevinmiş, habire ona yedirmeye çalışıyor, "Sen oralarda özlemişsindir bak enginar var, börek var, kısır da yaptım," diye çocuğu bunaltıyordu.

İlk kez onu bu kadar zamandır görmüyordum.

En son konuşmamızda baletten ayrılmıştı. Ama tabii onun işi belli olmaz yeniden buluşmuş ya da başkasını bulmuş olabilir. Yüzünden anlaşılmıyor. Mutlu mu, değil mi? Gizli sıtma. Belli etmez.

Anneanneme neşelensin diye hikayeler anlatıp dururken ona baktım.

Şeytan çekici dedikleri oydu herhalde.

Kendi içinde ne yaşarsa yaşasın işte böyle hemen girdiği yerin havasını değiştirir, insanı en kötü havadan bile çıkartıp güldürmeyi başarırdı.

"Aa ne bu haliniz canım, cenazeye mi geldik," dediği an herkesin keyfi yerine gelirdi.

Ama ne tuhaf onun keyfi yerinde değildi...

İçinde çok başka şeyler olduğunu ben biliyordum.

Keşke olmasaydı, keşke biz birlikte olsaydık, evlenseydik diye geçti içimden.

Kimbilir ne eğlenirdik...

İşin komiği ikimiz birlikteyken başkalarıyla olduğumuzdan daha çok eğlendik her zaman.

Söylesem ne güler buna şimdi.

O günlerde bilgisayar oyunları yeni çıkmıştı. Sonra yüzlercesini yaptılar.

Ama kendi hayatımızı yeniden kurmak için bir oyun yapsalar ne güzel olurdu.

Geri dönüp kimi günleri silmenin, kimi günleri yeniden oluşturmanın, şu yola girerken vazgeçip başka yoldan gitmenin mümkün olduğu bir oyun...

Şu yıkılan evi yeniden yapmanın, o kapanan kahveyi açmanın, bizi durup dururken bırakıp giden bir dostla yeniden buluşmanın... Hatta söylenmiş sözleri geri almanın mümkün olduğu...

Tabii biliyorum, olmuyor.

Hayat bizim istediğimiz gibi kurulmuyor.

Olsun, en azından hayal kurabilirim...

Hep öyle yapmadım mı?

Kendimi tavandaki aynada görüyorum. Ona ışıkları kapatmasını söylüyorum. İlk kez onunla yalnızım. Onun evinde. Onun aynalarla kaplı odasında. Hayır ne olacağını bilmiyorum. İstediğimin ne olduğunu bilmiyorum.

Sanki kendimi olacakların akışına bırakmış gibiyim.

İlk gençlik günlerinde aşktı sevişmek...

Birini okşamak, dokunmak, öpüşmek, yüzüne, gözlerine bakmaktan kendini alamamaktı. Kendiliğinden gelen sıcaklığın sizi yakması, durduramadığınız çarpıntının çekimiydi...

Korkuyla daha ileri gitmemek için, kendini bırakmamak için o yükselen sıcaklığı, adlandıramadığınız heyecanı durdurmaya çalışmaktı.

Şimdi yıllar sonra ilk öpüştüğüm sarışın oğlanı, saf, komik haliyle üstüme atlamaya çalışıp durduğunu ama yine de saatlerce oturup benim konuşmalarımı, şiir okumalarımı dinleyip umudunu kaybedene kadar beklemesini hatırlıyorum.

Zaman geçince artık o öpüşmenin devamının gelip gelmeyeceğini anlamak, ne istediğini öğrenmek, belki artık bunun aşk değil yalnızca istek olduğunu farketmekti...

Ancak Ferhat'la ikisini birarada yaşadığım zaman, birini gerçekten istemenin, seviştikten günler sonra bile onu içinde hissetmenin, nereye giderse gitsin aklına geldiğin an yeniden istemenin gerçek aşkla sevişmek olduğunu anlayabildim.

O yanımda yokken bile ona sarılmadım mı hep geceleri...

Kendi içindeki bir tünele girmek gibiydi çünkü. Orada kendi gizemini bulmak, gizlenmiş, örtülmüş, yasaklanmış şeyleri sanki içiçe geçmiş kutuları açıp içlerinden tek tek çıkartmak...

Hayır şimdi başka yerdeyim. Başka biriyle birlikteyim ve bunları artık düşünmemeliyim.

Onur bana bütün bunları unutturacak ve bu duyguların hayatta yalnızca birine ait olmadığını, kimsenin vazgeçilmez olmadığını gösterecek.

Onun için kendimi ona bırakıyorum.

Ama bu koku, bu dokunuş... İlk kez olduğu için mi... Beni sürekli yönetmesi, saçlarımı çekmesi, ağzımı kapaması... Kendimi bırakıyorum ama huzursuzum.

Onu tanıdıkça alışacağımı düşünüyorum.

Ama öyle olmuyor. Aradan geçen zamanda düşünmemeliyim dediğim şeyleri düşünüyorum hep. Karanlıkta, müziğin sesini açıp sevişirken aklımda, yanımızda birisi daha var.

Önceleri bundan utanırken, derin bir suçluluk duyarken giderek alışıyorum. Çünkü ancak onu düşünerek mutlu olabiliyorum.

O ilk günlerde, gecelerde bunun üzerinde çok fazla durmadım. Hayat yalnızca mutlu sevişmelerden ibaret değildi.

Yalnızca birkaç ay sonra bir akşam sakin sakin "Artık gelip burada benimle oturmanı istiyorum," dedi.

"Burada mı?" dedim şaşkın şaşkın.

Önce bunun evlenme teklifi olduğunu anlamadım.

Bunu bu kadar rahat söylemesine anlam veremedim.

Sonra gülerek, “Tabii gelip seni annenden istedikten sonra,” dedi.

Herhalde hiç kimse, hatta başımın etini yiyen Seda bile bunu yapacağımı düşünmüyordu.

Aslında teklifi bile sanki teklif değil de emir gibiydi. O karar vermiş ve başka türlü olamazmış gibi...

O gece benim evet demeyişime, hatta cevap vermeyişime şaşırmadı.

Sanki evet demişim gibi, düğünün nasıl olacağını anlatıyor, evde istediğim değişiklikler varsa onları hemen söylememi istiyor, balayı için nerelere gidebileceğimizden sözediyordu.

Bizim eve bir kere gelmiş, dışarı yemeğe çıkacağımız bir akşam elinde çiçeklerle yarım saat oturmuştu.

Annem tabii ki onu pek beğenmiş, Sare Hanım'sa yorum yapmamıştı.

Aslında kafasından neler geçtiğini merak ediyordum ama nedense sormak istemedim. Belki de duyacaklarımı az çok kestirdiğim için...

Yalnız Tolga, "Bu ne acele, biraz daha bekleseydin, daha ne kadar tanıyorsun ki bu adamı, okula geri dönersin diye umuyordum ama anlaşılan sen çoktan vazgeçmişsin," diye bozuldu.

Doğrusu ben evlilik konusunu neredeyse hiç düşünmemiştim ama öyle çok kafamda büyüttüğüm bir mesele de değildi.

Hem anneannemin hem de annemin evliliklerine bakınca öyle bir yastıkta kocanacak mutlu evlilik hayalleri filan da kurmamıştım.

Ne kız bebeklerini giydirdim ne bana aldıkları küçük evlerin içini eşyalarla doldurdum.

Mutsuz olursam boşanırım olur biter diye düşünüyordum.

Çünkü ne ona deliler gibi aşıktım ne de ondan büyük bir beklentim vardı.

Bildiğim şuydu ki biriyle evlenmenin nasıl olacağını evlenmeden anlamak imkansızdır.

Onur'la mutluydum. Onunla oturup konuşmaktan, gezip eğlenmekten, tatile gitmekten keyif alıyordum. Bana böyle davranan ilk erkek de oydu.

Onur'un geldiği akşam annem, "Böyle alelacele düğün olmaz, yakışık almaz, insanlar ne düşünür, önce nişan yapıp biraz beklemek lazım..." dedi.

O da buna fazla direnmedi. "Gerçi artık tanışmak için süreye ihtiyaç yok, bunlar eski adetler ama madem istiyorsunuz aile arasında nişan takalım, bir iki ay içinde de hazırlıkları bitirip nikah tarihi alalım, ben işlerin uzamasını sevmem..." dedi.

İşlerin?

Evet ona göre bu da bir işti. Bir işe karar verdiğinde nasıl davranıyorsa bunda da öyle yapacaktı.

Benim o akşam biraz içim sıkıldı. Çünkü aklıma gelmeyen bir sürü saçmalıkla uğraşmak zorunda kalacağımı, annemin tutturmalarını savuşturmak için ne yapacağımı, gelinlikmiş, çeyizmiş, düğün yeriymiş, davetli listesiymiş gibi zırvalarla bunalacağımı o akşam farkettim.

Sare Hanım uzun uzun Onur'u inceledi. Yalnızca birkaç soru sordu. Yaşlı dayısını kaybettikten sonra kimsesi kalmadığını öğrendi. Oturacağımız evin yakın olmasına sevindi. Eski günlerinde olsa kimbilir neler sorar, sonra bana neler anlatırdı ama artık hiç keyfi yoktu. Zaten günün büyük bölümünü uyuyarak ya da koltuğunda uyuklayarak geçiriyor, misafir istemiyor, biraz fazla konuşan oldu mu huysuzlanıyordu.

"İyi bir adama benziyor, madem sen seviyorsun..."

Madem sen seviyorsun cümlesini öyle bir söyledi ki aslında sanki "Seviyor musun gerçekten?" der gibiydi.

Neyse ki annem daha Onur kapıdan çıkar çıkmaz nişanın nasıl olacağını, nerede olacağını, kimlerin gelmesi gerektiğini anlatmaya başladığı için söz ortada kaldı.

Belki de bilinçaltımda bu evden de artık kurtulmak istiyordum. Anneannemin bu hali beni çok üzüyordu. Aynı zamanda evin o çok sevdiğim, neşeli, canlı hali gitmiş, kasvetli, sessiz garip bir hal almıştı.

Onur'un teklifini olsa olsa birkaç ay erteleyebilirdim. Ama sonunda istediği olmazsa benden ayrılırdı, bunu biliyordum.

Artık 40'lı yaşlarının ortalarındaydı ve çocuk istiyordu.

Doğrusu onunla tanışana kadar çevremde dolaşan, benimle görüşmek isteyen erkekler de beni hiç etkilememiş hatta kendi kendime bu insanlarla hayat geçiren kadınlar mı var, ben buna yemek süresince zor katlanıyorum diye düşünmüştüm.

Tabii Seda'nın sürekli "Adamın etrafı güzel kadınlarla dolu, senin bu saflığına çarpıldı, sakın bunu uzatma," deyip durması da ayrı.

Bir keresinde, "Hala aklında o deli ressam varsa unut, ondan insana hayır gelmez, kaçıp gitmiş, üstelik de yaşlı..." deyince kızdım, "Bir daha bu konuyu açma," dedim, sustu.

Ama aklımda birşey daha vardı.

Onur'la nişanı nerede yapalım, evde, bahçede küçük bir davet mi olsun diye konuşuyorduk.

Bu konulardan benim gibi sıkılmış değil aksine heyecanlanmış görünüyordu.

Hatta evi nasıl değiştireceğini, benim için çalışma odası hazırlayacağını anlatırken kağıt üzerinde çizip gösteriyordu.

Bir türlü lafa giremiyordum. Sonunda, "Sana söylemem gereken birşey var," dedim.

Durdu, yüzüme baktı.

"Benim de vardır mutlaka ama şimdi söylemenin zamanı değil, ben insanları kendim tanımak isterim, onların ya da başkalarının anlattıklarıyla değil," dedi.

Belki geçmişimden sözedeceğimi düşünmüştü. Belki de Ferhat'ı duymuştu.

"Benden önceki hayatın seni ilgilendirir, benim için önemli olan bundan sonrası..."

"Ama bu öyle birşey değil," dedim ve ona hastalığımdan ilk kez sözettim. Tabii oldukça hafifleterek.

Pek üzerinde durmadı. Elimi tuttu, okşadı. Belki de korktuğu şeyi söylemediğime sevinmişti.

"Gördüğüm kadarıyla hasta bir halin yok. Doktorların merakı bunlar hep. Gereken ne varsa birlikte araştırır buluruz. Herşeyin çaresi vardır..."

Evet o öyle düşünürdü. Herşeyin çaresi vardır.

O an böyle söylemesi beni çok mutlu etti hatta evlenme kararını verdiğim için kendimi ilk kez iyi hissettim ama tıpkı annem gibi onun da görmek istemediği şeylerden kaçtığını, belki de bu yüzden hayatını sürekli güzelleştirmeye çalıştığını, üzücü, tatsız anıları bile silip yokettiğini anlamamıştım.

Evliliğimizin ilk yazında bir deniz yolculuğuna çıktık. Üstümde bana son hediyesi renkli, uçuşan bir yazlık elbise, kafamda kocaman şapka, genç gelin olarak kaptanın masasında yenen yemek, yemekten sonra güvertede ayışığında içilen içki...

Onur her zamanki şıklığı ve havalı haliyle tanımadığı yabancı insanlarla sohbet ediyor, gemiler hakkındaki bilgisiyle kaptanı bile hayretler içinde bırakıyordu.

Herşey tam da filmlerdeki gibiydi.

Tam Onur'a yakışır cinsten.

E, o Cary Grant'sa ben de Grace Kelly olmalıydım tabii. Zaten neredeyse bütün gardırobumu baştan aşağı yenilemiş, en iyi modaevlerinden daha balayından önce yığınla şey alınmıştı.

Hoşuma da gitti. Bir tek son moda topuklu ayakkabılar ayağımı sıkıyordu o kadar.

Ama biraz sonra hava bozdu.

Vapur dalgaların üzerinde inip kalkmaya başladı.

Kamaraya geldik ve birden fenalaştım. Başım dönüyor, midem bulanıyor, titriyordum.

Üstümü başımı bile zor çıkardım.

"Deniz tutmuştur, belki de fazla şarap içtin, uyuyunca geçer," diyordu ama ben yatamıyordum. Yatınca daha beter başım dönüyordu ve paniklemeye başladım. Çünkü ne olduğunu anlamamıştım. Böyle vapurla yolculuk etmediğim için gerçekten deniz mi tuttu, zehirlendim mi yoksa yine atak mı geldi bilemiyordum.

Derin derin nefes almaya çalışıyordum ama sanki alamıyormuşum gibi geliyordu.

Ter içinde kusuyordum ama midemin bulantısı geçmiyordu.

Ona doktoru getirmesi için yalvarıyordum ama nedense "Birşeyin yok, geçer," diye inat ediyordu.

Ağlamaya başladım.

Sonunda gidip doktoru kaldırdı.

Tansiyonum ölçüldü, ateşime bakıldı, kalbim dinlendi.

"Korkacak birşey değil muhtemelen yemek dokundu ve hava da böyle olunca... Alıştığımız şeyler, merak etmeyin..."

Yaşlı doktor bana ilaç verdi ve sabah yeniden gelip göreceğini söyleyerek gitti.

"Gördün mü," dedi, "benim dediğim gibi, boşu boşuna kaldırdık adamı bu saatte, deniz tuttu işte..."

Zangır zangır titriyordum, hem üşüyordum hem ter içindeydim, bayılmamak için kendimi tutmaya çalışıyordum ama kulaklarımdaki ağrı dayanılmaz hale gelmişti.

Birden bana kızdığını anladım.

Doktoru uyandırdığım için mi?

Hayır, onun söylediğine inanmadığım için...

Ve daha da kötüsü, ertesi gün ve daha sonraki gün kamarada neredeyse bembeyaz olmuş yatarken, ne olur bir yerde inip geri dönelim diye yalvarırken öfkesi giderek arttı.

Bana özel haşlanmış patates, lapa getirtiyor, yiyemeyince daha çok sinirleniyordu.

"Herkesi deniz tutuyor, şımarıklığın lüzumu yok, doğru dürüst yemek ye, ilacını al kendine gelirsin..." diyordu.

Onunla tartışacak, "Sen ne biçim adamsın, ben burada ölüyorum, sen hala tatilin bozuldu diye söyleniyorsun," diyecek halim bile yoktu.

Farkettim ki onunla ilk kez yalnızız.

Yanımızda her zamanki gibi tanıdıklar, arkadaşlar yok.

Vapurun belki de en lüks, en havalı kamarasında yorganın altına girmiş yatıyordum.

Arada titreme geliyor, terliyorum, yüzüm gözüm şişmiş.. Benimle biraz oturuyor, sonra mavi beyaz çizgili gömleği, beyaz pantolonuyla yukarıya güverteye çıkıyor, saatler sonra geri geliyordu.

Kendimi zorluyordum ama ellerim ayaklarım tutmuyordu. Doktor bunun alerjik olabileceğini söyleyip başka ilaçlar vermişti ama onları değil gizlice kendi ilaçlarımı içtim.

Galiba asıl kızdığı, hastalanmam değildi. Ona göre ne olursa olsun söyledikleri yapılacak, böylece düzelecektim.

Onunla ilk kez yalnızdık.

Ama anladım ki asıl ben yalnızım.

Ve onunla hep yalnız olacağım.

Sonra yavaş yavaş anlamaya başladım. Aslında evlilik ona göre değildi. Bir yaşta yapılması gerekiyordu o kadar. Orada, o deniz yolculuğunda ilk kez karşılaştığım yüzünü gittikçe daha sık görmeye başladım.

Hastalığımın gerçekten ne kadar ciddi olduğunu anladığında işler daha da kötüye gitti.

Aslında onu anlıyordum.

Hayatına devam edecek, ben yanında olsam da olmasam da eskisi gibi gezip eğlenecekti.

Durup dururken başına sorumluluk aldığına pişman olmuştu ama açıkça söyleyemiyordu.

Korkuyordu ve bu onun için katlanılamaz birşeydi.

Erkekler korkaktır. Kendilerini kahraman gibi görürler ama en küçük acıya bile katlanamazlar.

Bense artık bambaşka biriydim. O bana kötü davrandıkça kendini ona beğendirmek için uğraşan, onun istediklerini giyen, onun istediği gibi konuşan hatta onun istediği gibi susan birine dönüşmüştüm.

Eskiden benimle oturup kafasındaki projeleri anlatırken, yapacaklarımı dinlerken, filmlerden, şarkılardan konuşurken keyfi yerindeydi.

Ama şimdi ya her akşam dışarı çıkmak istiyor ya birilerini çağırıyor, olmadı odasına çekilip çizim yapıyor, ben uykuya daldıktan sonra gelip yatıyordu.

Ona göre herkes beni kıskanırken ben mutlu olmayı bilmiyordum.

Aslında bir kadının bir erkeğe kendisini kötü hissettirmesi çok kolaydır. Ama bunu yapmak istemiyordum. O da yaptıklarından memnun değildi. Zaman zaman böyle davrandığı için üzüldüğünü, suçluluk duyduğunu farkediyordum.

Şimdi en başta görmemeye çalıştığım ne varsa artık gözüme batıyordu.

Başkalarını etkilemek için yaptıkları, anlattıkları artık bana ilginç gelmiyordu. Çünkü nasıl söze gireceğini, ne anlatacağını, hatta el kol hareketlerini bile artık biliyordum.

O görüntülerin prensiydi.

Çizdiği evler gibi, kendisini de çizmişti ve o kabuğu kırmanız imkansızdı.

Kimbilir belki de haklıydı. Kendi istediği hayatı kurmuş ve böyle devam etmek istiyor, bunu kabul etmeyenleri de hayatından çıkartıyordu.

Ama birşey daha vardı.

Tanıştığımız zaman herkes gibi o da içki içiyor ve çocukluğumdan beri anneannemin misafirlerini tanıdığım için bu bana doğal geliyordu.

Ama sonra giderek çok fazla içtiğini farkettim.

Başkalarının yanında kendisini kontrol ediyordu. Hatta sarhoş olunca çok neşeleniyordu. Ama eve gelip biraz daha içince birden değişiyordu.

O kibar adam gidiyor, yerine saldırgan, aşağılayıcı, kendisinden başka herkesi küçümseyen bambaşka biri geliyordu.

Bazen hiç olmadık bir konuda öylesine bir fikir söylediğimde birden çıldırıyor, bana etmedik hakaret bırakmıyordu.

Önceleri bunu çok önemsememiştim. Çünkü bu kadar çok içmenin hastalık olduğunu bilmiyordum.

Sarhoş oldu ve saçmaladı diyordum.

Zaten sabah uyanınca, "Dün ben zırvaladım mı, galiba yine fazla kaçırdım," diye gönlümü alıyordu.

Ama aslında ben iki ayrı insanla birlikteydim.

Ve bu gerçeği yalnız ben bildiğim için giderek daha çok kızıyordu.

Bir keresinde yeni yaptığı binayla ilgili konuşurken bana da ne düşündüğümü sordu. Ben de beğenmediğim birkaç ayrıntı söyledim.

Birden fırladı, içeri gitti, yeni yaptığım ebruları yerlere atıp bana hakaretler yağdırdı. Yeni aldığım büyük tekneyi devirdi. Sonra da çıkıp gitti.

İlk kez ondan korktum.

Birşey yapmam gerektiğini biliyordum ama ne?

Dedim ya iki ayrı insan vardı.

Ertesi sabah yüzlerce gülle uyandım. Karta "Senin gibi özel bir insanla birlikteyim ve bunu mahvediyorum, ne olur bana yardım et, bir daha olmayacak, söz veriyorum ve seni çok seviyorum..." yazmıştı.

Yazık ki bunların işe yaramayacağını bilmem gerekirdi.

Bir bahaneyle kavga çıkartıp nereye gittiğini, sabahın körü sarhoş nereden döndüğünü bilmiyordum ve sormak da istemiyordum.

Ne onunla konuşabiliyordum ne de başkasıyla.

Zaten kısa süre sonra Seda'nın sevgilisiyle araları açıldığı için onunla bile görüşemiyordum. Tolga'yla bir kez biraraya gelmişlerdi ama ondan da hiç hoşlanmamıştı.

Neredeyse annemlere gidip gelmeme bile söylenir hale geldi sonunda.

Bu oyunu neden oynuyordum bilmem.

Belki de yeni bir başarısızlığı daha kaldıramayacağımı düşündüğüm için...

Belki annem için söylediklerimin benim başıma gelmesine katlanamadığım için...

Belki ne olursa olsun aramızı düzeltebileceğime inanmak istediğim için...

Belki çaresizlikten...

Evet galiba bu daha doğru.

Hayatımdaki bütün erkekler beni bırakıp gidecek diye düşünmemin daha doğrusu derinde bir yerde böyle hissetmemin nedeni açıktı tabii...

O yüzden Onur'dan ayrılmak istemiyordum. Belki de o yüzden gözlerimi kapadım. Belki de başka bir kadının çoktan farkedeceği birçok ayrıntıyı görmezden geldim.

Gerçi görsem ne olacaktı ki?

Anneannem demez miydi hep, "Bizim ev kadınları kendisini ya hafiye ya yargıç sanır ve sonunda kapının önünde tek başına kalakalır," diye...

Gördüm sonunda...

Ama öyle her zaman olduğu gibi bir yerde onlara rastlamadım. Birilerinden de duymadım. Kadın da gelip bana itiraf etmedi, Onur da...

Ama ben gördüm.

Ve ne garip, gerçekle ötesinin karıştığı yerde hem de..

O akşam yine arkadaşlarıyla dışarı çıkmıştı. Lise yıllarından kalma alışkanlıkla en yakın arkadaşlarının doğumgünü ya da bilmemne gününün anısı olan gecelerde çıkar, sabaha kadar gezer ve genellikle zil zurna eve dönerdi.

Bir çizimle uğraşıyordum ama bilgisayarımda program kilitlendi ve ne kadar uğraşsam da açamadım.

Gidip onun bilgisayarından kendime mail atsam işe yarar mı diye düşündüm. Bunu niye düşündüm bugün de anlamış değilim çünkü gerçekten çok saçma...

Sanırım bazı şeyler böyle saçmalıklarla oluyor. Bazen birşey hiç beklenmedik bir anda karşınıza çıksın diye belki...

Çalışma odasına gittim, ona hediye aldığım antika masasına oturdum, bilgisayarının kapağını açtım.

Bilgisayarını kapamamıştı.

Uydurma birşeyler yazıp kendime yolladım. Tam kapamak üzereydim ki birden ekranın altında küçük bir kutu açıldı.

"Uyuyor musun?" yazıyordu.

Önce sanki gizli kapaklı birşey yapıyormuş da yakalanmış gibi korktum. Sonra şaşkınlıkla kutuya baktım.

"Orda mısın? Değilsen belki de daha iyi..." yazdı.

Kutuyu açtım. Büyüdü. Üstünde, yabancı bir kız ismi çıktı.

Ama herhangi bir isim değil. Benim bildiğim bir isim. Hayır tanıdığım değil. Bir film kahramanının, Onur'un en sevdiği filmdeki kadın karakterin ismi: Holly Golightly...

Bu da neydi böyle... Bir arkadaşı mı? Kim? Benim tanıdığım biri mi?

Ellerim titremeye başladı.

Bekledim.

"Belki daha iyi, çünkü sana anlatacaklarım var ve bunlara cevap vermek istemeyeceğini de artık çok iyi biliyorum," yazdı.

Bu bir arkadaşı değildi.

Arkama yaslandım. Koltuğun gıcırdaması bile beni korkuttu sanki duyulurmuş gibi...

"Uzun zaman oldu, biliyorum sen hiç söz vermemiştin, benim seçimimdi. Bunların hepsini biliyorum korkma..."

Ne yapacağımı şaşırmış ekranın karşısında büyülenmiş gibi yazılanları okuyordum.

Biri şu an bir yerde Onur'a birşeyler yazıyordu. Biri değil bir kadın.

Önce bilgisayarı kapatıp oradan kaçmak geldi aklıma. Tabii ki yapmadım. Kim yapar ki...

Bilgisayarın kilitleneceği tutmuştu, Onur'un arkadaşlarıyla çıkacağı geceye denk gelmişti, ben asla yapmadığım birşey yapıp onun bilgisayarını açmıştım, üstelik bilgisayar açıktı ve tam kapatacağım anda bu mesaj gelmişti. Tam on saniye sonra gelse görmeyecektim.

Bunların hepsi rastlantı mıydı?

"Bunları biliyorum ama senin bilmediklerin var ve sana onları anlatmak istiyorum."

İçimden "Kimsin sen," yazmak ve bu acayip durumu sona erdirmek geliyordu ama yapamıyordum.

Saate baktım daha geceyarısı bile değildi.

Önce Onur'un da pek çok erkek gibi sanal ortamda kırıştırdığını düşündüm tabii…

"Bütün bunlar, seninle ikimizin kurduğu bu özel tarikat, gizli yazışmalar, şifreler, başka isimlerle telefona kaydetmeler, herşeyi silme zorunluluğu beni, dünyayı ele geçireceğini sanan o delilerden birine dönüştürmedi ama uzun uzun düşündüm ve artık çocuk olmadığımızı, bütün bunların delilik olduğunu anladım."

Bacaklarımdan boynuma sanki sıcak su akar gibi hissediyordum. Tek korktuğum paniklemek ve yeni bir atakla burada bu durumda bayılmaktı. Sakinleşmek için birşey içmek istedim. Büfesinde içki vardı ama su ya da buz yoktu. Biraz konyak doldurup geri geldim.

Kalbim o kadar hızlı atıyordu ki yerinden çıkacak sanıyordum.

O devam etti,

"Güzeldi. Çok güzeldi. Hayatı belki anlamlı kılan, belki bütün kötülüklerden bizi uzak tutan şey: Mutluluk. Ve ben belki ilk kez mutluydum. Bir saat, iki saat, bir gece, bir kahve içimi, bir yemek süresi… Mutluydum. Hepsi için hazırlanırdım biliyor musun? Farkında bile değilsindir. Üstelik son saniye haber verirsin hep. Olsun. O kadar alıştım ki o anda giyinmeye, makyaj yapmaya, saçlarımı düzeltmeye…"

Başparmağımı emiyorum, ekrana bakıyorum ve bunların gerçek olup olmadığını yine bilmiyorum, kendi kendime, "Hayır bunlar yine senin rüyaların olmalı," diyorum.

"Ve biliyor musun, senin için hazırlanmaya bayılırım. Ne renk giysem, ne giysem, bunu mu beğenir yoksa bunu mu... Sonra birden mesaj gelir ve sen gelmekten vazgeçersin, birşey çıkmıştır, aslında yalan söylediğini bilirim, karından sözetmek istemezsin, işin vardır, toplantı uzamıştır, dünya kurulalı beri erkeklerin karılarına, sevgililerine, metreslerine söyledikleri yalanlar..."

Komik ama gerçekten o an gülümsedim. Sahiden de bunca yılda daha iyi yalan bulamamıştı hiçbiri...

Sessizlik oldu. Bir süre yazmadı. Sigara yaktığını ya da içki aldığını düşündüm. Konyaktan bir yudum aldım, boğazım yandı. "Yavaş iç, sakın sarhoş olma," dedim, kendi kendime.

"Sen gelemediğinde belki hemen yatıp uyursun ve unutursun ama ben üstümde evde giyilmeyecek giysilerle, topuklu ayakkabılarla, içimde garip çamaşırlarla, saçlarım yapılmış, makyajlı halde, masanın üstünde, orda burda yaktığım mumların ışığında oturup ne yapmalıyım diye düşünürüm. Aslında belki artık onu bile düşünmüyorum. Sadece oturuyorum ve gelemedi, aslında benimle olmak isterdi ama olmadı diye kendimce senin yerine bahaneler buluyorum. İşin tuhafı şu ki, senin bulmadığın bahaneler bunlar..."

Öyle garip bir duygu içindeydim ki kızgın mıyım, delirdim mi, üzgün müyüm, ağlamak mı istiyorum, gülmek mi, Onur'u arayıp bağırıp çağırıp buradan gitmeli miyim, yoksa sonuna kadar dinlemeli miyim bilmiyordum ve bilgisayarım gibi kendimi de kilitlenmiş hissediyordum.

"Sana bunları ilk kez anlatıyorum. Sen benim duygularımı sorar mısın? Ben seninkileri sorar mıyım? Hayır. Biz sanki bütün bunlar hiç yokmuş, buluştuğumuz anlarda dünyada yalnız biz varmışız gibi hissediyorduk ve belki de bunca zaman bunu sürdürebilmemizin nedeni buydu... Dedim ya aynı gizli tarikatlar gibi...

Çünkü konuşmaya kalkışınca herşeyin bir anda bizi sarmalayan o sihirden çıkıp çıplak, sıradan, alelade bir gerçek halinde karşımıza çıkacağını biliyorduk değil mi?

Onca konuşma arasında aldatma sözcüğü hiç geçmedi aramızda örneğin.

Ama yaptığımız buydu.

İki yalancı, bir başkasını aldatıyorduk. Sen ayrıca beni de aldatıyordun. Ben de belki bir anlamda seni, onu ve kendimi...

Biliyorum, sana sorsam, bunun neden bu denli önemsendiğini, insanların bu nedenle niye bu kadar mutsuz olduğunu, eğer biri seni aldatıyor ve sen buna katlanamıyorsan çekip gitmen gerektiğini söylerdin.

Ama sen karına onu aldattığını söyledin mi hiç?

Bunu doğrusu hala merak ediyorum. Belki de söylemişsindir. Belki de o hiç sormamıştır cevabını duymak istemediği için. Belki de yalan söylemişsindir.

İtiraf etmeliyim ki hiç tanımadığım bu kadın için bütün bu zamanda hiç de öyle büyük bir vicdan azabı duymadım. Ama senin duyduğunu biliyorum.

Zaten kimi zaman karından değil de sırtında taşıdığın o suçluluk duygusundan niye ayrılamadığını düşündüm."

Bir an Ferhat'ı düşündüm. Onunla yaşadıklarımı...

"Sen kötü bir insan mısın? Hayır. Kötü insan bana göre başkaları için kötülük düşünenlerdir. Sen öyle değilsin. Bütün bunlara aslında üzüldüğünü, karın ya da benim ya da ikimiz için vicdan azabı duyduğunu düşünüyorum. Bazen de umurunda olmadığını... Gerçekten belki de bu sorunun cevabını bilmiyorum. Bu senin için kaçış mıydı? Beni sevdiğini biliyorum. Çok kez ayrılmak isteyip ayrılamadığını, bir nedenle bana bağlandığını... Ama nedenini? Hayır."

Bağlanmak mı? Çok kez ayrılmak mı?

"İnsan bazen hiç aklına gelmeyen, kendisinin yaşamayacağını sandığı bir durumun içinde kalıyor ve anlaşılmaz biçimde o durumu sürdürüyor.

Bu aldatma hikayelerini ne çok dinlemişizdir hepimiz.

Kadınlar için neredeyse ölümcül olan bu durum erkekler için yumuşatılıyor. Hepimizin bildiği gibi onların yaptıklarına kendimizce isimler takıyoruz, bahaneler uyduruyoruz. Çapkın, hovarda, zampara sözcüklerini aşağılamak için değil de sanki afacan, yaramaz der gibi şımartma sözcükleri olarak kullanıyoruz.

Çocukken annemin arkadaşları geldiğinde konu açılır, kimi zaman orada olmayan birinin kocasının yaptıklarını sağır sultan duymuş olur, kimi zaman ağlayarak gelen kadın başına gelen felaketi anlatır ve onu sakinleştirmek, evliliğini kurtarmak, olayları yeniden yoluna koymak, o bilmemne kadının eline adamı bırakmamak, çocukları düşünmek gibi bin türlü neden bulunarak kadın sonunda ikna edilirdi.

Oysa aynısını kadın yapsa, o zaman bambaşka olur, herkesçe dışlanır, başına gelmedik kalmaz, artık hakkında tümüyle farklı sözcüklerle konuşulurdu.

Bütün bunların nedeni, kadınların aldatma dedikleri şeyin çok farklı olmasıyla mı ilgili yoksa?

Kocasını sırf eğlence olsun diye aldatan ya da iki günlük geziye gittiği anda bile hemen birini bulan kadın pek duymadım.

Kadınların çoğu iflah olmaz romantikler çünkü. Belki gerçekte nedenleri farklı bile olsa bir başkasına gittiklerinde ona aşık olduklarına inanıyorlar.

Ve hatta çoğu zaman gerçekten de oluyorlar.

Çünkü belki de senin söylediğin gibi, aşk kendimizi ve elbette karşımızdakini kandırmaktır."

Şaşkın şaşkın ekrana bakıyorum, ders dinler gibi... Komik ama bir an bu kadınla tanışıp karşılıklı konuşmak istiyorum. O devam ediyor.

"Sen belki karını aldattın bense kendimi...

Ama merak etme, bunu acıklı film cümlesi olarak söylemiyorum. Hayatımı senin yüzünden mahvettim, yıllarımı sana verdim anlamında değil.

Sen bana yalan söyledin mi? Evet söyledin. Ama onlar ufak tefek yalanlardı. Örneğin yılbaşında, örneğin doğumgününde bir yerlere gitmen gerektiği gibi... Elbette biliyordum karınla olacağını...

Ama bana ne söz verdin, ne gelecekle ilgili birşey söyledin, ne de bensiz yapamayacağını...

Sadece bazı geceler aramızdaki büyünün bize gerçekleri unutturduğu saatlerde ve tabii biraz içmişken, "Lütfen hayatımdan çıkma," derdin.

Keşke bunu söylerken gözlerimin içine öyle bakmasaydın... Galiba erkekler anlık tutkularda kayboluyor, kadınlarsa o tutkunun sonsuza dek süreceğine inanmak istiyor. Masallardaki gibi... Ama size o masalları okutmadılar değil mi?"

Bir aşk hikayesinin tam ortasında mıydım yoksa sonunda mı? Kocam sıradan bir çapkın mıydı yoksa gerçekten gizli aşkın kahramanı mı?

"Benimleyken ne kadar mutlu olduğunu, sarhoş olduğunda bana ne güzel şeyler söylediğini ama sonra birdenbire bambaşka birine dönüştüğünü, sabah uyanınca pişman olduğunu da biliyorum. Ne garip ama bütün bunlar aslında çok sahici... Öyle de olmalıydı. Çünkü benle mutluydun ama aslında yapmaman gereken birşey yapıyordun. Eğer hiç umurunda olmasa belki de seni bu kadar sevmezdim."

Birden afalladım. Bu kadın alelade bir metres değildi. Onur'a aşıktı. Bu sözler bir metresin değil aşığın ağzından çıkacak sözlerdi. Ve bu yeni değildi. Öylesine basit birkaçamak da değildi.

"Ebru..."

Birden irkildim. Yakalanmış gibi. Sanki bana sesleniyormuş benim burada olduğumu, bunları okuduğumu anlamış gibi....

"Birçok kadının senin peşinde olduğunu biliyordu, başından beri... Ve eminim ki onu aldattığını da düşünüyordur. Ama benden başka kimseyle olmadığını ben biliyorum. Yoksa bu kadar gelgitler yaşamazdın. Yalnızca daha çok kadınla yatarak başarılı olduğunu sanan erkekleri de tanıyorum çünkü, sen onlardan değilsin."

Bir yudum daha aldım. Bu kez daha büyükçe ve gerçekten boğazım yandı.

"Şimdi düşünüyorum da senin de kadınsı bir yönün var. Sen de iflah olmaz bir romantiksin. Seni ilgilendiren aslında kaçamak da olsa bir kadınla yaşadığın o an'ın duygusu... O duygu kaybolduğunda sen de kayboluyorsun.

Merak ettiğim ve cevabını hala bulamadığım birşey daha var. Ne zamandı bilmiyorum ama bir akşam bana, hayatımda ne yapmak istediğimi sormuştun? Önce anlamadım. Sonra, evlilikten, çocuklardan sözettiğini anladım. Bir anlamda benimle zaman geçiriyorsun ama hayatın da geçiyor demek istiyordun. O gece bunu benden artık kurtulmak istediğine yordum. Sonra vicdanını rahatlatmak için yaptığına inandım. İnsan kendisini her gördüğünde titreyen bir kadına gidip başka bir hayat kurmasını öğütler mi?

Gerçekte sen herkesi düşünen, herkesin hayatını hisseden biri miydin yoksa doğuştan taşıdığın bu garip suçluluk duygusu muydu sana bunları yaptıran bunu hiç anlayamadım."

İnsan kocasının aşk mektuplarını bulabilir, ona atılan mesajları yakalayabilir, karşılıklı konuşmaları sonradan okuyabilir ama böyle canlı olarak bir sevgilinin kocasına olan duygularını saniye saniye izleyebilir mi?

Anneannem olsa "Tam senin başına gelecek şey," derdi. Kalp atışlarım biraz yavaşlamıştı. Her nedense gülmek geliyordu içimden, kahkahalarla hem de... Bu da gelecekti başıma değil mi? Gelmiş işte...

Başka türlü olsa neler söylerdim de... Kıza bak, hazırlanıyormuş o gelecek diye... Beyefendinin hangi gömlekle hangi kravatı takacağına bile karar veren kim diye sormadın ama...

Ve hala yazıyor...

"Eminim gün içinde benim seni düşündüğüm gibi beni düşünmemişindir. Bense öyle çok düşündüm ki seni... Her gece uyurken bile sanki sana sarılırmış gibi uyudum."

Hayatımda hiç küfür etmedim. Bilmem bile... Ama doğrusu şimdi bu kıza küfretmek isterdim. Aslına bakarsanız garip bir durumdaydım. Hem kızıyordum hem dinlemek istiyordum hem de budalanın birine aşık olmuş bu kıza acıyordum.

Onur mu bütün bunları düşünecekti? "Gönül eğlendirmek," der geçerdi sorsam. Ama insan belki de en yakınlarındakini tanıyamıyor Ferhat'ın dediği gibi. Belki de onları hiç ilgisiz biri bizden daha iyi tanıyor.

Birden ayrıntıları merak ettiğimi farkettim. Neydi onu bu kıza götüren şey? Böyle gizli saklı, birkaç saate, bir geceye, belki bir tatil zamanına sıkışan? Aşksa, beni bırakıp gidebilirdi. Çocuğumuz da yok. Benden mi sıkılmıştı? Eh buna hayır diyemem. Ben de ondan sıkılmıştım aslında. Uzun zamandır sevişmediğimizi de düşünürsem...

"Belki de biz yalnızca hayatın güzel anlarını yaşadığımız için, yalnızca tutkuyu yaşadığımız için bu kadar uzun sürdü. İnsan bir evde birlikte oturduğu biriyle bunları hissedemez. Bazen gelirdin ve kravatını gevşetip ilgisiz şeyler anlatırdın, sanki seni başka kimse dinlemiyormuş ve o yüzden bana anlatıyorsun gibi gelirdi. Ben dinlerdim ama aslında ne anlattığını pek farketmezdim. Senin konuşmana, ellerine, dudaklarına bakardım. Sonra şarkılar dinlerdik. Eski, artık kimselerin bilmediği Türkçe şarkıları seversin. Bana da sevdirdin sonunda. Oysa annemler dinlerken nasıl sıkılırdım."

Yalnız ben de biraz sıkılmaya başlamıştım. Bir an aklıma birşey geldi. Galiba bu üçüncü ya da dördüncü yudumdan sonra oldu. İkircikteydim ama sonra neden olmasın dedim.

"Sonra beni öperdin ve o an çoktan başka bir dünyaya geçmiş olurdum. Buna ten uyumu mu deniyor bilmiyorum. Sanki artık orada değildim ve rüya görüyordum."

"Ben geldim" yazdım.

Sessizlik oldu.

Yalnızca gülümseme işareti geldi.

"Aslında kendi kendime konuşuyordum, istersen devam edeyim," yazdı.

"Biraz izin ver okuyayayım yazdıklarını," dedim.

"Oku ama cevap verme, seninle tartışmak için yazmıyorum bunları, bittiğini biliyorum, sakın hayır deme, sadece sana bunları söylemek istedim, belki de içimden çıksın istedim, yoksa yoluma devam edemem..."

"Bekle..." dedim.

Ne kadar sürerdi ki bütün bunları okumak. Başından beri okumaya çalıştım. Bittiğini biliyorum ne demek? Bir de ayrılık hikayesi dinleyecektim anlaşılan. Ne şans ama? Tam da bitirmişken yakalanmak.

Şimdi ben Onur olacaktım. Onun ağzından konuşacaktım. Ama nasıl? Acaba ne olmuştu? Ne konuşmuşlardı ki şimdi bitti diyordu. Kimdi bu kız? Kadın? Eski sevgililerinden biri mi? Kopamayan şu garip ilişkilerden mi? Hayır öyle olsa bu kadar uzak konuşmazdı.

"Evet asıl söylemem gerekeni geciktirdim yine. Hayatımın en mutlu günlerini yaşadım senle. Herşeye rağmen. Garip olan da buydu zaten. Bütün bunları düşünsem de kimi akşamlar sabahlara kadar kursam da aslında bambaşka bir havadaydım. İlk aşkını yaşayan genç kız gibiydim.

Kimi zaman haftada bir, kimi zaman onbeş günde bir, kimi zaman tatile denk gelirse ayda bir de görüşsek farketmiyordu. Her seferinde sanki düğüne gidecek gibi hazırlığa sabahtan başlıyordum.

Mantıklı açıklamalarla çözülecek, üstesinden gelinecek birşey değildi. Bu duygu beni esir almıştı ve onunla boğuşmamın anlamı yoktu. Seninle ilgili bile değildi aslında... Bu benim hayatımdı. Benim duygumdu.

Evet o duyguyu bana sen verdin ve beni değiştirdi.

Hiç bilmediğim yanlarımı ortaya çıkardı, yeniden kadın olmayı, yeniden aşık olmayı, yeniden sevmeyi, yeniden ağlamayı, yeniden kahkahalarla gülmeyi öğrendim o duyguyla..."

Ne tuhaf, demek sizin anlayamadığınız şeyleri bir başkası anlayabiliyor, belki sizin onda göremediğiniz özelliklerini görüyor, sizin sevemediğiniz adamı böylesine sevebiliyor.

"Aslında düşündüm ki birini aldatmak, hayatın içinde gizli bir hayat daha sürdürmek sanıldığı gibi eğlenceli değil.

Benim yanımda herşeyi unuttuğunu biliyorum. Ama aslında unutmuyordun. Yalnızca o an derinlere saklıyordun. Ama şimdi eminim ki bu seni giderek mutsuz etti.

Peki neydi o zaman?

Yalnızca bir zaaf mı?

Benden vageçememek ki?

Gün gelip hayatını değiştireceğini düşünmek ama birçok nedenle bunu sürekli ertelemek mi?

Eksik kalan birşeyleri tamamlamak mı?

Hala çocukluktaki gibi özgür olduğuna inanma isteği mi?

Ama çocuklar da özgür değildir ki..."

Evet doğru tesbit! Çocuk... Sorumluluk almak istemez hiçbir zaman. En küçük bir zorunluluktan bile kaçar. İleriye dönük planlar onu mutsuz eder. Belki de yalnızca anları yaşayarak, belki de yalnızca hayatın güzel bölümünü yaşayarak, hazların peşinden giderek mutlu olmak isteyen biri o...

Ama hayat buna izin verir mi?

Şimdi bu tanımadığım kadının Onur hakkında yazdıklarını okudukça aslında onu hiç böyle değerlendirmediğimi hatta hakkında hiç böyle derinlemesine düşünmediğimi farkediyorum.

İçimden, umarım ayrıntılara girmez, diyorum. Çünkü en çok ayrıntılar acıtır.

"Kimse bilemez," yazıyorum, "herkes bütün bunların nedeni olduğuna inanır ama aslında yoktur, bir gün bir şey olur, bir gün, bir koku, dokunuş, gülümseyiş seni başka bir yere çeker ve bazen gitmek istersin, hepsi bu.."

Yazıyorum ve şu anda gerçekten böyle düşünebildiğime, ağzımdan bu sözlerin döküldüğüne, böylesine sakin kalabildiğime ben de şaşırıyorum. Sadece yazarken ellerim titriyor ve bazı harfler karışıyor.

Bir Fransız arkadaşım bir gün, "Aldatmak yoktur, yakalanmak vardır," demişti. Kocasını kendi yatak odasında bir kadınla yakalamış, kıyameti kopartırken kadın sessizce giyinip çıkıp gitmişti. Belki çok komik ama kocası onun hayal gördüğünü, aldığı sakinleştirici ilaç yüzünden böyle olduğunu, aslında orada kimse olmadığını söylemişti.

"Biliyor musun buna daha çok delirmem gerekirken gülmeye başladım. Ve şimdi de gördüğün gibi gülerek anlatıyorum."

"Peki ne yaptın sonra?" dedim.

"Aslına bakarsan hiç birşey. Çünkü iki yıl önce ben de onu aldatmıştım ve o bunu asla öğrenemedi. Ama ben öğrendim. Bu olaydan sonra yazlık evi üzerime geçirdi ve ben de madem benden önce de ilişkisi olmuştu şimdi ne değişti diye düşündüm."

"Yani böylece artık ona kızgın değil misin?"

"Hayır, bazı adamlar çapkındır, aslında bence bütün adamlar öyledir ama bazıları bunu yapmaya cesaret edemez."

"İyi ama" diye itiraz ettim, "seni aptal yerine koymuş.."

"Hayır, hayır aksine kendisini aptal yerine koydu, kimsenin bu zırvaya inanmayacağını elbette biliyordu, bana o an, ayrılalım ben bu kadını seviyorum da diyebilirdi..."

"Bu daha dürüstçe olmaz mıydı?"

"Olurdu elbette ama ben onu gerçekten seviyorum ve onunla çok eğleniyorum, beni bırakıp gitmesi beni çok üzerdi, o zamandan beri artık bunlara cesaret edemiyor. Dürüst ama beni boğan bir kocayı tercih eder miydim diye sorarsan, ki ben kendime çok sordum, etmem..."

Evet o böyle söylemişti ve şimdi aslında dürüst olması gereken belki de bendim.

Ferhat'ı düşünmediğim tek gün bile olmuş muydu?

Sevişirken bile aklımdakinin o olduğunu söylememin zamanı gelmedi mi artık?

Ben zaten Onur'u sevmemiştim ki... Sevmek nedir biliyordum çünkü. Ben Ferhat'ı sevmiştim. Sevmek öyle birşeydi. Sürekli aklına gelmek, sürekli aklında olmak, uzaktayken de onu hatırlamak, alışveriş yaparken bile şu renk ona yakışır, bu gömlek ne güzel olur demek...

O aklıma geldiğinde yüzümde gülümseme belirir, içimde bilinmez bir duygu yükselirdi sanki.

Ama Onur'a doğumgününde hediye alırken bile iki saat dolaşırdım ve yine de bulamazdım.

Çoğu akşamlar yatsa ya da odasına geçip çalışsa da yalnız kalsam diye düşünürdüm.

Yatağa geç gitmek için sürekli bahaneler bulurdum.

Arkadaşlarıyla buluşmasına, iş gezilerine hiç sesimi çıkartmazdım.

Belki de bu yüzden aslında çok kızmadım.

Olmayacak bir işe kalkışıp onu da mahvetmemden daha doğal ne olabilirdi ki...

Tolga evleneceğimi duyduğunda deliye dönmemiş miydi?

Sare Hanım bana, "Birini yanında hep isteyecek kadar sevdiğine emin değilsen sakın evlenme sonra çok mutsuz olursun," demişti.

Bu evliliğin fazla sürmeyeceğinden herkes emindi aslında.

Bense kendimce oyun oynuyordum ve istersem yapabilirim diye düşünüyordum.

Belki de o güne kadar aslında kimse bana Onur gibi davranmadığı için aklımı çelmeyi başarmıştı.

Ferhat bana kadın gibi davranmazdı. Sevişmelerimiz dışında tabii. Yüzüme bile bakarken sanki çok sevdiği bir çocuğa bakar gibi bakardı.

O bana insan gibi davranırdı.

Onur bana ilk kez kadın gibi davranmıştı. İtiraf etmeliyim ki bu konuda oldukça başarılıdır.

"Evet," yazdım, "devam et..."

Onur'dum ya şimdi...

"İstersen yatabilirsin eminim yorgunsundur yine... Yarın hepsini okursun..."

"Hayır, dinliyorum," yazdım.

"En son Paris'teki otelde telefonda karınla konuştuğunda kendimi nedense ilk kez çok kötü hissettim. Orada hiç değilse tümüyle ikimize ait ilk tatilde, yalnızca benim olduğunu düşündüğüm anda telefonu alıp sakin sakin işlerinden sözedip onu sevdiğini söylediğinde macera bir anda bitti. O anda başı dönmüş, bayılacak gibi olmuş, korkmuş ve sana ne yapacağını soruyor, o saatte doktoru aramasını tavsiye ediyordun ve birkaç dakika sonra onu sakinleştirip beni öpecektin. Ama yapmadın. Sabah ilk uçakla dönmeye karar verdin, telefonu kapadıktan sonra sigara yaktın, kahve aldın ve benden özür diledin. Böyleydi. Gerçek, üstünü böyle tüllerle örterek gizleyebileceğimiz türden birşey değildi."

Gözlerimden kendiliğinden yaşlar akmaya başladı. O geceyi hatırladım. Çok uzak değil daha onbeş, yirmi gün önceydi.

Birden sırtıma bıçak saplanmıştı ve korkmuştum. O yüzden aramıştım Onur'u...

Hatta birden işleri iptal edip ertesi gün döneceğini söylemesine de şaşırmıştım. Benim ataklarıma yabancı değildi çünkü.

Şimdi bunları okurken o bıçak yeniden saplandı.

"Sen uçağı ayarlayıp bavulunu toplarken aslında onu çok merak ettiğin için değil kendi suçluluk duygundan yola çıktığını biliyordum artık. Bavulu toplayan sen değildin, vicdanındı."

Gözlerimi sildim. Aldatılan kadın, aldatan adam, vicdan, suçluluk… Ne çok dinlemiştik bu hikayeleri… Hiç boşuna bu havaya girme dedim kendi kendime. Her zaman alay ederdin bunlarla. Şimdi kendini bu duruma düşürmeyeceksin.

O devam etti yazmaya…

"Orada tek başıma iki gün geçirdikten sonra döneceğim akşam küçük kalabalık bir lokantada yemek yedim. Aklıma ne geldi biliyor musun? Bütün o geceler, sevişmeler, mutluluklar değil… Bir akşam beni sinemaya götürmüştün, patlamış mısırlarımızı alıp arka sırada oturmuştuk, karanlıkta elimi tutmuştun, lise yıllarımdaki gibi... Hüzünlü bir filmdi, sonunda kız ölüyordu ama ben ağlamadım, belki de seninle bunca zaman yaşadığım en güzel andı çünkü…"

Sinema mı? Bunca yıl beni hiç sinemaya götürmemişti. Her zaman sinemayı sevmediğini söylerdi çünkü. Ne garip, belki de bütün duyduklarımdan çok bu bana dokundu.

O yazıyordu:

"Yan masamda oturan adam bana kadeh kaldırıp birkaç şey sordu. Biraz sohbet ettik. Eşini kaybettikten sonra akşam yemeklerini artık bu küçük, şirin lokantada yediğini söyledi. Bana kısaca hayatından bahsetti, karısıyla en azından son yıllarda çok güzel tatiller yaptığını ve onu yıllarca ihmal ettikten sonra daha iyi tanıdığını ama geç kaldığını itiraf etti. Kalkarken onu öptüm ve teşekkür ettim. Neden teşekkür ettiğimi sordu.

Bilmiyorsunuz ama hayatımı artık tümüyle değiştirmeye karar verdim bu yemek sırasında, dedim. Elinizdeyken, yapabiliyorken yapın küçük hanım, yoksa sonra üzülürsünüz diye cevap verdi.

O yüzden bana açıklama yapmana gerek yok. Sana ne kızgınım, ne kırgınım, ne de artık bir beklentim var. Zaten olmamalıydı. Her zaman benim eski dostum, yakınım olarak kalacaksın, bunu silmek imkansız. Ve benim için vicdan azabı duyma, eğer merak ediyorsan, hiç beklenmedik birşey yapacağımı söyleyebilirim, yeniden Paris'e gidiyorum yarın ve bazen bir rastlantının hayatımı değiştirebileceğine yeniden inanmak istiyorum. Hoşçakal..." yazdı ve kayboldu.

Öylece biraz oturdum bilgisayarın başında. Sonra saate baktım. Onur birazdan gelirdi. Bu yaptığımı kendime yediremiyordum aslında. Hayatımda hiç böyle birşey yapmamıştım ve yapan kızlara da acırdım. İnsan büyük konuşmamalı dedikleri bu mu acaba?

Açıkçası içimden öfkeli olsam da bana bunu nasıl yapar diye düşünmedim. Konyağımı aldım, salona geçtim, koltuğa oturup sigara yaktım.

Demek Paris'e gidiyormuş.

Hem de aniden karar vererek.

Doğru mu, değil mi, Onur'u kışkırtmak için mi söyledi bilmiyorum ama bütün yazdıklarından sonra ona inanıyordum.

Henüz ne yapacağımı düşünmek için erkendi. Henüz yalnızca okuduklarımı düşünüyordum. Birçok ayrıntı şimdi aklıma geliyor, taşlar yavaş yavaş yerine oturuyordu ama bunu sürdürmek istemiyordum. Çünkü o zaman daha çok öfkelenecektim.

Ne gariptir ki üzgün değildim.

Hatta içimden bir ses bu senin kurtuluşun olacak diyordu.

Arkama yaslandım ve geçen yılları düşündüm.

O gelmeden gidip yattım. Geldiğinde uyumuş olmak istiyordum. Çünkü aslında o son kadehi içerken ne yapacağıma karar vermiştim.

Bu çok acayip gece benim için bitmişti.

Yalnızca bu gece değil, bu üç yıl da bitmişti.

Şimdi bunu ona nasıl söyleyeceğimi düşünmeliydim.

Tabii ki olan bitenden haberi yoktu ve hayatın kimbilir ne zamandır olduğu gibi sürüp gittiğini sanıyordu.

Aslında yarın hem sevgilisini hem karısını kaybedeceğinden de haberi yoktu.

Gerçi konuşmaya bakılırsa kadın bu ilişkiyi bitirmeye kalkışmıştı ama ben pek emin değildim. Biliyorum ki böyle ilişkiler kolay kolay bitmez. Sürüklenip gider. Kadın da bunu bildiği için hiç tanımadığı bir adamın yanına gidiyordu. Yoksa onun hala Onur'a aşık olduğundan adım gibi emindim.

Kimbilir Onur bunu öğrenince onun yanına koşacak ve belki beni de bırakacaktı.

Ama şimdi sıra bendeydi.

Kapının açıldığını duydum. Gözlerimi kapadım. Geldi, benim uyuduğumu gördü, banyoya girdi.

Her zamanki gibi üstünü çıkartmasını, pijamalarını giymesini, yanıma gelmesini duydum. Arkasını dönüp yattı.

Bunca yıldır sana arkasını dönüp yatan bir adamla yaşamanın suçu kimde olabilir ki?

Bir kere bile söyledin mi?

Sordun mu?

Evet ağlamak istiyordum hem de deli gibi...

Kendimi tutuyordum.

Hastaneye yattığım zaman bile bir an önce oradan kaçıp sevgilisinin yanına giden bir adamla yaşıyorum.

"Sen git, ben iyiyim," dediğim zaman "peki o zaman" diyen bir adamla..

Sabah kahvaltısında istediği peynir olmazsa, domatesleri istediği gibi dilimlenmemişse, yumurtası tam kayısı olmamışsa surat asan bir adamla...

Aynı tonda bin tane gömleğinden birini giymek istediğinde yakası güzel ütülenmemişse söylenen bir adamla...

Saçımı boyattığımda, kestirdiğimde, yaptırdığımda farketmeyen bir adamla...

Bana iki yıl üstüste doğum günümde aynı kolyeyi alan adamla...

Benden başka herkese iyi, nazik olan bir adamla...

"El iyisi" derdi Sare Hanım böylelerine...

"Aynanın karşısında bir kadından daha çok zaman geçiren adamlardan uzak dur," demişti Tolga...

Ağlamak mı, gülmek mi, onu uyandırıp kıyameti kopartmak mı, içimden gelenleri bilemiyorum artık.

Ne aşağılık olduğunu yüzüne söylesem mi?

Yoksa ne budala olduğumu kendime mi söylesem?

Horlamaya başladı bile. Tabii ki sarhoş...

Kalktım.

Salona gittim. Hayır bir kadeh daha içmeyecektim. Sarhoş olup onu uyandırıp kavga etmek istemiyordum.

Bütün bu karışık duygulara rağmen garip bir biçimde aslında kendimi iyi hissediyordum.

Bitmişti.

Biz birbirimizi sevememiştik.

Hepsi buydu.

Bu başıma gelen felaket değildi. Aksine bana hayatımı kurtarmam için verilmiş bir şanstı.

O kadına kızmam değil teşekkür etmem gerekiyordu.

Belki anlaması zor. Onur da niye bana katlanmıştı ki? Neden, sevdiği ya da yanında mutlu olduğu bir başkası varken hem de....

Sorumluluk mu? Düzen isteği mi?

Ama biz aile değildik ki? Bizim çocuğumuz bile yoktu.

O kadını da sevmiyordu aslında. Kendinden başka kimseyi sevmiyordu ki...

Eğer sevişmenin ne olduğunu bilmeseydim, kadın olmanın nasıl birşey olduğunu bilmeseydim şimdi o kadını çok kıskanırdım.

Ama biliyordum. Kimseye söylemesem de çok iyi biliyordum hem de...

Garip, beklenmedik bir geceydi. Sıradan gecelerden birinde birdenbire bunlar olmuştu işte. Belki de sıradan binlerce sıkıcı gecenin böylece sürüp gitmesini engelleyecek birşey.

Şimdi bütün bunları kafamdan silip atmalıydım. Babamın gidişinden ben sorumlu değildim. Onur'un bunları yapmasının nedeni de ben değildim.

Neredeyse gün doğuyordu.

Hayır yüzyüze konuşmak istemiyordum.

Bir kağıt aldım ve yazmaya başladım.

"Sevgili Onur, nedense bazı insanlar birbirleriyle herşeyi konuşamazlar. İkisi de içlerinden farklı şeyler düşündükleri halde bunu söyleyemezler. Hatta başkalarıyla konuşur, doktorlara gider ama yine de karşısındakine gerçeği anlatamazlar.

Seninle kimi zaman konuşmak istedim ama yapamadım. Belki de sen bu tür konuşmaları sevmediğin için... Belki de hep geçiştirdiğin için...

Geriye dönüp bakınca, beni ilk gördüğü andan itibaren peşimde koşan, ilgisiyle beni şaşırtan birini görüyorum. Kibar, sevecen, düşünceli, anlayışlı...

Yalnızca bir yıl sonra, beni neredeyse görmeyen, ilgilenmeyen, olur olmaz tersleyen, kabalaşan bir başka adam...

Evden sürekli kaçmaya, yalnız kaldığımız anları olabildiğince azaltmaya çalışan, başkalarının yanında yine eski eğlenceli, neşeli adamken benim yanımda somurtan...

Evlenmeye karar verdiğimizde sana pek çok insanın bilmediği şeyleri, hastalığımı anlatmıştım.

Kabul etmeliyim ki çoğu zaman, beklenmedik nöbetler geldiğinde, gecenin yarısı beni hastanelere taşımak zorunda kaldığında, bayıldığımda gerçekten öldüğümü sanıp deliye döndüğünde hep yanımda oldun.

Ama insan birbirine ağır gelir derdi anneannem. Zaman geçince bunlara katlanmak güç geliyor biliyorum. Bir çekmece dolusu ilaç içen, her gittiğimiz yerde yediklerine, içtiklerine dikkat etmesi gereken, vücut kokusu bile değişen, çoğu zaman yorgun, korkudan evden çıkmak istemeyecek kadar yorgun, vaktinden önce yaşlanmış bir kadını kim ister ki?

Tabii ki seninle evlenirken bunların düzeleceğine, iyiye gideceğine inanıyordum. Doktorlar anne olmanın bana iyi geleceğini söylüyorlardı. Ama ne yazık ki o da olmadı.

Aslında çoğu zaman en kötü anlarda bile sana yük olmamaya, gözlerimden yaşlar gelecek kadar acı çektiğimde bile senden gizlemeye çalıştım.

Ama artık itiraf etmenin zamanı geldi.

Birlikte mutlu değiliz. Ve senin bunu belki de yalnızca vicdan azabın nedeniyle sürdürdüğüne artık hiç kuşkum yok.

En yakın arkadaşının sana söylediği gibi belki de karşılaştıklarının arasında en düzgün, en iyi kız olduğum içindir.

Ama sana birşey söyleyeyim mi, ben iyi, düzgün bir kız olmak istemiyorum.

Yapmak istediklerimi, belki de beni bütün bu hastalıklardan, sıkıntılardan uzaklaştıracak, belki bana çok iyi gelecek şeyleri bile bu üç yılda erteledim durdum. Eve geldiğinde yüzünün gülmesi için, bana sarıldığın zaman mutlu olman için, açıkçası ne hazin ama beni sevmen için kendimi bir yana bıraktım. Arkadaşlarımdan bile uzaklaştım. Seninle olmak için yapayalnız kaldım.

Hayır, aşk emek vermekle ilgili değil. Bunu artık biliyorum. O, ne senin, ne benim kafese kapatıp zaman zaman seveceğimiz gizemli bir kuş değil.

Kimseye sormadan geliyor ve yine bir gün kimseye sormadan çıkıp gidiyor.

Seninle oturup bütün bunları konuşmak, hayatı yeniden yoluna koymak, belki birilerinden yardım istemek... Hayır bütün bunlar için çok geç.

Eğer her zaman içimdeki sesi dinleseydim, gerçek duygularıma inansaydım, onları düzenlemeye, hayata uydurmaya, bir biçime sokmaya çalışmasaydım daha mutlu olurdum.

Kimbilir belki bunu farketmem için de bu zamanın geçmesi gerekiyormuş."

Bunları yazdım, biraz durdum. Güneş doğuyordu. Kafam hem hiç olmadığı kadar karışık hem de aslında bu sabah gibi berraktı.

"Sana birşey daha itiraf edeceğim. Ben başkasına aşığım. Onun için de senden ayrılıyorum. Bir an önce boşanma işlerini halledersen beni çok mutlu edersin."

Yazdıklarıma yeniden baktım.

Evet böylesi daha iyi olacaktı.

Bu saatten sonra oturup da onun neler yaptığını yüzüne vurmaya, inkarlarını dinlemeye, iyice canımı acıtacak ayrıntıları duymaya hiç niyetim yoktu. Halim de... Zaten artık neye yarardı ki?

"Senden hiçbirşey istemiyorum. Her zaman benim için yaptıklarını, iyiliğini hatırlayacağım. Hoşçakal."

Tabii ki ağladım. Ellerim titredi yeniden okurken. Bunca zamanın özeti bu muydu?

Okulda koskoca romanların ana fikrini çıkartın dedikleri zaman yaptığımız gibi yazarın belki yıllarca en küçük ayrıntılarıyla uğraşarak yazdığı kitabı birkaç satırda özetleyivermek.

Evet böyleydi.

Mektubu masanın üzerine koydum.

Yalnızca çantamı ceketimi aldım ve çıktım.

Nereye gideceğimi, ne yapacağımı, şu an bile neler olacağını bilmeden, içimde hüzün, aynı zamanda beklenmedik bir heyecan vardı.

Yollar boştu. Ne zamandır bu saatte sokağa çıkmadığım için garip geldi bana. Pırıl pırıl güneş, hafif bir esinti vardı. Ürperdim ama yürüdükçe alıştım.

Yavru bir köpek peşime takılıp benimle oynamaya çalıştı.

Neden olmasın, dedim kendi kendime, bu belki de gerçekte olması gereken şeydir, yeni bir hayattır, senin yeni bir hayata ihtiyacın var.

Evet vardı. Bunca zaman sanki karanlıkta, bodrumda yaşamış gibi bu sabah ışığında gözlerimin kamaşması bundandı.

İşte yeni hayat önümde boş, uzun bir yoldu.

Bizim eve geldiğim o sabah aslında kendimi iyi hissettiğimi düşünüyordum ama sonra artık takatim kalmadı ve birdenbire kapının önünde yığılıp kaldım.

Tıpkı babam gittikten sonra olduğu gibi...

Sonra hatırladıklarım uyku gibi...

Daha doğrusu rüyadayken rüyada olduğunu bilmek gibi...

Sesleri duyuyorum. Annemle Seda konuşuyorlar. Fısıltıyla...

"Duymuyor," diyor Seda.

Sahi rüyaların sesi var mıdır?

Ama duyuyorum. Garip bir biçimde tıpkı rüyada bağırmak isteyip bağıramamak gibi duyuyorum demek istiyorum ama sesim çıkmıyor. Yine de bu beni korkutmuyor. Yalnızca inanılmaz yorgunken uyumak gibi...

Neredeyim? Hastanede mi? Evde mi? Bilmiyorum.

Bazen üstüste hızla görüntüler geçiyor, yüzler, televizyon görüntüleri, hayvanlar, geçmişe ait fotoğraflar, anılar, koşan bir çocuk... Sonra yeniden yavaşlıyor.

"Taner Bey gelecek mi?" diye soruyor annem. "Gelsin, ne olur gelsin," demek istiyorum.

"Evet bir saate kadar uğrarım dedi," diyor Seda, "isterseniz siz yiyin ben buradayım nasıl olsa..."

"Yok istemem kızım, doktor gelsin de... Onur nerede, kavga mı ettiler acaba?"

Bana birşey olmuş. Ne oldu ki?

Çiçeklerin arasında dolaşıyorum, evet hatırladığım bir yer burası, anneannemlerin evinin bahçesi, rengarenk güller var, uzakta çilek bahçeleri, kiraz ağaçları var.

"Merak etmeyin," diyor Seda, "bunu da atlatacak, üzmeyin kendinizi artık..."

"Artık benim de takatim kalmadı," diyor annem.

Benim de kalmadı anne.

Galiba bu kez benim de kalmadı...

Hiç kimseye asla söylemediğim birşey var, nedense aklıma o geliyor, ölmekten korkmadım hiç ama ölmeye yatmaktan korktum, kıpırdayamamaktan, ses çıkartamamaktan, gidememekten, orada kimsenin bilmediği bir yerde arada kalmaktan...

Hayır bu rüya olmalı, çok yorgundum çünkü hatırlıyorum, o kadar yorgunum ki yalnızca uyumak istiyorum, ellerimi bile kaldıramıyorum yorgunluktan...

Burada bir rüyanın içine hapsolup sonsuza dek kalmayacağım değil mi?

Ağlamaya başlıyorum. "Ama ben kimseye birşey yapmadım, ben hiç kötülük yapmadım, neden bütün bunlar bana oldu?" diyorum.

Sonra anneanneme çiçekler götürüyorum. Öylece yatıyor, elini tutmaya çalışıyorum ama kıpırdamıyor, bembeyaz kesilmiş, elinin damarları kaybolmuş, yalnızca kahverengi lekeler vardı ellerinde ve soğuk...

Odamın duvarına elimi sürüyorum ve jöle gibi yumuşadığını farkediyorum, sonra elimi içine sokabildiğimi...

Duvarın içinden geçiyorum ve gökyüzünden yere uzanan rengarenk çiçeklerle, sarmaşıklarla dolu bir tür ormana giriyorum.

Bütün o çiçeklerin kokusu, ormanın serinliği, o çiçeklere dokunurken hissettiklerim öylesine gerçek ki bunun rüya olmadığına inanıyorum.

Çocukken gördüğüm ve neredeyse tüm ayrıntılarıyla anlattığım rüyaları dinlerken herkes hayalgücümün ne kadar güçlü olduğunu söyler, bense benden başka kimsenin böyle rüyalar görmediğini düşünerek sevinirdim.

Büyüdüm ve bu hiç değişmedi.

Rüyalarım hala böylesine gerçek ve ben hala rüyayla gerçeği karıştırıyorum.

Şimdi bunca zaman sonra birdenbire bugün mü?

Onca şeye dayanmışken, onca şeyin üstesinden gelmeyi başarmışken, bütün bu acılarla, hep evet artık bitti derken yeniden başlamışken, neden şimdi?

İşte yine geldi... ellerim titriyor, kafam kayarmış gibi, belleğin içinde sanki birşey bütün anıları bir anda hızla sürüklüyor, sonra ağırlaşıyor, bütün bunları yıllarca anlattım ama kimse anlamadı, ne doktorlar ne başkaları, işte o küçükken gördüğüm rüyadaki gibi hep o uçurumun kenarından aşağı bakarken duyduğum his ve uyanmaya çalışmak, ama uyumuyorum, uyumadığımı, bunun rüya olmadığını biliyorum, keşke olsa, keşke hepsi, bütün bu hayat öyle olsaydı ve şimdi uyansaydım, ama değil, geri döndü biliyorum, adını bilmediğim şey, beni yoketmeye karar veren öteki ben mi, sebebini asla bilemediğim o uğursuz şeytan mı, yok yok yalnızca genetik bir bozukluk, sakin ol, paniğe kapılma, binlerce kez kendi kendime söyledim bunları, ama insan bedenini denetleyemediği zaman paniğe kapılır, sen biliyorsun, başkaları başına bir kez geldiğinde korkar ama sen biliyorsun, yürüyemediğin, yürümeyi unuttuğun anları düşün, çay fincanını tutmaya çalışıp düşürdüğün anları düşün, sen biliyorsun, gelen yabancı ama aslında senin için çok tanıdık, onu kaç kez yendin, bu oyunu kaç kez oynadın, yeniden oynayabilirsin, yeniden kazanabilirsin....

Evet bir oyun.

Yıllar önce birdenbire kendimi içinde bulduğum, hiç beklenmedik bir anda başlayan ve giderek korkunçlaşan bir oyun bu.

Ama zaten hayat da böyle değil mi? Sonunda, ne yaparsanız yapın kaybedeceğiniz bir oyun değil mi? Üstelik oyunlardaki gibi sizin yaptığınız hatalara bağlı değil.

Herşeyi doğru yapsanız da kaybedeceğiniz başından belli bir oyun.

İyi ama bazıları için en azından oynarken eğlenceli...

Son zamanlarda yaşadığım en güçlü ataktı ve kendime geldiğimde her yerim karıncalanıyor, bana neler olduğunu hatırlamaya çalışıyor ama hatırlamıyordum.

Önce çok korktular ama sonra yavaş yavaş kendime geldim.

Eve döndüğümüzde herkes Onur'u merak ediyordu ama ona haber vermemelerini söyledim. Gerçi zaten ortada yoktu ve beni aramayı bile düşünmemişti.

Onlara kavga ettiğimizi, Onur'un da iş gezisine gittiğini söyledim.

Tek istediğim sıcak suya girmekti.

Çocukluğumdan beri beni en çok rahatlatan şeyin su olması ve sonunda suyun içine yazılar yazmaya, resimler çizmeye kalkışmam ne garip...

Suya iz bırakılmaz derler. Ama işte bırakıyorum.

Anneanneme sorarsanız Ebru'nun bir anlamı bulut olduğu için, Seda'ya sorarsanız su burcunda doğduğum için...

Ama en kötü günlerimde, en hasta olduğum zamanlarda bile beni rahatlatan tek şey su...

O gün de sıcak suda uzandım.

Onur'la yeniden konuşmama gerek yoktu.

Bilirsiniz, Amerikan filmlerinin çoğunda bir yüzleşme sahnesi vardır.

Başına gelenlerin suçlusu olarak anne ya da babasını gören adam onlarla yüzleşir.

Kadın, hayatını mahvettiğini düşündüğü kocasıyla yüzleşir.

Gerçekte bir sır nedeniyle araları açılan iki eski dost yüzleşirler...

Ben kimseyle yüzleşmek istemem.

Beni daha da fazla üzecek gerçeği öğrenmek de istemem.

Sanki bütün hayat bir aldanma değilmiş gibi, çoğumuz gerçeği öğrenmek isteriz.

Ne yani, o astronotlar aya gerçekten gitmedilerse bunu öğrenip mutlu mu olacağım?

Zaten artık öğrenmem gereken ne vardı ki? Belki bana yalanlar söyleyecek, belki kadının delinin biri olduğuna ikna etmeye kalkışacaktı.

Gerçi o anda tam olarak neler olduğunu, kadının tüm yazdıklarını, benim verdiğim cevapları sonra ona bıraktığım mektubu da doğru dürüst hatırlamıyordum.

Daha geçen hafta Taner Amca'yla konuşmuştum.

Bana uzun zaman önce sözettiği o deneysel ameliyatın artık çok geliştiğini ve bunu düşünmem gerektiğini söylemişti.

Sanki arınması gereken benmişim gibi sıcak suyun içinde uzandım.

Su herşeyi taşır, alıp götürür ama onda birşey kalmaz.

Su unutmaktır aynı zamanda.

Ben de unutmak istiyordum.

Artık tüm bunları idare etmeye çalışmaktan, ataklarımı gizlemeye çalışmaktan, Onur hastalığımı öğrendikten sonra sanki suçluymuşum gibi ona belli etmemeye uğraşmaktan, bu evliliği aslında çok sıkıldığım halde yürütmekten, giderek anneme dönüşmekten çok yorgundum.

Evet ben bu değildim.

Olmak da istemiyordum artık.

Hayat anneannemin dediği gibi ya kendine yasaklayıp çile çektiğin ya da her ne olursa olsun, başına ne gelirse gelsin istediğin gibi yaşaman gereken birşeydi.

Demek öyleymiş, demek böyleymiş diye bir akşam önceki yazışmaları hatırlayıp kendimi daha fazla yıpratmayacaktım. Ona kızgın filan da değildim.

Ben de belki babam gibi günün birinde hayatımı değiştirecektim ama geç kalmadan ve onun gibi başkalarının hayatını bozmadan.

Yazdığım mektuptan sonra arasa da onunla konuşmayacaktım.

O gece ilaçlardan mı, yorgunluktan mı yoksa üzerimden aslında yük kalktığı için mi bilmem çok güzel uyudum.

Ertesi sabah tanıdık bir avukattan boşanma davası için neler yapmam gerektiğini öğrendim.

Sonra Taner Amca'yı aradım ve ameliyata gireceğimi ama annem dahil hiç kimsenin haberinin olmasını istemediğimi söyledim.

Telefonda sessizlik oldu.

"Birkaç gün sonra gidiyorum, gitmeden yüzyüze konuşalım, sen de biraz daha düşün, birlikte karara varırız," dedi.

Ama ben çoktan kararımı vermiştim.

Annem tabii ki çıldırdı. "Bir kavga yüzünden yuva yıkılır mı, biraz bekle elbet çıkıp gelecek, özür dileyecektir," deyip duruyordu.

Tabii ki onlara gerçekte neler olduğunu anlatmadım.

"İnsan sürekli mutsuzluğunu gizleyerek yaşayamaz anne," dedim sonunda, "herkes senin gibi değil..."

Yüzüme ters cevap verecekmiş gibi baktı ama vermedi.

Seda da merak içindeydi ama korkudan soramıyordu.

Annem, "Hiç değilse etrafa söylemeyelim, biraz bekleyelim, anneannene belli etme," gibi tam ona uygun lafları sırayla söylüyordu ama hiç umurumda değildi. Tabii ki anneanneme söyledim.

Belki biraz da vazgeçememek için yaptım bunu.

Zaten o sanıldığı gibi tepki vermedi.

"Sen kendin için iyi olanı bilirsin, bazen direnmek olsa olsa zaman kaybıdır," dedi.

Neyse ki annem yanımızda değildi.

Onur direnmedi. Gelip özür de dilemedi. Herhalde artık bunun yürümeyeceğinin farkındaydı ya da kimbilir belki benden sandığımdan çok sıkılmıştı ve söyleyemiyordu.

Boşanma işlemleri bitti, biraz zaman geçti. Artık kafamda tek şey vardı o da bir an önce ameliyata girmek.

Ama bir akşam eve geldiğimde annemi ağlarken buldum.

Anneannemle oturuyorlardı.

Acaba ameliyat olayını mı öğrendi diye düşündüm.

"Baban aradı..." dedi.

Çantamı yere bırakıp koltuğa yığıldım.

Babam mı?

Ne bu şimdi?

"Çok ağır hastaymış, seni görmek istiyormuş..."

Boşluğa baktım.

Benim babam var mı ki beni görmek istiyormuş?

Daldım gittim.

Bir keresinde Ferhat'a babamdan sözetmiştim. Neler anlattım şimdi hatırlamıyorum. Ama hiç ses çıkarmadan dinledi.

Sonra, o insanı sakinleştiren, yatıştıran, iyi hissetmesini sağlayan konuşma biçimiyle, "Biliyor musun," dedi, "bazen hayat hatta çoğu zaman bizim kurguladığımız gibi olmuyor, insan bazen verdiği sözleri tutamıyor, olan bitenlerle başedemiyor, zaaflarına yeniliyor..."

Babamın başına birşey gelmedi, onun başedeceği bir zorluk da yoktu yalnızca evet belki zaaflarına yenildi...

"Sana anlatmıştım," dedi, "babam sanki doğaya, bilime isyan etmiş gibi çocuklarının öleceğini ya da sakat kalacağını bildiği halde inat etti. Bunun için onu hiç affedemedim. Ama ne gariptir ki böyle yapmasaydı ben burada şimdi senin karşında oturuyor olmayacaktım. Ve hiç kuşku yok ki onlar için herkesten çok o acı çekti. Belki de savaşa giden bir komutan gibi bir mucize için o acılara katlanmayı seçti."

Gerçekten böyle düşünebiliyor muydu?

"Böyle düşününce ona daha farklı bakmaya başladım. Ve aldığı onca katlanılmaz cezadan sonra onu bir de benim cezalandırmaya kalkışmamın ne kadar saçma olduğunu farkettim."

Evet aslında onun anlattığı çok daha korkunçtu. Ölen kardeşler, yaşayan ama hayat boyu başkalarına muhtaç bir kardeş, mutsuzluklar, ayrılıklar, yalnızlıklar... Ve bütün bunları yaşayan anne...

"Tabii bunları düşünmemişti bence. Eğer düşünseydi benden sonra kardeşimin dünyaya gelmesini istemezdi. Belki de hayatı öylesine kabullenmiş, kadere inanmış, tüm bunların yaradandan geldiğine ve böyle olması gerektiğine inanmış biriydi. Yüzüne düşündüklerimi söylemedim. Ama çok zaman sanki karşımdaymış gibi kendi kendime konuştum."

Ne söyleyeceğini biliyordum.

Ve söyledi.

"Belki de günün birinde onunla karşılaşman, söyleyeceklerini o ölüp gitmeden söylemen iyi olur..."

Evet ben de onunla sanki karşımdaymış gibi ne çok konuşmuştum. Kimi zaman ben ölürken gelmiş ve yanımdaymış gibi ya da kimi zaman o ölürken...

Sanki bir gün bunun olacağını bilirmiş gibi anlatmıştı bana...

Ve şimdi babam ölüm döşeğinde beni görmek istiyordu.

O konuşma şimdi uzaklardan çıkıp gelmişti ve sanki yine orada onun evinde oturmuş konuşur gibi hatırlıyordum.

"O benim için çoktan öldü," dedim, "onun ölümünün yasını öyle uzun zaman tuttum ki yeniden o ölümü yaşamak istemem..."

"Belki de hala tutuyorsun," dedi...

Böyle söylüyordum ama doğru muydu? Gülümseyerek anlamış gibi bakıyordu yüzüme...

Yalandı çünkü babamın Seda'yla beni hayvanat bahçesine götürdüğü o günü, her yerimiz pamuk şeker ve dondurma olmuş halde eve geldiğimizde annemin söylenmelerini, eve gelirken babamın, bak şimdi annen neler söyleyecek, ne eğleneceğiz deyişini, çok istediğim konsere bana sürpriz yapıp en önden yer ayırmasını, Ajda'nın kulisine bizi sokup Tolga'ya imza attırmasını, şimdi yerinde gökdelenlerin yükseldiği dev çayırlıkta yaptığımız piknikleri, benim için yaptığı küçük tahta evi, geceleri mutlaka kısa da olsa yanımda oturup alnımdan öperek 'Allah rahatlık versin' deyişini, annemin dırdırları sırasında bana bakıp çaktırmadan aldırma der gibi göz kırpışını, maç izlerken söylenip heyecanlanmasını, bazen dalıp gidişlerini, 'her sabah kahvaltıda yedi zeytin yemek lazım,' demesini, saçını hep ceket cebinden çıkardığı metal tarakla taramasını, yolda yürürken boynumdan tutmasını, hemen her hafta bana aldığı kitapları...

Bunların hiçbirini unutmamıştım ki...

İnsan öyle her istediğini silemiyor. Bellek kendi bildiği bir oyunla istediğini istediği yere koyuyor, sizin o karmaşık tavanarasını yeniden düzenlemenize izin vermiyor.

Ferhat'ın uzaktan gelen sesiyle dalgınlığımdan sıyrıldım.

"İnsan çocukluğundan ayrılamaz, birçok şeyle vedalaşırız da onunla vedalaşamayız."

Kimbilir belki de haklıydı. Onun babası böyle davranmasa, benim babam çekip gitmese o an orada onunla olmayacaktım. Hayatım tümüyle farklı olacaktı.

İyi mi, kötü mü, artık bunu bilmek imkansız. Ama böyle olmuştu işte.

İçimde sanki iki Ebru vardı. Biri ne olursa olsun beş dakikalığına bile olsa gidip onu görmemi söyleyen, öteki kendi kendine yıllardır verdiğin sözü tut, gitme, o senin baban değil, diyen...

Ben onu mahkemeye çıkartmış, yargılamış ve mahkum etmiştim.

Buna hakkım var mıydı?

Üstelik savunmasını dinlememiştim.

Bir keresinde Sare Hanım, "bu konuyu fazla kafana takma, de ki baban kaza geçirdi, öldü," demişti.

Ama öyle değildi işte. Öyle olsa çok daha kolay olurdu.

Babam koca bir kamyonu üzerimize sürmüştü ve biz oraya buraya savrulup yine de hayatta kalmayı başarmıştık.

Ben Ferhat gibi düşünemiyordum. O bunların bir nedeni olduğunu düşünüyor, bunu yapanın aslında çok daha fazla acı çektiğine inanıyordu.

"Hayatı belirleyen şey ölümdür," demişti. "Ve ölüm herşeyi anlamsız kılar. Bütün bu konuştuklarımızı, suçlamaları, ihanetleri, kavgaları..."

Ona baktım, ellerini tuttum. Yanına oturdum.

"Ben şimdi buradayım, sen de burada mısın?" diye sordum.

"Artık hep tam da burada olacağım," dedi.

Eğilip beni öptü ve bütün bunların bizi getirdiği yerin burası olduğundan başka aklımda birşey kalmadı. Silindi gitti.

Ama herkes verdiği sözleri tutamıyor değil mi?

Şimdi tam da hayatımın bu en garip zamanında hiç beklenmedik biçimde babamın ortaya çıkıvermesi neyin işaretiydi?

O gece sabaha kadar yatakta dönüp durdum. Ne kaybedecektim? Çok mu üzülecektim onu görünce? Zaten yeterince üzülmemiş miydim? O kendi kendime yaptığım konuşmalarda neredeyse ezberlediğim cümleleri yüzüne söyleyebilecek miydim?

Hayatımın belki de en önemli kararını verdiğim bir anda ne değişecekti ki?

Küçük, eski, ahşap bir kutu.

Belki anneannemin çocukluğundan kalmış... İncecik solmuş renkli desenlerle bezeli...

Onu bana anneannem vermişti. Demişti ki verirken, "Bunun içine sence en değerli şeyleri koy, yıllar sonra büyüdüğün zaman onlara bakınca o kutunun içinde kendini göreceksin..."

Bu sözler o zaman bana sanki bir masalda, birden belirip kaybolan yaşlı bilgenin küçük kıza söylediği sözler gibi büyülü gelmişti. Ve o kutuyu büyülü bir hediye gibi saklamıştım.

Neler koymuştum içine?

Annemin bebekken kesip sakladığı bir tutam saç. Bebek patiklerim. Gümüş mama kaşığım. Çizdiğim ilk resimler. Seda'nın, Tolga'nın bana aldığı hediyeler. Küçük bir müzik kutusu, minicik bir hatıra defteri, birkaç fotoğraf, babamın en yakışıklı fotoğrafı (arkasında uçsuz bucaksız denizin göründüğü, bir geminin güvertesinde pipo içerken yüzünde düşünceli ama hafif mutlu bir gülümseme, daha çok genç...), annemin eteğine tutunmuş, evin kapısında herhalde babamın çektiği fotoğrafım, ilk gittiğim konserin bileti, mektuplar, annemle babama yazdığım ama hiç göstermediğim mektuplar, Tolga'nın bana yazdığı mektuplar, Sare Hanım'ın bana verdiği zümrüt küpeler, en sevdiğim, kurunca zıplayan küçük sincap, babamın bana ortaokula başlarken verdiği yeşil çizgili dolmakalem, zaman içinde anlamını, önemini yitiren ufak tefek şeyler...

O kutuyu yıllarca aradım ama bulamadım.

Sonunda kendi kendime dedim ki, okulunu bırakıp ülkene döndün, evliliğini bitirdin, yeni bir hayata başlamaya karar verdin. Kimsenin bilmediği, senin de sonunun ne olacağını bilmediğin bir ameliyata gidiyorsun.

Belki de o filmlerdeki gibi bir yüzleşme sahnesinin zamanı gelmiştir.

Gittim.

Berlin'e yakın bir hastaneye...

Babamın ölüm döşeğinin yanında sandalyede oturdum. Ne yapmam gerektiğini, ne söylemem gerektiğini bilemiyordum. Bunca yıl ne düşündüysem unutmuş gibi öylece oturdum.

Aslında yabancı gibiydi. Hatırladığım, çocukluğumdaki babaya benzemiyor. Çok kilo almış, saçları dökülmüş, bıyıklarını kesmiş.

Gündüz ama beyaz tavandan sarkan çıplak lamba yanıyor. Büyükçe ama hasta yatağı ve iki sandalye dışında birşey olmayan çıplak bir oda.

Yalnızca hüzün veriyor.

Dışarda yağmur.

Zorlukla konuşuyor. Çünkü boğazında birşey var. Boğazına delik açıp oraya birşey yerleştirmişler. Metalik bir sesle konuşuyor. "Geldiğin için teşekkür ederim," diyor ve ağlıyor. Gözlerinden yaşlar akıyor ama ağladığı bile zor anlaşılıyor.

Ve o ses, artık onun kendi sesi bile yok. Sanki robot konuşuyormuş gibi...

Odaya geldiğimde yüzünde oksijen maskesi vardı, onu çıkartmalarını istedi.

Kulaklarım ağrıyor. Başım dönüyor. Ne hissettiğimi kestiremiyorum.

Bütün düşündüklerim, gelirken yolda bile ona söylemeyi düşündüğüm cümleler anlamını yitiriyor.

Ben şu an ölmekte olan ve acı çeken bir adamın yanında oturuyorum.

Eğer bunca yılı birlikte geçirseydik ve şu an yine burada olsaydım ne değişirdi bilemiyorum.

Eminim daha çok üzülürdüm.

"Beni neden çağırdın?"

"Seni görmek için" diyor kesik kesik, "çok güzel olmuşsun, çok büyümüşsün..."

Sanki dışardan bir ses onun yerine konuşurmuş gibi...

Asıl bunun için ağlamak istiyorum. Neden daha önce çağırmadın? Neden bana ne olduğunu anlatmadın. Belki de anneme değil sana hak verirdim. Belki de aslında bütün bunlar bu kadar büyütülecek şeyler değildi... Belki kocamın daha üç yıllık evlilikte bana yaptıklarından beter değildi.

"Ben ölüyorum, bilmen gerekenler var..."

Buraya gelirken onunla konuşacaklarımı, yıllarca düşünüp durduğum şeyleri, soruları, cevapları kafamda canlandırmıştım ve onu affetmediğimi söyleyecektim değil mi?

Eliyle yanındaki dolabın çekmecesini gösteriyor. "Orayı aç," diyor... İlaç istiyor sanıyorum. Açıyorum ve kutuyu görüyorum. Bir an öylece kalakalıyorum.

Ne demişti Sare Hanım, "Bir gün, yıllar sonra büyüdüğünde o kutuya bakacaksın ve orada kendini göreceksin..."

Ne düşüneceğimi bilemedim. Sanki benim hayatımı alıp götürdüğü gibi kutudaki hayatımı da çalmıştı.

Ama yanına birkaç eşya alıp o evden bir akşam birdenbire çıkıp giden adam benim küçük kutumu yanında götürüp yıllarca saklamış mıydı?

Ne diyebilirdim ki?

"Onu senden gizlice almıştım, şimdi sana geri verme zamanı..."

Benden yalnızca özel büyülü kutumu aldığı için mi özür dileyecekti yoksa?

Sen benden yıllarımı aldın mı deseydim?

O yalnızca bir kutu. Büyülü filan değil. İçine küçük bir kızın mutsuzluklarını, küçük sevinçlerini, anlamsız üzüntülerini, anmalıklarını doldurduğu bir kutu.

Ona baktım. Yüzü çökmüş, zayıf, belki yalnızca gözlerinde ufak bir hayat kırıntısı kalmış bu adam benim babamdı.

Ve belki de o an, o kutuyu gördüğüm an ona olan tüm kızgınlığım geçti.

Çocuk gibi onu yıllarca saklaması acıklı değil komikti çünkü. Ben onun ölen kızı değildim. Ben yaşıyordum. Beni istediği an arayıp bulabilirdi. Ama onun yerine benden gizlice kaçırdığı çocukluk hatıralarımı saklamış ve kimbilir belki zaman zaman onları açıp ağlamıştı.

Bütün erkekler böyle korkak mı?

Ama ben şimdi ağlamayacaktım. Ona sormak istediğim tüm sorular artık anlamsız geliyordu. Uzak bir ülkede, kendi doğduğu, büyüdüğü yerlerden uzakta, bu eski püskü hastanede, sıvalar dökülmüş, eşyalar eskimiş, ölüyordu.

Belki bütün bu yaptıklarından pişmandı. Belki mutsuzdu. Kimbilir belki de gerçekte istediği hayatı sonunda yaşamayı başarmıştı...

Hayatta en çok korktuğum şey öldükten sonra sorguya çekilmek değil miydi? Şimdi onu ölmek üzereyken ben mi sorguya çekecektim. Ferhat'ın dediği gibi, "Kimin böyle bir hakkı olabilir ki?"

Nasıl böyle oluyor? Hayat birdenbire şu kırışmış ellerden, kemikleri çıkmış yüzden, belki daha birkaç gün önce gülerek bakan gözlerden çıkıp gidiyor ve sizi en yakın dostuna, ölüme teslim ediyor.

Ağlamayacak mıydım? Birdenbire gözlerimden yaşlar boşanıyor. Hayır o ölüm değil, o benim babam, kokusunu, buradaki bütün bu garip kokulara rağmen aldığım babam, ne yapmış olursa olsun onun şimdi benim kutumdaki yakışıklı resminden bu hale dönüşmesini istemiyorum.

Giderken nasıl elimden hiçbir şey gelmediyse şimdi de gelmediği için üzgünüm.

Elini tutmak için elimi uzatıyorum.

O sırada kapı açılıyor. Dönüp bakıyorum. Yaşlıca, iyi giyimli, bakımlı bir hanım elinden tuttuğu kız çocuğuyla içeri giriyor. Sarı saçları iki yandan örülmüş.

O an buraya neden çağırıldığımı anlıyorum.

"Beni," diyor, o garip metalik sesle, "affedebilecek misin?"

Ona, sonra kapıda ne yapacağını bilmeden duran o kadınla kıza, hiç tanımadığım küçük kızkardeşime bakıyorum.

Ve bilmiyorum neden, artık ağlamıyorum.

"Hayır," diyorum, "seni asla affetmeyeceğim..."

Başaramadım.

Onu bunca yıl sonra o halde gördüğüm için mi, birden karşıma çıkan o kadın ve küçük kız yüzünden mi, annemi düşündüğüm için mi?

Yaşadığım bütün bu hastalıkların, sıkıntıların, korkuların, yalnızlığın nedeni olarak onu gördüğüm için mi?

Ölmeden önce geride kalanlara birşeyler ayarlamaya çalıştığı ve beni yalnızca bu yüzden çağırdığı için mi?

Bilmiyordum.

Yalnızca bir tek söz söyleyecektim aslında.

Onlar o an kapıdan içeri girmese, elini tutup, "Bütün bunları unutalım artık, geçti, gitti," diyebilirdim.

Filmlerde, romanlarda kendi hayatını kurmak için çılgınca şeyler yapan insanları kahraman olarak görüp sevmemiş miydik?

Yazık ki insanın içindeki duygu, ona uzaktan bakarak verdiği anlamla bağdaşmıyor her zaman.

Neredeyse yeniden geri dönüp ona sarılmak ve "Hayır, affettim, tabii ki affettim," demek istiyordum.

İnsan ölmek üzere olan birine, düşmanına bile bunu söyleyemez mi?

Yalan bile olsa söyleyemez mi?

Kucağımdaki kutuya baktım. Sanki açmaya korkuyordum.

Sanki çok derinlere gizlenmiş, herkesten saklanmış, unutulmuş ne varsa oradan çıkıp üzerime gelecekti.

Açtım.

Hüzün de verse, canımı da yaksa o benim hayatım.

Kendime kızmayacaktım. İçimden ne geliyorsa onu söyledim. Belki asıl söyleyeceklerimi söylemedim. Ne kadar kendimi kandırsam da onu affetmemişim.

Sonra annemi düşündüm.

O bile böyle yapmazdı.

Bana, gitme demedi.

Bunca yıl onunla ilgili kötü söz söylemedi.

Ama tabii o anda, aslında babamın ona mektuplar yolladığını, bütün bunlardan haberi olduğunu ama bana söylemediğini bilmiyordum.

Ne derdi anneannem, "Hayatta hiçbir şey için geç değildir, sözler söylenir ve unutulur, yeter ki onları yeniden söylemeyi bilelim... Başkasına duyduğun öfke seni mutsuz eder, taşıması en zor yüktür..."

Ne yapalım ki başaramadım.

Berlin'deki o hastaneden çıkıp trene bindim.

Kısa bir süre için bir arınma kliniğine gittiğimi söyledim.

Annem tabii yine kıyametleri kopardı. Son başıma gelenlerden sonra tek başıma asla gidemeyeceğimi söyledi, beni ikna edemeyeceğini anlayınca kendisi de gelmek istedi ama sonunda pes etti.

Taner Amca'nın evinde kalacağımı söyleyince biraz rahatladı.

Aslında daha önce konuşmuştuk. Neler olacak, neler yapılacak, ameliyat nasıl geçecek, sonrası... Pek fazla dinlediğimi söyleyemem. Kafama bir delik açacaklardı işte. Sonrasını onların da bildiğinden emin değildim.

"Annenlerden bunu gizlemek bana hiç doğru gelmiyor, bunu söylemek istiyorum," dedi.

"Eğer intihar etmeye karar verseydim, bunu onlara söyleyecek birine benziyor muyum sizce?" diye sordum.

"Hiç güzel bir benzetme olmadı ama peki, artık küçük Ebru değilsin, sen böyle istiyorsan böyle olsun, ben yanında olacağım..."

Bir sürü acıya katlandım. Artık sabah uyandığımda ağzımdaki o metal tadı istemiyorum. Her an birşey olacak korkusuyla yaşamak istemiyorum.

Nereye varacağını tam olarak bilemeyen eski zaman kaşifleri gibi bilinmez bir yolculuğa çıktım ve bundan sonra ne olacaksa olacak...

İlk kez gördüğüm, eski evlerle dolu sokakta yürüyorum. Bu sabah biraz soğuk ama yine de güneşli. Taner Amca hastaneye giderken beni kasabanın merkezine bıraktı. Boynumdaki atkıyı iyice sarıyorum.

Evde oturmak yerine üşüsem de biraz dolaşmak, yeni yerler görmek daha iyi.

Paçalı atların çektiği arabalar, şık giysiler içindeki sürücüler, yüzyıllar öncesinden kalma gelenekleri yaşatmaya çalışan insanlar...

Beyaz, iki katlı bir evin önünden geçerken duruyorum. Bahçede minyatür bir ev var. Uzakdoğuda yaptıkları türden. Küçük figürler, azizler, rengarenk küçücük bir ev.

Ferhat'ın yaptığı o garip apartmanı hatırlıyorum.

Bundan biraz daha büyüktü. Belki iki ya da üç metre uzunluğunda beş, altı katlı bir apartman... Ama garip olan, her daireyi tek tek yapmasıydı. Kiminde bir adam tek başına televizyon izliyor, kiminde bir aile yemek yiyor, kiminde bir kadın pencerenin önünde sigara içiyor...

Hani gece bazı apartmanların önünden geçerken içlerindeki hayatı merak edersiniz ya, ışıkları yakınca öyle bir hisse kapılıyordunuz.

Böyle birşeyle ne kadar çok uğraştığına şaşırmıştım.

Dalmış bunları düşünürken bir kadın geliyor yanıma, bahçe kapısını iterken, gözlerimin içine bakarak, "Bana mı geldiniz?" diye soruyor.

Şaşkın şaşkın kadına bakıyorum.

"Yo, hayır, ben yalnızca..."

"Girin girin," diyor dinlemeden, "bana geldiniz..."

Ne yapacağımı şaşırıyorum.

"Gelsenize," diyor kadın, "merak etmeyin size çay ikram edeceğim... Burnunuz kızarmış, üşümüşsünüz... Belli ki yabancısınız..."

Sanki tutulmuş gibi arkasından yürüyorum. Kapıyı açıyor, beyaz kabarık tüylü bir kedi mırıldanarak kapıda onu karşılıyor ve içeri giriyoruz.

Eski püskü eşyalar, sanki öylesine toplanıp getirilmiş gibi birbirine uymayan ıvır zıvırla dolu bir ev.

Birşeyleri itiyor, elindekileri bir yere koyuyor, beni kırmızı kadife koltuğa oturtuyor.

"Çok uzaktan geliyorsunuz değil mi?" diye soruyor.

"Evet," diyorum, "İstanbul'dan..."

Kayboluyor. Kendi kendime "Neler oluyor?" diyorum.

Elinde tepsiyle geri geliyor. Kaynayan su, minik fincanlara konulmuş çaylar... Güzel bir koku duyuluyor.

"Uzaktan gelen insanlar hep bir yerleri özler," diyor.

Çayın demlenmesini beklerken, birkaç dakika daha geç kalsa karşılaşamayacağımızı, üstelik birinin onu çarşıda lafa tuttuğunu anlatıyor.

60 yaşlarında olmalı. Gençliğindeki haliyle yaşıyor. Yalnızca biraz şişmanlamış, saçları beyazlaşmış, gözlerindeki kırışıklar artmış.

"Ben," diyorum, "aslında öylesine geziyordum ve bu sokağa girdim, ne çok falcı var burada.."

"Öyle olmalı, çoğu insan bu sokağa bunun için gelir ama ben fal bakmıyorum," diyor, sonra çayı demlerken, "yani uzun zamandır bakmıyorum..."

Portakal kokulu çaydan koyuyor küçük fincanlara...

"Kimsiniz siz?" diyorum.

"Bugün rastlaman gereken biriyim belki," diyor, "falcılar gerçekten geleceği bilselerdi bu sefil mahallede oturmazlardı diye düşünüyorsun değil mi?"

Gülümsüyorum, çaydan bir yudum alıyorum. Ilık ve çok güzel kokuyor, çok hafif, belli belirsiz tarçın tadı var.

"Çok güzelmiş, teşekkür ederim," diyorum.

"O da çok uzaklardan geldi senin gibi ve uzakta hep bizimle hiç tanımasak da benzer düşünceleri olan dostlarımız vardır."

Şimdi Seda olsa eminim bunun büyülü bir karşılaşma olduğuna inanırdı.

"O boynundakini çıkar sonra dışarıda üşüyeceksin," diyor, öyle rahat, annem gibi söylüyor ki ister istemez dediğini yapıyorum.

Karşımdaki koltukta oturmuş çayını içerken, "Sonradan anlatırsın, bir gün sefil bir mahalleye gittim ve sokaktan geçerken deli kadının biri beni evine davet etti, çay ikram etti, sonra ben uyudum ve böbreklerimi mafyaya sattı," diye... Kahkaha atıyor.

Gülümsüyorum. Aslında ne yapacağımı bilemediğim için...

"Gözlerin uzakta dedim, ama yalnızca gözlerin değil, ruhun da çok uzaklarda..." diyor.

Gerçekten delinin teki mi? Korkmalı mıyım? Hiç tanımadığım bir yerde, hiç tanımadığım bir kadının evindeyim...

"Uzakta derken kendi ülkende, şehrinde demek istemiyorum, ruhun senden uzakta..."

Birden bu garip sabahta bu garip evde içimden ağlamak geliyor. Çünkü belki de ne zamandır söylemeye çalışıp anlatamadıklarımı söylüyor.

"Ama onu sana biri geri getirecek... Hem de hiç ummadığın biri..."

Dut yemiş bülbül gibi karşısında oturuyorum. Hah, diyorum, şimdi fala başladı, birazdan bana daha da garip şeyler anlatacak ve sonra da para isteyecek...

Ama öyle olmuyor. Bana artık yapması gereken işler olduğunu ve istediğim zaman oraya yeniden gelebileceğimi söylüyor.

Sokağa çıktığımda hem şaşkınım hem de keyifli. Annemin çok eskiden benim duymadığımı düşünerek teyzeme anlattığı o kehanet hikayesi geliyor aklıma...

Ben bebekken gittiği falcının ona, Emirgan'daki evin bahçesini, bahçedeki gizli geçitleri ve yıllar önce orada yaşanan korkunç olayı anlattığı...

Annem her ne kadar etkilense de çok üzerinde durmuyor falcı kadının söylediklerinin... Ta ki birdenbire hastalandığım güne kadar... O zaman yıllar sonra gerçekten de evin olduğu yerde, tarihi köşkte çok eskiden korkunç bir olay olduğunu, bir kadının çocuklarıyla birlikte kendisini yaktığını, bunun gizlendiğini ama sonunda ortaya çıktığını ve çocuklar ölüp kadın kurtulsa da sonsuza dek lanetlendiğini öğreniyor...

Annemin bu hikayeyi benden gizlemesinin nedenini sonradan anlıyorum. Çünkü başıma gelenleri aslında bu hikayeye bağlıyor ama bunu söylemeye dili varmıyor.

Ürperiyorum.

Yetiştiğim okullarda ve evde bana hep bütün bu safsatalara inanmamam öğütlendi. Anneanneme sorulacak olsa dünya göründüğü gibidir ve olanların bir nedeni vardır. Bilinmeyenler, gizemli şeyler, başka dünyalar onu ilgilendirmez.

Ama şimdi bunca yaşantıdan sonra hiç de öyle düşünemiyorum. Kimbilir belki de başka şeylere inanmak istiyorum.

Üstelik bu benden saklanan kehanetteki gizli geçitlerde az zaman geçirmedim.

Yalnız çocukken değil büyüdüğüm zaman da gizli geçitlerde dolaşmayı hep heyecan verici buldum. Hayatımda değilse bile en azından hayalimde...

Yalnızca görünenlerin gerçek olduğu bir dünya sıkıcı değil mi zaten?

Ben, evet, gerçek hayatı rüyayla karıştırdım çoğu zaman. Hatta bunu bilerek yaptığım, öyle sanıyormuşum gibi davrandığım zamanlar da çok oldu.

Bazen birinin aslında ne yapmaya çalıştığını, ne düşündüğünü anlayıp başka şeyler anlattığında farkında değilmiş gibi yaptım. Bazen gayet iyi anlasam da anlamamış gibi davrandım.

Herşeyi bilen ve bunun kibriyle dolaşan biri olacağına biraz budala olmanın ne zararı var?

Falcıların sokağından çıkıyorum ve nereye gittiğimi bilmeden öylesine yürüyorum.

Kendimle başbaşayım ama o garip kadının söylediği gibi aslında kendimden çok uzaktayım.

Çıkarken bana ismimin ne anlama geldiğini sordu, "Bulut gibi birşey," dedim.

"Ne güzel bir isim, benimki de Juliette, hani şu ünlü aşk hikayesindeki..." dedi gülerek...

Bir yere doğru giden insanları izliyorum ve rengarenk bir sokağa giriyorum.

Festival mi, panayır mı? Karnaval mı?

Duvarları boyayan çocuklar, yerlere yayılmış tuvallere resim çizenler, sokak çalgıcıları...

Birileri isteyenin resmini çiziyor, genç müzisyenler caz çalıyor. Kafalarında kocaman şapkalar var. Önlerindeki kutuya birkaç kuruş atıyorum.

Küçük, sevimli arabada satılan kahveden alıyorum. Biraz acı ama olsun, içimi ısıtıyor.

Bir kadınla erkek tüm bedenleri altın yaldız kaplanmış, birbirlerine sarılarak farklı heykeller yaratıyor.

Elele tutuşmuş yaşlı çiftler, sarılmış gençler, elleri cebinde sanatçı görünümlü tipler, öğretmenlerinin peşinde pek de etrafa aldırmadan şakalaşan çocuklar...

Birden unutuyorum. Buraya neden geldiğimi, nerede olduğumu, kim olduğumu... Sanki hep buradaymışım ve hayat hep böyle renkli, neşeli bir festivalmiş gibi geliyor.

Oysa yalnızca birkaç gün sonra buradan biraz uzaktaki kliniğe yatacağım ve neler olacağını bilmiyorum.

Biraz yoruldum. Bizim simitimize benzeyen, tuzlu birşey satıyorlar. Ondan alıyorum ve küçük bir tabureye oturuyorum. Keşke o tombul sabah simidi olsaydı.

Tezgahlarda hepsi el yapımı yüzükler, bilezikler, boncuklar, kolyeler, küpeler satılıyor. Birileri dövme yapıyor.

Bir palyaço elindeki akordiyonla vals çalarak önümden geçiyor.

Yaşlıca, eski ama şık giysileri olan dalgalı, beyaz saçlı adam bana gül veriyor. Bana söylediklerini anlamıyorum. Simitçiyle gözgöze geliyoruz, gülüyor. Adam yalnızca gülü verip gidiyor.

Bütün ülkeler böyle olsa keşke, diye düşünüyorum.

Hep karnavalda gibi...

Bu insanların belki hiçbiri zengin değil. Hatta giysilerine bakılırsa çoğu yoksul. Ama farklı renklerden, farklı ırklardan, farklı ülkelerden, yaşlardan insanlar bu garip karnaval havasında, bu küçük kasabada biraraya gelmiş eğleniyorlar...

Kafalarında kukuletalarla, yerlere kadar uzanan bol, geometrik desenli giysileriyle üç, dört kişi geliyor, hemen karşımda oturup eskiden çok güçlü bir uygarlıkken birdenbire yokolup giden o insanların müziğini çalmaya başlıyorlar.

Ellerinde antik çalgılar...

Gizemli ormanların, kimsenin çıkmak istemeyeceği kadar yüksek dağların içinde belki de ilk büyük kentleri kuran insanlar sonra nereye gitmiş olabilir ki?

Belki de saklanmak işe yaramıyor.

Artık eve dönsem iyi olur. Kalkıyorum. Elimde, kırmızı gül, gülümsüyorum.

Kalabalığın içinde yürüyorum.

Birkaç kişi duvarı boyuyor. Ellerini başının arasına almış, dizlerini göğsüne çekmiş bir kadın, tam olarak adlandıramadığınız, tanıyamadığınız hayvanlar, her türlü yiyecekle dolu bir masada tıkınan şişman, zengin adamlar, çoktan türleri tükenmiş sürüngenler, saçları sakallarıyla ünlü bir rock topluluğu, birbirini öldüren askerler, elleri, ayakları olmayan, yerde sürünerek yürüyen çocuklar, köpeğini gezdiren çok güzel bir kadın, farklı dillerde yazılar...

Oraya toplanmış kalabalığın içinde resmi anlamlandırmaya çalışıyorum. Öyle çok ayrıntı var ki...

Resim önümüzde çizilmeye devam ediyor. Bir resmin, bu andan sonra neler olacağını bilmediğiniz bir hayatın kurulmasını izliyoruz.

Birden...

Yine mi?

Yine rüyayla gerçeği karıştırıyor muyum?

Bu benim tanıdığım bir duygu.

Ona, beyaz gömleklerinin üzerine takması için verdiğim şey.

Başım dönüyor.

Bir yerlere tutunsam...

Elinde kocaman bir fırçayla orada.

Boynunda benim ona verdiğim fular.

Herşey yanıltsa da o yanıltmaz.

Gülerek resim çizen adamlarla konuşuyor ve boşlukları dolduruyor.

Saçları iyice beyazlaşmış, kısalmış, biraz yorgun yüzü...

Bazen...

Bazen mi?

Hep hayaller kurarsın Ebru...

Burada, hiç tanımadığın bir yerde, yıllar sonra, hayatının en büyük yolculuğuna çıkmışken, öylesine sokaklarda dolaşırken...

Bu gerçek olabilir mi?

Araya birileri giriyor.
Önüme geçen şişman kadını itiyorum.
Onu görmeye çalışıyorum yeniden..
Sakın düşme!
Dönüyor.
Kısa bir an.
Beni görüyor.
Görüyor değil mi?
O palyaço akordiyonuyla neşeli bir şarkı çalıyor.
Donmuş kalıyorum orada.
O an gözgöze geliyoruz.
Elindeki fırçayı atıyor, bana doğru geliyor.
Düşeceğim.
Bu sen misin?
Yıllar önce sana verdiğim fularla...
Saçların kısalmış... Bembeyaz olmuş...
Yine o beyaz, uzun gömlek...
Yine o gülümseyiş...
Yine o içime saplanan bakış.

Sanki yavaş çekim gibi... Elindeki fırçayı atıyor...
Bana doğru geliyor.
Bayılacağımı biliyorum.
Yine rüyada mıyım onu bilmiyorum.
Kendimi onun kucağında buluyorum.
O garip sirk müziği, kalabalık, karmaşa...
Hep böyle rüyalar gördüm.
Ama bu gerçek.
Çünkü kokusunu alıyorum.
Ne demişti Juliette?

"Ruhun şimdi senden çok uzakta ama onu hiç beklenmedik biri sana geri getirecek..."

Böyle şeyler olur mu?
Oldu işte.

Ona kızgın mıyım?

Onun yüzünden mi oldu bütün bunlar?

Ona soracağım çok fazla soru var mı?

Hayır. Artık ne anneme, babama, ne Onur'a ne başka birine, hiç kimseye kızgın değilim.

"Burada ne yapıyorsun?" diyor.

"Asıl sen burada ne yapıyorsun?" diyorum.

Zayıflamış. Gözlerinin altında torbalar var. Kısa saç çok yakışmış.

Ne çok zaman geçti.

Benim sana sormam gereken sorular var.

Bu belki de pek çok insanın başına gelen, kırık bir aşk hikayesiydi. Öylece kalacak, zamanla unutulacak, yıllar sonra belki küçük bir sızı gibi hatırlayacağınız...

Şimdi bütün olanlardan sonra, bir anda biten bir evlilikten çıkıp, ani bir karar verip, uzak bir kasabaya gelip yeniden onunla karşılaşmak yalnızca rastlantı mı?

Tabii ki ona niye burada olduğumu söylemeyeceğim.

"Gel," diyor, "üşümüş gibisin, evim hemen şurada..."

Üşümüş mü?

Şu anda başıma geldiğini söyleyebileceğim en son şey bu olurdu.

Keşke o kadar basit olsaydı.

Kalabalığın içinden geçerken koluma giriyor. Belki on, onbeş dakika yürüyoruz.

Büyük, demir kapıyı açıyor. Depo gibi bir yere giriyoruz.

"Sana sıcak birşey yapayım, çay ister misin?"

Hayır, daha sert birşeye ihtiyacım var.

Bunca yıl sonra inanılmaz bir biçimde karşılaştık ve sen bana çay ister misin diye mi soruyorsun?

Yüksek tavanlı, soğuk, eski binanın içindeyiz.

Köşede tavana dayanan dev, ahşap bir top var.

Yine İstanbul'daki gibi bir sürü garip şey etrafta.

Küçük kadehe şeffaf bir içki koyuyor. Ne olduğunu bilmiyorum. Alıp kafama dikiyorum.

Sonra bir tane daha...

"Şimdi bana herşeyi anlatacaksın," diyorum.

"Neden gittiğini, neden bana hiçbir şey söylemediğini... Artık birşey söylemeyen insanlardan, birşey soramadığım insanlardan, kimseye bunları söyleyememekten çok yoruldum..."

Bunları ben mi söylüyorum?

Kimseye söyleyemediklerimi şimdi ona mı söylüyorum?

Gülümsüyor.

"Anlatırım ama uzun ve sıkıcı bir hikaye aslında," diyor.

"Kendi ülkemden sürüldüm... Sürülmek ne kelime, kaçmak zorunda kaldım. İnsan kendi ülkesinden kaçıp hiç tanımadığı bir yere neden sığınsın? Bundan daha büyük utanç olabilir mi?"

Hayır artık gülümsemiyor.

Taner Amca'yı aradım, bir arkadaşıma rastladığımı, merak etmemelerini söyledim.

Aslında ne anlatacağı umurumda bile değildi.

Uzaktan geldim. Uzağa, belki de hayatımın sonuna doğru bir yolculuğa çıkıp... Yılların içinden... Ve orada böyle bir anda en olmayacak şey gibi birden onu gördüm.

Unuttuğumu sanmışken...

Artık bütün kırgınlıklar geride kalmışken...

Daha doğrusu öyle sanırken...

İnsan bunca yıl sever mi birini?

Biliyorum ki onu düşünmeden geçen tek günüm bile olmadı. Yalnızca unutmak istedim. Derinlere gizleyip... Babamda yaptığım gibi... Alınyazısı gibi...

O da beni bırakıp gitmişti. Ne garip, hayatımı en çok etkileyen iki erkekten biri kendi isteğiyle bütün hayatını değiştirdi ötekiyse hiç istemediği halde başka bir hayata başlamak zorunda kaldı.

İnsan birini seviyor, bir başkasına belki bir süre aşık oluyor, birini yanında istiyor ama zamanın içinde bir yerdeki o duygu yalnızca size onu verene ait kalıyor.

O aslında ne kadar uzakta da olsa, kaybolmuyor. Sanki dönüp baksan orada durduğunu görecekmişsin gibi...

O duyguyu tanıdım.

Ve gerçek olduğunu biliyorum.

Onunla karşılaştığım anda yıllar öncesinde her gördüğümde ne hissettiysem o...

Biliyorum çünkü hayattaki hiçbir bilgi böylesine gerçek olamaz.

Ve yine biliyorum ki aşkın geçmiş zamanı yoktur. Çünkü gerçekten aşık olmuşsan her zaman aşıksındır.

Ben hayal bile olsa onu yanımda taşımıştım. Rüzgarı tutmak gibiydi oysa.

Ama işte şimdi o yılların içinde hep bana onun kokusunu getiren rüzgar yeniden esiyordu ve sanki kendi ülkemi, çocukluğumu da buraya taşıyordu.

Sanki güçlü olmamı sağlamak için...

Birden kendime geliyorum. Tren duruyor.

Paltomu giyiyorum. Küçük bavulumu alıyorum.

Taner Amca istasyonda beni bekliyor.

O çok sevdiğim yazarın söylediği gibi, yaşamın ucuna yolculuktayım.

"Madem merak ediyorsun," dedi Ferhat ve bana neler olduğunu anlattı.

Bir arkadaşının hem de en güvendiği yardımcısının onu ihbar ettiğini, kaçmak zorunda kaldığını, buraya gelince bilmediği bu ülkede, bilmediği bir dilde ne yapacağını şaşırdığını...

Öylesine tanıştığı bir arkadaşının sayesinde buraya gelmişti.

Bir gece barda içtikten sonra sokakta yürürken biri ona saldırmış, bacağından bıçaklamış, onunla kavga ederken iki genç gelip onu kurtarmış. Yalnızca yabancı olduğu için...

Sabah kendisini onların evinde bulmuş.

"Uyandığımda şişman, yaşlı bir kadınla karşılaştım. Bana tatlı çörekle kahve getirmişti. Hemen yanlarındaki bu döküntüye taşındığımı, ressam olduğumu biliyorlardı yalnızca... Beni kurtaran çocuklardan birinin annesiydi."

Bilmediği bir ülkede, kimsenin onu tanımadığı, kimseyi tanımadığı bir yerde, herşeyden kaçıp gizlenmeye çalışırken...

Sonra onlarla ve daha küçük çocuklarla resim çalışmaya başlamıştı. Yakınlardaki okulun müdürü ona destek olmuştu. Onlar da uzak ülkelerden gelen sığınmacılardı.

Şimdi o çocuklar için uzaktan gelmiş bir lider gibiydi.

Haftasonları hep birlikte yoksul mahallelere yemek götürüyor, atölyedeki resim çalışmalarına katılan çocuklara ne biliyorsa öğretmeye çalışıyordu.

O benim sevdiğim adamdı.

Ben babamı bile affedememiştim ama o kendisini ihbar eden arkadaşını affetmişti.

"Şimdi sen söyle," dedi, "burada ne arıyorsun?"

Doktorumu ziyarete geldiğimi söyledim.

"O zaman," dedi, "onları da al, iki gün sonra sergi açılışım var, birlikte gelin..."

Orada gördüğüm o kocaman ahşap top ünlü bir sergi salonunun önüne konacaktı.

Yalnızca ahşap bir top.

Sana artık söylemek istiyorum. Bana söylemediklerini, beni korumak için bana haber yollamadığını, hayatıma girdiğin gibi çıkıp gitmeye çalıştığını biliyorum.

Ama artık bütün bunlar umurumda bile değil.

"Hadi gel," diyor, ben bunları söyleyemeden, "seni götüreyim, yolları bilmezsin, cumartesi akşamı bekliyorum..."

Kalabalık...

Eski bir sarayın önündeyiz... Soğuk.

Avludaki kalabalığın içinde ilerliyoruz.

Binanın önünde üzeri örtülü birşey var.

Dev birşey...

Karanlıkta...

Çok şık kadınlar, erkekler...

Özel giydirilmiş garsonlar, genç kızlar ellerindeki tepsilerle içki ve kanepe dağıtıyor.

Yağmur yağdı yağacak.

Önce müzik başlıyor.

Bir köşede orkestra çalıyor.

Bu kentin simgesi olan adamın yazdığı bir şarkı.

Ve sonra renkli ışıklar yanıyor.

Örtü çekiliyor.

O ahşap top yavaş yavaş ortaya çıkıyor.

Herkes merakla bakıyor.

Bu yalnızca dev, ahşap bir top.

Birisi gelip topun içindeki kapıyı açıyor.

O yeraltına gömülmüş terakota askerler gibi, topun içinde yine ahşaptan oyulmuş askerler var.

Işık onları aydınlatıyor.

Hepsinin yüzü farklı.

Kimi kaygılı, kimi sert, kimi öfkeli, kimi boş bakıyor.

Ama aynı üniformaları giymişler.

Neredeyse topun içinden çıkacak gibi görünüyorlar.

Bunun adı "Truva Topu".

Birden hatırlıyorum.

Tam anlam veremediğim resimlerini... Heykellerini...

Bir resmini görmüştüm. Kendi portrelerini çizmişti. Aynı tuvalin içinde yüzlerce küçük portre... Hepsinde başka görünüyordu.

"Bunun ismi var mı?" diye sormuştum.

"Hayır," demişti, "benim yüzlerim..."

"Binbir Surat," koy adını demiştim. Çok gülmüştü.

Şimdi anlıyorum. Bütün o resimlerde aslında aynı şeyi anlatmaya çalışıyordu.

Renkli ışıklar yanıp söndükçe topun içindeki yüzler değişiyordu.

Herkes bir başkasıydı.

Onun evinde gördüğüm, aynaya bakan kadın resmini hatırladım.

Aynaya bakıyor ama aynada başka bir yüz görüyor.

"Artık dönelim," diyor Taner Amca, "yolumuz uzun, yarın sabah erken kalkacaksın..."

Yine o uçurumun kenarındayım.

Yine rüyayla gerçek arasında bir yerde...

Ferhat diyor ki, "Korkma düşmek yok, buradan atlayacağız ve uçar gibi bizden başka kimsenin bilmediği bir ülkeye gideceğiz..."

Ama korkuyorum.

İlaçların etkisi, rüya görüyorsun, diyorum kendi kendime...

Anneannemi, annemi görüyorum.

Hayır hiç biri burada değil.

Buraya yalnız geldim, hatırlıyorum.

"Düşmek yok..."

Çok uzun, sayısız merdiveni tırmandım ve sanki sonunda inanılmaz bir manzarayla karşılaşacağımı, bundan böyle yalnızca görmek istediklerimi göreceğimi düşündüm. Kimseye söylemeden, bütün o kırgınlıkları, üzüntüleri, kaybedişleri kendi kendime yaşadım.

Şimdi bu anda, uçurumdan, bu, hayatımın en büyük kabusundan aşağı düşemem...

Hayatında hiç uçurum görmemiş birinin uçurumlardan deli gibi korkması ne tuhaf!

Birden hafifliyorum.

Bana sayı saymamı söylediler, en son hatırladığım bu...

"Kendine geliyor," diyor biri... Taner Amca adımı söylüyor, "Geçti," diyor. Biraz yankılanır gibi sesler...

Çocukluğun bahçesi, gizli geçitler, sanki tam düşerken biri elimden tuttu...

Gözlerimi açıyorum.

Biri sahiden de elimden tutuyor.

Biri değil o!

Bu nasıl olabilir ki...

Hala rüyada mıyım?

Hem rüyamda hem burada nasıl elimi tutmuş olabilir?

Bunu yapacağımı, burada olacağımı bilmiyor ki...

O garip iki renkli gözleriyle bana bakıyor.

Evet o, şimdi eminim, şimdi rüyada değilim, çünkü kokusunu duyuyorum.

"Artık burada mısın?" diye soruyor.

Burada mıyım?

Gözlerimi iyice açıyorum. Gülümseyen yüzler var.

Gerçek olduğuna inanmak için elini sıkıyorum.

"Evet," diyorum, "ben geldim, buradayım..."

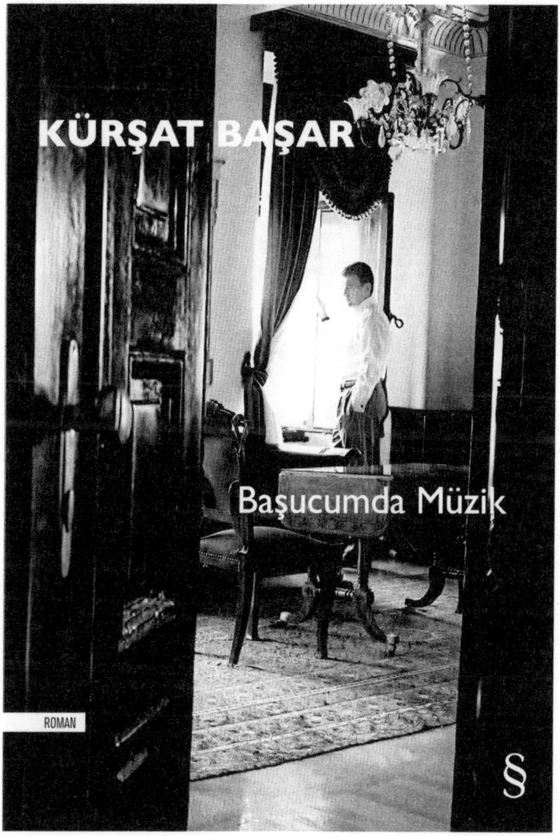
KÜRŞAT BAŞAR
Başucumda Müzik
ROMAN
§

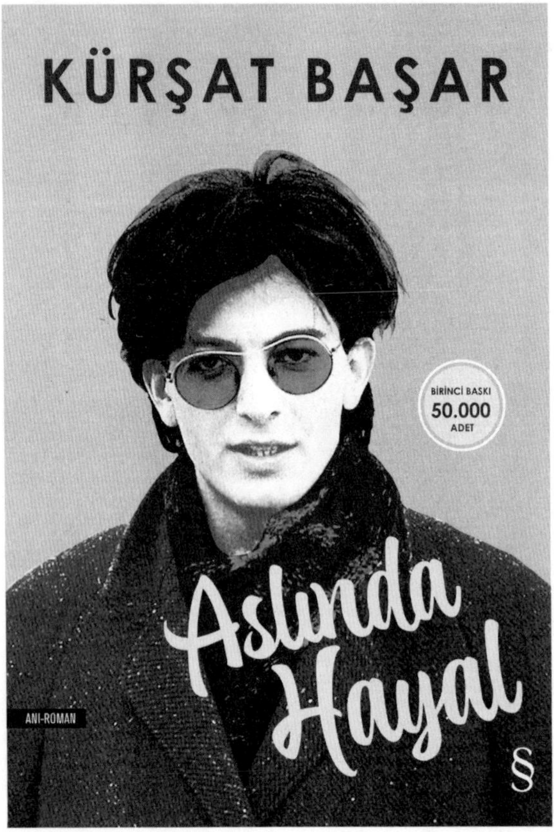
KÜRŞAT BAŞAR
BİRİNCİ BASKI
50.000
ADET
Aslında
Hayal
ANI-ROMAN
§

KÜRŞAT BAŞAR
YAZ
Sanki yıllar öncesindeki o sabah, onu gördüğüm, tanıdığım o ilkyaz günü zamanın akışına kapılıp gitmedi de, hep benimle kaldı.
ROMAN
BİRİNCİ BASKI 100.000 ADET
§

KÜRŞAT BAŞAR

YAĞMURLAR

Bazen

YILLAR

Unutmak

SOKAKLAR

İstersin

DENEME

YARIM KALAN ŞEYLER

§